T0311626

Economic Liberties and Human Rights

The status of economic liberties remains a serious lacuna in the theory and practice of human rights. Should a minimally just society protect the freedoms to sell, save, profit and invest? Is being prohibited to run a business a human rights violation? While these liberties enjoy virtually no support from the existing philosophical theories of human rights and little protection by the international human rights law, they are of tremendous importance in the lives of individuals, and particularly the poor. Like most individual liberties, economic liberties increase our ability to lead our own life. When we enjoy them, we can choose the occupational paths that best fit us and, in so doing, define who we are in relation to others. Furthermore, in the absence of good jobs, economic liberties allow us to create an alternative path to subsistence. This is critical for the millions of working poor in developing countries who earn their livelihoods by engaging in independent economic activities. Insecure economic liberties leave them vulnerable to harassment, bribery and other forms of abuse from middlemen and public officials. This book opens a debate about the moral and legal status of economic liberties as human rights. It brings together political and legal theorists working in the domain of human rights and global justice, as well as people engaged in the practice of human rights, to engage in both foundational and applied issues concerning these questions.

Jahel Queralt is a Serra Hunter Lecturer in Law at Pompeu Fabra University. Previously, she has been a postdoctoral fellow at the Centre for Advanced Studies Justitia Amplificata at the Goethe-Universität of Frankfurt and at the Ethik Zentrum at the University of Zurich. Her research interests include liberalism, distributive justice, productive justice and human rights. Her work has appeared in journals such as *Law and Philosophy*, *Ratio Juris* and *Analyse und Kritik*.

Bas van der Vossen is Associate Professor in the Smith Institute of Political Economy and Philosophy, and the Philosophy Department at Chapman University. His research is in political philosophy. He is the co-author of *In Defense of Openness*, with Jason Brennan (2018) and *Debating Humanitarian Intervention*, with Fernando Tesón (2017) and co-edited the *Routledge Handbook of Libertarianism* (Routledge, 2017). He is currently an Associate Editor of the journal *Social Philosophy and Policy*. Bas earned his DPhil from the University of Oxford.

Political Philosophy for the Real World
Edited by Jason F. Brennan
Georgetown University

Unequivocal Justice
Christopher Freiman

Justice and the Meritocratic State
Thomas Mulligan

Unjust Borders
Individuals and the Ethics of Immigration
Javier S. Hidalgo

Economic Liberties and Human Rights
Edited by Jahel Queralt and Bas van der Vossen

For more information about this series, please visit: www.routledge.com/Political-Philosophy-for-the-Real-World/book-series/PPRW

Economic Liberties and Human Rights

Edited by Jahel Queralt and Bas van der Vossen

NEW YORK AND LONDON

First published 2019
by Routledge
605 Third Avenue, New York, NY 10017

and by Routledge
2 Park Square, Milton Park, Abingdon, Oxon OX14 4RN

First issued in paperback 2021

Routledge is an imprint of the Taylor & Francis Group, an informa business

Publisher's Note
The publisher has gone to great lengths to ensure the quality of this reprint but points out that some imperfections in the original copies may be apparent.

Library of Congress Cataloging-in-Publication Data
A catalog record for this book has been requested

ISBN 13: 978-1-03-209262-1 (pbk)
ISBN 13: 978-1-138-57439-7 (hbk)

Typeset in Sabon
by Apex CoVantage, LLC

Contents

1 Introduction*

Jahel Queralt and Bas van der Vossen

1. Economic Liberties as Human Rights

Suppose you are poor and live in a poor country. You are struggling to put food on the table for you and your family. The kids are crying, the roof (assuming you have one) is leaking. What are you to do?

"Find a job" might seem the obvious answer. But poor countries being poor, jobs typically aren't abundant and those that are available to the poorly educated and unskilled do not offer a steady and predictable income. They tend to be casual jobs with unsafe and difficult working conditions that only last for several weeks or days. "Start your own business, then" one might follow up. And to be sure, that may be possible. Find some things to sell on the side of the road is one way to get started. It's hard to make a living that way, but at least start-up costs are low.

Poor people around the world are incredibly inventive at finding ways to eke out a living, despite a lack of decent jobs. They scrounge metals from local dumps to sell to those who might need them, at a small profit. They roam the streets collecting cardboard, selling it for tiny amounts of money. They cook snacks and produce handcrafted objects for those who may be willing to pay for them.

The lack of jobs in poor countries is an institutional failure. Their governments fail to adopt the policies that are needed to facilitate job creation and increase the productivity of existing jobs. They are unwilling or unable to remove the obstacles that prevent the private sector from creating jobs. They do not give priority to health and education, which are the cornerstones of human capital. They neglect critical investments in communications and infrastructure without which individuals and firms cannot seize the benefits of technological progress. And, most importantly, they fail to provide a stable legal framework in which companies can effectively do business. They do not protect, and frequently violate, property rights, freedom of contract and other economic liberties.

However, it's not just the lack of jobs that makes poor people's lives so precarious. Those who decide to start a business of their own, as an alternative path to making a living, face further barriers that hinder their prospects. Their governments adopt cumbersome and onerous business regulations that push them towards the informal economy, where they operate without legal or social protection.

To be sure, operating a formal business always entails some regulatory costs—for example, license fees, compliance with bureaucratic procedures, payments for public utilities and taxes. When adequately designed, however, those regulatory costs ensure that commercial activities meet minimum standards to provide a good or a service (Pigou, 1938). But most poor countries have excessive and rigid bureaucratic systems that have little if anything to do with higher quality of goods. Their main effect is to push work and workers into informal sectors (Djankov et al., 2002). To compare: starting a business in New Zealand takes only 1 step, half a day and nearly nothing in fees; doing it in Venezuela takes 20 procedures, 230 days and 350 percent of the average citizen's annual income (World Bank, 2018).

Such onerous business regulations create a division between, on the one hand, large companies and wealthy individuals who can handle regulatory costs and are able to navigate through red tape with legal aid, and, on the other hand, poor entrepreneurs who cannot afford formalizing their businesses. The effect is to trap those who are already economically vulnerable in even more precarious positions, make it harder for them to escape these, and reduce competition and innovation.

This still understates how bad things are for poor people in poor countries. The informal status of their businesses makes them particularly liable to extortion and bribery. Informal entrepreneurs have to devote between 10 and 15 percent of their gross income to bribe local authorities, whereas formal entrepreneurs pay an average of 1 percent in bribes (De Soto, 1989). Street vendors are particularly liable to these actions. They are victims of direct repressive and arbitrary actions that range from police simply taking products off of their stands for their own consumption to more harmful forms of harassment such as confiscation of their stock or violent evictions.

Trade repression, direct and indirect, not only hampers the economic prospects of the poor, it also moves societies away from the conditions that lead to development and rising living standards. It's commonly accepted among economists that basic individual rights, and economic liberties in particular, are among the most important conditions needed for development. In their influential book, *Why Nations Fail*, Daron Acemoglu and James Robinson classify economic institutions into two kinds: extractive institutions, in which a small number of individuals exploit the rest of the society; and inclusive institutions, in which a "great mass of people [participate] in economic activities that make best use of their talents and skills and that enable individuals to make the choices they wish" (Acemoglu and Robinson, 2012: 74). Inclusive institutions enable and foster economic growth; extractive institutions, prevalent in poor countries, frustrate it. The economic prosperity of poor countries depends on their capacity to replace their extractive institutions based on corruption, extortion and fraud, by inclusive institutions that secure an unbiased system of law and the economic liberties of all—property rights, freedom of contract and protected rights to profit from savings and investments (Acemoglu and Robinson, 2012; North, 1990; De Soto, 1989). Without these liberties, then, the entrepreneurial forces of development stand no chance. Countries that violate them thereby retard the economic development and growth that provides countries their only real shot at escaping poverty (Pritchett, 2018).[1]

Citizens of poor countries might vote or petition their governments to move in that direction, of course. But even at the best of times, voting one way or another has very little effect in terms of actually bringing about a change. At least not in time to get food on the table. And these are very far from the best of times. The very dysfunction of poor countries' governments that leads them to continue to be mired in poverty also makes them insensitive to the interests of their inhabitants.

In fact, economic liberties are instrumental to improving political systems. In contexts where they are adequately protected, there is less room for rent-seeking behavior because the ability of politicians to reward their cronies and redirect resources towards their own interests is constrained by the property rights and contracts of others. Secure economic liberties prevent the concentration of excessive economic power in the hands of government and, in so doing, they diminish the incentives for infighting in order to seize that power and benefit from it. Some of the worst violations of economic liberties that we see in poor countries are aimed at precisely that: perpetuating the privileges of predatory elites at the expense of ordinary citizens.

We are still understating things. It's not just governments that are enemies of people's economic liberties. International law and institutions aren't offering much stronger protections. Human rights law does recognize the right to private property, but it provides weak protections in practice and has a highly attenuated connection to other economic liberties, such as the right to profit from transactions or the right to start a business.[2]

Three reasons support this contention. First, although Article 17 of the Universal Declaration of Human Rights (UDHR) protects the right to hold property "alone as well as in association with others,"[3] the two International Covenants that followed it—the Civil and Political Covenant (ICCPR) and the Economic, Social and Cultural Covenant (ICESCR)—omit this right.[4] As a consequence, the monitoring mechanisms established under the two Covenants do not cover the implementation of property rights. The Human Rights Committee has addressed the right to property only indirectly, that is, in examining complaints related to violations of other rights that raised issues concerning ownership, particularly related to the right to a fair trial (Article 24), the right to no discrimination (Article 16) and minority rights (Article 27).[5] Complaints directly related to the right to property have typically been dismissed on the basis that the right is not included in the ICCPR and, thus, potential violations of it are beyond the jurisdiction of the Committee.[6]

Second, while rights related to property appear in other international human rights documents, such as prohibitions on economic discrimination against vulnerable groups,[7] a human right to private property, let alone to other economic freedoms, cannot be inferred from these non-discrimination provisions. On the one hand, the provisions in these treaties are consistent with strict limits on private property and economic liberties. An equal and non-discriminatory access to private property can be achieved by leveling down, that is, by granting a meager access to all. On the other hand, an extensive interpretation of these treaties is at odds with the circumstances in which they were adopted, as in the years in which they were signed the Soviet bloc would certainly have opposed the derivative recognition of the right to property (Sprankling, 2014).

Third, the protection of the right to private property and other economic liberties has been left to regional instruments, and with mixed results. The strongest protection is the European Court of Human Rights (ECHR) jurisprudence, which upholds limited rights to basic possessions, economic interests, certain contractual agreements and claims of compensation against private and public parties.[8] However, the ECHR, like other courts, gives the widest interpretation to national prerogative to regulate and curtail private property. Only in egregious cases of government expropriation, interference and curtailment does the court see cause to step in. The Inter-American Court of Human Rights case law regarding the right to property is less extensive, yet it has largely followed the jurisprudence of the ECHR (Janis et al., 2008: 519–520).

Finally, the status of the right to property and other economic liberties in the African System of Human Rights is very precarious. The African Commission has enforced the right in only a few isolated instances and its jurisprudence is still far from achieving the standards of the European and Inter-American Courts (Olaniyan, 2002: 238–241). The precarious status of the right to property in the African System of Human Rights is largely due to its formulation in the African Charter of Human Rights (Article 14), which is considerably narrower than the corresponding provision in other regional documents. It does not make any reference to adequate compensation in case of expropriation and leaves the enforcement of this right to the will of national and municipal authorities (Naldi, 2001).

In a nutshell, a universal formal and legally binding criterion protecting the right to property and other economic liberties is nowadays lacking and the protection of these rights by the regional instruments is highly uneven, being particularly weak in poor countries.

This situation is, to a large extent, a hangover from socialist Utopianism. At the time of the UDHR's drafting there was strong ideological opposition to including the right to property, including from the communist delegations as well as the principal drafter of the Declaration, John Peters Humphrey. An avowed socialist, Humphrey sought to insert a socialist conception of personal property (excluding or strongly limiting private ownership of productive property) into the UDHR, and even proposed a human right to an "equitable share of the national income."[9] Such attempts were successful at other times, leading to Article 23 of the *American Declaration of the Rights and Duties of Man* limiting the right to property to what "meets the essential needs of decent living and helps to maintain the dignity of the individual and of the home."

Perhaps it was once reasonable to hold out hope for such socialist Utopianism (although opinions surely differ on that). But it has been overtaken by events. Since the collapse of the Soviet Union and the fall of the communist regimes in Eastern Europe, countries across the world have dismantled command economies and gradually embraced freer markets and private enterprise. This turn towards the capitalist road was largely motivated by a change in empirical beliefs: economic growth is the best strategy towards social and economic development.

Of course, unlocking economic growth is no simple task. No one has the recipe for making a country prosper. But we do know the recipe for making a country poor. The best evidence available shows that without economic liberties it simply does not happen. Market economies have proved to be able, under certain circumstances, to generate inclusive and pro-poor economic growth. Socialist economies had only promised it.

If human rights law is ambivalent about the economic liberties, theorists speak much more univocally. While the academic literature is rife with proposals of new human rights, it remains largely silent or critical about economic liberties and property rights.[10] Indeed, the very term "economic rights" has come to refer to rights to adequate standards of living, food, clothing, shelter, basic health care and so on.

Some theorists present the poor as passive beneficiaries of foreign aid and, consequently, put forward strongly redistributive theories that see economic liberties as barriers to the achievement of justice. (Some literally compare the world's poor to children who need to be saved by Westerners.) Others show greater concern for the role of the poor as economic agents but they invariably depict them as wageworkers employed in sweatshops and focus on standard labor rights as means to protect their interests. They ignore the fact that those rights are of little significance to the poor who are not subject to an employment relationship. But this concerns half of the workforce in poor countries, and the working conditions of this group are often worse than those of sweatshop workers (Wiego, 2018).

This constitutes a very serious failure. Initially, the human rights regime was primarily intended to constrain arbitrary state power. International legal norms provide a set of rights that offer backup protections in case national governments fail to adequately carry out the task of protecting their subjects. The state of affairs described above, however, means that in the economic arena such backup protections are sorely lacking. Despite governments around the world trampling on these rights, international law does not offer adequate backup support. To name but one example: there are no explicit prohibitions on bribery and other corrupt government activities that are obstacles to economic activities (Buchanan, 2013: 167–168). As a result, rapacious regimes can extract resources from their people in order to pay off their supporters, do not have to contend with a strongly developed rule of law when dealing with property rights and so on.[11]

In a sense, a strange inversion has occurred, then. Where the main purpose of human rights seems to be protecting people by *constraining* the power of the states under which they live, in the economic domain human rights have come to *empower* states. They call for provisions and protections that require states to arrange, order and interfere in the economic affairs of their subjects.[12] Clearly, such calls for empowerment without the accompanying constraining protections can be highly dangerous.

No doubt, many important and difficult questions remain. Even if the property rights and economic liberties are to be recognized as human rights, there remain questions about how strong these protections should be. There remain questions about what parts of economic life should be protected by them. There remain questions about how much discretion states should have in terms of regulating these rights. There also remain important theoretical questions. What grounding might be given to these rights? Can we affirm these rights in a way that's fully respectful to different countries and cultures around the world? What is the connection between these rights and other rights? How should the actual practice of these rights influence our theorizing about them? How do these rights function in practice, and what can we learn from that?

These and related questions lie at the heart of this volume. Our hope is that, by bringing together authors who are engaging in an open-minded and constructive discussion of these topics, we can move in the direction of a discussion of these rights that is more constructive and, to be frank, more honest.

2. Overview

This book is divided into five parts. The chapters in Part I are concerned with economic liberties as legal human rights. They explore different issues concerning the legal status, nature and justification of these liberties, as well as their relationship to other human rights. At present, only the right to property is legally recognized as a human right. It has been enshrined in 21 human rights instruments—including some of the most widely ratified—and more than two thirds of countries are under the jurisdiction of regional human rights courts that can enforce property rights. Despite these facts, however, legal scholars, political theorists and human rights advocates are generally ambivalent, if not hostile, towards the human right to private property. In the opening chapter, José E. Alvarez argues that this resistance is fueled by a caricature of the right to property as a simplistic, uniformly applicable set of prescriptions that aims to export Western values to the rest of the world and often hurts the interests of the most vulnerable. He shows, however, that this understanding of the right to property is belied by the existing human rights treaties and the international jurisprudence that emerges from them. The human right to property that results from his analysis is a complex and nuanced idea. It encompasses state obligations involving private, common and communal property. It differs among nations and even among communities. It extends to the rich no less than the poor. And it can be trumped by the rights of others, just like other human rights.

In Chapter 3, Samantha Besson examines the nature and justification of economic rights as international human rights law. She criticizes two standard approaches to these rights. The first sees them as mirroring real or natural moral rights. Besson is critical of this view, contending that it would lead to an overly liberal interpretation. Instead, Besson prioritizes attempts to promote social justice. The second downgrades economic rights to "moral goals" and, in so doing, it reinforces the conception of social rights as passive subsistence or anti-poverty rights that has been common in the international system of human rights since the 1960s. Besson offers a third view. She argues that legal economic rights recognize and/or specify universal moral rights that are not natural or real but conventional: their justification is instrumental to the value of the social practice they belong to. Her conventional reading of economic rights seeks to re-unite them with social rights and hence, alleviate possible tensions between the two.

In the next chapter, Carol Rose continues exploring the connection between economic rights and other rights. How might property rights advance, or fail to advance, human rights? Contrary to the view of many human rights theorists, who often cast property as a villain, Rose claims that property protections play very important roles in supporting other human rights. She focuses on three such roles. First, secure property rights are a fundamental part of the background conditions in which the realization of social rights is both economically and politically feasible. Second, the recognition of indigenous and traditional communities' land claims can, with some caveats, protect them from encroachments that threaten their livelihoods and cultures. Third, expropriation can create constituencies for repressive regimes that engage in mass atrocities of displacement, murder and other gross violations of human rights.

Besides their specific connections with other rights, economic liberties are often grounded on a simple reason: they provide fertile soil for economic growth. The question of how to unlock economic growth, particularly in lagging world regions, has become a central focus in global development discussions among practitioners and policy makers. This, however, raises concerns among certain political philosophers and legal scholars who fear that the quest for growth will threaten the realization of other fundamental rights. While the worry may be reasonable, it should not lead one to ignore the tremendous importance of these rights, in terms of supporting both economic growth and other human rights. A more promising view, then, sees the two classes of rights as compatible and indeed mutually reinforcing.

The chapters in Part II vindicate this role and value of economic liberties. Dan Moller explains the nature of economic growth and draws some lessons from economic history about its importance for realizing justice and economic well-being. He points out that prominent philosophical work on global justice persistently ignores those lessons and focus instead on altruism and foreign aid, despite the widespread evidence that the latter often hurt, rather than benefit, the world's poor. His contribution is an important invitation for philosophers to rethink their approach to problems of global justice.

The connection between economic liberties, economic growth and human rights is further explored in Francis Cheneval's contribution to the volume. His chapter argues that the realization of social rights such as the rights to education, subsistence and health care, which he subsumes under a right to assistance, is only possible if a sizable group of people contributes to the creation of wealth that in turn allows expenditures on individual well-being. Wealth creation necessarily involves the economic activity of individuals, alone or in cooperation with others, which can be either forced or free. Economic liberties ensure that individuals are free to decide which economic activities they pursue—as well as how and with whom—in order to create the wealth necessary to assist others. Without economic liberties, the demands of the right to assistance can only be satisfied by means of forced labor. Cheneval contends that this is a reason to recognize some economic liberties, in particular entrepreneurial rights, as human rights on a par with the social rights they serve.

The essential role of economic liberties in achieving poverty reduction, economic prosperity and human rights is the starting point of Fernando Tesón's contribution as well. In his chapter, he makes the case for overcoming the economic agnosticism that characterizes international human rights law, which gives economic liberties a low status for the sake of remaining neutral between capitalism and socialism. The best empirical evidence shows the superiority of markets over alternative arrangements in advancing social and economic development and this should be enough reason to eradicate socialism's influence on international human rights law. Attempts to justify economic agnosticism as a form of public-reason liberalism that preserves the economic sovereignty of the states are, according to Tesón, bound to fail for two reasons. First, public-reason tolerance should apply to normative beliefs, not to empirical ones. Second, whatever the merits of public-reason liberalism when applied to individuals, its extension to states has serious problems.

Part III presents moral arguments in favor of acknowledging some economic liberties as human rights. The authors interrogate existing accounts of human rights and offer compelling reasons to extend them to specific economic liberties. Amanda Greene's pioneering chapter focuses on the right to livelihood understood as the ability to exercise some control over how one generates sufficient income for providing for one's own material well-being. The right livelihood entails specific claims that are different from those entailed by other economic rights like freedom of occupation, the right to work or the right to own means of production, and thus deserves a separate defense. First, Greene argues that the right to livelihood is a moral right because having a livelihood is good in itself and contributes to individual well-being directly, through providing social contribution esteem and a sense of self-provision, and indirectly, through the collective good of the free market. Second, she shows how the right to livelihood can be effectively protected and enforced as a constitutional right and as a human right.

The next two chapters discuss the right to productive property. Chris Freiman and John Trasher understand this right as the liberty to acquire, own, use, transfer and benefit from means of production. They argue that such a right ought to be considered a human right because it is one specification of other well-established human rights: the right to personal property and the right to freedom of occupational choice. The former derives from the latter two just as the right to work as a motivational speaker derives from the rights to freedom of speech and occupational choice. Thus, they conclude, the decision of socialist or authoritarian regimes to outlaw private productive property always constitutes a violation of two fundamental human rights that liberals of all stripes should condemn.

Nien-hê Hsieh rejects the interpretation of the right to productive property as a liberty or a privilege and makes the case for acknowledging the claim to an adequate share of productive property that ensures an adequate standard of living as specified by other human rights. He embraces a political account of human rights and seeks to justify the right to productive property by interpreting the role it would play in the human rights practice. His main argument is that recognizing such a right would be decisive to realize the ideal of status egalitarianism, which he sees as a central feature of the contemporary human rights regime. In contrast to

Freiman and Trasher, Hsieh claims that ensuring the right to own means of production may actually require restricting the economic liberties associated with capitalism.

Finally, in their chapter Robert Cooter and Benjamin Chen seek to ground economic freedom in the value of economic creativity. Human rights documents refer to creativity almost exclusively in the context of the arts, hence disregarding the role it plays in the economic sphere. Economic creativity is intrinsically valuable as an expression of individual freedom and as form of human flourishing. It is also instrumentally valuable to human well-being to the extent that it improves the capacity of our economic systems to deliver goods. Assuming a naturalistic account of human rights, Cooter and Chen argue that economic freedom is a moral human right, which ought to be acknowledged as a legal human right, because it allows, protects and fosters economic creativity.

In Part IV, authors consider worries about the status of economic liberties as human rights. Daniel Attas is concerned about economic liberties being too parochial to be codified in international human rights law. The legitimacy of such law depends, in part, in its capacity to accommodate the deep-seated fact of cultural pluralism that characterizes the global order. According to Attas, economic liberties are not general freedoms to participate in economic activities but specific freedoms to commodify, that is, to take part in production and consumption through economic exchange. Such liberties, he contends, protect individual interests that are common in capitalist societies, but they are not distinctly human, timeless or culture-independent. The objection of parochialism applies to both naturalistic and political conceptions of economic liberties as human rights.

The next chapter focuses on the liberty to engage in market exchange. Rowan Cruft discusses two questions about the status of this liberty as a moral right. The first is about the importance of this liberty vis-à-vis other rights such as freedom of association, health, education and life. The second is about the centrality of the interests it protects to our human nature. Cruft's answers are connected. He claims that freedom of exchange is less fundamental than other rights because our interest in being unimpeded in exchanging fails to ground the right in the ways he considers essential. His argument is compatible with acknowledging that in the present circumstances freedom of exchange plays a vital role in advancing individual well-being.

Finally, Part V offers a practice-based discussion of the implementation of some economic liberties with a special focus on their potential to protect the interest of vulnerable groups. Martha Chen draws attention to the fact that nearly half of the global workforce are self-employed workers that run informal business with no legal or social protection. This reality defies the assumption on which the economic rights of workers are premised, namely, a wage relationship. Self-employed workers, Chen argues, need a greater variety of economic rights than wageworkers. Her chapter suggests a basic bundle of economic rights for the self-employed based on the demands triggered by the working conditions of some these workers—home-based workers, street vendors and waste pickers—and offers a roadmap for realizing them.

Karol C. Boudreaux shifts the focus towards other vulnerable groups, namely, women and indigenous people. She offers an empirically informed discussion that probes the significance of land rights in advancing the human rights agenda, particularly regarding those groups, who often see their ability to access, use, manage and transfer land heavily constrained. Weak or insecure land rights are often the result of unequal and discriminatory treatment; create poverty and hunger; hamper economic and social opportunities; and fuel different kinds of disputes and conflicts. Despite their limited recognition under the human rights framework, land rights deserve a prominent role in human rights policies and discussions.

Notes

* Earlier versions of some these chapters were presented at the workshop Economic Liberties and Human Rights, at the Ethik Zentrum of the Univerity of Zurich, May 25–26, 2017. Funds were provided by the Swiss National Science Foundation as part of the project Entrepreneurial Rights, Legal Rights and Legal Empowerment of the Poor.

1 We set aside here the important fact that people's (not countries') best opportunity for escaping poverty is migration. For extensive discussion and defense, see van der Vossen and Brennan, 2018. See also Pritchett, 2018.

2 An exception is the Charter of Fundamental Rights of the European Union that recognizes the freedom to conduct businesses (Article 16).

3 The qualification was intended to make the right consistent with communist regimes—which, essentially, denied these protections to their subjects.

4 The covenants include property-related rights such as property rights of peoples over natural wealth and resources (Article 1.2 ICCPR), intellectual property rights (Article 15 ICESCR) and mention property as a prohibited ground for discrimination (Article 2 and Article 26 ICCPR).

5 See, for example, *Ominayak (Lubicon Lake Band) v. Canada*, Communication N°. 167/1984; *Länsman (Ilmari) et al. v. Finland*, Communication N°. 511/1992; *Länsman (Jouni E.) et al. v. Finland*, Communication N°. 671/1995; *Mahuika et al. v. New Zealand*, Communication N°. 547/1993; *Oló Bahamonde v. Equatorial Guinea*, Communication N°. 468/1991; *Ackla v. Togo*, Communication N°. 505/1992; *Diergaardt et al. v. Namibia*, Communication N°. 760/1997; *Simunek et al. v. The Czech Republic*, Communication N°. 516/1992; *E. and A.K. v. Hungary*, Communication N°. 520/1992; and *Somers v. Hungary*, Communication No. 566/1993.

6 See *E. and A.K. v. Hungary*, Communication N°. 520/1992; and *Anton (Armand) v. Argelia*, Communication N°. 1424/2005.

7 Article 15 of the *International Convention on the Protection of the Rights of All Migrant Workers and Members of Their Families* affirms the right to

property for migrants. Articles 15 and 16 of the *Convention on the Elimination of All Forms of Discrimination Against Women* hold that women must have equal rights to men concerning property and economic freedom.

8 Although even in the European case, these rights were initially excluded from the main Convention (and relegated to the optional First Protocol) because several European nations at the time were engaged in nationalizing industries.

9 Johannes Morsink (1999) writes: to Humphrey "socialism. . . [was] a religion" (133. See also: 139, 191 ff and ch. 4).

10 For extensive discussion, see van der Vossen and Brennan, 2018: ch. 7.

11 Acemoglu and Robinson (2012) discuss the way in which stable property rights constrain extractive regimes (which is partly why such regimes oppose these rights). De Soto (2000) writes about how a stable property regime will have positive spill-over benefits in terms of creating a rule of law.

12 We owe the point to Fernando Tesón.

References

Acemoglu D and Robinson J (2012) *Why Nations Fail*. New York: Crown Business.

Buchanan A (2013) *The Heart of Human Rights*. Oxford: Oxford University Press.

De Soto H (1989) *The Other Path: The Economic Alternative to Terrorism*. New York: Harper and Row.

De Soto H (2000) *The Mystery of Capital: Why Capitalism Triumphs in the West and Fails Everywhere Else*. New York: Basic Books.

Djankov S et al (2002) The Regulation of Entry. *Quarterly Journal of Economics* 117: 1–35.

Janis M, Kay R and Bradley A (2008) *European Human Rights Law: Text and Materials*, 3rd ed. Oxford: Oxford University Press.

Morsink J (1999) *The Universal Declaration of Human Rights: Origins, Drafting, and Intent*. Philadelphia: University of Pennsylvania Press.

Naldi G (2001) Limitation of Rights Under the African Charter on Human and Peoples' Rights: The Contribution of the African Commission on Human and Peoples' Rights. *South African Journal of Human Rights* 17: 109–118.

North D (1990) *Institutions, Institutional Change, and Economic Performance*. Cambridge: Cambridge University Press.

Pigou, AC (1938) *The Economics of Welfare*, 4th ed. London: Palgrave Macmillan.

Pritchett L (2018) *Alleviating Global Poverty: Labor Mobility, Direct Assistance, and Economic Growth*. CGD Working Paper 479. Washington, DC: Center for Global Development. Available at: www.cgdev.org/publication/alleviating-global-poverty-labormobility-direct-assistance-and-economic-growth.

Olaniyan (2002) Civil and Political Rights in the African Charter: Articles 8–14. In: Evans M and R Murray (eds) *The African Charter on Human and Peoples' Rights, the System in Practice, 1986–2006*, 2nd ed. Cambridge, MA: Cambridge University Press, pp. 213–244.

Sprankling JG (2014) *The International Law of Property*. Oxford: Oxford University Press.

Van der Vossen B and Brennan J (2018) *In Defense of Openness: Why Global Freedom Is the Humane Solution to Global Poverty*. Oxford: Oxford University Press.

Wiego (2018) Informal Economy Monitoring Study. Available at: www.wiego.org/wiego/informal-economy-monitoring-study-iems-publications (accessed 20 December 2018).

World Bank (2018) Doing Business Rankings. Available at: www.doingbusiness.org/en/rankings (accessed 20 December 2018).

Part I

Economic Liberties and International Law

2 Property Rights as Human Rights

José E. Alvarez

Imagine no possessions, I wonder if you can . . . the brotherhood of man.
—*Imagine*, John Lennon

1. Introduction

While progressives in the West like to imagine an idyllic world without property, international lawyers like to imagine a world grounded in respect for human rights. Neither sees property protections as part of their ideal. This is so even though (1) every society in recorded history has seen fit to establish mechanisms for protecting property for private, common or communal use; (2) rights to property are now embraced by some 95 percent of national legal systems (most commonly in their constitutions); and (3) property protections feature in a large number of international legal regimes, including at least 20 human rights instruments.[1] International human rights law, at least in the form of treaties, protects forms of private, common and communal property. This chapter explores what the human right of property is and is not.

2. Ambivalence or Hostility

As is indicated by Table 2.1 included at the end of this chapter, the human rights instruments containing an explicit right to the protection of "property" include the texts that started the 20th-century human rights revolution, namely the Universal Declaration of Human Rights and the preceding American Declaration of the Rights and Duties of Man. Such treaties include regional human rights regimes that enable permanent international courts to hear such claims as well as some of the most widely ratified treaties in existence that seek to protect refugees, prisoners, indigenous peoples, racial minorities, women, migrant workers and the disabled (Table 2.1). As Table 2.1 indicates, more than two thirds of nations have accepted the jurisdiction of a regional human rights court that can rule on property rights (under the American Convention on Human Rights, the European Convention of Human Rights, the African Charter or the Arab Charter) and only two states—Palau and

South Sudan—are not party to at least one treaty that bars discriminatory treatment with respect to property rights.

The right to property protection under international law is the subject of a growing body of jurisprudence in both national and supranational courts and tribunals. One in six of the 19,750 rulings issued between 1959 and 2016 by the European Court of Human Rights (ECtHR) involve claims to property, for example (Alvarez, 2018: 657). UN human rights treaty bodies, including the committee under the Convention on the Elimination of All Forms of Discrimination Against Women (CEDAW), have addressed the right of property in the course of monitoring state reports, issuing "views" pursuant to individual complaints, or in their general comments.[2] Property protections are also addressed by national and international bodies with jurisdiction to consider the other internationalized property rights regimes in Table 2.2, including WTO panelists addressing intellectual property, ILO monitoring committees and national and international courts prosecuting war crimes involving the deprivation of property owned by prisoners of war, pillage or the destruction of cultural property.[3] Of course, the rights of foreign-owned property are also the subject of a burgeoning arbitral case law under thousands of international investment agreements (IIAs) (see, e.g., Bishop et al., 2005).

International property protections cut across traditional public/private divides. Like other treaties, those that include property protections impose inter-state obligations and may permit states to file claims against each other for alleged breach. Violations of treaty-based property rights, like any other treaty breach, constitute traditional "international wrongful acts" that, unless ousted by *lex specialis* remedies (such as authorizations to engage in tariff retaliation by the WTO's dispute settlement system), trigger remedies under the rules of state responsibility.[4] But some property-protecting treaties authorize their non-state beneficiaries to bring claims for breach. These include individuals under optional protocols to UN human rights treaties, individuals or other legal persons (such as corporations) before the ECtHR, individuals and some shareholders before the IACtHR and foreign investors and investments under IIAs. In some instances (e.g., under regional human rights treaties or IIAs), the anticipated remedies include legally binding awards for damages or other forms of reparation for property deprivations. In other cases, property rights breaches elicit, as do violations of other human rights, efforts to mobilize shame against violators, such as public criticism by human rights treaty committees, ILO committees or UN bodies (such as the UN Human Rights Council, UN special rapporteurs, the General Assembly or the Security Council). As noted, some breaches of internationalized property rights may even trigger individual criminal accountability.[5]

To the extent scholars have focused on international property rights, most of their attention has been on the specialized regimes of trade and investment. The economic rights of traders of goods, makers of intellectual property and foreign investors have drawn the most attention.

Internationalized property rights are also associated with the advice of economists working in development agencies or international financial institutions such as the World Bank or the IMF. Ronald Coase, Harold Demsetz, Douglass North and Hernando de Soto, among others, have stressed the value of formal title to property, particularly land, for purposes of economic development (see Upham, 2018: 1–9, discussing these scholars). Advice from these quarters continues to emphasize that legally recognized rights to property promulgated by legislative authority and enforced by courts are indispensable to economic growth, are essential elements of 'good governance' and/or the 'rule of law' and needed to protect the stable expectations that support sound planning and inter-state commerce (Upham, 2018:1–2).

These instrumentalist defenses of property rights have a venerable history. Their intellectual forebears include Aristotle, Aquinas, Francisco de Vitoria, Domingo de Soto, Hugo Grotius and Adam Smith—all of whom argued in their respective ways that the protection of property incentivizes diligence, promotes efficiency, order and stability and enables common interests in peaceful commerce to emerge (Koskenniemi, 2011, 2017). Similarly functionalist rationales have justified the internationalization and treatification of rules in defense of the property rights of aliens, particularly foreign investors. Alien property has been protected under customary international law (e.g., the "international minimum standard" of treatment or the rule requiring "prompt, adequate and effective compensation" upon expropriation), numerous bilateral or regional agreements (from the OECD's Code of Capital Movements to bilateral investment treaties (BITs) to the NAFTA's investment chapter) and many forms of "soft law" (e.g., the World Bank's Guidelines for the Treatment of Foreign Investment) (Alvarez, 2017).

It is therefore not surprising that internationalized property protections on behalf of aliens, particularly Western investors, are associated with "Western" values. James Madison and John Locke both famously proclaimed that one of the chief aims of establishing a government was to preserve property and that idea found its way into the U.S. Constitution (in its takings and contract clauses) to make sure that the young Republic would protect the rights of national *and* foreign property owners (Alvarez, 2018: 598–599). The nation's earliest treaties with Britain shared the same goals (Alvarez, 2018: 600–602). As Alexander Hamilton argued in the course of defending the 1794 Jay Treaty—whose provisions included defending the rights of British creditors and investors from actions by state legislatures and courts—international rules to protect foreign investors were necessary to protect the reputation of the nation and to ensure continued flows of foreign capital (Alvarez, 2017). For over 200 years the United States has pursued this agenda through Friendship, Commerce and Navigation treaties (FCNs), (generally unsuccessful) efforts to conclude multilateral treaties in defense of foreign property, the 1995 transformation of the GATT into the WTO (along with incorporation of intellectual property into that regime) and the conclusion of IIAs with access to investor-state dispute settlement (ISDS) (Alvarez, 2018: 602–604). U.S. negotiators of BITs argued that adherence to such treaties would demonstrate a state's willingness to adopt the "minimum conditions" needed to engage in modern commerce (see e.g., Vandevelde, 1998).

To be sure, the protection of foreign capital under today's IIAs owes a considerable historical debt to classic texts associated with what became, after WWII, "human rights."[6] Property rights were essential to both the "pursuit of happiness" in the U.S. Declaration of Independence and the 1789 French Declaration of the Rights of Man and of the Citizen.[7] But, over time, the links between international instruments to protect foreign investors and those seeking to protect the rights of all humans from abuses committed by their own governments were relegated to historians. The respective legal communities dealing with international investment law and international human rights drew apart and, to some extent, became estranged. Today, suggestions that foreign investors, and possibly corporations, enjoy "human rights" (as under IIAs) are fighting words to most human rights scholars and advocates, while defenders of the international investment regime or the WTO's protection of intellectual property, for their part, tend to associate demands for protecting human rights as defenses raised by states charged with interfering with free capital and trade flows.[8]

For most scholars of investment law, property protections under IIAs stem from 19th-century diplomatic espousal practice that considered maltreatment of one's nationals abroad to be an affront committed by a host state against the investor's home state. These scholars, the most significant group within international law that examines the "right to property," do not see that right as a claim arising simply from the condition of being human. They ignore the reality that, at least as far as contemporary international law is concerned, property rights are *human* rights.

The lack of attention to the property-respecting aspects of the human rights treaties in Table 2.1 and the close association with internationalized property rights with the rights of foreign traders and investors have made international law's protection of property rights easy to associate with development experts who emphasize the need to allocate formal land title. Those who criticize efforts to export hard enforceable property rights argue that this prescription ignores alternatives that have worked elsewhere (as in China), namely more flexible forms of property protection characterized by periodic evolutions from collective to private possession, reliance on decisions taken by policy makers and not legislatures or courts and the use of soft law and remedies (Upham, 2018: 83–105). Similar critiques have been made of ISDS rulings that seem intent on protecting property simply because its holders happen to enjoy first possession or requiring governments to pay "prompt, adequate, and effective compensation" for all takings of property no matter the motive. For critics like Upham, such applications of traditional "status quo" property rights prevent or unduly delay the periodic "destruction" of prior property rights that even in the West has been essential for long-term growth, such as to promote manufacturing or mining (Upham, 2018: 34–60).

To the extent the human right to property is associated with such development advice, it leads to predictable criticisms. The international right to property eludes inevitable contestations over what "property" is among nations and the need for relevant protections to evolve over time and in response to technological developments. The human right to property seems to assume worldwide consensus on what is the legitimate content of the right to property.[9] Of course, for those who are aware of the considerable differences even within Western nations with respect to how governments should respect, ensure or fulfill the property rights of their citizens, this universalist conception, even if it were affirmed in treaties, strains credulity.

And, despite the varied nature of international property rights demonstrated in Tables 2.1 and 2.2—and the diverse views of those who interpret such treaties—the international protection of property is today most closely associated with the strict property protections accorded to investors by investor-state tribunals under IIAs. Such rulings are easy to criticize as the continuation by other means of international law's longstanding "civilizing"-cum-"imperialist" project.[10] They can be seen as the modern-day deployment of law to promote the interests of powerful multinational enterprises—much like a contemporary version of 19th-century justifications to enable "gun-boat" diplomacy directed at forcing debt payments from the global south (see Johnson and Gimblett, 2012: 649). If internationalized property protections are but thinly veiled tools that defend the West's economic interests and its supranational enforcement tools merely species of "gun-boat arbitration," they can be readily dismissed as imperialist cudgels to colonize, tools that privilege only one kind of market state, or enablers of incomplete, misleading or dangerous recipes for development (Upham, 2018: 1).[11] And if the international protection of property is associated only with the WTO and ISDS regimes, growing doubts about those regimes—about whether "free trade" agreements are really in the interest of all nations or the interest of the poorest persons in any nation—is bound to undermine the credibility of claims that property rights are genuinely "human" rights.

Even without such associations, the human right to property protection has much to answer for. Since ancient times, philosophers and theologians have worried that property protection has often been a tool to discriminate against the vulnerable or the property-less (as to deny the vote or to target slaves, refugees, stateless persons, women or members of minorities). Quite apart from skepticism about the very idea of human rights, there have been perennial concerns about whether property rights in particular can be "genuine" human rights. Does it make sense to suggest that the right of property is a "fundamental" one that can be demanded from governments when such rights exist only because they are created by governments? Why protect private property, a creature of society, from society and society's own needs to sometimes take property? How can property protection be a human right when, unlike others, property rights are not "inalienable" and, indeed, are typically defined by one's capacity to sell, trade or destroy them? Some have suggested that, unlike genuine human rights like the right not to be tortured, the right to property does not derive from the human condition but rather from the mere material, arbitrary and possibly trivial fact that someone has managed to secure first possession and secure title. Property ownership, some say, is not *essential* to being human; its deprivation does not offend human dignity in the way that torture does. Further, if one defines genuine human rights as those which bind or connect individuals to one another by reminding them of their common humanity, how does recognizing the right to exclusive possession achieve that?[12]

All of this helps to explain the considerable ambivalence, including among human rights advocates, about the human right to property protection—despite its widespread appearance in widely ratified treaties. Consider, as one example of that ambivalence, the treatment of property by U.S. courts. Unlike, for example, the case law of the IACtHR with respect to indigenous peoples, the international human right to property plays no role in American Indian law.[13] Worse still, U.S. courts are reluctant to accept the reality that international law protects the right of property for a state's own citizens. The most prominent cases involve the exception from sovereign immunity provided in the U.S.'s Foreign Sovereign Immunities Act, enabling certain suits to proceed against foreign states in U.S. courts involving rights to property "taken in violation of international law."[14] U.S. courts have uniformly resisted finding that a government taking of property owned by its own national violates international law. Despite the language of the FSIA, they have created, through judicial interpretation, an exception for "domestic takings," indicating, as stated in a leading case, that this is because "[w]ith a few limited exceptions, international law delineates minimum standards for the protection only of aliens; it does not purport to interfere with the relations between a nation and its own citizens."[15] U.S. courts have affirmed that "domestic takings" do not violate international law even when dealing with countries, such as Venezuela, that are parties to the American Convention of Human Rights, a treaty which like many others clearly indicates that a state's own nationals have a right to property.[16] While some U.S. courts have carved out a limited exception to their "domestic takings" jurisprudence, that exception—permitting claims against states for "genocidal takings"—indicates the lesser status of the international right of property under U.S. jurisprudence.[17] U.S. courts, like international lawyers who focus only on the property rights of foreign traders or investors, appear to believe that international law protects only alien property.

3. International Law's Response: What the Human Right to Property Protection Is and Isn't

The treaties in Table 2.1 suggest one response to property rights' unequal application. History did not end when the two covenants, the International Covenant on Civil and Political Rights (ICCPR) and the International Covenant on Economic, Social and Cultural Rights (ICESCR), came to a Cold War compromise by rejecting the Universal Declaration's right to property (favored by Western states).[18] As demonstrated by the proliferation of human rights treaties, international lawyers responded to the complaint that property rights have often hurt the vulnerable by concluding treaties designed to respect the property rights of the most vulnerable: racial minorities, women, refugees, stateless persons and the disabled. International law has also attempted some responses to ancient concerns over property rights. While the ICCPR did not include the protection of property because of Cold War divides, it still managed to ban the use of property as a precondition for voting and, of course, treaties negotiated long before the human rights revolution prohibited turning human beings into someone else's property by banning the slave trade.

The suggestion that the human right of property is a simplistic, uniformly applicable set of prescriptions that ignore the absence of genuine consensus on such matters is a caricature that is belied by the diverse property instruments at Tables 2.1 and 2.2. These treaties do not presume a single definition of which bundle of rights amount to a "property" right or on precisely how governments must balance the right of private property vis-à-vis the sovereign right to regulate. Far from presuming that the West's view of hard property rights can be exported to the world, the distinct instruments in these tables, drafted by and ratified by separate numbers and groups of states and subject to very different hard and soft remedies, recognize that the concept of property—and individuals' right to it—is deeply contestable within societies and naturally among them.[19] The property-respecting instruments that we now have are built on the lessons learned from numerous failed efforts to negotiate comprehensive global rules regarding even a subpart of the subject, namely rules to govern the property of foreign investors.[20] The emerging international property jurisprudence under these treaties recognizes that, as Upham would recommend, property rights sometimes need to be destroyed; that even the "fundamental" right of property, like other rights, can be "trumped" by the rights of others; that private property can co-exist alongside common and communal property; that the right of first possession does not always prevail; that property can be protected by soft, as well as hard, law or remedies; that the instantiation of the human right of property differs among nations and even among communities within them; and that the deprivation of property by the state does not always require "full" compensation.

Consider, as one example, the rich and nuanced property jurisprudence of the Inter-American Court of Human Rights (IACtHR). Article 21 of the American Convention of Human Rights, as interpreted by the IACtHR, protects both communal and private property.[21] It protects certain groups (indigenous peoples) as well as individuals. While in some instances (such as with respect to allocating certain "sacred lands" to indigenous peoples), that Court has found a right *to* certain property, most of the time, the remedy for property deprivations in that Court (as well as in other supranational forums that enforce property rights) is some form of reparation, including damages. Property, as interpreted by the IACtHR, is not an excuse to maintain the "status quo." Property protections evolve over time in accordance with the Court's view of the American Convention as a "living instrument" responsive to changing technology, changing national laws establishing certain entitlements and "current living conditions" within the region's democracies.[22] Through 2017, the IACtHR has found protected property to include "sacred" lands farmed (but not formally owned) by identified indigenous peoples, forms of intellectual property, certain rights enjoyed by corporate shareholders, tangibles seized from individuals in the course of law enforcement and civil forfeiture and distinct forms of "acquired rights" provided by welfare states. In protecting these forms of property, that Court has treated as relevant (and not only in cases involving indigenous peoples), the economic, social and "affective" associations formed between property and persons, the expectations for continued enjoyment of property established under national law on behalf of either groups or individuals and the satisfaction of fair process requirements within established democracies (Alvarez, 2018: 606–633). In certain cases, the Court has protected expectations to property, including to government pensions, on the basis of a presumed connection between the freedom to work and the right to secure the benefits of one's labor.[23] Whether a claimant enjoys "first possession" of the property in question or even has formal title to it has not always proven determinative.[24]

The IACtHR's property jurisprudence differs from U.S. Indian law jurisprudence or even U.S. jurisprudence involving direct or indirect takings.[25] Under the IACtHR's case law, governments are not expected merely to refrain from doing harm to property (as by refraining from expropriations), they are expected to be more proactively protective of property to the extent vulnerable groups (such as those living in poverty) are affected or legitimate expectations have been generated by the government's prior laws (e.g., by its establishing entitlements to pensions at a certain level) (Alvarez, 2018: 646–647). States' duties to protect some forms of property (such as the historic rights of indigenous peoples) are perceived as overlapping with governments' affirmative obligations to satisfy "essential" human needs, as for shelter and access to natural resources.[26]

The IACtHR's application of Article 21 has led to supranational review over politically sensitive actions taken by governments, as in response to crime or economic or other crises.[27] In such cases the Court has noted that property rights are "not absolute" and need to be judged relative to the competing rights owed to other persons, as well as the right of governments to regulate in the public interest (Alvarez, 2018: 646). In undertaking this balancing, the Court appears to proceed on a "case-by-case" basis in which a number of legal and even social factors (e.g., burdens of proof in criminal cases, the relative poverty of the claimant or the seriousness of the property deprivation) are considered both for purposes of determining whether a treaty breach has occurred as well as to decide the appropriate remedy, which need not always require payment of full, fair market value compensation.

Despite the IACtHR's frequent references to the case law of the ECtHR,[28] that Court's property jurisprudence differs from that of the ECtHR for obvious reasons. The ECtHR has not needed to address the rights of indigenous peoples nor the types of property cases involving "special gravity" that the IACtHR has faced,[29] even while needing to address unique property claims arising from the transition from communism and distinct claims for restorative justice in Eastern Europe.[30]For these reasons the two regional human rights courts that have produced the largest body of case law on the human right of property cannot be seen as producing harmonious property jurisprudence. Neither regime purports to find "universally" applicable property rules, even as it applies a "human right" of property. As is suggested by the absence of a single comprehensive property treaty on point, there is no such thing as a single global regime for property protection. The diversity of these instruments and the forums charged with interpreting them impose formidable obstacles towards reaching such a goal, even if such a prospect were desirable. The protecting instruments in Tables 2.1 and 2.2 differ with respect to whether distinct forms of property recognized as meriting international protection should be seen as a "human" right. And even the human rights instruments in Table 2.1 differ to some extent among themselves. Those with a global aspiration, such as CEDAW and CERD, encompass only non-discrimination guarantees with respect to property and only provide access for individual claimants to committees of experts with no authority to issue legally binding judgments.[31] Other instruments impose limits only with respect to governments' "arbitrary" deprivations of property.[32]

Instruments that tackle property within the framework of equality differ considerably from the Inter-American and European human rights systems. CEDAW and its committee, for example, reframe property rights by targeting the specific ways that women's property rights have been violated throughout history, that is, during marriage and divorce and inheritance.[33] CEDAW, and the wide network of human rights institutions that it reaches, have encouraged an evolving understanding of the different ways national laws, cultural and religious practices make women less likely to achieve their full potential for self-realization.[34] Interpretations by the CEDAW committee target the blind spots promoted by traditional "public"/"private" distinctions in law, the focus on formal but not substantive equality, presumptions of male-headed households and the emphasis on only financial contributions for assessing entitlement to marital property (Mason and Carlsson, 2005: 114). The CEDAW committee's insistence on contextualizing how property rights relate to the unequal status of women and girls and on "accommodating differences" not only between men and women but between different women (and girls) in different places and time cast doubt on the wisdom of *uniform* property rules for all persons irrespective of context.[35]

This critical take on property rights, a considerable departure from the individualistic property jurisprudence of countries like the United States, may also emerge from other "equality" instruments in Table 2.1. Such instruments require, as CEDAW does, evaluating how the right to property promotes or detracts from the enjoyment of equal treatment for a particular group of persons; these compacts demand that property rights be treated as one among others. Such treaties, embedded in institutional settings that include expert committees, special rapporteurs and periodic consideration of state reports, encourage continuous conversations on how property rights impact vulnerable groups.[36] They are, as the IACtHR would put it, "living instruments" for *revisable* property rights that are attentive to evolving ideas of what "equal property rights" demand, for example, for women.[37]

For these reasons, the human right of property is, in general, more akin to the rights encompassed by the ICESCR than those included in the ICCPR. Like the former, property protections yield to progressive development over time and are dependent on the resources of the country in question (see ICESCR, Article 2). Accordingly, fears that acceptance of a human right of property leads to overly constricted and ideologically loaded development prescriptions seem overstated. The human right of property is not one idea but many. While the 132 states that are parties to at least one of the four major regional human rights treaties, the additional three states that are parties to the Commonwealth of Independent States Convention on Human Rights and Fundamental Freedoms and the 189 countries (including the United States) that are state parties to at least one treaty that prohibits discrimination with respect to property (such as CEDAW or CERD) have accepted the idea that a human right to property protection exists, they have left its instantiation to treaty by treaty elaboration and have only sometimes delegated its enforcement to an international judicial body (see Table 2.1). The à la carte and treaty-based nature of international property rights means that this capacious right remains responsive to sovereign consent—and, at least to this extent, to the discrete needs, cultures and histories of nations. The capacity of states to pick and choose among property rights and for each treaty regime to define them over time is international law's way of responding to the complexity of property rules as well as to concerns about exporting a particular version of them without due regard to context.

Table 2.1's human rights instruments do not insist, as would the strongest defenders of private property rights like Hernando de Soto, that the only route to economic development lies in allocating private title to holders of land (De Soto, 2000: 49–51). Nor does the human right of property protect only the right to private property. As noted, instruments like the American Convention embrace rights to *communal* property in some instances.[38] Other treaties, such as those within international humanitarian law, protect some forms of common property—such as cultural artifacts that help define a culture, a religion or an ethnic group. The 1954 Hague Convention for the Protection of Cultural Property in the Event of Armed Conflict recognizes that certain property needs protecting because there is, as the IACtHR has recognized in other contexts, often a "close association" between a culture or way of life and property, and the enemies of that group should not be permitted to systematically destroy either living persons or the things they build to remind others that the group exists.

As is clear from the case law of the ECtHR and the IACtHR, the right of property in some contexts and under some treaties may indeed protect private property and may even require governments to provide fair market value to the extent it is taken. To that extent some of this regional case law is consistent with some of the arbitral case law produced under IIAs. But as scholarly debates over the extent of compensation that is owed even under the ECtHR regime reveal, even when compensation is due for property deprivations, the extent to which that compensation must reflect "fair market value" or whether it should, in addition, pay the injured party for the subjective value of particular property varies among the human rights adjudicators that have addressed it (Alvarez, 2018: 664–666). The human rights instruments in Table 2.1 do not require recognition of "entrepreneurial freedom," "freedom of commerce" or a right to democracy. [39] In theory and in fact (given the diversity of states that have ratified many of these treaties), these instruments extend to all forms of government, capitalist or not, and presumptively accommodate diverse approaches to allocating the powers of the state versus the market. Some international property rights regimes may be *components* of the so-called Washington Consensus recipe for development designed to encourage privatization, respect for property rights, along with other forms of "good governance" promoted by the West, but the diverse property instruments in Table 2.1 should not be *conflated* with these efforts. Despite the historical connections between some property-respecting treaties (such as IIAs) and the drive by Western states to support the free market, the human rights treaties in Table 2.1 and those in Table 2.2 that appear to share human rights aims, such as those protecting labor rights or the rights to property during conflict, fulfill many distinct purposes apart from the pursuit of "economic freedom."

Caution is also required with respect to equating the human right of property with "hard enforcement" at the hands of national or international courts. International legal remedies, even when deploying relatively strong enforcement tools like regional human rights courts or ISDS, are subject to considerable possibilities for "exit and voice." Like most forms of international law, internationalized property rights rely on "managerial" or "experimentalist" tools to give them effect that complicate assessments of what "compliance" means (see Chayes and Chayes, 1995; de Búrca, 2017: 277; Howse and Teitel, 2010: 127, 136). A substantial number of the human rights treaties in Table 2.1 are subject to informal or soft enforcement tools that resemble, in many respects, those which Upham examines in the context of the Chinese approach to property (Upham, 2018: 83–105). International legal regimes' notorious enforcement gaps and capacity for treaty reservations make the human right of property a malleable instrument that does not always "trump" the state—or threaten its sovereignty. The texts of many human rights instruments, such as CEDAW, are circumspect with respect to constraints on sovereign discretion. These are suggested by the prevalence of hedge words such as only requiring "appropriate" measures in CEDAW's text, that treaty's abundant (if regrettable) reservations, as well as the potential for defiance of the CEDAW committee's non-binding views and recommendations. Admittedly, these concessions to sovereignty threaten to make that treaty, as well as other human rights instruments, toothless tigers. But this weakness means that the threat that these pose to legitimate regulatory concerns should not be exaggerated. The human right of property as applied in places like human rights committees is not a sword of Damocles hanging over conscientious regulators bent on fulfilling the public good.

4. Conclusions

John Lennon's call for a "brotherhood of man" without property asks us to imagine the impossible. As the eminent theologians who wrestled with the morality of property rights ultimately recognized, once humans came to exist in society the allocation of forms of property—private, common and communal—became essential. Far from being antithetical to bringing people together, rights to property enable people to commune. Societies—Western, Eastern, indigenous or other—cannot do without property rights, even if they sometimes choose to protect them through executive not judicial or legislative action and through revisable soft norms rather than hard title. As this suggests, the human right of property serves, at bottom, instrumentalist purposes. It makes modern society—China's no less than the United States'—possible. Nor were classical philosophers wrong to suggest that at key moments, the right to property—particularly private property—may incentivize efficiency, promote stability and encourage commerce over the turn to war. Protecting property may also serve to protect other rights. It can protect Franklin Roosevelt's Four Freedoms: it may protect us from want, ensure the right to work, enable freedom of expression and help to free us of certain governmental threats that inspire fear.

But the human right of property is not merely something needed to protect other, more "genuine," human rights, such as a publisher's right to a free press by protecting that press. Like other fundamental rights, it is derived from or inspired by core moral intuitions about what human dignity requires.[40] This is so even if human rights to property protection apply only to the extent particular states have agreed to them via treaty and do not apply as a matter of universal customary law or general principles of law. Although some have tried to ground the human right of property in global sources like custom, there are doubts on that score and universal property rights would, in all probability, encompass only the most minimalist of rights, perhaps capable only of protecting a person's entitlements to basic needs (Alvarez, 2018: 683–689).

But the piecemeal recognition, treaty by treaty, of certain human rights does not render them non-existent. We accept that, at least for those states that have ratified the Rights of the Child Convention or the ICESCR, those states owe treaty-based human rights that may be all the better for being more precisely defined and more clearly applicable temporally. This is no less true for the human right of property. That right does not need to be globally applicable to exist.

Nor does its treaty basis make the human right of property less grounded in human dignity. The dignitarian moral intuitions that inspired many of the property-protecting treaties in Tables 2.1 and 2.2 are not hard to discern. A number of them—the Refugee Convention, the treaty on indigenous peoples and for Stateless persons—recognize that the right to property is not dependent on sovereigns to give or withhold. These treaties recognize that, as Thomas Jefferson said, these rights are inherent to persons and not dependent on their nationality or lack of one. Such treaties usefully remind us that foreigners are people too and that governments don't get to decide unilaterally who a *person with rights is*.

Many of the property-protecting treaties resist other distinctions between their human beneficiaries. The right to property extends to the rich no less than the poor. It does not defer to racist or sexist cultures or stereotypes; even prisoners cannot be completely denied the core right to their personal effects. Even a seemingly minimal demand for non-arbitrary, non-discriminatory application of property rights rests on the need to respect human dignity equally—because this helps to avoid treating persons as mere objects, and accords respect to the autonomy of all persons to make decisions over their lives. These goals are also shared by treaties protecting industrial property, workers' wages and the right of farmers to use their land. All these instruments—and even IIAs—presume a strong connection between the right to work and the right to benefit from that work.

That the human right of property rests on treaty elaboration and that the bundle of entitlements that it confers differs by the status of persons (e.g., refugee, stateless person, citizen) does not mean that it is any the less "fundamental" or generally applicable to "humans." Many other human rights rest only on a treaty (rather than universal customary) basis; other human rights make comparable status distinctions (Waldron, 2013: 25). That states continue to differ with respect to what kind of property and what part of its bundle of sticks are entitlements owed by society makes the right of property no different from many other fundamental rights in the canon. States (and adjudicators) differ on the scope of many rights contained in the ICCPR; they differ on the permissible limits on free speech or what it means to allow persons the right to "participate" in their choice of government. If, as indicated, the human right of property is subject to variable geometry, so are many of the rights in the ICESCR, for example—from its right to an "adequate standard of living" to that treaty's right to health. That particular property entitlements are defined by governments does not make the right to property protection unique. Entitlements to sanitary water, to health or to basic education are all created at the behest of society and yet are, under human rights treaties, no less credible demands owed by the state to individuals. Human rights can include, or be based upon, benefits created by welfare states. Nor is it unusual that the right of property is limited by the rights of others. Indeed, the Universal Declaration of Human Rights' Article 29(2) recognized as much at the very beginnings of the human rights revolution. That property rights are often defined by the power of property rights holders to alienate their property is also not a fatal objection to including them as human rights. Persons can choose to renounce or trade away many other human rights, including those that rely on government largess set out in the ICESCR or even some of those included in the ICCPR. The freedom to practice religion includes, after all, the right to convert or to denounce religion altogether.

At the same, the variable geometry of the human right of property does not weaken its intuitive and intellectual connections to ideas associated with human dignity. The treaties in Table 2.1 (and some in Table 2.2, whether or not they are formally classified as "human rights" instruments) presume that it is not right to discriminate with respect to the right to communal or community property but also that it is essential to recognize certain private property rights because anything less than that fails to respect the dignity of persons, in groups or as individuals. These instruments give effect to the Scholastics' arguments that a right to personal property is essential to persons living in common because it deflects or avoids conflict (see generally Koskenniemi, 2011). They presume, along with Amartya Sen, that the right to property permits people to lead the kind of lives people value.[41] They follow Hegel (and Kant) in the belief that personal property enables the exercise of one's moral autonomy; that is, the right to property enables persons to express their personality, achieve their independence and master a degree of self-government (Monteagudo, 2013: 8; Waldron, 1990: 343–389). Like Aristotle, they suggest that without non-discriminatory access to a basic core right to property, people are slaves (see generally Koskenniemi, 2011).

Even if states continue to pick and choose which property-respecting treaties to recognize and global consensus on what "property" requires protecting is lacking, the human right of property exists. It cannot be imagined away.

Table 2.1 Human Rights Instruments with Property Protections

#	Instrument			Defined Right	Beneficiaries
	Year	*Name*	*State Parties*		
1	1948	**Universal Declaration of Human Rights,** Article 17.	**	• Right to own property. • Right not to be deprived of property arbitrarily.	• Individuals • Groups ("in association with others")
2	1948	**American Declaration of the Rights and Duties of Man,** Article XXIII.	35*** (Parties to the OAS Charter)	• Right to own property.	• Every person
3	1951	**Convention relating to the Status of Refugees**	145	• Right to treatment which is (i) as favorable as possible, and (ii) not less favorable as other aliens in the acquisition of property and other rights pertaining thereto. • Right to movable and immovable property (industrial property also protected by Article 14).	• Refugees
4	1952	**Protocol to the European Convention for the Protection of Human Rights and Fundamental Freedoms,** Article 1.	46	• Right to the peaceful enjoyment of possessions. • Right not to be deprived of possessions (with exceptions).	• Every natural or legal person

(*Continued*)

Table 2.1 (Continued)

#	*Instrument*			*Defined Right*	*Beneficiaries*
	Year	*Name*	*State Parties*		
5	1954	**Convention relating to the Status of Stateless Persons,** Article 13.	90	• Right to treatment which is (i) as favorable as possible, and (ii) not less favorable as other aliens in the acquisition of property and other rights pertaining thereto. • Right to movable and immovable property (industrial property also protected by Article 14).	• Stateless persons
6	1955 (adopted by ECOSOC in 1957 and 1977, and revised by UNGA in 2015)	**Standard Minimum Rules for the Treatment of Prisoners**	-	• Right to a safe custody of money, valuables, clothing and other effects.	• Prisoners
7	1957	**ILO Convention concerning the Protection and Integration of Indigenous and Other Tribal and Semi-Tribal Populations in Independent Countries (No. 107)**	27	• Right of ownership of lands traditionally occupied. • Respect to traditional mechanisms of transmission of rights.	• Indigenous peoples: both individuals and collectives
8	1961 (revised in 1996)	**European Social Charter**	43	• Right to fair remuneration for work.	• Workers

9	1965	**International Convention on the Elimination of All Forms of Racial Discrimination,** Article 5.	179*	• Right to own property without racial discrimination. • Right to inherit without racial discrimination.	• Individuals • Groups ("in association with others")
10	1969	**American Convention on Human Rights,** Article 21.	24****	• Right to the use and enjoyment of property. • Right not to be deprived of property unless under certain conditions.	• Everyone
11	1979	**Convention on the Elimination of All Forms of Discrimination Against Women,** Articles 15 & 16.	189****	• Equal right to administer property. • Same rights as men in respect of the ownership, acquisition, management, administration, enjoyment and disposition of property.	• Women
12	1981	**African Charter on Human and Peoples' Rights,** Article 14.	53	• Right to property.	• Human beings
13	1989	**ILO Convention Concerning Indigenous and Tribal Peoples in Independent Countries (No. 169)**	23	• Right of ownership and possession over the lands traditionally occupied. • Right to safeguard the lands not occupied, but accessed for subsistence and traditional activities. • Right to participate in the use, management and conservation of natural resources pertaining to their lands.	• Indigenous peoples

(Continued)

Table 2.1 (Continued)

#	*Instrument*			*Defined Right*	*Beneficiaries*
	Year	*Name*	*State Parties*		
14	1990	**International Convention on the Protection of the Rights of All Migrant Workers and Members of Their Families,** Article 15.	51	• Right not to be deprived of property arbitrarily.	• Migrant workers and members of their families
15	1995	**Commonwealth of Independent States Convention on Human Rights and Fundamental Freedoms**	4	• Right to own property	• Natural and legal persons
16	1994/ 2004	**Arab Charter on Human Rights,** Article 25 (1994 version, which never entered into force), Article 31 (2004 version, entered into force in 2008)	12[42]	• Right to own private property.	• "Every citizen"

17	2000 (legally binding as of 2009)	**Charter of Fundamental Rights of the European Union**	28	• Right to own, use, dispose of and bequeath lawfully acquired possessions. • Right to intellectual property.	• "Everyone"
18	2003	**Protocol to the African Charter on Human and Peoples' Rights on the Rights of Women in Africa**	36	• Right to acquire and administer property during marriage. • Right to an equitable sharing of property deriving from marriage. • Right to property over land. • Right to inherit.	• Women
19	2006	**Convention on the Rights of Persons with Disabilities,** Article 12.5	177****	• Equal right to own or inherit property. • Equal right to control their own financial affairs and have access to credit. • Equal right not to be arbitrarily deprived of property.	• Persons with disabilities
20	2012	**ASEAN Human Rights Declaration,** Article 17	(ASEAN has 10 member states)	• Right to own, use, dispose of and give lawfully acquired possessions. • Right not to be arbitrarily deprived of property.	• "Every person"

References

*: The United States is a party to this treaty.

**: The United States voted in favor of this declaration.

***: This declaration is now incorporated into the OAS Charter. Thus, the United States is a party to it (and therefore subject to the jurisdiction of the Inter-American Commission (but not Court) of Human Rights).

****: The United States signed this treaty, but has not ratified it.

Table 2.2 **Other Select International Instruments with Property Protections**

#	*Instrument*			*Defined Right*	*Beneficiaries*
	Year	*Name*	*State Parties*		
1	1883	**Paris Convention for the Protection of Industrial Property** (revised in 1900, 1911, 1925, 1934, 1958, 1967, 1979), Article 1	177	• Right to *industrial property*.	• Nationals of member states and nationals of others domiciled or established in the member states (Article 3)
2	1886	**Berne Convention for the Protection of Literary and Artistic Works**[*] (revised in 1896, 1908, 1914, 1928, 1948, 1967, 1971, 1979)	176	• *Protection* of literary and artistic works, e.g., exclusive right to translate, make reproductions, to broadcast, to perform in public dramatic and musical works, to make motion pictures, adaptations and arrangements of the work.	• Authors of literary and artistic works
3	1891	**Madrid Arrangement Concerning the International Registration of Marks** (revised in 1900, 1911, 1925, 1934, 1957, 1967, 1979), Article 1(2)	55	• Right to *protection* for marks.	• Nationals of member states and nationals of others domiciled or established in the member states

4	1907	**Hague Convention Respecting the Laws and Customs of War on Land**	38	• Right of prisoners of war to *property over personal belongings*. • Prohibition to *destroy or seize enemy property*. • Prohibition of *confiscation of enemy property during capitulations*. • Right to *private property of municipalities, and institutions dedicated to religion, charity and education, the arts and sciences*.	• Prisoners of war • Parts in hostilities • Capitulating parties to hostilities • Municipalities, and institutions dedicated to religion, charity and education, the arts and sciences
5	1949	Convention (IV) Relative to the Protection of Civilian Persons in Time of War (Fourth Geneva Convention)	196*	• Right not to *have property destroyed*. Internees: • Right to *possession of articles of personal use and of those who have a personal or sentimental value*. • Right to *remuneration*. • Right to *retain a certain amount of money, to be able to make purchases*.	• Individuals and groups during armed conflict or military occupations • Internees

(*Continued*)

Table 2.2 (Continued)

#	*Instrument*			*Defined Right*	*Beneficiaries*
	Year	*Name*	*State Parties*		
6	1949	**ILO Convention Concerning the Protection of Wages (No. 95)**	98	• Right to *receive wages* directly, regularly, in legal tender and without deductions. • Right to *dispose freely of wages*.	• "[A]ll persons to whom wages are paid or payable" (Article 2.1)
7	1954	**Hague Convention for the Protection of Cultural Property in the Event of Armed Conflict with Regulations for the Execution of the Convention**	132*	• Obligation to *protect cultural property*.	• States
8	1961	**Rome Convention for the Protection of Performers, Producers of Phonograms and Broadcasting Organizations**, Article 7(1).	93	• Right to *the protection of performances*.	• Performers, producers of phonograms and broadcasting organizations
9	1961	**Vienna Convention on Diplomatic Relations**	191*	• Right to *inviolability of property, residence, papers and correspondence*. • Right to *be exempt from taxation*.	• Diplomatic agents
10	1962	**ILO Convention Concerning Basic Aims and Standards of Social Policy (No. 117)**, Article 4.	33	• Right to *ownership and use of land*, which must serve certain social purposes.	• Agricultural producers

11	1970	**Convention on the Means of Prohibiting and Preventing the Illicit Import, Export and Transfer of Ownership of Cultural Property**	134****	• Right to *the protection of cultural property*.	• Everyone
12	1971	**Geneva Convention for the Protection of Producers of Phonograms Against Unauthorized Duplication of Their Phonograms,** Article 2.	79*	• Protection against the duplication and distribution of phonograms.	• Producers of phonograms
13	1994	**North American Free Trade Agreement (NAFTA),** Chapter 11	3*	• Extensive rights (FET, non-discrimination, prompt, adequate and effective compensation upon expropriation).	• Foreign investors and investments from the three NAFTA countries
14	1994	**Agreement on Trade-Related Aspects of Intellectual Property Rights**	164*	• Right to *the protection of intellectual property*.	• Everyone entitled to intellectual property
15	1995	**Unidroit Convention on Stolen or Illegally Exported Cultural Objects**	43	• Right to *compensation for returning a stolen or illegally exported cultural object*.	• Possessors of stolen or illegally exported cultural objects
16	2000	**United Nations Convention Against Transnational Organized Crime**	189*	• Implies the existence of a right to *acquisition, possession or use of property*.	• Everyone

References

*: The United States is a party to this treaty.

**: The United States voted in favor of this declaration.

***: This declaration is now incorporated into the OAS Charter. Thus, the United States is a party to it (and therefore subject to the jurisdiction of the Inter-American Commission (but not Court) of Human Rights).

****: The United States signed this treaty, but has not ratified it.

Notes

1 Table 2.1 attached to this chapter lists instruments containing an explicit "property" protection that are commonly described as protecting human rights. This list is admittedly idiosyncratic as international lawyers have not come to uniform agreement on what a "human rights treaty" is. See Alvarez, 2018: 651–652. In recognition of this, Table 2.2 lists an additional 16 prominent treaties that protect property, including some promulgated by the International Labor Organization (ILO) and others that protect cultural property during conflict that many would include within the human rights family. Table 2.2 is not exhaustive; it includes, for example, only one representative of the over 2,300 international investment agreements (IIAs) that protect foreign investments. The numbers of state parties to the instruments listed in Tables 2.1 and 2.2 were current as of June 12, 2018.

2 See, e.g., Commission on the Elimination of Discrimination Against Women, *General Recommendation on Article 16 of the Convention on the Elimination of All Forms of Discrimination Against Women (Economic Consequences of Marriage, Family Relations and Their Dissolution)*, ¶¶ 37–38, 55 U.N. Doc. CEDAW/C/GC/29 (October 30, 2013) [hereinafter *General Recommendation on Article 16*].

3 See, e.g., Hague Convention (IV) Respecting the Law and Customs of War on Land (1907) Articles 4, 22–23, 35, 56; 36 Stat 2227; Hague Convention for the Protection of Cultural Property in the Event of Armed Conflict with Regulations for the Execution of the Convention (1954), 249 U.N.T.S. 215.

4 See Crawford J (2002) *The International Law Commission's Articles on State Responsibility*. Cambridge: Cambridge University Press. (Articles 28–38 and commentaries).

5 See, e.g., Situation in the Republic of Mali, *The Prosecutor v. Ahmad al Faqi Al Mahdi*, International Criminal Court, Trial Chamber VIII, ICC-01/12-01/15, 27 September 2016, available at www.icc-cpi.int/CourtRecords/CR2016_07244.PDF (accessed 7 June 2018).

6 Notably, a number of the classic applications of the "international minimum standard" in favor of aliens that continue to be regularly cited in investor-state rulings under IIAs would today be seen as unexceptional human rights cases. See, e.g., *Neer v. Mexico*, 4 R.I.A.A. 60 (1926) (an arbitral ruling under the General Claims Commission involving the alleged maltreatment of a U.S. national in Mexican court).

7 Thus, the Virginia Declaration of Rights, an obvious inspiration for the U.S. Declaration of Independence, explicitly identified property as an essential right. Virginia Declaration of Rights, 1776, available at www.history.org/almanack/life/politics/varights.cfm (accessed 7 June 2018).

8 For an attempt to address the divide, see, e.g., Alvarez, 2011.

9 For a suggestion that the "international law of property" should attempt to secure global agreement on its precise bundle of entitlements, see Sprankling, 2014.

10 See generally, Anghie A (2005) *Imperialism, Sovereignty and the Making of International Law*. Cambridge: Cambridge University Press. 113–114 (describing international "rule of law" efforts as contemporary examples of the "civilizing mission" initially pursued by colonial powers on those they identified as "the other").

11 For a more specific critique of ISDS, see van Harten G (2007) *Investment Treaty Arbitration and Public Law*. Oxford: Oxford University Press.

12 For more thorough consideration of these critiques, see Alvarez, 2018: 588–597.

13 Indeed, a recent Harvard Law Review Note proposing greater use of international law with respect to the interpretation and enforcement of American Indian law does not even mention the possibility of using the property protections of international human rights instruments. See Alvarez, 2018: 635.
14 For a summary of these cases, see Alvarez, 2018: 636–644.
15 *De Sanchez v. Banco Central de Nicaragua*, 770 F.2d 1385, at 1395 (5th Cir. 1985).
16 *Mezerhane v. República Bolivarian de Venezuela*, 785 F. 3d 545 (11th Cir. 2015).
17 See, e.g., *Abelesz v. Magyar Nemzeti Bank*, 692 F.3d 661, at 675 (7th Cir. 2012). That some U.S. courts would only consider redress in cases involving "genocidal takings" suggest that to such courts international property rights are either a lesser right not worth protecting unless more worthy human rights are implicated or that the only kind of cognizable international property right that arises for a state's own citizens emerges under international criminal law and not human rights law.
18 See Sprankling, 2013: 470–472, for the oft-told story of how the right to property disappeared from the texts of the ICCPR or the ICESCR (both adopted and opened for signature, ratification and accession by UN G.A. Res. 2200A (XXI) on 16 December 1966).
19 See, e.g., Waldron, 1990: 30 ("The objects of property—the things which in lay usage are capable of being owned—differ so radically in legal theory, that it seems unlikely that the same concept of ownership could be applied to them all, even within a single legal system."). Nonetheless, in his book, Waldron proceeds to provide a right-based argument for a right to private property. See Waldron, 1990: 62–105.
20 For one such ambitious attempt that failed to lead to a successful treaty negotiation, see Sohn LB Baxter (1961) Responsibility of States for Injuries to the Economic Interests of Aliens, *American Journal of International Law* 55: 545–560.
21 American Convention of Human Rights, Article 21, signed by the Organization of American States on 22 November 1969, Series No. 36, at 1.
22 See, e.g., *Mayangna (Sumo) Awas Tingni Cmty v. Nicaragua*, Merits, Reparations and Costs, Judgment, Inter-Am. Ct. H.R. (ser. C) No. 79, ¶ 146 (31 August 2001).
23 See, e.g., *Palamara-Iribarne v. Chile*, Merits, Reparations and Costs, Judgment, Inter-Am. Ct. H.R. (ser. C) No. 135, ¶¶ 102–03 (22 November 2005).
24 See, e.g., *Sawhoyamaxa Indigenous Cmty. v. Paraguay*, Merits, Reparations and Costs, Judgment, Inter-Am. Ct. H.R. (ser. C) No. 146, ¶ 128 (29 March 2006). In this instance, as in others dealing with the rights to communal property for the indigenous, the Inter-American Court did not find either the absence of formal legal title or the right of innocent third-party purchasers to preclude the obligation of the Paraguayan state to pursue some appropriate remedy for indigenous peoples deprived of their lands.
25 Scholarly analysis of both is voluminous. On U.S. Indian law, see Prucha, 1984. For an introduction to U.S. takings jurisprudence, see, e.g., Rose, 1996: 329.
26 In this sense, some of the IACtHR's property jurisprudence is consistent with the views of the ICESCR Committee which sees the rights under the ICESCR as subject to progressive development over time.
27 Scc, c.g., *Furlan & Family v. Argentina*, Preliminary Objections, Merits, Reparations and Costs, Judgment, Inter-Am. Ct. H.R. (ser. C) No. 246, ¶ 222 (31 August 2012).
28 The IACtHR has relied on ECtHR rulings for the proposition, for example, that human rights instruments like the American Convention are "liv[ing]

instruments" that evolve over time. See, e.g., *Yakye Axa Indigenous Cmty. v. Paraguay*, Merits, Reparations and Costs, Judgment, Inter-Am. Ct. H.R. (ser. C) No. 125, ¶ 125 (June 31, 2005).

29 These cases of "special gravity" involve deprivations of property in the course of mass atrocities committed by government or rebel groups. See, e.g., Alvarez, 2018: 630–633.

30 See, e.g., *Jahn and Others v. Germany*, App. Nos. 46720/99, 72203/01, and 72552/10, ECtHR, 22 January 2004, 43 ILM 522 (2004).

31 See, e.g., CEDAW General Comment on Article 16.

32 See Convention on the Protection of the Rights of All Migrant Workers and Members of Their Families, 18 December 1990, 2220 U.N.T.S. 3, Article 15.

33 Under Articles 15 and 16 of CEDAW, states "shall give women equal rights to conclude contracts and to administer property" and "shall take all appropriate measures to eliminate discrimination against women in all matters relating to marriage and family relations," in particular to extend "[t]he same rights for both spouses in respect of the ownership, acquisition, management, administration, enjoyment and disposition of property . . ." Convention on the Elimination of All Forms of Discrimination Against Women, 18 December 1979, 1249 U.N.T.S. 20378 (entered into force 3 September 1981) [hereinafter CEDAW].

34 For analysis of how CEDAW's scrutiny of national laws has been impacted by that Convention's inclusion of property, see, e.g., Goonesekere, 2012: 388–407; Freeman et al., 2012: 432–436.

35 Indeed, CEDAW's contextualization of property—that is, its insistence that, for example, property rights during marriage or for rural women should be addressed in those particular contexts—has in turn been incorporated within other international instruments such as General Assembly resolutions. See, e.g., G.A. Res. 70/132, para. 2 (17 December 2015).

36 See e.g., CEDAW, Article 11.

37 *Ituango Massacres v. Colombia*, Preliminary Objections, Merits, Reparations and Costs, Judgment, Inter-Am. Ct. H.R. (ser. C) No. 148, ¶ 155 (1 July 2006). This means that matters that might have been originally omitted from treaty texts in order to secure agreement—such as mention of inheritance rights in CEDAW's Article 16—may re-emerge in the course of later treaty interpretations. See, e.g., Freeman, 2014: 414.

38 See, e.g., *Kichwa Indigenous People of Sarayaku v. Ecuador*, Merits and Reparations, Judgment, Inter-Am. Ct. H.R. (ser. C) No. 245, ¶ 146 (27 June 2012); *Sawhoyamaxa Indigenous Cmty. v. Paraguay*, Merits, Reparations and Costs, Judgment, Inter-Am. Ct. H.R. (ser. C) No. 146, ¶¶ 118, 121 (29 March 2006); *Mayagna (Sumo) Awas Tingni Cmty. v. Nicaragua*, Merits, Reparations and Costs, Judgment, Inter-Am. Ct. H.R. (ser. C) No. 79, ¶ 149 (31 August 2001).

39 Compare, for example, Henkin et al., 2009: 1521 (including, as a contested potential human right, "freedom of enterprise") or Franck, 1992 (discussing an "emerging right to democracy").

40 For the author's efforts in this respect, see Alvarez, 2018: 666–683.

41 For one attempt to connect the right to property to Amartya Sen's views, see Monteagudo, 2013.

42 The author has not been able to locate an official source indicating the number of current state parties to the Arab Charter. One scholar indicates that as of 2013, 12 of the 22 members of the Arab League (Algeria, Bahrain, Iraq, Jordan, Libya, Palestine, Qatar, Saudi Arabia, Syria, the United Arab Emirates, Yemen and Kuwait) have ratified the Charter. Matta, (2013): 91.

References

Alvarez JE (2011) Are Corporations "Subjects" of International Law? *Santa Clara Journal of International Law* 9: 1–36.

Alvarez JE (ed) (2017) *International Investment Law*. Leiden: Brill.

Alvarez JE (2018) The Human Right of Property. *University of Miami Law Review* 72: 580–705.

Anghie A (2005) *Imperialism, Sovereignty and the Making of International Law*. Cambridge: Cambridge University Press.

Bishop RD, Crawford J and Reisman WM (2005) *Foreign Investment Disputes Cases, Materials and Commentary* (Vol. 20142) The Hague: Kluwer Law International.

Chayes A and Chayes AH (1995) *The New Sovereignty*. London: Harvard University Press.

Crawford J (2002) *The International Law Commission's Articles on State Responsibility: Introduction, Text and Commentaries*. Cambridge: Cambridge University Press.

de Búrca G (2017) Human Rights Experimentalism. *American Journal of International Law* 111(2): 277–316.

De Soto H (2000) *The Mystery of Capital: Why Capitalism Triumphs in the West and Fails Everywhere Else*. New York: Basic Civitas Books.

Franck TM (1992) The Emerging Right to Democratic Governance. *American Journal of International Law* 86(1): 46–91.

Freeman MA, Chinkin C and Beate R (eds) (2012) *The UN Convention on the Elimination of All Forms of Discrimination Against Women: A Commentary*. Oxford: Oxford University Press.

Goonesekere S (2012) Article 15. In: Freeman MA, Chinkin C and Beate R (eds) *The UN Convention on the Elimination of All Forms of Discrimination Against Women: A Commentary*. Oxford: Oxford University Press, 388–407.

Henkin L et al (2009) *Human Rights*. St. Paul, MN: West Academic.

Howse R and Teitel R (2010) Beyond Compliance: Rethinking Why International Law Really Matters. *Global Policy* 1(2): 127–136.

Johnson Jr OT and Gimblett J (2012) From Gunboats to BITS: The Evolution of Modern International Investment Law. *Yearbook on International Investment Law and Policy* 649–692.

Koskenniemi M (2011) Empire and International Law: The Real Spanish Contribution. *University of Toronto Law Journal* 61(1): 1–36.

Koskenniemi M (2017) Sovereignty, Property and Empire: Early Modern English Context. *Theoretical Inquiries in Law* 18(2): 355–389.

Mason KO and Carlsson HM (2005) The Development Impact of Gender Equality in Land Rights. In: Alston P and Robinson M (eds) *Human Rights and Development: Towards Mutual Enforcement*. Oxford: Oxford University Press.

Mattar MY (2013) Article 43 of the Arab Charter on Human Rights: Reconciling National, Regional, and International Standards. *Harvard Human Rights Journal* 26: 91–147.

Monteagudo M (2013) The Right to Property in Human Rights and Investment Law: A Latin American Perspective of an Unavoidable Connection. SECO/WTI Academic Cooperation Project Working Paper Series 21013/06.

Prucha FP (1984) *The Great Father: The United States Government and the American Indians* (Vol. 2). Lincoln: University of Nebraska Press.

Rose CM (1996) Property as the Keystone Right? *Notre Dame Law Review* 71: 329–369.

Sohn LB and Baxter RR (1961) Responsibility of States for Injuries to the Economic Interests of Aliens. *American Journal of International Law* 55: 545–560.

Sprankling JG (2013) The Global Right to Property. *Columbia Journal of Transnational Law* 52: 464–505.

Sprankling JG (2014) *The International Law of Property*. Oxford: Oxford University Press.

Upham FK (2018) *The Great Property Fallacy: Theory, Reality and Growth in Developing Countries*. Cambridge: Cambridge University Press.

Vandevelde K (1998) Investment Liberalization and Economic Development: The Role of Bilateral Investment Treaties. *Columbia Journal of Transnational Law* 36: 501–527.

Van Harten G (2007) *Investment Treaty Arbitration and Public Law*. New York: Oxford University Press.

Waldron J (1990) *The Right to Private Property*. Oxford: Clarendon Press.

Waldron J (2013) Is Dignity the Foundation of Human Rights? New York University Public Law and Legal Theory Working Papers. Paper, 374: 1–29.

3 In What Sense Are Economic Rights Human Rights?

Departing From Their Naturalistic Reading in International Human Rights Law

Samantha Besson

1. Introduction

International (universal and regional[1]) human rights law (IHRL) protects economic rights (and liberties[2]) (ER), such as the right to property or freedom of contract. What is striking, however, is that it is not the case in all international human rights treaties and regimes,[3] and that, even when it is, the kind of ER protected varies a lot across regimes[4] (see Donnelly, 2007). Interestingly, the same may be said about ER in domestic human rights law (DHRL) (see Daintith, 2004: 61 ff; O'Connell, 2011).

As a result, even an exemplary list of ER is difficult to establish.[5] ER are not as readily identifiable as "civil and political rights" or even as "social rights" (SR). As a matter of fact, the group of rights they are usually associated with are SR. One often speaks of "socio-economic rights" (SER) or "welfare rights" to refer to both ER and SR, for that matter, and, in common human rights language, the term "social rights" is mostly used to include ER, or even vice versa in some cases (e.g., Buchanan, 2013: 167–171).[6] This is, of course, because of the grouping of ER with SR in the 1966 International Covenant on Economic, Social and Cultural Rights (ICESCR) (Craven, 1995; Riedel et al., 2014). This association between SR and ER under the term SER dates back, however, to the recognition of labor rights in the 1920s (e.g., International Labour Organization (ILO) law),[7] but also to the discussions that ensued in the 1940s[8] and led to the adoption of the 1944 Declaration of Philadelphia and of the 1948 Universal Declaration of Human Rights (UDHR).[9]

Importantly, none of the most recent international human rights treaties have protected ER specifically, except for the right to property in international non-discrimination treaties.[10] The Millennium Development Goals (see Alston, 2005b) and their successors, the 2030 Sustainable Development Goals, do not include ER and hardly even mention SR (see Alston, 2016a, 2016b). As a matter of fact, international economic law (IEL) is the regime where the most specific protection of individual economic rights has been introduced in recent years (e.g., World Trade Organization (WTO) law[11] and European Union (EU) law[12]) (see Alston, 2002: 821–823; Howse and Teitel, 2010).[13]

While indeterminacy about the nature and justification of a given human right or group of human rights is not unusual in IHRL, ER amount to a subset of international legal human rights (ILHR) whose existence, content and scope are the least self-evident in contemporary IHRL. This indeterminacy reveals, this chapter submits, a deeper controversy about the "moralization" or, more accurately, moral "naturalization" of the law of the market (Murphy, 2016), but also, more generally, about the details of the relationship between moral and legal human rights.

The uneasiness pertaining to ER in IHRL does not come as a surprise to those familiar with the controversial nature of contract and property rights in moral and legal philosophy (see Murphy, 2016) and, more broadly, in political theories of justice (see Waldron, 2010b). While some authors have considered them as "natural," i.e., genuine or real,[14] moral rights (for this Lockean reading, see Nozick, 1974),[15] others have disparaged them as "false" rights that belong to market ordering (for this Rousseauan reading, see Marx, 1862), whereas yet another group understands them as "conventional" moral rights whose justification is instrumental to the value of the relevant social practice (for this Humean reading, see Murphy, 2016; Dagan and Dorfman, 2017). This debate notably pervades private law theory for it affects what the law's normative take on those rights should be and especially how it should relate to their moral counterparts provided there are any (see Murphy, 2016; Scheffler, 2015). It has actually been reactivated by the recent opposition between neo-naturalist approaches to promising and contract (e.g., Bernstein, 2011) and the conventional approach that had become largely undisputed in the second part of the 20th century.

Curiously, however, that controversy about the moral nature and justification of contract and property rights has not yet reached current discussions of ER in human rights theory. This is surprising given the strong ideological debates about the relationship between the economy and social justice that pervaded the 1920s and 1940s.

True, some human rights theorists have discussed whether ER actually amount to "human rights."[16] So doing, however, they have approached those rights mostly as "natural" or real moral rights (e.g., Nickel, 2007: 123; Hertel and Minkler, 2007: 7–9; Risse, 2009; Pogge, 2009; Mantouvalou, 2012, 2015; Gilabert, 2016; Queralt, 2017), for this is the kind of rights ILHR are usually held to be. Trapped into what one may refer to as a "naturalistic" reading or interpretation of IHRL (see, however, Buchanan, 2013: 162–164), those authors have faced a binary choice and quandary: either they justify ER as natural moral rights (e.g., Mantouvalou, 2012, 2015; Collins, 2015; Gilabert, 2016; Queralt, 2017) and thereby qualify them as "human rights" or, provided they argue against such a direct grounding in human interests or values, they are reduced to justifying them as "moral goals" instead of rights (e.g., Nickel, 2013, 2015).

In fact, discussions of ER in human rights theory have mostly focused on other topics, and in particular on the differences between ER and "other" human rights and on ER's complementarity to the latter. That focus actually mirrors the critical discussions of SER of the 1960s (e.g., Cranston, 1967). Lately, however, empowered by a bolder self-perception of the success of SER,[17] contemporary debates among international human rights lawyers have moved away from questions of feasibility, justiciability and universality.[18] Regrettably, the new directions chosen have not always been the best ones, and it is time therefore for their companion discussions in human rights theory to shift focus as well.

In this chapter, I would like to go back to the original question of the nature and justification of ER as ILHR, and link that discussion to current debates in private law theory. My aim is to clarify ER's international legal normative regime and their ties to various kinds of moral rights, either real or conventional, but also to other moral principles such as social justice (see Waldron, 2010b; Supiot, 2016). I purport to explore the various relationships (of recognition, specification and/or creation) between the legal and moral norms that protect ER. The chapter proposes to nuance the standard "mirroring" (Tasioulas, 2017) approach to the relationship between moral and legal human rights, according to which the latter unidirectionally transpose or specify the former without retroaction on the moral rights themselves, and especially without distinction between whether the moral rights recognized, specified or created as legal rights are real or conventional moral rights.

Based on this more nuanced account of the normative structure of human rights, this chapter's aim is to extract current interpretations of ER from the naturalistic moral reading that has become predominant among international human rights lawyers and theorists. As I will argue, that reading risks either corseting their interpretations of ER *qua* human rights into a neoliberal straightjacket, on the one hand, or, conversely, by depriving their understanding of SR from their co-constitutive relation to ER *qua* SER, to reducing the remaining SR into a desocializing program of assistance to the poor and the passive role they have been assigned in IHRL since the 1960s, on the other. Instead, the proposed conventional moral reading of ER in IHRL should help, on the one hand, channeling their legal interpretations towards the social and egalitarian considerations that fit their conventional moral quality and, on the other, revealing the crucial role the law, including IHRL, can and should play in specifying and enforcing them as active and relational rights.

Accordingly, the chapter's argument is five-pronged. In a first section, it discusses the underpinnings of the naturalistic reading in the origins of ER, before arguing against it (1.). In a second section, and in a search for an alternative non-naturalistic account of human rights, the chapter discusses the normative nature and layers of human rights in general, and explores the multiple and mutual relationships between moral and legal human rights and, more specifically, between real or conventional moral rights and legal human rights (2.). In the third step, the chapter turns to a normative qualification of ER, and argues that ER are best considered as conventional moral rights justified by reference to the value of the social and economic practice they are part of, but also as conventional moral-legal human rights (3.). In the fourth and final section, the chapter explores various implications of the proposed conventional moral reading of ER in DHRL and IHRL, and especially consequences for the egalitarian- and social justice-oriented interpretation of ER and for the development of international legal regulation of markets that could be better aligned with the social practice whose value justifies the protection of conventional ER in IHRL (4.).

For the purpose of this chapter, ER in IHRL may be understood to cover rights to have economic activities (that have to do with money or the market), i.e., rights to relate to others (i) in activities pertaining to economic goods (e.g., that may become the object of property or of contract), (ii) provided those activities, and the social practice they are part of, protect important human interests. Following Nickel's taxonomy, the proposed conception of ER includes three clusters of rights: "using and consuming" (consumption); "transacting and contracting" (contract); and "acquiring, holding and alienating" (property) (Nickel, 2007: 125). One may add a fourth one that does not amount to a right to a commodity, to quote the 1944 Declaration of Philadelphia: exchanging one's labor (work). In turn, those may be spelled out further to include four bundles of ER: rights to buy, sell, use and consume goods and services; to engage in independent economic activity; to hold both personal and productive property; and rights to sell one's labor (Nickel, 2007: 123). They encompass, in particular, and based on contemporary regimes of IHRL, the following rights and liberties: freedom of contract (e.g., Article 16 EUFRC. See Elster, 1994: 211), the right to property (e.g., Article 17 UDHR; Article 1 Protocol 1 ECHR; Article 17 EUFRC; Article 21 ACHR; Article 14 ACHPR; Article 16 CEDAW; Article 5 CERD; Article 15 CRPMW; Article 12 CRPD. See Waldron, 2013; Dagan and Dorfman, 2017) and the right to work (e.g., Articles 6–9 ICESCR; Article 15 EUFRC. See Gilabert, 2016; Mantoulavou, 2015; Collins, 2015).[19]

A final methodological *caveat* is in order. The present chapter amounts to an exercise in normative legal theory applied to IHRL (Besson, 2017): it interrogates and organizes the content of the international legal normative order of human rights, and ER in particular, from the point of view of moral rights. It assumes, indeed, that IHRL *qua* law amounts to a normative order within morality, but to one that is distinct from others. More specifically, it considers that legal reasoning about human rights, like legal reasoning in general, is (moral) reasoning of a special kind. The chapter approaches IHRL, accordingly, as containing, enveloping and constituting normative justifications: it does not just borrow them from morality. Things that appear to be normatively "deeper" (e.g., Nickel, 2007: 126) about IHRL are not necessarily genuinely moral or "natural": the law *qua* normative social practice[20] encompasses both real and conventional morality[21] and may even mold the latter or add normative material of its own (see Waldron, 2012). The law's pivotal role in the framework of moral normativity (see Raz, 2012) illuminates in turn how IHRL may be both an object of moral critique and a resource for moral reform with respect to the international recognition and interpretation of ER.

2. Nature, Rights and the Economy: The Naturalism Trap

The naturalistic reading of ER, as this chapter understands it, amounts to interpreting them as legal human rights corresponding to natural or real moral rights. It has become predominant lately among international human rights lawyers and theorists alike (e.g., Mantouvalou, 2012, 2015; Nickel, 2015; Gilabert, 2016; Queralt, 2017).

That reading traps human rights theorists into either excluding ER *qua* non-natural rights from the scope of human rights, and hence reducing the scope of SER to "subsistence" (e.g., Shue, 1996)[22] or "anti-poverty" (e.g., Beitz, 2009)[23] rights, on the one hand, or including ER *qua* natural rights within the scope of human rights, and hence turning moralized economics into human rights (e.g., Collins, 2015), on the other. The former leads to the pursuit of the *desocializing naturalism* that has plagued the recognition and development of SER in IHRL since the 1960s, to the extent that it approaches SER as rights "to be" (and receive) and not "to do." The latter, by contrast, threatens to undermine SER in IHRL by endorsing another kind of naturalism, i.e., the *individualistic naturalism* that is built into economic neoliberalism and that approaches features of individual economic behavior as natural moral ones (see Fouillée, 1899: 48).

As the second and third sections of this chapter will demonstrate, there is actually a third way to approach ER. It liberates human rights theorists from having to choose between the Charybdis and Scylla of naturalistic justifications of ER: ER should be considered, I will argue, as moral and legal rights that belong with SR to SER in IHRL, but their moral justification should not be approached as natural or real, but as conventional and instrumental to the value and, in particular, to the social justice of our economic practices, both local and global.

Of course, the threat arising from the naturalistic reading of ER is not new. Its first instantiation, i.e., desocializing naturalism, has led, since the 1960s, to the setting aside of SER from other human rights in IHRL. Contrary to a widespread view that this was a compromise—a view that actually reveals a deep misunderstanding of social justice and of the alleged interest of all states in promoting the latter—this movement was supported by both Western and communist states alike (see Donnelly, 2007: 41–43; Moyn, 2014: 149, 155–156).

The former, dominated by the liberal ideology of the market and the corresponding approach to property and contract, resisted the idea that human rights could enter the economic sphere and that states could owe duties to individuals therein, except with respect to a basic natural minimum protected by the subsistence-approach to SR. They clearly rejected in particular the idea of protecting economic liberties against the market and other private actors, and hence the project of state regulation in order to protect the market against itself. Communist states also opposed the idea of states owing economic duties to individuals, albeit on different grounds. They rejected the project of protecting any individual economic liberties against State intervention in the market. Both sides contributed therefore equally, albeit for different reasons, to the undermining of SER soon after their recognition in the UDHR in 1948 and to cutting SER off from civil and political rights and by framing them into the different and less demanding regime of the ICESCR. Over time, this has led to reducing SER to a so-called core (e.g., Shue, 1996: 5; Hertel and Minkler, 2007: 3–4) of individual and passive SR, minimizing their corresponding positive duties and depriving them from their relational (and, actually, social) and active economic dimensions (see Supiot, 2016).

Some authors have argued that IHRL and economic liberalism actually worked hand in hand to that effect ever after. It is true that international human rights lawyers' distrust of, and even resistance to, the State has led them to undermine the power of the sole potential duty bearer of positive duties corresponding to SER. Over time, this has contributed to turning human rights into "powerless companions" (Moyn, 2014: 155–160) to economic liberalism, thereby paving the way for the empowerment of the market and private actors outside the reach of states' human rights' duties. It is difficult, however, to construct this as anything but a case of historical contingency.

Today, however, the juncture between the desocializing naturalism of IHRL and the individualistic naturalism of economic liberalism is no longer accidental. It is actually celebrated on both sides. True, for a long time, neoliberals had but very little interest in human rights law (e.g., Hayek, 1978), and social justice supporters avoided moralizing the realm of private law and market regulation. After a long stand-off between international trade lawyers wanting to absorb human rights (e.g., Drache and Jacobs, 2014) and international human rights lawyers resisting that move, however, the latter, and at least socio-economic rights lawyers, seem to have given in.[24]

Indeed, what is new in the second kind of naturalistic reading of ER currently at play, i.e., individualistic naturalism, is the neoliberal embrace of IHRL combined with the surrender of international human rights lawyers to the market. International investment lawyers, for instance, have recently developed an arbitration practice around a strong international human right to property (e.g., Alvarez, 2018; Sprankling, 2014), and international social rights lawyers have, conversely, worked towards the economic standardization of social rights protection (e.g., Riedel et al., 2014: 37 ff, 44 ff; O'Connell, 2011: 552–553). That international moralization of the law of the market is unprecedented and difficult to resist to, especially when it is facilitated by IHRL and its own naturalistic moral language as it is the case with ER.

3. Human Rights as Legal-Moral Rights

Departing from the naturalistic reading of ER in IHRL requires exploring the normative nature and layers of human rights in general. To do so, this section addresses the relationship between moral (real or conventional) and legal rights (2.1.), and then turns, more specifically, to that between moral (real or conventional) and legal human rights (2.2.).

3.1 The Relation Between Moral and Legal Rights

Just as moral rights are moral propositions and sources of moral duties, legal rights are legal propositions and sources of legal duties. They are (moral) interests recognized by law as sufficiently important to generate (legal and moral) duties (see Raz, 1984: 12, 2010a).

Generally speaking, moral rights can and actually may exist independently from having counterparts in legal rights, but legal rights do not exist, at least if they are to be able to give rise to legitimate legal duties, without also amounting to moral rights and duties at the same time. As such, legal rights should always also amount to moral rights, whether by recognition (i) or specification (ii) of pre-existing moral rights, or even by creation (iii) of moral rights at the same time as legal rights (see Raz, 1984: 16–17).

To the extent that all law is normative, for it is a matter of rules, duties and rights, the exact nature of the relation between moral and legal rights may sound redundant. However, we do not in all cases see legal rights and duties as reflecting or "mirroring" (see the debate between Buchanan, 2013: 17–18; Tasioulas, 2017) independent underlying moral rights and duties. This differentiated normative layering within legal rights in turn affects the ways we can and should reason with them. Of course, in some cases, there will be mirroring of real moral rights, but not in others where there is creation of moral rights through legal ones. Even when there is "mirroring," moreover, the reflection will not always be perfect for the legal rights specify the corresponding moral ones. Finally, there may also be mutual transformations between moral and legal rights rather than a pure unilateral reflection or even specification, thereby making the "mirroring" analogy actually inexact in those cases.

Importantly, within moral normativity itself, some moral rights may be considered "natural," genuine or real because they derive directly from some human interest, while others are "conventional" or instrumental to the value of the social practice they belong to, and in particular to the collective goods and human interests that that social practice promotes. An example of the former is the right to life whose justification is to be found in a direct human interest in living independently from any social practice, while an example of the latter may be, as I will argue in the third section, the right to individual property whose justification is instrumental to the value of the social practice of property over things, for instance the promotion of (the human interest in) autonomy through that practice. It is worth emphasizing that conventional moral rights are grounded in interests like any other moral rights, but the grounding in those interests is indirect and mediated through the appeal to the value of the social practice they are part of and to how that practice promotes those interests. Crucially, therefore, their not being "real" or "genuine" moral rights does not mean that they are "fake" or "artificial" rights, and of a lesser moral nature or quality than other moral rights, nor that they should be ranked second in moral priority or legal hierarchy.

That distinction between real and conventional moral rights has an impact on the corresponding legal rights. First of all, some legal rights recognize or specify real moral rights, while others recognize or specify conventional moral ones. In the latter case, since the law itself amounts to a social rule-based or normative practice, the legal rights that correspond to moral rights, whether real or conventional, are themselves inherently conventional. When legal rights recognize or specify conventional moral rights, therefore, two conventional normative orders meet and influence one another: one social and pre-legal and the other political and legal. Importantly, however, the two levels of normative ordering and rights are never redundant: they share the values they are promoting and that justify them, but do so in complementary ways.

Second, some legal rights (and hence also moral rights) may not actually recognize and/or specify any pre-existing (real or conventional) moral rights. Rather, they create (conventional) moral rights by themselves. This is the case of legal parking rights, for instance, that have no independent (conventional or real) moral existence before the law generates them by organizing the social practice that gives rise to the protection of the related moral interests as rights.

3.2 Human Rights as Legal Subset of Universal Moral Rights

Qua rights (that give rise to legitimate moral duties), legal human rights are best conceived as being at once moral and legal rights (Besson, 2011: 211–245, 2015, 2017). Like legal rights, legal human rights are (moral) interests recognized by the law as sufficiently important to generate (moral and legal) human rights duties.

Four elements may be identified from the practice of (international and domestic) human rights law to qualify the protected interest that should be sufficiently important to give rise not only to simple duties and hence to a simple right, on the one hand, but also to give rise to a human right and the kind of duties it grounds, on the other. Those four elements are the fundamental and general nature of the individual interest protected; the existence of standard or generalized threats against which it should be protected; the feasibility of the protection of the interest against standard threats; and the fairness of the burden placed on the duty bearer by the protection of the interest. In a nutshell, therefore, human rights amount to a subset of universal moral rights that protect fundamental interests (importance) (i) against standard threats (urgency) (ii) and which belong to all human beings (universality) (iii) merely on the basis of their humanity (generality) (iv) (Besson, 2013a).

By reference to the relationship between moral and legal rights discussed in the previous section, the first question to address is whether there is something inherently legal about human rights so defined, and hence a (moral) duty to legalize the universal moral rights that are then recognized, specified or created as legal human rights.

I have argued elsewhere that, unlike other moral rights that may not be recognized and/or specified as legal rights and should not always be, universal moral rights considered as moral human rights should also be legal at the same time (Besson, 2015, 2017). In short, and although scope precludes making a full argument here, this is, first of all, because the universal moral rights that will become human rights create moral duties for all of us and therefore primarily for our institutions, and hence for the law as well, to recognize and protect human rights (see Raz, 2010a, 2010b: 321–337). Second, and more fundamentally, the legalization of human rights is the only way to be true to their central egalitarian and hence democratic dimension. Human rights constitute our status of basic moral equality and that equality being relational calls for its public recognition as political and legal equality (Besson, 2013b).[25]

The second question to address is whether human rights *qua* legal and moral rights always correspond to independent universal moral rights recognized or specified, whether real or conventional, or whether they may also create the corresponding universal moral rights in some cases.

First of all, one should stress that most legal (and moral) human rights recognize or specify independent universal moral rights. The universal moral rights recognized or specified by human rights are not necessarily only real universal moral rights, and some may be conventional universal moral rights. Thus, the human right to life recognizes or specifies the real moral right to life, whereas the human right to property recognizes or specifies the conventional moral right to property.

Of course, this only applies provided those conventional moral rights recognized and/or specified by legal human rights fit the structural dimensions of (moral and legal) human rights, and in particular the universality and generality of the interests protected and the equality of the threats weighing on them. Both conditions may be fulfilled by the universality and generality of the social practice they are part of, as we will see, and by the latter's universal instrumental justification through the promotion of universal human interests.

When legal (and moral) human rights correspond to conventional universal moral rights, they often do more than recognizing and/or specifying them. Their legalization could also have a retroactive impact on the conventional universal moral rights themselves. This is not only a consequence of their dual conventional nature as it is the case for conventional moral and legal rights in general. The legal conventionality of human rights, in this understanding, is not merely redundant to the moral one: it is about recognizing and enhancing the relational equality of participants in the relevant social practice.

Second, but exceptionally so, however, some legal (and moral) human rights may be created as such without having pre-existing (conventional or real) universal moral rights as counterparts. In the absence of an independent moral normative order and of a non-legal social practice in which those rights could exist, the corresponding conventional moral human rights are created as part of a legal social practice. As an example, one may mention the human right to democratic participation that cannot be justified by reference to an independent (real or even conventional) universal moral right to democracy outside of our political and legal practice of democracy, but whose moral justification may be said to lie in the instrumental value of existing democratic procedures themselves and in particular by appeal to how they promote the universal individual interest in equality.

It is more difficult, at first sight at least, but not impossible, as we will see, for such legal rights to fit the structural dimensions of (moral and legal) human rights. Provided they do, however, those rights are to be considered as legal (and moral) human rights, with all their categorical consequences in IHRL, and it would be wrong to reduce them to mere moral goals (see Nickel, 2015: 146) or principles (see Buchanan, 2015).

4. Economic Rights as Conventional Human Rights

Departing from the naturalistic reading of ER requires re-qualifying them normatively. This section argues that economic rights are best considered not only as conventional moral rights (3.1.), but also as conventional legal (and moral) human rights (3.2.).

4.1 Economic Rights as Conventional Moral Rights

While some authors have considered individual economic rights as "natural" or real moral rights, others have disparaged them as "false" rights that belong to market ordering, while yet another group, with whom I side, has considered them as "conventional" moral rights whose justification is instrumental and based on the value of their relevant social practice and on how it promotes fundamental individual interests.

Scope precludes rehearsing this discussion in full in a chapter that pertains to the justification of ER *qua* human rights in IHRL in general (see, however, Murphy, 2016).[26] What I will do, however, is, first, debunk the idea that owning, promising, consuming and working are pre-social and pre-institutional human interests whose protection as rights is required independently from the value of the social practice they are part of, and, second, argue that there is a moral value in that social practice that may provide an instrumental justification *qua* conventional moral rights of the economic rights that are part of that practice.

First of all, there are no individual objective interests sufficiently fundamental to give rise alone and directly to real individual economic rights. The latter do not make sense in the same immediate way as other moral rights that clearly protect human interests outside of any social practice, such as the interest and right to life (see Murphy, 2016).

This argument is not particularly difficult to make for property rights or other consumption rights that pertain to things. There can, indeed, be no direct or pre-social human interests in things or natural ties to them. This is not to say, of course, that there are no objective human interests at stake in this context (e.g., self-preservation).[27] What is clear, however, is that, in the current and non-ideal social and political circumstances of human life, those are mediated as social interests (e.g., owning), and the latter ground rights to the social relations pertaining to those things (see also Waldron, 2010a: 10, 14). Of course, it has long been part of the liberal economic ideology to transform relations between people and things into relations among people (see Dumont, 1985).[28]

By contrast, the same thing is more difficult to argue with respect to other economic rights like contractual freedom or the right to work. Those rights pertain indeed to social relations among people and, as a result, the grounding in individual interests does not seem as indirect as in the case of rights to things. Moreover, consent and the right to consent with the duties it generates are usually invoked as examples of a direct human interest and of a natural or real moral right grounded in that interest. Still, direct human interests of that kind are more difficult to establish with respect to promises and other kinds of contractual relations: outside of the specific circumstances of consent (e.g., to an intervention in one's bodily integrity), it remains unclear indeed how human will alone can bring moral rights and duties into existence without reference to the social relation that vests that will with normative power. What is normative about promises stems from the moral value of the social practice of promising rather than from that of promising itself (see Raz, 2015). There is no human interest in promising, at least directly and without reference to how the social relationship it is part of may benefit other human interests.[29]

Second, even if the rights in those economic relations are not directly or immediately grounded in objective interests,[30] there is actually some moral value in the social practices economic rights are part of.[31] Those social practices may protect other objective interests indirectly and in a mediated fashion, and this may therefore provide an instrumental moral justification to economic rights *qua* conventional moral rights.

Among potential candidates for such justifications, one may mention the contribution of economic rights, and the socio-economic practice they belong to (e.g., a property regime, a contractual practice, labor conditions), to fundamental individual interests such as individual autonomy (e.g., Raz, 2015), individual self-realization (e.g., Dagan and Dorfman, 2017; Nickel, 2007: 125–129, 2015: 140–141; Gilabert, 2016: 178; Collins, 2015: 32–37) or individual well-being (e.g., Queralt, 2017; Gilabert, 2016: 178). More generally, socio-economic practices, such as property, contract or labor, and the economic rights they entail, may be regarded as important instruments of social and economic justice (e.g., Scheffler, 2015; Waldron, 2010b) and even as collective goods.[32]

On the proposed conventional reading, economic rights are participatory rights: they are rights to participate in a given social relationship with other right-holders and to be included, respectively not excluded from it.[33] This is particularly clear for property rights (see Waldron, 2013: 10) or the right to work. Their collective dimension relates to the value or good protected, however, and not to the interests themselves, the subjects of the rights or their exercise that may all remain individual. To that extent, while they may be regarded as collective rights in that respect, their collective dimension does not prevent approaching them as individual moral rights grounded indirectly in the protection of individual interests through that collective practice.

Importantly, there is nothing utilitarian in this account of economic rights corresponding to conventional moral rights (contra: Buchanan, 2013: 171–172; Alston, 2002: 826; Collins, 2015: 19–20, 28–37). The value of the social practice they are part of and of how that practice promotes human interests is not itself a matter of economic efficiency (see Murphy, 2016; Raz, 2015).

Moreover, those instrumental justifications of economic conventional moral rights should not be conflated with two other kinds of instrumental moral "justification" of those rights. First of all, they should not be conflated with relations of mutual reinforcement between independently justified rights. Indeed, relations between basic and non-basic rights (Shue, 1996: 22–25), linkages (Nickel, 2007: 129–131) or, more generally, the indivisibility (Nickel, 2008) of rights in their implementation all rely on and build upon the pre-existing justification of the moral rights at stake and cannot replace it. Second, instrumental moral justifications for economic rights *qua* moral rights should be distinguished from the instrumental moral justifications for the creation of conventional, including legal, so-called rights based on other moral principles or goals than (conventional or real) moral rights (Nickel, 2013). What is justified in such cases are not *stricto sensu* moral (and legal) rights, not even of a conventional kind. As a result, the justifications and reasoning pertaining to the latter are bound to be very different and unrelated to corresponding moral rights.

As any other conventional moral rights, individual economic rights may be recognized, specified or even created by legal rights. Most of them are actually legalized to the extent that the social-economic practices they are part of benefit from the formalization and stability that legal rights bring with them.

As I argued before, the dual conventionality of pre-legal economic moral rights recognized or specified as economic legal rights brings some further layers of complexity into their relations to economic legal rights. In some cases, indeed, the legal practice and rights will dominate the non-legal one and its corresponding rights so much that they become inseparable and their moral conventionality is masked. When it happens, it is important to keep moral and legal economic rights in alignment with one another (see Murphy, 2016). Any misalignment of one or the other practice may indeed undermine the ability of both of them to promote the values and interests that justify the conventional moral rights they comprise.

4.2 *Economic Rights as Conventional Moral and Legal Human Rights*

ER are best approached as legal (and moral) human rights recognizing, specifying or creating the corresponding economic conventional universal moral rights, and hence as a subset of conventional universal moral rights rather than as a subset of real universal moral rights.

This reading differs from most existing theoretical accounts of ER. Some authors approach some ER *qua* legal human rights protecting moral goals instead of natural rights (Nickel, 2015: 146).[34] Others approach them *qua* legal human rights protecting liberal natural rights at a minimum, on the one hand, and complemented by external moral justifications in well-being or in equality, on the other (Buchanan, 2013: 167–171). Yet other authors approach ER, or at least some of them, entirely as natural rights (Gilabert, 2016: 178–180). All three accounts fall prey to the naturalistic trap I criticized in the first section. Of course, it is important for the conventionalist argument to succeed to establish that ER, indirectly or instrumentally grounded in this way, can actually fulfill the structural criteria of human rights.

First of all, the interests they protect albeit indirectly, such as autonomy, well-being or self-realization, are clearly fundamental enough to ground human rights (see Nickel, 2007: 145, 135–136, 2015: 139;

Queralt, 2017). Earning money through one's labor, being able to own and concluding contracts to sell and buy clearly promote those fundamental human interests. Second, those interests are shared generally in each society, independently of people's status and position in the market, and universally irrespectively of the prosperity of their country (see Nickel, 2007: 132–133; Gilabert, 2016: 177–178). Of course, to the extent that ER are conventional rights and hence part of a social practice in a given society, there may be more important national and regional variations among those social practices and the corresponding conventional moral rights than in the case of real moral rights. Those variations can be accommodated, however, by the fact that the content of ER in IHRL only has to be minimal.

Third, those fundamental human interests may be considered under general threat, be it by the State itself or, as it is more likely, by other private actors, and hence as equally vulnerable in all segments of the population, whether poor or rich, and across the globe (see Nickel, 2007: 145, 131–132, 2015: 139). Finally, the fairness and feasibility of the burden of protecting ER as rights are given (see Nickel, 2007: 148–152). The duties, negative or positive, that arise from ER may vary depending on the context and hence on the resources of every country, and they can and should therefore be adapted to the abilities of domestic authorities. Despite their name, ER *qua* human rights do not require from states that they provide jobs to all (contra: Nickel, 2015: 139–140, 144–146), complete property protection or full performance of contracts, but only, as we will see in section 5, that they regulate the market and, more broadly, economic practice so as to make it function and as to organize the respective rights and duties of other private participants in the practice.

Moving back to the first prong of the structure of human rights and to their moral-legal nature, ER also qualify as inherently legal and moral rights, and hence as equal human rights. The necessary institutional and egalitarian and hence legal dimension of human rights fits the conventional nature of economic moral rights particularly well. What characterizes economic (human) rights by comparison to other conventional legal and moral rights is, indeed, the greater interaction between the two levels of social practice, and how the promotion of the values of the non-legal social practice may only be met through legalizing the corresponding rights. It is the very egalitarian dimension of human rights that pleads in favor of including ER into IHRL (see also Dagan and Dorfman, 2017), and that distinguishes this kind of legal protection from that provided by other domestic and international legal regimes guaranteeing economic rights.

5. Implications for Economic Rights in International Human Rights Law

Protecting ER as full-fledged human rights that recognize and specify conventional moral rights has important legal implications in IHRL. First of all, there are consequences for the implementation and interpretation of those rights by *domestic* authorities.

The first set of implications is *institutional*, and pertains to the existence and form of design and regulation of the market and economic relations in domestic law. It is one of the consequences of the conventional dimension of ER that, even before being recognized and specified as human rights by IHRL, they are conceived of as a pre-institutional social normative order and hence as inherently regulatory. Their instrumental justification implies, in other words, that they be practiced and regulated to promote a certain value and hence to arise as rights. What this means is that states are called to regulate more over ER than other human rights if they are to abide by their corresponding duties, either in order to protect the valuable socio-economic practice or, most likely, to specify it and formalize it further. Regulating ER generally requires adopting general legislation, but may also occur, depending on the circumstances, through adjudication. As a result, the conventional reading of ER turns the ("everyday") libertarian concern about the regulation of economic rights and liberties on its head (see Murphy and Nagel, 2002: 15, 31–37). It disqualifies, for instance, resistances to alleged public law "expropriations" grounded in the idea of pre-legal natural property or to public law taxation based on the legitimacy of one's pre-legal natural possessions.

Another important institutional feature of ER that stems from their conventional nature is the states' positive duty to regulate the market so as to recognize and/or specify not only the rights, but also the duties of private actors related to the socio-economic practice regulated (e.g., property, contracts, labor). To that extent, ER do not only amount to vertical rights like all other human rights: they are meant to be mediated institutionally into horizontal rights and duties as well. This can take place through domestic private law, but also criminal law in some cases. Generating private duties for economic actors actually echoes the collective dimension of ER that amount to rights to participate in a social practice of economic exchange where participants do not only have rights, but also duties towards one another.

A second set of implications of the proposed conventional reading of ER is *substantive*, and pertains to the content of domestic law regulating the market and economic relations. The conventional reading of ER binds domestic authorities, including the legislature and judges, to interpret them in a way that takes into account the values that justify them in the first place, and in particular equality and social justice. This means, for instance, regulating the domestic property regime so as to accommodate social considerations that are part of the value of the socio-economic practice of property (see Dagan and Dorfman, 2017). This relational and egalitarian interpretation of domestic property rights has clear implications, for instance, for the social housing dimension in land planning.

As a matter of fact, the proposed egalitarian and social justice-oriented interpretation of ER goes hand in hand with the reverse economic interpretation of SR, and both sets of rights are best applied together as indivisible rights (see Nickel, 2007: 139, 131–132). Bringing the two sides of the same coin back together could contribute to the re-socialization of SR by making them more active and less passive, on the one hand, and more relational and less individual, on the other. This regained interpretative complementarity between SR and ER could even alleviate the alleged contradictions between them (see Waldron, 2010b: 5; Nickel, 2007: ch. 8 and 9). For instance, the co-application of SR with ER could give rise to duties to secure equal access to education or equal access to the job market, and, conversely, to duties to organize self-help on the part of individual ER holders and their access to micro-credit.

Of course, under IHRL, ER *qua* human rights only give rise to minimal duties that correspond to a transnational consensus on ER. As a result, there is a broad margin of appreciation of states and scope for diversity in the regulatory organization of the economic social practice and the market domestically. For instance, individual property rights may be organized so as to co-exist with forms of collective or common property (see Waldron, 2013: 11 ff), rather than as competing with the latter, provided the core egalitarian dimension of human rights and social justice are respected.

Importantly, ER do not generate human rights duties only within the territorial jurisdiction of states. Extraterritorial duties may arise when states exercise jurisdiction abroad. Moreover, states also incur responsibilities for human rights' protection outside of their jurisdiction, and this includes assisting other states to respect, protect and fulfill ER. What this includes arguably are responsibilities to help other states to set up regimes of property, contract or labor law that abide by the egalitarian and social underpinnings of the corresponding protected economic practice. Those extraterritorial duties and responsibilities could help, for instance, fighting back current practices of land-grabbing by foreign private investors in the absence of indigenous property regimes (see de Schutter, 2011) or of production and export of land products in the absence of indigenous agricultural regimes (see Wenar, 2015).

Second, the proposed conception of ER in IHRL also has implications for the *international* regulation of the market. Importantly, abiding by ER duties does not mean merely including economic individual rights into international trade regimes such as WTO or EU law as it has long been done. It also means taking ER *qua* human rights seriously in the institutional design of international trade institutions and regulation. Besides their obligations to revisit international trade law's existing approach to ER and to resist the latter's absorption under individual market rights in IEL, states also incur duties under ER to regulate areas that have been left untouched to date by international law. After all, examples of successful global regulation of economic rights abound in IEL to protect the real or intellectual property rights of multinational corporations or investors, and in areas as diverse as deep-sea minerals or satellite orbits. More active social regulation of ER in other areas of international trade law is not only feasible, therefore, but also required. One may think, for instance, of developing a new regime of international land (property) law to prevent property-regime voids and land-grabbing (see Wenar, 2015: 175–177; de Schutter, 2011) or of re-invigorating international labor law that has been left to erode since the 1920s (see Supiot, 2016).

Of course, given how important domestic private law and the duties of private actors are for the effective implementation of ER, the duties of states under IHRL also include drafting private international law instruments applicable to transnational circumstances (e.g., agricultural products' exports, labor migration). Domestic legal regimes pertaining to property or contract are bound to differ, indeed, and hence to compete with one another, thus inevitably leading to a race to the bottom. States are therefore, one may argue, under ER positive duties to develop private international law rules that restrain private law shopping in the fields of property law, contract law and labor law (see Wenar, 2015: 184–185).

6. Conclusion

The moralization and, more specifically, the moral naturalization of the private law of the market as a result of "everyday libertarianism" (Murphy, 2016) has recently been denounced by private law theorists. While such understandings had long been disparaged to the profit of conventional ones, property and contract rights are now predominantly approached again as "natural" or real moral rights mirrored by domestic private law. The return of this form of individualistic naturalism may be approached as the resurgence, in a new guise, of a now century-old phenomenon of combination of the natural laws of science with those of morality (see Supiot, 2009). Only this time, what is taking place is the marriage between the alleged natural laws of the economy with those of morality, with the complicity of positive human laws.

Interestingly, the same development may now be observed in the field of IHRL. One may coin it the moral naturalization of ER *qua* human rights. The difficulty is greater in this context, however, to the extent that human rights are usually held to be the epitome of "natural" or real moral rights. This makes the combination of both kinds of naturalistic readings even more irresistible. The problem is that the alliance of the individualistic naturalism of economic liberalism with the desocializing naturalism of most existing human rights theories constitute a great risk for social justice and the effective protection of SR. The latter rights have indeed progressively been reduced to passive and atomized subsistence and anti-poverty rights.

In response, this chapter has identified a third way for human rights theorists interested in supporting a reading of ER that can promote social justice. The choice is not, unlike what the few human rights theorists discussing ER to date have argued, between either considering ER as natural or real moral rights, and hence recognizing individual market rights as human rights and entrenching some form of economic naturalism into IHRL, on the one hand, or approaching them as mere moral goals and not as proper human rights, and hence condemning social rights to the passive and individualized role they have been assigned since the 1960s, on the other. Human rights like ER may also be considered to recognize and/or specify universal moral rights that are not natural or real moral rights, but conventional moral rights whose justification is instrumental and grounded in the value of the social practice and normative order they are part of.

The proposed conventional reading of ER has important repercussions for human rights theory, more generally, because it provides a morally nuanced understanding of the relations between moral and legal rights in human rights law. It is also bears on the future practice of SER both domestically and internationally and, with respect to the latter, in IEL as much as in IHRL. Interpreting ER in the proposed conventional way reunites ER with SR and approaches SER as the active and relational rights they were first conceived to be. In turn, this revives the hope of finally putting ER, and arguably IHRL, to the task of promoting social justice.

Notes

1 The regional regimes discussed in this chapter are primarily the Convention on the Protection of Human Rights and Fundamental Freedoms (4 November 1950; 213 UNTS 221) (European Convention on Human Rights; ECHR), the European Social Charter (3 May 1996; ETS Nr 163) (ESC) and the Charter of Fundamental Rights of the European Union ([2012] OJ C326/391) (EUFRC).

2 In this chapter, ER include "economic liberties" (e.g., freedom of contract), but also other "economic rights" (e.g., the right to property). This is why it is the latter and most encompassing group, i.e., rights, that is discussed under the name of ER. Contra: Nickel, 2007: ch. 8 (who only refers to "economic liberties"); Buchanan, 2013: 167–171 (who refers to them as "economic liberties" and uses "economic rights" to refer to social rights); Waldron, 2010b.

3 Thus, while universal human rights law protects ER among SER in the Universal Declaration of Human Rights (10 December 1948; UNGA Res 217 A(III)) (UDHR) and, albeit in a different way, in the International Covenant on Economic, Social and Cultural Rights (16 December 1966; 993 UNTS 3) (ICESCR), regional human rights law does not always include them. For instance, the ECHR does not include any ER, except for the right to property and then only under Article 1 of its First Optional Protocol, notwithstanding, of course, their protection by the ESC. The American Convention of Human Rights (22 November 1969; 1144 UNTS 123) (ACHR) and the African Charter on Human and People's Rights (21 October 1986; 1520 UNTS 217) (ACHPR) only protect the right to property (Article 21 ACHR; Article 14 ACHPR).

4 For instance, the right to property that is protected in the UDHR (Article 17), and in the three regional human rights treaties mentioned before, is not

protected in the ICESCR or anywhere in universal human rights law, even though, by contrast, the ICESCR protects more SR (Articles 6–9, 10–12 and 13–15) than the UDHR (Articles 23, 25 and 26), and the latter are not protected by regional human rights treaties either (except by the ESC). By contrast, the EUFRC, that is more recent, protects the freedom to exercise a profession, the freedom of enterprise and the right to property (Articles 15, 16 and 17 EUFRC).

5 The CESCR distinguishes, in its monitoring process of state reports, between three clusters of ESCR: Articles 6–9, Articles 10–12 and Articles 13–15. Some have argued the first cluster could be considered as ER, and the latter respectively as SR and CR: see Riedel et al., 2014: 8–10.

6 In some traditions, "property rights" are used to include all ER: see Daintith, 2004: 59–61; Nickel, 2007: 125.

7 See the ILO 1998 Declaration on Fundamental Principles and Rights at Work, 37 ILM 1233.

8 See FD Roosevelt's *Economic Bill of Rights* 1944 speech (www.fdrlibrary.marist.edu/archives/address_text.html): "necessitous men are not free men." See also Sen, 2009 on "socio-economic unfreedoms."

9 On ER in Roosevelt's 6 January 1941 *Four Freedoms* (http://docs.fdrlibrary.marist.edu/od4frees.html) and 11 June 1944 *Economic Bill of Rights* speeches, in the 10 May 1944 *Declaration of Philadelphia* (ILO)(http://blue.lim.ilo.org/cariblex/pdfs/ILO_dec_philadelphia.pdf) and in the 1948 UDHR, see Donnelly, 2007: 38–41; Supiot, 2016.

10 See e.g., Article 16 Convention on the Elimination of All Forms of Discrimination Against Women (18 December 1979; 1249 UNTS 13) (CEDAW); Article 5 International Convention on the Elimination of All Forms of Racial Discrimination (7 March 1966; 660 UNTS 195) (CERD); Article 15 International Convention on the Protection of the Rights of All Migrant Workers and Members of Their Families (18 December 1990; 2220 UNTS 3) (CRPMW); and Article 12 Convention on the Rights of Persons with Disabilities (13 December 2006; 2515 UNTS 3) (CRPD).

11 This is the case of intellectual property rights under the Marrakesh Agreement establishing the WTO (15 April 1994; 1867 UNTS 3) (TRIPS).

12 This is the case of the freedom to exercise a profession, the freedom of enterprise and the right to property in the EUFRC (Articles 15, 16 and 17), but also of two of the four EU fundamental freedoms, i.e., free movement of workers and free movement of service providers (Title IV of the Consolidated Version of the Treaty on the Functioning of the European Union (TFEU); [2012] OJ C326/47).

13 This ambiguity is even heightened in the EU given the mere transformation of some EU fundamental (economic) freedoms into EU fundamental rights: see Weatherill, 2013.

14 Because the present chapter argues against the naturalistic reading of ER, including on grounds of the many conflations the invocation of "natural laws" (of morality, religion, science or the economy) give rise to (see Supiot, 2009: ch. 2), it is better not to refer to "genuine" or "real" moral rights as "natural" rights.

15 For discussions about the Lockean origins of this position, see Waldron, 1990: 282–283, 2013.

16 See Daintith, 2004; Waldron, 2010b; Nickel, 2007: ch. 8; Hertel and Minkler, 2007. Most of them, however, are specific to some ER, such as the *right to property* (see e.g., Dagan and Dorfman, 2017; Waldron, 1990, 2010a, 2013); the *right to work* (see e.g., Gilabert, 2016; Collins, 2015; Nickel, 2015; Mantouvalou, 2012, 2015; Risse, 2009; Pogge, 2009; Alston, 2005a; Elster, 1988; Nickel, 1978–79); or *entrepreneurial rights* (see e.g., Queralt, 2017).

17 For a critique of this self-confidence following the entry into force of the Optional Protocol to the ICESCR, see Alston, 2016b.
18 Contrast the 1990s and 2000s discussions (e.g., Craven, 1995) with recent ones (e.g., Riedel et al., 2014).
19 While Nickel, 2007 used to include the right to work among SR, Nickel, 2015 declassified it from human right to "moral goal" or "goalish right."
20 By "social practice," I mean any rule-governed social activity where the rules are generally complied with. See Murphy, 2016; Raz, 2012.
21 By "conventional morality," I mean the set of moral norms that is generally accepted in a society and which is typically realized in a social practice. See Murphy, 2016.
22 For a critique and on the complementarity between ER *qua* rights to self-help and SR *qua* rights to provision, see Nickel, 2007: 131–132; Alston, 2016b.
23 For a critique of this conflation between poverty and SER violations, see Alston, 2005b: 784 ff, 2016b.
24 See for an early warning about "marrying, almost symbiotically" trade and human rights, Alston, 2002: 818, 843–844.
25 Importantly, and contra Tasioulas, 2017's critique of Buchanan, 2013, the egalitarian dimension of (legal and moral) human rights should be conflated neither with a basic human right to equality or non-discrimination (non-discrimination rights exist as specific human rights in IHRL, because they protect specific interests to non-discrimination) nor with a ground of human rights themselves (equal moral status and human rights are mutually constitutive). See Besson, 2013b.
26 Unlike Murphy, 2016, my concern in this chapter is primarily with naturalism, and not necessarily only with "libertarian" naturalism. What one may argue in reaction to non-naturalist or conventionalist libertarian arguments for ER, however, is that the egalitarian dimension of human rights makes it a requirement of ER under IHRL that they be regulated over in domestic law and that thereby the mutual duties of private actors be specified by reference to social justice, as I explain in the final and fourth section of the chapter.
27 See e.g., Stilz, 2018 for a "hybrid" natural-conventional view of property rights. Unlike her, I think there are other (especially egalitarian) ways to justify states' territorial sovereignty and the corresponding "rights" (that need not actually be approached as proprietory in kind) than through the (even minimal) natural rights of first occupancy of their individual subjects.
28 On the "labour theory of property," see Locke, 1690. For a critical discussion, see Waldron, 1990: 171–177.
29 See Murphy, 2016 referring to Raz, 2015: "[t]he performance [of a promise] interest is a normative interest, not a real material interest. It would be question-begging to explain the duty to keep promises by saying that promisees have an interest that promises be kept, since promisees only have that interest if promisors have that duty."
30 Even if the first prong of the argument is rejected, the second prong may be taken to establish that the conventionalist account of ER is at least superior to the naturalist one for the reasons presented in the first and final sections of the chapter, but also in the remainder of this section.
31 Importantly, the instrumental justification of ER by reference to the value of the economic practice does not imply that those rights themselves are (solely) constitutive of the value of that practice.
32 See Raz, 1986: 247–248, 251–253: "the right to economic freedom, or the right to freedom of contract, does not exist in opposition to collective goods. Far from its purpose being to curtail the pursuit of collective goods, it presupposes and depends for its value on the existence of at least one collective good: the free market."

33 This does not imply a right to the setting up of the economic practice itself: it relies on a pre-existing social practice economic conventional moral rights are a part of.

34 See, however, Nickel, 2007: 126 for a dual justification for those rights *qua* human rights: both instrumental to the promotion of other values (126–29) and linkage-based (129–31).

References

Alston P (2002) Resisting the Merger and Acquisition of Human Rights by Trade Law: A Reply to Petersmann. *European Journal of International Law* 13(4): 815–844.

Alston P (2005a) Labor Rights as Human Rights: The Not So Happy State of the Art. In: Alston P (ed) *Labour Rights as Human Rights*, 1st ed. Oxford: Oxford University Press, pp. 1–24.

Alston P (2005b) Ships Passing in the Night: The Current State of the Human Rights and Development Debate Seen Through the Lens of the Millennium Development Goals. *Human Rights Quarterly* 27(3): 755–859.

Alston P (2016a) Phantom Rights: The Systemic Marginalization of Economic and Social Rights. Available at: www.opendemocracy.net/openglobalrights/philip-alston/phantom-rights-systemic-marginalization-of-economic-and-social-rights (accessed 6 October 2017).

Alston P (2016b) Third Report of the Special Rapporteur on Extreme Poverty and Human Rights. A/HRC/32/31.

Alvarez J (2018) The Human Right to Property. *New York University School of Law, Public Law Research Paper* No. 18–21.

Beitz C (2009) *The Idea of Human Rights*. Oxford: Oxford University Press.

Bernstein D (2011) *Rehabilitating Lochner: Defending Individual Rights Against Progressive Reform*. Chicago: The University of Chicago Press.

Besson S (2011) Human Rights: Ethical, Political . . . or Legal? First Steps in a Legal Theory of Human Rights. In: Childress III D (ed) *The Role of Ethics in International Law*, 1st ed. Cambridge: Cambridge University Press, pp. 211–245.

Besson S (2013a) Justifications of Human Rights. In: Moeckli D and Shah S (eds) *International Human Rights Law*, 2nd ed. Oxford: Oxford University Press, pp. 34–52.

Besson S (2013b) The Egalitarian Dimension of Human Rights. *Archiv für Sozial- und Rechtsphilosophie Beiheft* 136: 19–52.

Besson S (2015) Human Rights and Constitutional Law: Mutual Validation and Legitimation. In: Cruft R, Liao SM and Renzo M (eds) *Philosophical Foundations of Human Rights*, 1st ed. Oxford: Oxford University Press, pp. 279–299.

Besson S (2017) Legal Human Rights Theory. In: Brownlee K, Lippert-Ramussen K and Coady D (eds) *A Companion to Applied Philosophy*, 1st ed. Chickester: Wiley Blackwell, pp. 328–341.

Buchanan A (2013) *The Heart of Human Rights*. Oxford: Oxford University Press.

Buchanan A (2015) Why International Legal Human Rights? In: Cruft R, Liao SM and Renzo M (eds) *Philosophical Foundations of Human Rights*, 1st ed. Oxford: Oxford University Press, pp. 244–262.

Collins H (2015) Is There a Human Right to Work? In: Mantouvalou V (ed) *The Right to Work: Legal and Philosophical Perspectives*, 1st ed. Oxford and Portland, OR: Hart Publishing, pp. 17–38.

Cranston M (1967) Human Rights, Real and Supposed. In: Raphael D (ed) *Political Theory and the Rights of Man*, 1st ed. London and Melbourne: Palgrave Macmillan, pp. 43–55.

Craven M (1995) *The International Covenant on Economic, Social and Cultural Rights: A Perspective on Its Development*. Oxford: Clarendon Press.

Dagan H and Dorfman A (2017) The Human Right to Private Property. *Theoretical Inquiries in Law* 18(2): 391–416.

Daintith T (2004) The Constitutional Protection of Economic Rights. *International Journal of Constitutional Law* 2(1): 56–90.

de Schutter O (2011) The *Green Rush*: The Global Race for Farmland and the Rights of Land Users. *Harvard International Law Journal* 52(2): 503–559.

Donnelly J (2007) The West and Economic Rights. In: Hertel S and Minkler L (eds) *Economic Rights: Conceptual, Measurement and Policy Issues*, 1st ed. Cambridge: Cambridge University Press, pp. 37–55.

Drache D and Jacobs L (eds) (2014) *Linking Global Trade and Human Rights*. Cambridge: Cambridge University Press.

Dumont L (1985) *Homo aequalis I. Genèse et épanouissement de l'idéologie économique*, 2nd ed. Paris: Gallimard.

Elster J (1988) Is There (or Should There Be) a Right to Work? In: Gutmann A (ed) *Democracy and the Welfare State*, 1st ed. Princeton: Princeton University Press, pp. 53–77.

Elster J (1994) The Impact of Constitutions on Economic Performance. *The World Bank Economic Review* Supplementary Volume: 209–226.

Fouillée A (1899) L'idée de justice sociale d'après les écoles contemporaines. *Revue des deux mondes* 152: 47–75.

Gilabert P (2016) Labor Human Rights and Human Dignity. *Philosophy and Social Criticism* 42(2): 171–199.

Hayek F (1978) *Law, Legislation, and Liberty, Vol. 2: The Mirage of Social Justice*. Chicago: The Chicago University Press.

Hertel S and Minkler L (2007) Economic Rights: The Terrain. In: Hertel S and Minkler L (eds) *Economic Rights: Conceptual, Measurement and Policy Issues*. Cambridge: Cambridge University Press.

Howse R and Teitel R (2010) Global Justice, Poverty and the International Economic Order. In: Besson S and Tasioulas J (eds) *The Philosophy of International Law*, 1st ed. Oxford: Oxford University Press, pp. 437–450.

Locke J (first published in 1690; 2016) *Second Treatise of Government*. Oxford: Oxford University Press.

Mantouvalou V (2012) Are Labour Rights Human Rights. *European Labour Law Journal* 3(2): 151–172.

Mantoulavou V (2015) Introduction. In: Mantouvalou V (ed) *The Right to Work: Legal and Philosophical Perspectives*, 1st ed. Oxford and Portland, OR: Hart Publishing, pp. 1–10.

Marx K (first published in 1862; 1972) *Theories of Surplus Value*. London: Lawrence and Wishart.

Moyn S (2014) A Powerless Companion: Human Rights in the Age of Neoliberalism. *Law & Contemporary Problems* 77(4): 147–169.

Murphy L (2016) *Private Law and Public Illusion*. Frankfurt Lectures. Unpublished manuscript, on file with author.

Murphy L and Nagel T (2002) *The Myth of Ownership*. Oxford: Oxford University Press.

Nickel J (1978–79) Is There a Human Right to Employment? *Philosophical Forum* 10(2): 158–170.

Nickel J (2007) *Making Sense of Human Rights*, 2nd ed. Malden: Blackwell Publishing.

Nickel J (2008) Rethinking Indivisibility: Towards a Theory of Support Relations Between Human Rights. *Human Rights Quarterly* 30(4): 984–1001.

Nickel J (2013) Goals and Rights: Working Together? In: Langford M, Summer A and Yamin A (eds) *The Millennium Development Goals and Human Rights: Past, Present, and Future*, 1st ed. New York: Cambridge University Press, pp. 37–48.

Nickel J (2015) Giving Up on the Right to Work. In: Mantouvalou V (ed) *The Right to Work: Legal and Philosophical Perspectives*, 1st ed. Oxford and Portland, OR: Hart Publishing, pp. 137–148.

Nozick R (1974) *Anarchy, State and Utopia*. Oxford: Blackwell Publishing.

O'Connell P (2011) The Death of Socio-Economic Rights. *Modern Law Review* 74(4): 532–554.

Pogge T (2009) Comment on Mathias Risse: "A Right to Work? A Right to Leisure? Labour Rights as Human Rights." *Law & Ethics of Human Rights* 3(1): 40–47.

Queralt J (2017) Protecting the Entrepreneurial Poor: A Human-Rights Approach. Unpublished manuscript, on file with author.

Raz J (1984) Legal Rights. *Oxford Journal of Legal Studies* 4(1): 1–21.

Raz J (1986) *The Morality of Freedom*. Oxford: Clarendon Press.

Raz J (2010a) Human Rights in the Emerging World Order. *Transnational Legal Theory* 1: 31–47.

Raz J (2010b) Human Rights Without Foundations. In: Besson S and Tasioulas J (eds) *The Philosophy of International Law*, 1st ed. Oxford: Oxford University Press, pp. 321–338.

Raz J (2012) *Normative Variations*. Unpublished manuscript, on file with the author.

Raz J (2015) Is There a Reason to Keep a Promise? In: Klass G, Letsas G and Saprai P (eds) *Philosophical Foundations of Contract Law*, 1st ed. Oxford: Oxford University Press, pp. 58–77.

Riedel E, Giacca G and Golay C (2014) The Development of Economic, Social and Cultural Rights in International Law. In: Riedel E, Giacca G and Golay C (eds) *Economic, Social and Cultural Rights in International Law*, 1st ed. Oxford: Oxford University Press, pp. 3–50.

Risse M (2009) A Right to Work? A Right to Leisure? Labour Rights as Human Rights. *Law & Ethics of Human Rights* 3(1): 1–39.

Scheffler S (2015) Distributive Justice, the Basic Structure and the Place of Private Law. *Oxford Journal of Legal Studies* 35(2): 213–235.

Sen A (2009) *The Idea of Justice*. Cambridge, MA: Harvard University Press.

Shue H (1996) *Basic Rights: Subsistence, Affluence, and U.S. Foreign Policy*, 2nd ed. Princeton: Princeton University Press.

Sprankling J (2014) A Global Right to Property. *Columbia Journal of Transnational Law* 52(2): 464–505.

Stilz A (2018) Property Rights: Natural or Conventional? In: Brennan J, Schmidtz D and van der Vossen B (eds) *The Routledge Handbook of Libertarianism*. New York: Routledge, pp. 244–258.

Supiot A (2009) *Homo Juridicus: Essai sur la fonction anthropologique du droit*. Paris: Seuil.

Supiot A (2016) What International Social Justice in the Twenty-First Century? In: Blanpain R, Hendrickx F and du Toit D (eds) *Labour Law and Social Progress Holding the Line or Shifting the Boundaries?* 1st ed. Alphen aan den Rijn: Wolters Kluwer Law & Business.

Tasioulas J (2017) Exiting the Hall of Mirrors: Morality and Law in Human Rights. In: Campbell T and Bourne K (eds) *Political and Legal Approaches to Human Rights*. London: Routledge, pp. 73–89.

Waldron J (1990) *The Right to Private Property*. Oxford: Clarendon Press.

Waldron J (2010a) Property Law. In: Patterson D (ed) *A Companion to Philosophy of Law and Legal Theory*, 2nd ed. Oxford: Wiley-Blackwell, pp. 9–28.

Waldron J (2010b) Socioeconomic Rights and Theories of Justice. *New York University Public Law and Legal Theory Working Papers Paper* 245.

Waldron J (2012) *Dignity, Rank and Rights*. Oxford: Oxford University Press.

Waldron J (2013) To Bestow Stability upon Possession: Hume's Alternative to Locke. In: Penner J and Smith H (eds) *Philosophical Foundations of Property Law*, 1st ed. Oxford: Oxford University Press, pp. 1–12.

Weatherill S (2013) From Economic Rights to Fundamental Rights. In: de Vries S, Bernitz U and Weatherill S (eds) *The Protection of Fundamental Rights in the EU After Lisbon*, 1st ed. Oxford: Hart Publishing, pp. 11–36.

Wenar L (2015) Coercion in Cross-Border Property Rights. *Social Philosophy and Policy* 32(1): 171–191.

4 Property's Relation to Human Rights

Carol M. Rose

1. Introduction

Commentators on property typically take the perspective of a property owner, often citing the famous passage in William Blackstone's *Commentaries* that describes property as the "sole and despotic dominion" that the owner enjoys over things, to the exclusion of all others (Blackstone, 1765: 2:2). Blackstone himself immediately expressed grave doubts about this description, however, and particularly about the supposed origins of any such dominion (Rose, 1998: 604–605). Even if we put Blackstone's doubts to one side, however, we might observe that these famous lines concern not only the owner but the non-owners as well. Implicitly, property is a social institution in which individuals may play the role of owners but much more frequently play the role of non-owners, who must acknowledge and defer to the claims of others to control specific resources (Rose, 2013: 272).

What does this social institution do for us? Sometimes, nothing at all. There is no point in having property in things that are boundlessly available. But where resources are even somewhat scarce, the institution of property plays the very important role of deflecting conflict, instead encouraging forbearance and negotiation. Beyond that, property can serve a variety of important and to some degree overlapping functions: safeguarding a zone of autonomy for individuals (Claeys, 2006: 722); protecting their dignity and the signals of respect that they gain from others (Atuahene, 2016); creating a basis for undertaking projects in the world (Radin, 1982); diffusing political authority among many actors and thus deflecting concentration of power (Friedman, 1962: 7–21); maintaining individuals' independence and shielding them from subservience to others (Craig-Taylor, 1998). Perhaps best known, however, is the economic role of property. Especially when taken together with trade and commerce, property incentivizes the creation of wealth by rewarding an owner's effort, planning and careful management of resources (Bentham, 1891: 109–119; Blackstone, 1765: 2:7; Posner, 2014: 40). This economic role entails a recognition of the importance of self-interest in motivating individuals, but self-interest is not the only motivator in property relations; people invest in their property for the sake of others, including their families, friends, churches, communities and causes.

But from the perspective of rights, as is implicit in the Blackstonian lines, the institution of property roots itself not only in assertions of one's own claims but also in deference to the claims of others. In that sense, property relations act as a practical education in what it means to have and to respect rights.

It is especially interesting, then, that in contemporary human rights literature, property plays a role that is at best ambivalent. Some human rights advocates assert that property must itself be considered a human right (Alvarez, 2018). But often property appears as a bully, as where advocates decry international enterprises that harp on property claims and investment agreements at the expense of local populations' well-being (Kaushal, 2009: 522–532); or they chastise property owners who resist redistributive measures that might support human rights claims to essential resources (Pashkoff, 1989: 88; Moyn, 2010: 17–22, 64); or they assert that developed-world technologists find local agricultural or medicinal products and then close them off with claims of intellectual property (Brown, 2003: 95–143).

How, then, might property relate to human rights? Is property an impediment to human rights? Or is it a human right itself? Or something else? Let me say immediately that I have no particular expertise in human rights, and I am sure I will make many errors in describing the conceptions and literatures that are at stake. But from a superficial look at some to the contemporary works, it seems to me that the idea of human rights—as background rights that should naturally belong to all human beings—describes what is primarily a moral framework and only secondarily a matter of legal prescription (Shelton, 2008; Regan and Hall, 2016: 2020–2027). Having said that, however, human rights *are* legally prescribed insofar as governments have adopted laws binding themselves to human rights. This has occurred with sufficient frequency that such leading international law scholars as Jose Alvarez (2018) and John Sprankling (2014) can make the case that as a positive matter, there is already an international human right to property in a general sense. These and other commentators, however, point to substantial qualifications on property's legal status as a human right, given that different political regimes vary widely in their treatment of property, and given that sanctions for violation are at best doubtful (Penalver, 2000: 146–147).

My own intuition is that the strongest moral case for property as a human right relates to independence; the ability to acquire and own property is a bulwark against subservience to others. But aside from that minimalist consideration, I will remain agnostic on the issue whether property is or should be defined as a human right as a legal matter or even a moral one. So far as I can see, the modern human rights discussion after the Second World War (hereinafter WWII) began with issues with little obvious connection to property: first denouncing atrocity and official oppression, and later expanding to encompass ever more elements of a full and meaningful life. These are admirable aims, and insofar as there are controversies about human rights, they seldom concern these overall goals but rather question whether a rights-based approach is the appropriate means to achieve those goals (Kennedy, 2002: 101, 104, 125; cf Moyn, 2014a: 61–62, 2014b: 151).

This pragmatic approach seems to me to be particularly appropriate with respect to property. Hence in this chapter I will take the position that the most fruitful way to look at property's relation to human rights is practical—that is, to consider how the protection of property might or might not advance the general goals of a human rights agenda, whether or not one regards property as a human right in itself, or what such a right might mean.

I will begin with a few very brief comments on my understanding of the rather ambiguous place of property in the modern debates over human rights. I will then take up three topics that especially probe the role of property in advancing human rights ideals. The first topic concerns a fairly well-known issue: property's relationship to claims for social and economic rights, where property is often cast as a kind of villain or obstacle. Here I will observe that while property claims can indeed be too rigid, the protection of property actually can help to create the background economic progress that supports economic and social well-being. This is a well-known position, but less intuitively, I will also argue that more secure property rights can create conditions in which it is *politically* feasible to fulfill those social and economic claims.

The second topic is somewhat more recent in human rights discussions, that of claims for cultural preservation of tradition or indigenous peoples. My argument here takes an opposite trajectory: in connection with these claims, human rights proponents treat property as the hero of the story. But here too I will again take a partially contrarian position, arguing that property recognition can indeed be helpful in a larger sense of protecting the group, but that some serious caveats are in order. Not only may group-based property fall short in an economic role, but equally important, group property can carry some dangers for human rights as a matter of democracy.

The third topic is only a very brief sketch, in which property is neither villain nor hero, but rather a signal or bellwether that links to the more central modern human rights concerns about atrocities. Here I will observe a point that I believe has not yet been much explored in human rights literature: that property deprivations threaten to accelerate other kinds of human rights abuses by creating constituencies for those abuses. Greater attention to property, on the other hand, might help to keep some of these massive human rights violations from spiraling out of control—or even better, might make them less likely in the first place. In keeping with this pragmatic observation, I will conclude that while property has a rather murky place in the world of human rights, attention to property rights can act as an important support for other kinds of rights.

2. The Backdrop: Where Has Property Been in 20th-Century Human Rights Discussions?

Human rights histories often point to two major sources: the first is the set of universalist pronouncements coming from the 18th-century American and French Revolutions, which followed an Enlightenment philosophical tradition in treating property as one of the essential rights of human beings and indeed as one of the bases for the societies they form.[1] The second is the array of declarations and decrees of international organizations at the end of WWII, much enhanced in the 1970s and thereafter, which were to become the starting point for modern human rights claims (Sprankling, 2014: 468–469; Moyn, 2010: 120–121, 2018: 120–124).

My impression of these sources is that they differed in their contexts and their goals. To put it in an overly crude way, the 18th-century activists and reformers aimed at changing their own governing institutions, whereas the mid-20th-century human rights activists and reformers aimed to set a standard not only for their own governing institutions but just as importantly, for other people's governments. The Allied victory in WWII gave the discussion of universal human rights a very different focus from that of 18th-century revolutionaries. The immediate context was not reform at home, but rather the question how the Allies might come to grips with the atrocities perpetrated by the Axis powers—among other things justifying the postwar trials of Axis officials for the newly created "crimes against humanity." The new discussion of human rights thus initially centered on the horrific acts associated with the Axis regimes: displacement, enslavement, starvation and outright murder of whole population groups; imprisonment and torture of adversaries; suppression of dissent on all fronts.

Finding a just rebuke for these acts necessitated jettisoning a longstanding "Westphalian" tradition in international law, that of nonintervention into the internal affairs of other regimes.[2] The modern human rights movement builds on this transformation. For example, human rights theorist Leif Wenar specifically argues that human rights must put aside the Westphalian tradition. In his view, human rights violations in one nation may require others to intervene at least in the form of moral suasion, moral disapprobation and moral support for the victims; or in the most serious cases trade sanctions or possibly (if very rarely) military intervention (Wenar, 2005; Twiss, 2004: 51–53). Other human rights advocates have been more cautious, arguing that human rights do not controvert sovereignty (Alvarez, 2018). Still, human rights language has affected sovereignty not only because sovereign entities have ostensibly bound themselves to human rights principles through laws and treaties, but also because human rights language now serves as a medium through which external political figures and non-governmental organizations can criticize those sovereign entities.

Property has been much less prominent in 20th- and 21st-century human rights discourse than it was in the Age of Revolution, however. Property seizures and destruction played some role in the picture of totalitarian abuses in the post-WWII discussions, but these paled by comparison to other much more dramatic horrors. In any event, the war alliance with the Soviet Union meant that in the postwar period, property seizures would not be a central topic in human rights pronouncements. In the United Nations 1948 Universal Declaration of Human Rights (UDHR), Article 17 made the anodyne assertion that everyone has the right to own property and to be free of arbitrary seizures, but subsequent UN rights declarations omitted property until the end of the Cold War (Alvarez, 2018; Sprankling, 2014: 471–474).

Moreover, other human rights guarantees in the UDHR itself created some ambiguity about the status of property ownership as a human right, particularly the articles guaranteeing access to such social support as housing, nutrition and education (Articles 25–26). These claims for access to resources potentially entail redistributive demands on the property of existing owners. Insofar as that is the case, it would seem that these kinds of claims raise questions about how, whether and the degree to which human rights ideals can include both a right to property on the one hand, and redistributive rights on the other.

These ambiguities, however, are generally not at the forefront of ordinary news invoking human rights. As with the totalitarian abuses of the 1930s and 1940s, human rights stories after WWII have continued to focus most sharply on issues of mass murder and the brutal suppression of dissent, particularly in connection with outbreaks of violence in such places as Rwanda, Cambodia and Bosnia, or in arbitrary detentions and murders in military dictatorships in Latin America and elsewhere. Property seizures have been a part of these terrible events, but murder and genocide command far greater attention.

In the burgeoning human rights discussions since the 1970s, scholars and activists have increasingly highlighted the very kinds of claims that render ambiguous the role of property in a human rights order. First, human rights proponents have expanded the conception of social and economic resource access rights that were initially stated in the UDHR. The Declaration enumerated rights to basic subsistence, education, health, meaningful work, among others, and these are now joined by claims to a growing list, many relating to environmental resources. As with any claimed right to resource access, these expanded claims have a potential impact on property insofar as they call on current property owner A to give up portions of her assets to assist recipient B; as such they lead to more questions how claims to social and economic rights relate to a purported human right to own property.

A second type of emergent claim grows out of UDHR's Articles 1 and 27, describing a right to equal dignity and to a right to participate in culture. Over the last few decades, these precepts have been memorialized in other documents and have come to center on property rights in groups, as a means to protect the dignity and lifeways of traditional peoples and especially indigenous populations. Property claims for these groups often include claims of land rights and sometimes intellectual property, and here they can confront the property claims of other persons and groups, repeating those A vs. B issues. But aside from these distributive issues, group rights pose other kinds of dilemmas for conventional property rights, relating to membership in the group and the authority of some group members over others.

In the next two parts of this chapter, I turn to these two relatively recent expansions of human rights discussions in an effort to discern their implications for the relationship between property and human rights. In both these claim areas, conflicts and convergences—including some unexpected examples of each—emerge between conventional property and human rights concerns. In the next and last part, I will outline another unexpected convergence: that between property and the prevention of the kinds of dramatic abuses—including murder and displacement—that drove human rights thinking immediately after WWII and that now continue to dominate the news cycle.

3. Property and Human Rights Claims to Resource Access; or, What Looks Bad About Property May Have a Good Side

Since WWII, human rights discussions have asserted that these rights include not only life and liberty, but also access to resources sufficient to guarantee a decent mode of living—food, shelter, education and health. These kinds of social and economic claims have been controversial even within the literature on human rights, but controversy has not halted more recent elaborations, some expanding the list to include access to a clean environment, to protection and restitution from the ravages of climate change, to specific resources such as water, as well as access to knowledge (Larson, 2017: 1307, 1318; Helfer, 2007:1012–1014).

Claimed rights to resource access are sometimes called positive rights—as distinguished from "negative" rights, like freedom from arbitrary detention or torture or homicide, which basically call on governments to refrain from unjust activities. A major reason for their controversial nature is that all involve substantial expenditure of funds and demands on taxpayers, and in a context of finite resources, all expenditures require priorities and budgeting. A "rights" designation for resource access is unhelpful in prioritizing; instead, in the first instance, that designation would suggest that each matter requires maximal effort towards fulfillment, perhaps requiring more in taxes, and perhaps trumping more mundane expenditures like pothole repair.

Resource access demands on public budgets clearly involve property owners as taxpayers. To be sure, some claims to resource access focus on goods for the public at large—e.g., clean air or public sewerage systems; in many cases, as environmentalists observe, a shift of private funds to these public goods actually increases the total wealth of a society, and implicitly compensates taxpayers by making everyone better off, even if some feel the costs more than others (Rose, 1997: 57–58). But positive human rights claims often have a more focused distributional component, and these are the ones on which I wish to concentrate. Human rights claims may mean that some group of As are to pay for the B's food or housing—or pay B's water bill or give up intellectual property to B. And that is the major rub for property: insofar as B's access to these resources are called human rights, and insofar as A has to pay for them, A is very likely to object that these demands amount to an involuntary and uncompensated taking of A's property. In this rather simple scenario, if property is itself considered a human right, then the scenario pits one human right against another.

It is worth noting that some Marxist critics have depicted the movement for social and economic human rights as a coverup for the abuses of capitalism itself—a sop that excuses the wealthy As by requiring no more than a pittance in the pot for poverty-stricken Bs. Historian Samuel Moyn rejects the view that the human rights movement has an evil twin in neoliberalism, but he nevertheless argues that the human rights movement gives up too easily, satisfying itself with the paltry goal of *sufficiency* of personal welfare. Instead, according to Moyn, the real goal should be much grander, that is to say, *equality*, placing the As and Bs are on an equal plain (Moyn, 2018: 6, 174–176, 216–220).

But then, one might want to think why the As or anyone else has all that wealth in the first place. Economic thinkers have long associated property and contract, the building blocks of capitalism, with greater social wealth. The crude version was mentioned above: property rewards effort and planning with gains, while punishing carelessness and shortsightedness with loss. Contracts expand the range of this dynamic: by contracting with others, A can find more markets and opportunities, and can thus enhance the productivity of her efforts and the incentives to make more. But if successful A has to divide the gains from her efforts with unsuccessful B, she loses at least some of the incentive that drives her success. Similarly, if A's contractual relationships can be upended easily, she cannot make credible commitments and potential contracting partners will melt away; consequently she will not be able to generate much wealth, or interest others in investing in her efforts. At the extreme, one can see the result on a national scale in a place like Venezuela in 2018, where governmental disruptions of property and contract have dramatically reduced the nation's wealth—and the willingness of others to invest.

On the whole, property and contract are not zero-sum games; commerce thrives where the payoffs go not only to A but also to the Bs and Cs and Ds, her business clients and associates and employees too; hence collectively, individuals' wealth turns into Adam Smith's Wealth of Nations. But well-being and even riches are the carrot while the threat of penury is the stick for the As, the Bs and all the others; and the prospects of both carrot and stick are essential parts of what makes property/contract regimes generate wealth, both individually and socially.

Thus if property is to act as an economic driver—and it is widely thought that this is a chief function of property—the unpleasant truth is that inequality is baked in. Regimes can certainly insist that all the As and Bs reduce the external harms from their activities and pay their share for public goods, and thus A and B have less for their private activities, but the implicit compensation is that all are better off from the resulting increase in public wealth. More controversially, regimes can even insist on transfers from the As to the Bs, and they can even structure property so as to incorporate transfer duties. The result will be greater equality, but very possibly at a price. That price would come from a trade-off between equality and wealth generation. As Jeremy Bentham observed, the regime of thoroughgoing equality may well mean an equality of poverty—not desirable for either A nor B, even for the modest goal of sufficiency (Bentham, 1891: 119–122).

But is the trade-off actually so sharp? Even capitalist A may wish to make some transfers, if for no other purpose than to quiet the discontented rumblings of the Bs (Michelman, 1977–1978: 154). There is a less obviously self-interested reason, however, why the As may be willing to transfer wealth to the Bs in a capitalist regime: as Aristotle observed, greater possessions make liberality possible. It is not that poor people are ungenerous—far from it, there are many, many examples of great generosity among impoverished people—but simply that having more makes it easier to give more (Aristotle, 1962: 85 [Book 4, ch. 1]). Early proponents of capitalism expanded on related ideas, pointing out that trade accustoms people to consider what other people want, as opposed to what one can force others to do; in the 18th-century parlance, commerce "softens manners" (Hirschman, 1977: 56–63). In spite of Marx's mid-19th-century ridicule of "gentle commerce," historians have linked capitalism to the origins of modern philanthropy in the 18th century, as traders vastly widened their commercial circles and grew interested in and sympathetic to people very different from themselves (Haskell, 1985: 555–563).[3] Hence we might expect wealthier societies to engage in more charitable giving or alternatively, to give greater political support for redistributive taxation for social welfare or public goods, though the picture is certainly mixed (Eaves, 2008; Frohlich et al., 2016).

How then are we to understand property's relation to human rights in this context? Adam Smith's lectures on jurisprudence ([1766] 1978: 7–9) divided rights into perfect and imperfect rights, with the perfect rights being those that one is entitled to compel by natural and civil justice (including property), and imperfect rights being those that one claims through appeals to a common humanity. There is no reason to think that Smith thought that imperfect rights were a null set; despite his sometimes acid comments on the morals of the rich (Smith, [1759] 1976: 183–185), it is more likely that he thought that imperfect rights might be better fulfilled where secure property and contract resulted in the creation of wealth that could be directed to the well-being of those in need.

With regard to some of the specific claims of the newer human rights thinking, as in a right to a healthful environment, some economic theories sound a faint echo of the old Aristotelian observation that property lubricates liberality. The idea of a "Kuznets curve" argues that environmental quality suffers in the early stages of economic development, but then recovers and prospers as a nation grows wealthier and as its residents turn their attention to issues of quality of life. The underlying idea is that environmental quality is something of a luxury good—only feasible when wealth grows to a certain level. There is certainly room for skepticism about the Kuznets curve and its applicability to the environment, but one does see some support in the recent turn of China to long-neglected environmental issues (Kysar, 2003: 249–251; Percival, 2011).

Thus with respect to human right claims for social and economic rights, property appears in an ambiguous position. Property claims can certainly be set up as an unwelcome obstruction to what are called positive rights—or what Adam Smith would have called imperfect rights—which call for a transfer of resources from wealthier persons to poorer persons, or from private goods to public goods like environmental quality. But at the same time, secure rights to individual property help to generate the social wealth that makes those transfers possible both economically and politically.

At the same time, property should not be understood as an untouchable and unchangeable right, and indeed the contents of property have always been in some flux depending on resource pressure and the need to reduce common pool losses, as economists have noted (Libecap, 1989: 12–16). The balance between private and public goods thus differs with a whole range of varying conditions. Even more sharply, the balance between security for existing property rights on the one hand, and transfer programs on the other, may implicitly or explicitly entail a choice between wealth and equality. Political decision makers may strike these balances differently under different circumstances, and they require more flexibility about property than a static and rigid human rights designation for property would entail.

Nevertheless, considerable security for individual property is important and even essential to move towards the human rights goal of resource access, even if this means that social and economic claims to human rights are softened to the Smithean sense of imperfect rights. Even the modest goal of sufficiency demands this.

4. Property and Human Rights Claims of Traditional Communities; or, What Looks Good About Property May Have Some Problems

In 2001, the Inter-American Court of Human Rights (IACtHR) decided the landmark human rights case of *Awas Tingni v. Nicaragua*. The case pitted an indigenous community against the government of Nicaragua after the latter had granted a logging concession on lands occupied by the community, without the community's consent. Although the Awas Tingnis' lands had never been formally titled, the Court's decision required Nicaragua to recognize their communal land rights and their traditional modes of tenure (Anaya and Grossman, 2002: 11–12; Alvarez, 2018: 27–31). Following that case and three similar IACtHR cases over the next few years, the UN General Assembly adopted a resolution in 2007 entitled the Universal Declaration of the Rights of Indigenous Peoples. The Declaration, while not legally binding in itself, signaled the growing human rights interest in the claims of indigenous populations—including indigenous land claims, reflecting these groups' spiritual and cultural connections to their lands (UNDRIP Articles 25–26). In subsequent years, other indigenous groups have successfully deployed human rights arguments to vindicate communal property rights to customarily occupied lands.

The Awas Tingni victory and its successors would appear to give a clear and welcome signal that property is a human right insofar as it protects the integrity of indigenous groups, whose dispossession and oppression has been a matter of concern at least to some since the beginning of colonization (Marks, 1998: 164–172). Whatever the complaints of disappointed modern concessionaires, here too the problem has not been too much property but too little, in that traditional and customary communal claims have gone unrecognized or unappreciated in modern states. There are many reasons for this. One is a history of colonialism, supported by the self-serving doctrines that have treated indigenous territory as "empty"; or theories that have treated indigenous land use practices as wasteful and unproductive; or more sympathetic if paternalistic claims that if indigenous groups had full property rights, they would sell out too cheaply and without understanding the consequences (e.g., Banner, 2007: 20–28, 62–63, 73–78). Then too there are issues arising from the entrenchment from past encroachments—the established settlements that have already created expectations of permanence, the international trade and development agreements that are disrupted by recognizing indigenous claims.

Hence recognition of indigenous and traditional communities' land claims has been late in coming. But one could also explain this tardiness with modern economic theories about the evolution of property as an institution. These evolutionary theories begin with the observation that property regimes always entail costs for demarcation and defense, and that they do not emerge until the costs of such regimes are outweighed by their benefits, which for economists principally mean such matters as incentivizing effort and reducing conflict and common pool losses (Demsetz, 1967). Indeed, even then, property regimes may not materialize (Libecap, 1989: 19–26). But when they do, in the standard evolutionary stories, property rights move from none at all for plentiful and uncontested resources, through group-based communal property, to modernist property; the last is relatively firmly demarked, owned by identifiable individuals or entities, alienable to other individuals or entities and typically backed by organized governmental enforcement (Schorr, 2018: 508–514).

In this evolutionary picture, group-based or communal property generally precedes modern individual property chronologically, but in practice, communal property finds only limited recognition in formal, modernist property. Modernist formal regimes can adjust to property held by groups, but generally only insofar as the group is a collectivity of identifiable individual claims, as in corporate shares or condominium units. Traditional groups' property arrangements are different: membership in the group may be difficult to define; the members' individual entitlements are only held according to internal communal norms and allocations; and individual holdings may not be alienable to outsiders if they are alienable at all. With those characteristics, traditional group-based property is quite alien to formal regimes (Rose, 2011: 34–35).

Since the costs of defining or even recognizing traditional group property are high for formal regimes, standard economic theory would suggest that traditional communal property would arrive late if at all to the modernist, formal property table. On the other hand, once the costs of the modernist disregard of communal property become more visible—as in displacement of traditional communities, and in conflicts and protests that stymie national development projects and international concessions—then one might expect that governmental institutions would begin to find ways to bestow formal property status on indigenous communal claims.

Thus theories about the evolution of property rights take us some distance in understanding the earlier lack of recognition of traditional peoples' property claims. But let us also look more closely at other complications arising from the differences between traditionalist and modernist property regimes. We can put to one side such expensive but relatively uncomplicated matters as paying off international concessionaires who find their projects halted by newly recognized indigenous claims—not uncomplicated politically, but uncomplicated in the sense that we know how to do this in modernist property systems. But consider the issue of membership: if an indigenous communal group claims property on a group basis, who is and who is not a member of the group?

The experience of the United States in dealing with indigenous claims is instructive. In the early contacts between indigenous peoples and European settlers, quite a number of the latter joined indigenous communities, possibly leading to the conclusion that membership might be defined by cultural assimilation and adherence to customary practices. But this is a vague and uncertain way to define who may enjoy entitlements, and it is not easy for modernist property to recognize. Indeed, modernist property has long rejected uncertain definitions of indefinite group membership. A case in point is something called the Rule Against Perpetuities (RAP) in property law. The rather complicated RAP appears chiefly in legal issues over wills and estates, because it aims to limit the control that a current property owner can exercise over future heirs. It does this in part by requiring the owner to specify exactly who the heirs will be, and denies inheritance rights to anyone in a group defined so loosely as "the members of the PTA" or even "my grandchildren." In the case of American indigenous communities, the government of the United States has fallen back on other measures to specify membership, notably blood quotients—that is, racial definitions that are rejected in other contexts in U.S. law, that were not a part of historic Native American practice and that are rejected by some as a repellant colonial holdover (Jarvis, 2017; Lyte, 2016).

An instance of the membership issue emerged in the late 1960s and early 1970s when oil was discovered on Alaska's North Slope. Officials in the United States realized that because native Alaskan land claims had never been formally settled, those claims might impede the construction of a pipeline to carry oil across the state. In the Alaska Native Claims Settlement Act of 1971 (ANCSA), Congress created a complex system of native Alaskan corporations to control land and resources; membership in these corporations was allocated to persons of native Alaskan heritage who were alive in the year that the law passed—that is to say, to specifically identifiable persons rather than those later accepted through indefinite communal norms (Blair, 2016).

ANCSA's insistence on individually defined entitlements has been controversial among native Alaskans, and more generally, the modernist limitation of rights to specific individuals seems somewhat obsessive. But there are reasons: one is that modernist property deals with claims that may become extremely valuable, by comparison to the generally modest value of traditionalist communal entitlements like fishing or grazing rights. Specific membership criteria thus become important in order to fend off opportunistic claimants, a point that Native American groups themselves have recognized, as for example when some tribal groups began to invest in casino gambling (Jarvis, 2017).

Moreover, while group ownership may serve well one purpose of property institutions—the protection of dignity—it is less likely to serve others. Group-held property dilutes a major function of property regimes, that is, incentivizing individual efforts to manage resources so as to enhance their value, given that the group shares at least part of any payoffs. Similarly, traditional group-held or group-constrained property often presents obstacles to purchase by outsiders, with the result that group-held property may limit the insiders' market activities, and thus indirectly lesson their incentives for effort and investment.

But there is also another and more profound reason for the modernist insistence on individual claims, a reason that sounds in democratic values. Potential conflicts between group rights and individual rights have been observed in human rights literature more generally (Twiss, 2004: 41–47), but they have a special salience in connection with property. At the extreme, simply allocating property to a communal group effectively designates *governance* to the community's norms and practices about property holdings, including the community's norms of authority and its practices of resource allocation. Communal leaders may be wise and just and environmentally sensitive in their decisions about the allocation of property rights and duties, but they may also be misogynist or dismissive of claims of community members considered less worthy. Leaders may be selected only by and from among a privileged few. Those leaders may insist on their own power to distribute access to resources, and they may not permit members to alienate their individual claims. In turn, this means that dissatisfied members cannot depart with assets from their prior efforts, which may mean that they cannot depart at all. In short, recognizing property in a communal group may result in substantial departures from the democratic practices of the larger community (Rose, 2011: 33–34; Sunder, 2000: 75–76, 96–98). One finds a trace of this concern in some 19th-century American courts' rejection of custom as a basis for property ownership; as one such court stated, in a democratic nation, property claims cannot be governed by customary practice but must follow constitutional norms in which leaders are elected and accountable (*Delaplane v Crenshaw, 1860*: 475; Rose, 1994: 123–124).

In the intellectual property area, one can find a similar mixture of concerns about traditional groups' property as a human right—some positive developments for traditional group claims, but also some potentially troubling matters. Indigenous people's cultural productions and references have long been fair game for non-native enterprises that have appropriated indigenous symbols and artwork for brands and labels, with neither compensation to native communities nor heed for cultural sensitivities. Crazy Horse adorns malt liquor, joined by Jeep Cherokee and a Zuni symbol on New Mexico's state flag, to name only a few. Similarly, commercial entrepreneurs have sometimes found and refined traditional peoples' medicinal and agricultural practices without consultation or compensation (Brown, 2003: 69–109). It is thus a very welcome development that traditional peoples have been able to exercise some control over these productions and take some gains from their use by others, as for example the Maori assertion of control over the Haka warrior dance—approved for the New Zealand All Black rugby team, but disapproved for Fiat automobiles (Connolly, 2009).

Insofar as traditional groups demand compensation, their claims are not markedly different from any other IP claims. IP regimes, like other property regimes, rest in large part on a theory of incentives. They are supposed to encourage creativity by allocating rights to creators and inventors, and it seems only fair that traditional groups too should be able to assert a right to compensation. On the other hand, some aspects of traditional people's intellectual property claims fit only uneasily into the modernist statutory regimes for copyright, patent and trademark. As with land claims, issues of membership and identity arise. Traditional productions often result from long accretions of practice by many different persons; moreover, they may have diffused over time to many groups. Who are the creators who deserve control and recompense? Even well-meaning commercial enterprises have found themselves buffeted by numerous community claims that they cannot easily sort out. When traditional groups seek not compensation but rather privacy or secrecy, the claims are even less suitable for modernist IP regimes, which generally aim at the dissemination of useful information and the creative arts (Brown, 2003: 11–35, 111–114, 119–125).

Finally, in traditional groups' IP claims, some hints of democratic concerns echo those of land claims. Consider *Bulun Bulun and Milpurrurru v. R & T Textiles* (1998), an important intellectual property case decided in Australia 20 years ago. The case concerned an Aboriginal artist who created one of the "Dreaming" paintings that have come into much demand in recent decades. While non-Aboriginal entrepreneurs initially copied these paintings at will for such items as t-shirts, Australia now quite properly recognizes them as artistic productions deserving copyright protection. Leaders of Bulun Bulun's Aboriginal community, however, claimed along with Bulun Bulun himself that his Dreamings originated in their legends and culture, and that the community along with the artist had a claim to ownership rights in the artist's work. The Australian court acceded to this claim and conceded some rights to the community, including a right to consultation and consent before the Dreaming painting could be sold (Bulun Bulun and Milpurrurru, 1998; Brown, 2003: 43–67). However happy the conclusion for the Aboriginal parties involved in this case, including the artist, similar cases could easily pit the traditional group leadership against one of their own members, not only potentially disincentivizing his artistic production but also potentially controlling his work, restricting the kinds of art he produced and limiting his ability to engage in an independent profession (Sunder, 2000: 90–93).

I want to stress that the emerging grants of property recognition to traditional groups is a substantial advance over the lack of any such recognition. Riding roughshod over these groups' claims has been the rule for centuries. Past practice has led to terrible displacements and disruptions of the lives of people who in all justice should have been asked for consent before their lands or creative works were taken or simply destroyed. The evolutionary story about property is correct insofar as it suggests that modernist property regimes have only recently begun to come to terms with the terrible costs associated with non-recognition of traditional claims. In pointing out the remaining problems, I wish only to note that recognition of group property, while clearly preferable to nothing at all, carries problems of a different sort for property regimes within democratic governments.

The democracy problem, if I may call it that, emerges in particular because the recognition of group-based property rights is a kind of concession of sovereignty, to be exercised by whoever leads the group, and in a manner that is independent of and possibly quite different from the constitutional order of the recognizing state. One must ask, how is this compatible with the underlying idea of human rights? After all, human rights thinking is a major step away from the old Westphalian consensus, according to which sovereign states avoid interfering with the ways that other sovereigns deal with internal matters. On the contrary, the modern effort to assert universal human rights implicitly or explicitly rejects the immunity of sovereign states from exterior judgment, whatever the pronouncements to the contrary (e.g., UNDRIP, 2007: Article 46). Recognition of property rights in traditional groups, while clearly an advance over practices that trampled those groups' livelihoods and cultures, nevertheless looks very like a return to Westphalia on a smaller scale—now at the level of the governance practices of traditional groups *within* modernist states (Shachar, 1998: 287–288).

I would suggest that the set of issues associated with recognition of traditional groups' property—identity of members, institutional purposes and governance practices—generate many of the conflicts that arise between traditional customary property arrangements on the one hand, and modernist, state-secured property regimes on the other. Are there ways around these problems? I am not sure any are entirely satisfactory, but several paths come to mind.

One well-known path is trusteeship, in which the larger government holds title to the traditional community's property but in trust for the community members. This is roughly the relationship of the United States government to Native American tribal reservations, which formally are part of the public lands of the nation but are "reserved" for the use of tribal members. The history of these reservations, however, is not promising for the trusteeship model. Quite aside from its numerous broken promises, the United States has found the trusteeship role uncomfortable, and for a time even tried to shuck it off by breaking up the reservations into individually owned plots (Dawes Severalty Act, 1887). The current regime is something that one might call supervised self-government, but it is at best a dubious model. Tribal populations are among the most poverty-stricken in the nation; among other things, the fact of trusteeship means that tribes and tribal members generally cannot alienate reservation lands to non-tribal members, and in turn this means that they cannot use reservation lands to leverage conventional outside financing for economic development. Moreover, the implicit paternalism of the trusteeship model makes it seem an unlikely model to satisfy the dignitary concerns raised by modern human rights thinking.

A second path is more individualistic, as was described above with corporations. The organization as a whole owns property, but each of the members also own individual shares in the whole, and those shares can be cashed out individually. This approach contrasts sharply with traditional common property practices, but perhaps out of disappointment with the trusteeship model, the United States took this path with ANCSA in 1971, when it established the large Alaska native corporations as owners of natural resources in major parts of the state, and designated then-living Alaska natives as individual shareholders. After a somewhat rough beginning, Alaska's native corporations by now have become economically formidable. One should note, however, that ANCSA's corporate structure has raised serious doubts among Alaska natives, particularly over the very issues that separate ANCSA's corporate form from ordinary practices in traditional communities. Notable points of contention have concerned the initial exclusion from share allocation of native Alaskans born after the Act took effect, and the possible alienability of native shares to non-natives—contemplated by the original statute after a 20-year period, but still not permitted as of 2018 (Blair, 2016: 273–278).

Still a third path is suggested by what legal scholars Michael Heller and Hanoch Dagan have called the "liberal commons." This kind of common property regime retains the collective's ability to regulate the whole, but it diverges from traditional property regimes by incorporating a limited right to *exit*, which in turn indirectly protects individual members' rights vis-à-vis the group (Heller and Dagan, 2001: 567–570, 597–603). One contemporary model approximates something like the co-op form most often seen in some older residential communities. A right to exit, however, is linked to the twin issues of membership and alienability: a member of a community cannot realistically exit unless she has assets that she can alienate and then take the proceeds. As presented by Dagan and Heller, the liberal commons community may regulate but not entirely ban the individual insider's right to exit and the purchaser's or donee's concomitant right to enter.

If we think of the liberal commons as one intermediating model for the relationship between traditional communities and the metropolitan modernist state, we see a hint at the relationship between property and human rights. Property in this model plays a role at two levels: the community's property protects its claims as a group over against outsiders, but within the group, the individual members' property protects each member's ability to decide on his or her relationship to the group. One might see property at these various levels as an essential support to other human rights—rights to the community's cultural identity, but also rights to life, liberty and individual choice within the cultural community.

5. Property and Atrocity—A Brief Discussion

In this chapter so far, I have digressed quite far from the issue that made me interested in writing on the topic of property and human rights in the first place, and which I can only briefly describe here: that is, a particularly *political* aspect to expropriation of private property. To put it bluntly, expropriation can create constituencies for violations of other kinds of rights, along with support for the regimes that engage in those violations.

If we think back to the post-WWII development of human rights, the issues of greatest concern were massive atrocities of displacement and murder, particularly directed at minority populations. But expropriation had a role in these atrocities, sometimes as a precursor, often as a means to create support for the regime and hatred of those forced out. Expropriation was an overt part of the Nazi treatment of Jews, as "Aryanization" took business properties from Jewish owners and transferred those properties to others with better so-called Aryan credentials. The new "owners" certainly had no interest in the return of the former owners, and no real interest in considering their fate. On the contrary, their new endowments turned them into constituents for expulsion and supporters of the expelling regime, whatever the consequences to the former residents.

One sees variations on this theme in other sites of atrocity, as in the war in Bosnia, where Serbs took over Muslim properties, or in Rwanda, where Hutu neighbors moved into the homes and plots of their murdered Tutsi neighbors. Notoriously repressive East German and Cuban governments transferred the property of "class enemies" to others, thereby creating a class of new possessors to support existing governments—for all their repressions—and fueling fear of any regime change that might restore the prior owners while sharply complicating ultimate resolutions (Penalver, 2000: 213–214). As I write, Myanmar's rulers are brutally forcing long-standing Rohinga migrant communities from their lands, and I have every expectation that those lands will soon be occupied by other Burmese, who will then staunchly support Myanmar's rulers in resisting human rights–based calls for Rohinga repatriation.

Daniel Sharfstein has argued that people can come to feel especially entitled to property not in spite but rather *because of* the hurtful and even vicious acts involved in its acquisition. Among his numerous examples are the appropriations of lands that followed the murders and terrorization of both Native Americans and African Americans—actions that the United States government all too often tolerated in fact if not in principle (Sharfstein, 2012: 660–665, 682–683). In an especially chilling illustration of the point, Sharfstein quotes a statement made by a white man who resisted the voting rights activism in Mississippi in the 1960s: "We killed two-month old Indian babies to take this country and now they want to take it away and give it to the Niggers" (Sharfstein, 2012: 637). Few would be so coarse, but the statement is telling in its link of purported property entitlement to the grossest of human rights violations.

Sharfstein's citation chiefly concerned white settlers who took a bloody shortcut to what they saw as economic opportunities, abandoning property's fundamental practice of negotiation and trade, at the terrible expense of indigenous communities—and then rooting their claims in the acts of atrocity themselves. But readers will observe that this citation sounds an echo in the mid-20th-century human rights focus on totalitarian atrocity. Nowadays, one often hears of dictatorial leaders who enrich themselves by transferring their opponents' property to themselves and their cronies, and who then resist any change to the new status quo for fear of their own impoverishment. But what I wish to stress is that these same regimes can benefit from expropriative transfers in a subtler way. Expropriations and transfers can serve to create political constituencies for murderous and repressive regimes—constituencies of persons who at worst enthusiastically promote further rights violations and at best simply avert their eyes (e.g., Arsenault, 2011). Even without the active leadership of elites, governments' simple neglect of involuntary transfers can create constituencies for treating some groups as "other," and denying those groups recognition and dignity within the polity. Thus I would suggest that the politics of constituency-construction should be a major reason for human rights concern about the treatment of property.

This is not to say, however, that property rights can never change, or even to condemn all transfers. As a practical matter, there are many good reasons why property rights may change shape and extent. Indeed, property owners know this even if they do not like it. Owners know about property taxes and about the public's power of eminent domain and police powers; they know that they may lose their properties if they neglect them for a long time and someone else mistakenly moves in; they know that public policies may support some level of redistribution for purposes with which they do not necessarily agree. What is important in protecting property is the protection of reasonable expectations, taking into account that expectations evolve over time. Thus a very important component of property's security is adherence to a rule of law even as property expectations change, or at a minimum adherence to normal or customary practice—and the avoidance of sudden and unusual or violent intrusions. The property transfers that signal and promote human rights violations are often exactly that: sudden and unusual, and often violent.

6. Conclusion

David Hume once observed that the virtue of justice, on which property depends, is not natural to human beings, because it requires a kind of self-restraint not inborne to individuals. But he also observed that this foundation of property *is* natural in the sense that people together are naturally inclined to invent useful and necessary institutions, of which property is clearly one (Hume, 1948 [1739]: 54–55, 61–62). Property's relation to human rights might best be seen in this light—as an institution that is very useful in the protection of other rights, but whose justifications are pragmatic rather than natural.

In principle, in a rights-based ideal world, each piece of property would be rooted in a just origin, followed by a sequence of voluntary transfers up to the present (Nozick, 1974: 150–172). But as Henry Smith has pointed out, it is unrealistic to expect that we can find such a heroic record with respect to most property (Ellickson et al., 2014: 74).[4] It was with good reason that Blackstone had anxieties about the origins of title. Like it or not, much property has an equivocal past, tolerated in the present because people have gotten used to a current arrangement and based significant decisions on it, and because righting one historic injustice may cause a current injustice or unveil another injustice in the more distant past. There is of course a limit to toleration and sometimes good reasons to alter existing property relations; but the past casts a shadow on property that has no equivalent with claims against murder or torture. With respect to those issues, rights-based thinking is much cleaner.

All the same, though it may be murky by comparison to matters normally considered as human rights, property plays very significant roles in supporting those human rights. This chapter has touched on some of these roles: a regime of reasonably secure property can encourage the wealth production that in turn permits expenditures on general economic well-being and environmental quality; recognition of traditional people's property claims can help to prevent the encroachments that impoverish them economically as well as culturally; recognition of property rights can protect these groups as well as other despised minorities from expropriation—and also from the emergence of constituencies that tolerate or applaud other rights violations.

In these areas and others as well, property presents contradictions and ambiguities if considered a human right in itself. Nevertheless, there may be pragmatic reasons for naming property as a human right in order to advance other elements of a wider human rights agenda. But if I may revert to the early pages of this chapter, it is important to recall that property is not merely the dominion of owner A over resource X; even more importantly, property entails the recognition of A's rights by *non*-owners B, C, D, . . . Property thus is an institution through which we learn that other people have rights, and we learn to respect them. In that educative capacity as in others, property is not the enemy of human rights. Property is a friend, indeed an essential friend.

Notes

1 The French Declaration of Rights of Man and of the Citizen (1789) included property; the American Declaration of Independence did not, but contemporary state declarations of rights did, and property was essential in American political thinking in the founding period (Sprankling, 2014: 468–469).

2 "Westphalian" is named for the 1648 Treaty of Westphalia, which concluded a century of religious wars in Europe and permitted each ruler to determine the religion of his principality. The principle then generalized to one of non-intervention in internal affairs.

3 Insofar as modern Marxist commentators criticize today's human rights discussions as an artifact of late 20th-century global capitalism (Moyn, 2014b: 149–150, 155–160), they curiously recall the parallel growth of commerce and philanthropy two centuries earlier.

4 Smith wrote the note that makes this observation.

Statutes and Cases

Dawes Severalty Act (1887) 24 United States Statutes at Large 24: 388; 25 U.S.C. ch 9 par 331 et seq.

United Nations General Assembly (1948) Universal Declaration of Human Rights (UDHR).

United Nations General Assembly (2007) Declaration of the Rights of Indigenous Peoples (UNDRIP).

Delaplane v. Crenshaw, 56 Va. 457 (1860).

Mayagna (Sumo) Awas Tingni Community v. Nicaragua, Inter-Am. Ct. Hum. Rts. (Ser. C) Case No. 79, para. 103(k) (Judgment of Aug. 31, 2001).

Bulun Bulun & Milpurrurru v. R & T Textiles Ltd., 41 I.P.R. 513, 86 F.C.R.244 (1998).

References

Alvarez JE (2018) The Human Right of Property. New York University Public Law and Legal Theory Research Paper Series, Working Paper, 18–21.

Anaya J and Grossman C (2002) The Case of Awas Tingni v. Nicaragua. *Arizona Journal of International and Comparative Law* 19(1): 1–15.

Aristotle (1962) *Nicomachean Ethics*, M Ostwald (trans). Indianapolis and New York: Bobbs-Merrill.

Arsenault C (2011) Socialism to Opportunism? *Al Jazeera*, 8 November.

Atuahene B (2016) Dignity Takings and Dignity Restoration: Creating a New Theoretical Framework for Understanding Involuntary Property Loss and the Remedies Required. *Law and Social Inquiry* 41(4): 796–823.

Banner S (2007) *Possessing the Pacific: Land, Settlers, and Indigenous People from Australia to Alaska*. Cambridge: Harvard University Press.

Bentham J [1840] (1891) Principles of the Civil Code. In: *Theory of Legislation*, 7th ed. R Hildreth (trans). London: Kegan Paul, Trench, Trübner, pp. 88–236.

Blackstone W (1765–1769) *Commentaries on the Laws of England* (4 vols.). Oxford: Clarendon Press.

Blair M (2016) Issuing New Stock in Alaska Corporations. *Alaska Law Review* 33: 273–286.

Brown MF (2003) *Who Owns Native Culture?* Cambridge, MA, and London: Harvard University Press.

Claeys ER (2006) Natural Property Rights and Privatization. *St. Louis University Law Journal* 50(3): 721–734.

Connolly E (2009) Maori Win Battle to Control All Blacks' Haka Ritual. *The Guardian*, 11 February.

Craig-Taylor P (1998) To Be Free: Liberty, Citizenship, Property, and Race. *Harvard Blackletter Law Journal* 14: 45–90.

Demsetz H (1967) Toward a Theory of Property Rights. *American Economic Review (Papers and Proceedings)* 57(2): 347–359.

Eaves E (2008) Who Gives the Most? *Forbes*, 26 December.

Ellickson R, Rose CM and Smith HE (2014) *Perspectives on Property Law*, 4th ed. New York: Wolters Kluwer Law & Business.

Friedman M (1962) *Capitalism and Freedom*. Chicago: University of Chicago Press.

Frohlich TC, Sauter MB and Comen E (2016) Countries with the Most Generous Welfare Programs, *24/7 Wall St*, 30 November.

Haskell TL (1985) Capitalism and the Origins of the Humanitarian Sensibility, Part 2. *American Historical Review* 90(3): 547–566.

Helfer LR (2007) Toward a Human Rights Framework for Intellectual Property. *University of California at Davis Law Review* 40(3): 971–1020.

Heller MA and Dagan H (2001) The Liberal Commons. *Yale Law Journal* 110(4): 549–623.

Hirschman AO (1977) *The Passions and the Interests: Political Arguments for Capitalism Before Its Triumph*. Princeton: Princeton University Press.

Hume D 1948 [1739] A Treatise of Human Nature. In: Henry DA (ed.) *Hume's Moral and Political Philosophy*. New York: Hafner, pp. 1–169.

Jarvis B (2017) Who Decides Who Counts as Native American? *New York Times*, 18 January.

Kaushal A (2009) Revisiting History: How the Past Matters for the Present Backlash Against the Foreign Investment Regime. *Harvard International Law Journal* 50(2): 491–534.

Kennedy D (2002) The International Human Rights Movement: Part of the Problem. *Harvard Human Rights Journal* 15: 101–126.

Kysar DA (2003) Some Realism About Skepticism: The Implications of Bjorn Lomborg's *Skeptical Environmentalist* for Environmental Law and Policy. *Ecology Law Quarterly* 30(2): 223–278.

Larson RB (2017) Law in the Time of Cholera. *Notre Dame Law Review* 92(3): 1271–1322.

Libecap GL (1989) *Contracting for Property Rights*. New York: Cambridge University Press.

Lyte B (2016) Native Soil. *The Atlantic*, 25 September.

Marks G (1998) Law, Theology, and Justice in the Spanish Colonies. *Australian Journal of Legal History* 4(1): 163–174.

Michelman FI (1977–1978) Political Markets and Community Self-Determination. *Indiana Law Journal* 53(2): 145–206.

Moyn S (2010) *The Last Utopia: Human Rights in History*. Cambridge: Harvard University Press.

Moyn S (2014a) The Future of Human Rights. *SUR-International Journal on Human Rights* 20: 57–66.

Moyn S (2014b) A Powerless Companion: Human Rights in the Age of Neoliberalism. *Law and Contemporary Problems* 71(4): 147–170.

Moyn S (2018) *Not Enough: Human Rights in an Unequal World*. Cambridge: Harvard University Press.

Nozick R (1974) *Anarchy, State, and Utopia*. New York: Basic Books.

Pashkoff L (1989) Human Rights Versus Property Rights: The South African Conflict. *ILSA Journal of International Law* 13: 85–110.

Penalver EM (2000) Redistributing Property: Natural Law, International Norms, and the Property Reforms of the Cuban Revolution. *Florida Law Review* 52(1): 107–216.

Percival RC (2011) China's "green leap forward" Toward Global Environmental Leadership. *Vermont Journal of Environmental Law* 12(3): 633–658.

Posner RA (2014) *Economic Analysis of Law*, 9th ed. New York: Wolters Kluwer Law & Business.

Radin MJ (1982) Property and Personhood. *Stanford Law Review* 34(5): 957–1016.

Regan MC and Hall K (2016) Lawyers in the Shadow of the Regulatory State: Transnational Governances on Businesses and Human Rights. *Fordham Law Review* 84(5): 2001–2037.

Rose CM (1994) *Property and Persuasion*. Boulder: Westview Press.

Rose CM (1997) Property Rights and Responsibilities. In: Chertow MR and Esty DC (eds) *Thinking Ecologically*. New Haven, CT: Yale University Press.

Rose CM (1998) Canons of Property Talk, or, Blackstone's Anxiety. *Yale Law Journal* 108(3): 601–632.

Rose CM (2011) Ostrom and the Lawyers: The Impact of *Governing the Commons* on the American Legal Academy. *International Journal of the Commons* 5(1): 28–49.

Rose CM (2013) Psychologies of Property (and Why Property Is Not A Hawk/Dove Game). In: Penner J and Smith HE (eds) *Philosophical Foundations of Property Law*. Oxford: Oxford University Press.

Schorr D (2018) Savagery, Civilization and Property: Theories of Societal Evolution and Commons Theory. *Theoretical Inquiries in Law* 19(2): 507–531.

Shachar A (1998) Group Identity and Women's Rights in Family Law: The Perils of Multicultural Accommodation. *Journal of Political Philosophy* 6(3): 285–305.

Sharfstein D (2012) Atrocity, Entitlement and Personhood in Property. *Virginia Law Review* 98(3): 635–690.

Shelton DL (2008) Soft Law. *George Washington University Law School Public Law and Legal Theory Working Paper* No. 322, Washington, DC.

Smith A (1978) [1766] *Lectures on Jurisprudence*, Meek RL, Raphael DD and Stein PG (eds) Oxford: Oxford University Press.

Smith A (1976) [1759] *The Theory of Moral Sentiments*, Raphael DD and MacFie AL (eds) Oxford: Clarendon Press.

Sprankling JG (2014) The Global Right to Property. *Columbia Journal of Transnational Law* 52(2): 464–505.

Sunder M (2000) Intellectual Property and Identity Politics: Playing with Fire. *Journal of Gender, Race and Justice* 4(1): 69–98.

Twiss SB (2004) History, Human Rights, and Globalization. *Journal of Religious Studies* 32(1): 39–70.

Wenar L (2005) The Nature of Human Rights. In: Føllesdal A and Pogge T (eds) *Real World Justice: Grounds, Principles, Human Rights, and Social Institutions*. Dordrecht: Springer, pp. 285–294.

Part II

Economic Liberties, Growth and Human Rights

5 Global Justice and Economic Growth

Ignoring the Only Thing That Works

Dan Moller

1. Introduction

This chapter argues that philosophers have widely ignored the only thing that has worked to bring large numbers of people out of poverty—economic growth—and that this is an important mistake. Most philosophers instead focus on altruism and foreign aid, even though these don't seem ever to have worked at scale. Britain, Botswana, Japan, China and Brazil escaped absolute poverty overwhelmingly through internal economic growth, not through external assistance (which isn't to say aid can't do some good).

I begin by explaining the nature and importance of economic growth, and the way in which economic history should affect our thinking about international poverty. I go on to consider prominent work on global justice, and point out that such work rarely mentions economic growth, or engages any of the literature on the subject. However, I also acknowledge that things are not so straightforward: economic growth may seem to lack practical valence in light of how hard it has proven to reliably *induce* growth. Perhaps we are like neighbors rescuing people from a burning building: what we need is a firetruck, but if we don't have one, rescuing some people one at a time is better than nothing.

I conclude with some lessons that growth and the invisible hand have to teach us about global justice all the same. In particular, focusing on growth can help us avoid offering counterproductive solutions to problems of dire poverty, and misguided criticisms of other people's solutions. More importantly, a focus on growth suggests changes in how we respond, both institutionally and individually. Although unlocking growth is difficult, almost everyone agrees that growth-oriented policies in poor countries will include promoting property rights and encouraging an entrepreneurial class, e.g., by making it easier to start and run a business. To the extent that advocates of global justice insist that severe poverty is a human rights violation, it is puzzling why they wouldn't see these kinds of economic rights, liberties and norms as subsidiary rights. And yet this connection it is still too rarely made by philosophers.

To put it another way, a time-traveling altruist would recognize that 18th-century Britain had many malnourished children worthy of assistance. But there would be a serious case to be made that he should instead devote his efforts to promoting commerce and economic growth. Buying railroad stock and so capitalizing firms participating in industrialization would be an eminently worthy (if unsentimental) approach to take. The same lesson applies today, as I argue. Altruism disconnected from the ultimate aim of growth is senseless.

2. Economic Growth

A large body of historical and economic research suggests that most of humanity has lived under conditions that readers would consider abysmal for most of our species' history. There have been exceptions, periods of relative affluence, especially for a fortunate aristocracy or royalty that managed to capture a surplus off the backs of a peasant-class or slaves (Roman aristocrats, say, or urban elites in Tang-era China), or the occasional hunter-gatherer group blessed by an absence of warfare, famine or disease. But the average human has lived a life that most of us would regard as deeply unfortunate until very recently, as recorded in life-expectancies, caloric intake, average height and disease burden.[1] We are all beneficiaries of what the economist Angus Deaton calls "the Great Escape," which he documents in rich detail (Deaton, 2013: chs. 2–4). This escape is overwhelmingly associated with economic growth. The phrase "economic growth" may connote industrial activity, exploited workers and wealthy capitalists, but the evidence suggests otherwise. As Gregory Clark sums up, "the biggest beneficiary of the Industrial Revolution has so far been the unskilled. There have been benefits aplenty for the typically wealthy owners of land or capital, and for the educated. But industrialized economies saved their best gifts for the poorest" (Clark, 2007: 2–3). For those societies lucky enough to have escaped abject poverty—workers and owners alike—the vehicle has largely been growth of the sort we now associate with macro-level facts and figures like GDP, employment rates and consumption levels. To be sure, it is possible to envision forms of growth that are more or less favorable to the worse off, and it is reasonable to favor the former over the latter. But historically, it is hard to think of examples of societies experiencing sustained high growth that didn't also raise up the worst off. Raising GDP *per capita* without raising the fortunes of the many is difficult over the long term, especially at the earlier stages of growth, if only because those benefiting will increasingly require higher degrees of social cooperation, infrastructure and investment opportunities for self-interested reasons.

There is, to be sure, room for some debate and qualification here (see e.g., Deaton, 2013: 87–100). I am focusing on poverty, but there is a complicated relationship between affluence and other aspects of development, for instance health and science and technology. It is possible to argue that these have advanced for reasons independent of material prosperity, and in ways that could be replicated in poor societies simply by drawing on the relevant knowledge. Examples of such advancements might include the germ theory of disease and public health, basic physics and the invention of the steam engine. Disentangling these elements is of course difficult, and this is not the place to do so. But as a matter of simple association, it is striking how rarely materially poor societies manage to take advantage of pure knowledge; there seem to be many subtle connections between material prosperity and what at first glance seems like independent advancements.

Consider, for instance, the level of prosperity required for universal education, rapid transmission of goods and information, and an incentive framework to seek out and promote these advancements. Without these, it seems doubtful that pure knowledge will translate into improved welfare. (If Aristotle had done a little less metaphysics, he could perhaps have invented the germ theory of disease through a series of experiments, but it would have remained difficult to construct water purification systems or to fund extensive testing regimes.) Nevertheless, let me simply concede that it is in principle possible to advance along some dimensions of welfare independent of material prosperity, and that we should leave room for at least some contribution to the Great Escape that is genuinely independent of economic growth. The point remains that the proximate reason most people in developed countries aren't poor by absolute standards (and enjoy at least some big chunk of their good health) is that we live in societies that have experienced economic growth. We can call this the *Growth Thesis*.

This thesis may seem true by definition. What is prosperity if not the end-result of growth? But this certainly isn't a conceptual truth. We can imagine societies that have sustained prosperity for 1,000 years without seeing much growth, even if that is unlikely in practice. At the end of the 1,000 years, it is not economic growth that explains this steady-state prosperity in any interesting sense. Things are rather different with us, whose grandparents were dramatically poorer. (I grew up polishing my grandfather's trophy for door-to-door salesman of the month—an occupation he used to provide for a family of five, and not unusually so.) Or again, certain remote communities—military compounds, oil towns—are rendered prosperous entirely from the outside, by an external supply. We naturally associate prosperity with growth, but the association is contingent.

What *is* growth? In a narrow sense, it is simply an increase in the goods and services available in a society per capita. (We usually think of this as resulting from an increase in production, but it's also worth noting increases due to efficiencies in consumption, as when there is more energy available to us because of longer-lasting lightbulbs; it's possible to get richer by making *less* stuff.) More substantively, growth reflects an increase in productive activity that people value. Sheer activity isn't the point, of course—frantically digging holes and filling them in again does not constitute a form of prosperity (even if encouraging this could be a last-best solution to an economic crisis). Growth means that people are generating more and more value through what they do and create. For this reason, growth, it seems to me, is always intrinsically good, which doesn't mean it can't have negative side-effects. Even after growth has saved us from absolute poverty, growth means we are creating something of value—new ideas and technologies that let us do more, learn more and grow more in the personal sense. It is growth that allows for the Large Hadron Collider, international travel, *Blade Runner*, and cancer treatment.

In this more substantive sense, economic growth is distinct from getting rich in the accounting sense, and this may tempt us to think that there are ways to get rich or at least escape poverty outside of economic growth. Natural resources come to mind. It is a conventional wisdom that supposed petro-states or diamond-states like Botswana have obtained middle-income status largely through extraction. These cases, however, are complicated. According to the World Bank, natural resources account for only around 20 percent of the wealth of developing countries (World Bank, 2011: xi). Using slightly different criteria, "natural" capital forms an insignificant part of the wealth of rich countries (about 2%) but isn't a massive contributor for middle- or low-income countries either (about 15% to 30%), and of course the tendency is to transition from stocks of natural capital to intangible assets, like an educated workforce (World Bank, 2011: 7). Individual country studies confirm this. In Botswana, for instance, famous for its diamond resources, the World Bank estimates that minerals make up less than 16 percent of economic output (World Bank, 2015a: 17). Of course, 15–30 percent is enough to offer a boost in the early phases of development, and the public-finance impact of these resources can be greater than the 15–30 percent might suggest, since natural resources may be the only source of exports and of hard currency, or they may substantially fund the budget. For example, in Nigeria, oil and gas make up less than 15 percent of GDP, contrary to stereotype, but they constitute 90 percent of Nigeria's exports and contribute 70 percent of the government's budget revenue (World Bank, 2015b: 2). But these facts must in turn be treated carefully, since, e.g., using natural resources to fund the national budget is often the result of bad policy, not necessity, as when people living in petro-states become addicted to huge fuel subsidies.

Overall, the evidence suggests that economic growth, not just in the statistical sense, but in the sense of becoming more innovative and productive, is key to escaping poverty, especially when the population is simply too large for natural resources to make a big dent, as in India or

Nigeria, as opposed to Trinidad and Tobago or Botswana; but even in smaller countries, as we have just seen, natural resources are unlikely to be enough. These have their place early in economic development, but no country is likely to escape dire poverty without substantive and exponential economic growth.

This should not seem surprising, in light of how currently rich or middle-income countries got that way. Consider Western Europe, the United States, Japan, China, Mexico, Turkey and Brazil. They all escaped poverty through economic growth. To a good approximation, economic growth is the only way anyone has ever escaped poverty. We can't consider this an iron law since it isn't a conceptual truth; perhaps some small island nation has gotten or could get by on natural resources and tourism alone, but again, to a good approximation, economic growth is the only thing that has worked. We can call this the *Only Growth Thesis*. Since it is obvious that sustained economic growth is *sufficient* for prosperity (you can't grow at 7% a year forever and remain in absolute poverty), we have arrived at a biconditional: at least to a good approximation, economic growth is both necessary and sufficient to escape poverty.

3. Philosophers and Growth

Given the crucial role of economic growth in escaping poverty, it comes as a surprise that most philosophers seem uninterested in the subject.[2] There is a vast literature on global justice, international poverty, the responsibilities of the rich countries and so on, and yet hardly any of this literature discusses the only thing that works.

Peter Singer's book-length discussion of effective altruism, for instance, never mentions economic growth, apart from a few sentences on "capitalism," despite being very much focused on global poverty (Singer, 2015: 50). Instead, the emphasis is overwhelmingly on individual donations. Of course, it's not fair to criticize someone for writing the book they wrote instead of some completely different book, but it's not as if Singer registers the facts described above and then suggests we should offer aid as well. The entire topic is simply passed over. Other prominent work in this area follows suit: there are stern rebukes of rich countries for not rendering enough aid to end global poverty, condemnations of colonialism and more recent foreign-policy debacles, critiques of institutions like the IMF and the World Bank (e.g., conditional loan policies and the Washington Consensus) and sometimes there are even positive proposals, such as Thomas Pogge's Global Resource Dividend, which would tax the use or consumption of natural resources such as oil in order to help alleviate global poverty. But there is little or no discussion of economic growth, or anything like the Only Growth Thesis, or the ramifications for global poverty and justice. It's hard to demonstrate this negative if anyone should question it, but the 700-page anthology *Global Justice*, which collects major works in the field, clearly illustrates this neglect, which is substantial, if not absolute, as we will see further on.[3]

This may still all seem unfair. Perhaps it's just too obvious to be worth stating that economic growth is the antidote to poverty, and what are discussions of Global Resource Dividends, criticisms of trade policy and histories of iniquitous American meddling overseas if not discussions of impediments to and prospects for growth? The mere fact that the phrase "economic growth" rarely occurs doesn't demonstrate the absence of substantive engagement with the relevant issues. But although this last point is certainly correct—the issue isn't one of vocabulary—there really is a difference between fully recognizing that it is the productive, innovative, commercial activities within the countries themselves that are key to any serious hope of escaping poverty, on the one hand, and criticizing or proposing particular policies on moral grounds on the other. For example, once we are focused on growth, it makes much less sense to bicker over particular policies—trade agreements, agro-tariffs, debt forgiveness and the like. These policies may or may not be individually defensible, but it isn't plausible that wide swathes of rural India are poor because of these kinds of details. Few economists think that the growth rate of India is exquisitely sensitive to rich country policies, or that there is much to be done systemically for India's rural poor besides growing the economy as rapidly as possible. They are poor because India has not yet grown rich. Nor is it likely that we will focus on a Global Resource Dividend based on natural resources if we have growth in mind, both because wealth resulting from growth is overwhelmingly a product of services, not natural resources (Moller, 2017), and because the main problems for poor countries are impediments to growth, not a lack of access to capital. Both of these points matter. To the extent that we're struck by the vast disparities between rich and poor countries, we're confused if we seek to trace these back to differences in natural resources that should accordingly be taxed. Neither Japan, Israel, Germany or the U.S. is rich because of gold or oil deposits—their wealth resides in productivity that manifests itself in the service sector (the U.S. economy is 80% services by GDP). If we want to tax the rich, we should simply announce a global progressive tax on utilitarian grounds. And the main problem for desperately poor countries isn't access to the money needed to spur growth; there is plenty of capital available to fund investment in factories or infrastructure. The problem is that these investments don't reliably work in situations of abject poverty. This means that the funds generated by the Dividend would amount to charitable aid—which may be good, but that hardly can count as a form of acknowledging the importance of growth. At the very least, the appropriate way of discussing such topics is to analyze their impact on growth rates and to cite the relevant economic literature, which is not what happens in this body of work.

Perhaps the closest thing to a discussion of economic growth occurs in Henry Shue's *Basic Rights* (excerpted in *Global Justice*, it's worth noting), in the course of addressing economic deprivation. Shue discusses cases that involve complex international interactions, e.g., a peasant who takes up a contract to grow flowers for export instead of a food staple, whose price consequently rises, which causes local malnutrition, thus, it is suggested, violating people's subsistence rights. Shue concludes that this type of malnutrition is a "social disaster," as opposed to a natural disaster, and thinks that this kind of story is "typical" of what is (or was in 1980) happening around the world to people who were "threatened by forms of 'economic development' that lower their own standard of living" (Shue, 1980: 40–46). He goes on to cite a then-current analysis of Latin America, which identifies an "illiberal state capitalism" that is said to pursue a strategy of industrialization, export-led growth and the accumulation of hard currency to repay foreign debtors, all at the local population's expense. But although this discussion does touch on economic growth, at least tangentially, the point of the argument is actually to direct our attention *away* from the fact of growth and towards what Shue sees as instances of unjust growth or growth-associated policies. (It's not as if Shue elsewhere champions high-growth policies done in the right way; the impression left is that technocratic policies encouraging export-led growth, a good credit rating, and so on, are themselves dubious.) And neglecting the prime importance of growth is once again a mistake. Growth is associated with escaping the very subsistence conditions Shue decries, and although one can always challenge any given policy, the real tragedy isn't the kind of case Shue describes, but the absence of sustained growth, which, when it does occur, far outweighs the kinds of worries Shue has. It's crucial to consider not just farmers made worse off through the freedom to contract with exporters, but those, mostly invisible to us, who *aren't* going hungry *because* of such contracts—what matters is the net, which is what is captured in numbers like per capita GDP. For example, Shue mentions Brazil as an instance of the kind of development-pathologies highlighted by the flower-contract story. But while Brazil does face many challenges around crime, inequality, corruption and much else besides, it is crucial to observe that per capita GDP has risen by a factor of *four* since 1980, in real terms. Life expectancy has risen by *12 years* in the same period. Malnutrition rates have plummeted. Nor is this surprising—the same trends were obvious in 1980 when Shue was writing. (Growth was especially rapid during some periods of post-1985 civilian rule, but per capita GDP also grew by a factor of eight under the military dictatorship.) We shouldn't be cavalier about the many problems still outstanding, but it would be a gross error to neglect growth and the concrete benefits like rising life expectancy associated with it. Surely something is going right, over and above particular pathologies, when the life expectancy, per capita income and health are going through the roof.

Alternatively, some writers who focus on aid rather than growth may simply reject the Only Growth Thesis. For instance, they may not feel bound by existing examples of escaping poverty, and they might assert that the aid they are calling for *would* make the relevant countries at least tolerably well off, if rich countries really did their duty. It's no fair, they might argue, to claim that growth is the only thing that works, if that is only so in virtue of rich countries refusing to do their bit! But could aid lift a country out of poverty without economic growth? Some economists doubt whether aid is even *helpful*. Angus Deaton, for instance, is skeptical: "The correlation between aid (as a share of national income) and growth remains *negative* even when other important causes of growth have been taken into account" (Deaton, 2013: 288). He worries that we face a kind of dilemma: "when the 'conditions for development' are present, aid is not required. When local conditions are hostile to development, aid is not useful, and it will do harm if it perpetuates those conditions" (Deaton, 2013: 273). If it turns out that the main driver of growth is the presence, say, of good institutions, and that large flows of aid do more harm than good in the presence of bad institutions, it certainly won't seem persuasive that we could help countries escape poverty without economic growth, just by aid. William Easterly (2006, esp. 37 ff.), a former World Bank economist, likewise argues that the effect of aid on development can often be negative, as does Dambisa Moyo, the Oxford-trained economist, who refers to "the vicious cycle of aid" that "chokes off desperately needed investment, instills a culture of dependency, and facilitates rampant and systematic corruption, with deleterious consequences for growth" (Moyo, 2009: 49). Of course, others disagree—more on them below—arguing that the problem lies with how aid is directed, that "aid" often consists of thinly disguised attempts to pursue national interest rather than genuinely help recipients, or that we just need one more big push (see, e.g., Sachs, 2014 and his Millennium Villages Project). Still, it is worth registering the remarkable fact that the data is messy enough that experts are divided over whether large aid flows do more good than harm, *let alone* whether aid might lift a country out of poverty absent economic growth. And even the optimists don't think aid will be enough independent of internal growth.

A plausible conjecture, in my view, is that aid can do a great deal of local (as opposed to systemic) good: outside groups can facilitate eradicating specific diseases, assist with infrastructure projects like building a dam, or solve short-term financial problems, but are more or less incapable of doing much systematic good. From this perspective, you cannot grow an economy for someone from the outside, or do much to improve systemic institutional problems by fiat. (Of course, this isn't a reason not to invest in fighting malaria or AIDS for reasons that have nothing to do with growth or international poverty.)

4. Engineering Growth

What explains philosophers' lack of interest in economic growth? I suspect there are boring sociological explanations—disciplinary parochialism, the scholar's traditional aversion to the merchant-class. More importantly, philosophers have long focused on distribution and redistribution in their discussions of poverty, which tends to blind us to the significance of creating wealth in the first place. This point bears some emphasis. It tends to be assumed that the reason others are in poverty is distributive—we (or someone else) haven't given them enough. Sometimes this *is* the right explanation, as when parents with an obligation to provide for their young children simply refuse. But the deep reason that Bangladesh or large swathes of China remain quite poor isn't that Germany or Japan hasn't sent them money—could anything be more condescending?—it's that the people themselves haven't managed to generate significant wealth of their own as yet. An imperfect comparison: your child graduates and enters the labor force, and starts off in a cramped apartment living hand to mouth—perhaps you should help out, but it would be bizarre to analyze the overall state of affairs in terms of wealth distribution rather than wealth creation, even if you could gift your child a lavish lifestyle. But set these sociological speculations aside. A sober reason to focus on effective altruism, say, or on foreign aid, is that there may not be much we can *do* about growth.

Even if we grant the Growth and Only Growth theses, it doesn't follow that those concerned about global justice should focus their efforts on growth. If there is no way we can impact growth rates, then we might reluctantly conclude we should go back to emphasizing personal charity. More subtly, growth rates are affected by things like public health and education, and it may be easier for us to affect those than to encourage growth directly. And in fact, some economists have suggested that there are sharp limits to our ability to make growth happen by fiat. Easterly, for instance, has argued at length not just that aid hasn't worked well, but that attempting to promote growth from the outside generally doesn't work, and that the reasons for this aren't (as the global justice literature might suggest to us) malice, indifference or gross negligence. In his aptly titled *The Elusive Quest for Growth*, he catalogues successive theories of economic growth and how the best minds (of academics and institutionalists—not politicians) have thought about promoting growth in poor countries. And he shows how unsuccessful these ideas have been. It is easy to dismiss official country-level aid as misdirected or inadequate, but what is striking in Easterly's catalogue is that *there isn't even a good theory* of how to successfully promote growth, and trying to do so has rarely worked at scale.[4]

In the modern period, when academics began theorizing about the nature of growth the focus was initially on investment. The theory was that growth would be proportional to investment in machinery, which fit the recent experience of the U.S. and Western Europe (the Harrod-Domar model). But perhaps unsurprisingly, investment in physical systems like machines or infrastructure is no panacea, and seems related to growth only under specific conditions that rarely obtain in very poor countries. Institutional literature continues to emphasize the importance of investment, which is no doubt a necessary condition for growth, but has proven far from sufficient. The growth-theorist Robert Solow pointed out that increasing the machinery available per worker runs into diminishing returns, and that calculations of capital income as against wages suggest that investment isn't the limiting factor in the United States, but rather technological change, which produces a general increase in productivity. But this, too, is unhelpful from an international development standpoint: clearly the problem isn't the mere availability of new technology, but complicated facts about its utilization. (North Koreans don't live in the dark because they lack the technology for light.)

In general, mono-causal recipes and panaceas have usually turned out to be misguided. As one specific example, debt forgiveness was a fashionable approach not long ago, praised by rock stars and the Dalai Lama. Intuitively, it seems wrong to press poor countries to repay their debts when they are already desperate. But, as Easterly argues, forgiving countries their debts often does them no good at all or does harm. The absence of debt simply means that leaders can go into debt once more, which they frequently do, and whatever general causes of being in debt in the first place that were operative before continue to operate (Easterly, 2002: 128). There are, of course, many other ideas to pursue, like education and human capital, which might seem like the missing ingredient besides investment and technology, but comparatively massive increases in education levels in many poor countries did not result in growth in the 1960s, 1970s and 1980s. And even if we are suspicious of the numbers on education (classroom time doesn't equal real education), there is little evidence that rich countries are good at increasing human capital from the outside.

Theories of growth tend to be designed to explain growth across time in countries that are already in relatively good shape, like the United States 1900 to 1950, or across advanced countries, where the main issues are simply adopting technology invented elsewhere, and investing to make use of it. By contrast, the challenges in very poor countries are often entirely different, involving sui generis problems with health care, political organization or culture that are not well addressed by technical work drawing on mathematical economics ("How much investment will produce X% growth next year?"), and which are probably better studied under the headings of history, politics or anthropology.

Not everyone agrees with this pessimistic take on foreign aid. There is an optimistic school of "aid empirics" that holds that recent advances allow us to claim that aid *does* contribute to economic growth. A representative overview finds that, "The weighted average result from these studies indicates that a sustained inflow of foreign aid equivalent to 10 percent of GDP is expected to raise growth rates per capita by about one percentage point on average" (Arndt et al., 2016: 469). However, these empirics are in turn disputed. A recent meta-analysis reports that:

> The AEL [Aid Effectiveness Literature] is now 43 years old. Our study covers 141 papers with 1,777 estimates of the effect of aid on growth. When corrected for censoring the average is + 0.03 + 0.01. This result has proved remarkably stable over time. Thanks to the large number of estimates the average is statistically significant, but it is economically negligible.
>
> (Doucouliagos and Paldam, 2015: 345)

Suffice it to say, there is no social science consensus as of yet. The important thing to bear in mind is that even those who think aid does something don't think it does all that much relative to the escape from poverty, meaning internal growth really is crucial, and that there's plenty of room for the skepticism that motivates the objection about growth we've been entertaining.

From another, positive point of view, many economists emphasize institutions as crucial to explaining success and failure at the national level. Institutions, especially in the form of political and economic arrangements, structure people's incentives to innovate, save, educate and invest, which in turn shapes growth. But this, too, is cause for pessimism in the current context, since institutions are very difficult to mold from the outside. All kinds of techniques have been tried, like making loans conditional on institutional improvements of various sorts, without much success. Towards the end of their survey of the institutional approach, Daron Acemoglu and James Robinson write that, "foreign aid is not a very effective means of dealing with the failure of nations around the world today. Far from it. Countries need inclusive economic and political institutions to break out of the cycle of poverty." Moreover:

> Attempts by international institutions to engineer economic growth by hectoring poor countries into adopting their policies and institutions are not successful because they do not take place in the context of an explanation of why bad policies and institutions are there in the first place.
>
> (Acemoglu and Robinson, 2012: 454, 447)

However, they don't suggest easy solutions to these problems, even when the requisite understanding *is* in place.

I should mention, in all candor, that I am skeptical of this now-popular institutions approach, which seems to me either to conflate institutions with culture (especially if *informal* institutions count, like attitudes towards taking bribes, or showing up to work on time), or else simply to underestimate the role of culture, which is difficult to measure and often has a politically incorrect flavor, but which seems to me essential all the same. Germany isn't richer than Spain because of formal institutional differences, nor northern Italy than southern Italy, nor Massachusetts than Oklahoma, nor Nigerian Americans than average Americans. Since institutions in very poor countries are typically bad for all kinds of reasons, everyone can agree that it would be good to improve them, and that in cases like Zimbabwe this would make a great difference. But if teachers don't show up to their jobs, or women are excluded from economic activity, or clan structures retard political reform, it's unclear that formal institutions are the place to look for fixes, or that these are more than a symptom. Still, this only buttresses the pessimistic suggestion we have been pursuing, since nebulous formations like culture are even harder to meaningfully influence or export.

5. Why Growth Still Matters

However, in my view, ignoring growth remains a mistake, for three main reasons. First, it is crucial to have a clear understanding of what the goal is in addressing international poverty, and how our actions relate to that goal. Discussions of global justice typically take the form of inveighing against the iniquities of the rich countries in light of extreme poverty, and issuing calls for remediation in the form of more foreign aid (directed towards development, not the cultivation of military allies), or else reparations, or schemes like the Global Resource Dividend. But if we conclude that the real issue is economic growth, there are several ways in which such proposals should be reframed, if not rejected. First, none of these proposals seems likely to succeed at its self-given aims. It is unclear whether foreign aid produces growth, or doesn't in fact produce *harm*, even in countries where there is proportionately a lot of it, even when it is designed to advance the recipients' interests. And in the absence of growth, poverty will remain. It's probably fair to say that there are no or exceedingly few long-term success stories at the national level. (This may surprise us less when we consider natural experiments, like Nigeria or Congo turning out to be resource-rich, which is analogous to getting large aid flows.) There is no undisputed evidence that the main problem for severe international poverty is a lack of access to capital or investment, and plenty to the contrary. Or to put it the other way around, it is hard to think of plausible cases of societies showing promise for growth but failing to do so because of a lack of aid or savings to fund investment, improved human capital and so on. Setting up a fund to send lots of money to countries with severe, systemic institutional problems seems unlikely to be successful in light of the evidence we have reviewed.

More generally, attaining growth is just very difficult. The countries that first discovered sustained growth, like Britain, did not do so through deliberation, but by stumbling into it more or less by accident, and often while doing almost anything they could to suppress growth (e.g., by mercantilism or colonial misadventures). Even a century after clear, sustained growth *had* been shown to be possible, places like China found it impossible to copy for various cultural and institutional reasons. There is no simple recipe. This means that there probably isn't a real substitute for leaving countries to stumble towards growth as best they can, while being supportive whenever possible, and addressing specific, technical obstacles that can be overcome by parachuting in expertise or equipment, e.g., specific medical technologies, like antiretrovirals or disease-eradication campaigns.

Finally, many of the obvious policies that would have to be part of any sensible plan for growth—even if they function only as necessary and not sufficient conditions—are ones we hear very little about in philosophical work. These include economic rights, liberties and norms that would encourage entrepreneurship, business activity and free trade. Growth broadly reflects productivity, and it is impossible to foster productivity without the appropriate incentive structures. No one will start a business if they cannot enforce contracts, own capital or reap a decent share of the profits. The World Bank's Doing Business rankings (2018) attempt to chart this particular dimension of economic liberty, and make it clear that there is a vast difference between what it is like trying to run a business in Bangladesh rather than Romania, say, meaning there is ample but non-obvious room for improvement and public discussion (World Bank, 2018). Philosophers concerned about global justice should urge attention to this type of consideration to the extent that they care about growth and escaping poverty, and draw on economic literature in doing so (see e.g., Rodrik, 2007: 99–152; Easterly, 2006: 341–364). (They should also continue to criticize particular failings in rich countries that pose barriers to international development, such as indefensible subventions, particularly of agriculture, even if these don't in themselves seem to explain persistent poverty.)[5] To the extent that we think that severe poverty constitutes a human rights violation, we should presumably insist on economic liberties and growth-oriented property regimes as correlative rights. So, to sum up this first point, many existing positive proposals are inconsistent with a focus on economic growth and what is (not) known about the subject, and many analyses of the problem and attendant calls for short-order solutions look similarly misguided, or ignore institutions and norms that are prerequisites for growth.

The second point is complementary to the first: many policy *criticisms* emerging from global justice circles are misdirected, because they don't sufficiently attend to growth. I mentioned the case of Brazil earlier, which was lamented as an example of baleful policies hurting the poor even as it was in the midst of a growth miracle. The problem here isn't criticizing a military dictatorship or any particular devaluation policy, say. Dictatorships are bad, and devaluation policies can be wrong. The problem is rather failing to recognize the importance of growth, and recognizing that this is what we should be tracking for purposes of international poverty. From a global justice perspective, it makes no sense to rail against a regime for impoverishing its people, and against rich countries for their complicity in the form of institutional support or financial cooperation, in the midst of a growth spurt. To take the present case of China, there's plenty of room for human rights–based criticism, but not for denouncing the WTO, say, for some nefarious role in keeping the people of China down.

The confusion involved here sometimes seems more systematic. To stick with our Latin American example, one standard history of Nicaragua, focused on the bête noire of American influence, describes the goal as one of turning Nicaragua into a client-state focused on generating wealth for rich elites by producing an economy "overwhelmingly externally oriented, placing great emphasis on the production of products for export" (Walker and Wade, 2011: 85–86), while neglecting domestic consumption entirely. Citizens are viewed as insignificant laborers for production, instead of valued consumers. This has the flavor of Henry Shue's remarks noted earlier. But the main problem for Nicaragua hasn't been an excess of production, alas. *Re*distributing its product more widely wouldn't make much difference since there isn't much to distribute in the first place. Once again, the focus on distribution has blinded us to the importance of creating wealth in the first place. The tragedy isn't that Nicaragua is a successful export-oriented economy, but that it isn't. Countries like Britain, Japan and now China got or are getting rich precisely by becoming productive enough to engage in free trade at scale. China is getting rich by harvesting European and Americans surplus wealth, not by trying to extract the (non-existent) native riches and keeping them.

This misunderstanding is endemic in certain quarters of popular consciousness. Naomi Klein argues that the system of cheap labor in sweatshops produces the mirage of growth, one that disappears as labor is chased to ever-cheaper sources: when "the multinationals first landed in Taiwan, Korea and Japan, many of their factories were owned and operated by local contractors" (Klein, 2009: 224). But following pressure for higher wages, "the swallows once again took flight" (ibid.), only to repeat this performance in places like China and the Philippines. The frontiers are Indonesia, Thailand and eventually Vietnam (ibid.). But what Klein is tracing is the course of development. The "victims" she cites keep getting rich. Klein and others eagerly seize on the Asian financial crisis or other local setbacks. But the trend is unmistakably towards growth, and the problem for a Nicaragua is that it *hasn't* gotten to participate in these export-dominated and often elite-led enterprises that made Britain, the U.S. and now swathes of Asia prosperous.

A somewhat different confusion can be seen in some of the criticisms of Bretton Woods institutions and neoliberalism, notably the 1980s/1990s-era Washington Consensus, which emphasized things like fiscal discipline, tax reform, privatization of state markets, deregulation, securing property rights and trade liberalization. Economists like Joseph Stiglitz (2003) have subjected these policies and their implementation to withering criticism, precisely for being inimical to growth; a UN report declared that, "The emphasis of the Washington Consensus-related policies on static comparative advantage virtually amounted to a prescription for non-development in the sub-Saharan region" (UNCTAD, 2010: 123). Clearly there is room for criticism of the merits of these policies. But philosophers like Richard Miller have drawn the normative conclusion that rich countries' "restraint in imposing prescriptions of submission to market forces has not kept pace with evidence undermining warranted confidence in their efficacy" (Miller, 2010: 151). As a result, he says, the U.S. has both shaped the landscape of poor countries for the worse (through structural adjustment loans and the like), and now has incurred an enormous obligation to fix things in the developing world. The problem with this kind of view is that it neglects the *good faith effort* to promote growth, and how incredibly difficult it has proven to promote growth from the outside, as reviewed earlier. Obviously, there are plenty of specific cases to criticize—instances in which ill-considered foreign-policy objectives impede development. But institutional ideas like the Consensus aren't like that, and criticizing serious attempts to promote growth just because they end up failing or aren't immediately revoked is incompatible with the evidence on jump-starting growth from the outside, and risks disincentivizing further work on the problem.

It's worth going into a little more detail. To be clear, I am not asserting the Washington Consensus (or austerity measures, or various conditional loan policies) really *are* good. In fact, I'm rather impressed by the evidence that lots of rich countries have gotten or are getting rich without observing the neoliberal shibboleths (e.g., Japan and the Asian Tigers), and that countries that have off and on tried haven't always done well (Chile's record has been mixed). This suggests we shouldn't be too doctrinaire beyond the kinds of basic economic rights and liberties fundamental to enterprise and should instead emphasize a pragmatic, experimental approach (see Chang, 2007; Rodrik, 2007: 16–35). We can insist that China wouldn't have grown while it yet discouraged enterprise and ownership, while allowing for disagreement about various austerity programs.

My point is merely that it's a mistake (both backward- and forward-looking) to read into the evidence something nefarious rather than the elusiveness of growth—as the more reasonable critics like Stiglitz tend to concede. The term "Washington Consensus" and the core prescriptions are due to the British think-tank economist John Williamson, who was offering his best suggestion on how to promote growth, not due, say, to lobbyists for American corporations. Williamson's career includes stints at the UK treasury, the IMF, MIT, as chief economist for the World Bank South Asia, and as a UN planning director; his publications include *Reference Rates and the International Monetary System*, *Delivering on Debt Relief*, *The Crawling Band as an Exchange Rate Regime*, *Estimating Equilibrium Exchange Rates*, *Currency Convertibility in Eastern Europe*, and *Targets and Indicators: A Blueprint for the International Coordination of Economic Policy*. Williamson, I submit, isn't very promising as a Machiavellian architect of imperial domination. (In personal communication, Williamson admits he overestimated the degree of consensus in the Consensus, noting, inter alia, that the Japanese contested some of the policies, but he still thinks the evidence supports many of its key features.) Conflating the severe epistemic limitations on the quest for growth, and technocratic failure of the sort Easterly documents, with nefarious intent can only discourage the ongoing search for solutions.

The first two reasons for being clear about growth involve analytical clarity in our positive proposals and our negative criticisms. The third reason is that we should consider growth even in our personal decision-making about what to spend our time and money on. It may seem as if health or malnutrition programs should always get priority, if nothing else because sick and malnourished people aren't in a position to participate in the economy. (Though, in fact, it is unclear whether improving health does much for economic growth [Ashraf et al., 2009].) These are obviously worthy efforts, but it is useful to think more carefully about the wisdom of the invisible hand in this context. When we reflect on growth, we realize that what we really are after, in the end, is mainly self-interested commercial activity; growth in per capita GDP, which is reflected in roads, plumbing, X-ray machines and other nice things that economic activity and a tax base make possible, is mostly the result of people responding to incentive structures and idiosyncratic personal interests. There is no need to declare that *all* of this is selfish or even self-interested; plenty of teachers and doctors are motivated by a complicated mix of wanting to help others and to earn a living. But what is happening when a society moves from deep poverty to middle income is fundamentally economic activity that individuals are being *paid* for (hence the economic value of the goods and services). Britain didn't go from being an impoverished agricultural society to being well off through acts of altruism, but through commercial activity (supported by, and supporting, we can acknowledge, non-commercial or impurely commercial activities like medical and STEM research). Given all of this, there is a case to be made that we can promote international development and global justice simply by promoting commerce. Altruism didn't work for Britain or Japan; those of us eager to see other countries join them in development might consider helping them do what those countries did.

How might we do this, apart from donating to health or nutrition-focused organizations? Ideas like microfinance perhaps gesture in the right direction, but I have more directly commercial proposals in mind. These might range from scholarships for business students in developing countries—not the most intuitive or worthy-seeming recipient-class—to promoting telecom development in sparsely populated areas that are candidates for leapfrogging technology platforms, e.g., by guaranteeing loans to firms interested in exploiting such opportunities. At the level of aid, such proposals could take the form of funding tax breaks for certain types of companies or business ventures. At a more personal level, altruists sometimes urge their students to get rich and then donate to famine relief. But the lessons of growth suggest a better strategy: promote business development overseas, for instance by going to work for a company that does business in a way that promotes local commerce (say, by facilitating transportation or communications). Or go to work for a business in a developing country that you can help make profitable. Or buy products from businesses in developing countries, while avoiding "sustainable" or "fair trade" products that incentivize uncompetitive industries.

We can close by considering the measurement problems that beset attempts to be effective in promoting prosperity. Effective altruism is a bit like "evidence-based medicine"—who would want any other kind? But there are serious problems with the suggestion that we measure the good that we are doing, say, with randomized controlled trials of different kinds of interventions. Consider, once again, Britain before growth, at the dawn of the Industrial Revolution. Even in retrospect, it is hard to compare the good done by feeding orphans, say, rather than sponsoring the construction of railways or steam engines. Should the time-traveling altruist buy bread for orphans, or help capitalize a railway company, or sponsor steam engine R & D? It seems to me unclear that the answer isn't the latter. But of course, this would be extremely difficult to demonstrate, and in the short term it would seem quite irresistible to spend on feeding the life in front of you rather than promoting abstract and distant well-being in the future. Essentially, we face a trade-off between aiding identifiable individuals in the present or taking more abstract, growth-oriented measures that we believe will produce greater good in the future. (As I have noted elsewhere, more generally, all of us face a difficult trade-off between helping fewer people now or more people in the future [Moller, 2006].) But I take it to be obvious that there *is* a serious case to be made for the time traveler to focus on accelerated industrial development, just not one it is easy to capture in terms that can survive a faux-rigorous comparison with more immediate measures. The same point applies, mutatis mutandis, to us and international poverty.

Notes

1 See, e.g., Clark, 2007; Morris, 2010. See Moller, forthcoming: ch. 12 for details and further argument.
2 With important exceptions, of course. See, e.g., Brennan and van der Vossen, 2018, esp. chs. 1 and 10.
3 Pogge and Moellendorf, 2008. On the Dividend, see pp. 466–471. Other anthologies that demonstrate a similar neglect include Barry and Lawford-Smith, 2012; Brock and Moellendorf, 2005 (whose index is a testament to the absence of growth from the discussion).
4 The following paragraph is loosely based on Easterly, 2002: chs. 2–4.
5 See Moyo, 2009: 114–125 for discussion and criticism.

References

Acemoglu D and Robinson J (2012) *Why Nations Fail*. New York: Crown Business.

Angus D (2013) *The Great Escape*. Princeton: Princeton University Press.

Brennan J and van der Vossen B (2018) *In defense of Openness: Why Global Freedom is the Humane Solution to Global Poverty*. New York: Oxford University Press.

Brock G and Moellendorf D (eds) (2005) *Current Debates in Global Justice*. Dordrecht: Springer.

Chang H (2007) *Bad Samaritans*. New York: Bloomsbury.

Channing A, Jones S and Tarp F (2016) What Is the Aggregate Economic Rate of Return to Foreign Aid? *The World Bank Economic Review* 30: 446–474.

Christian B and Lawford-Smith H (eds) (2012) *Global Justice*. Farnham: Ashgate.

Clark G (2007) *A Farewell to Alms*. Princeton: Princeton University Press.

Doucouliagos H and Paldam M (2015) Finally a Breakthrough? The Recent Rise in the Size of the Estimates of Aid Effectiveness. In: Arvin M and Lew B (eds) *Handbook on the Economics of Foreign Aid*. Cheltenham: Edward Elgar.

Easterly W (2002) *The Elusive Quest for Growth*. Cambridge: MIT Press.

Easterly W (2006) *The White Man's Burden*. New York: Penguin.

Klein N (2009) *No Logo*. New York: Picador.

Miller R (2010) *Globalizing Justice*. Oxford: Oxford University Press.

Moller D (2006) Should We Let People Starve—For Now? *Analysis* 66: 240–247.

Moller D (2017) Property and the Creation of Value. *Economics and Philosophy* 33: 1–23.

Moller D (Forthcoming) *Governing Least: A New England Libertarianism*. Oxford University Press.

Morris I (2010) *Why the West Rules—For Now*. New York: Farrar, Straus and Giroux.

Moyo D (2009) *Dead Aid: Why Aid is Not Working and How There is a Better Way for Africa*. New York: Farrar, Straus and Giroux.

Pogge T and Moellendorf D (2008) *Global Justice*. St. Paul: Paragon House.

Quamrul A, Lester A and Weil D (2009) When Does Improving Health Raise GDP? *NBER Macroeconomics Annual* 23: 157–204.

Rodrik D (2007) *One Economics, Many Recipes*. Princeton: Princeton University Press.

Sachs J (2014) The Case for Aid. *Foreign Policy*. Online.

Shue H (1980) *Basic Rights*. Princeton: Princeton University Press.

Singer P (2015) *The Most Good You Can Do*. New Haven: Yale University Press.

Stiglitz J (2003) *Globalization and Its Discontents*. New York: WW Norton.

United Nations Conference on Trade and Development (UNCTAD) (2010) Trade and Development Report: Employment, Globalization and Development. United Nations Publication. New York and Geneva.

Walker T and Wade C (2011) *Nicaragua: In the Shadow of the Eagle*. Boulder: Westview Press.

World Bank (2011) The Changing Wealth of Nations. Available at: https://siteresources.worldbank.org/ENVIRONMENT/Resources/ChangingWealthNations.pdf (accessed 26 August 2018).

World Bank (2015a) Botswana: Systematic Country Diagnostic. Available at: http://documents.worldbank.org/curated/en/489431468012950282/Botswana-Systematic-country-diagnostic (accessed 26 August 2018).

World Bank (2015b) Nigeria Economic Report. Available at: http://documents.worldbank.org/curated/en/684961468197340692/Nigeria-economic-report (accessed 26 August 2018).

World Bank (2018) Doing Business Rankings. Available at: www.doingbusiness.org/en/rankings (accessed 26 August 2018).

6 Entrepreneurial Rights as Basic Rights

Francis Cheneval

1. Introduction

In this chapter, I conceptualize entrepreneurial rights (sections 2 and 3) and justify them as basic rights grounded in the duty of assistance and freedom of occupation (section 4). This argument is different from—although not necessarily opposed to—the justification of economic freedoms as necessary for the exercise of the moral powers of the person (Tomasi, 2012). The argument presented is the following: if *A* has a duty of assistance towards *B*, then *A* also holds the right to create the economic surplus value necessary to assist *B*, and vice versa. I conceptualize the right to create economic surplus in a bundle of "entrepreneurial rights" and will explain this in more detail in the first and second part of the chapter. This bundle of rights is constrained by overriding conflicting rights and the principle "do no harm." The possibility of denying entrepreneurial rights by totally delegating the duty of assistance to the state as sole detainer of entrepreneurial rights is ruled out by freedom of occupation. According to my argument entrepreneurial rights are "enabling rights" of a duty bearer (Rawls, 2007: 144), not duty-less rights that stand alone. But the duty of assistance is a fundamental humanitarian duty. My argument thus follows a natural kind of justification, it is not limited to highly contingent social roles subject to possible duty-loss or change (Wenar, 2013: 218–219). Furthermore, freedom of occupation is a basic right in all accounts of liberalism. These considerations support the claim to consider entrepreneurial rights as basic rights. I will offer a more elaborate explanation of this point in section 5 of the chapter. Section 6 will give an outlook and discuss the societal relevance of my findings.

2. Entrepreneurial Activities

I use "entrepreneurial" to characterize activities that aim at creating economic surplus value while putting resources at risk. Economic surplus value is created when the combining of resources results in benefits that exceed the value of invested resources including costs of capital. Entrepreneurial activity concerns human and material resources. The former are not and ought not to be objects of property. Hence, entrepreneurial activities cannot be reduced to the use of property and, as will become clear in the next section, entrepreneurial rights are not totally reducible to property rights. They are a bundle of person-related and object-related rights.

Usually the cause for value creation can be traced back to some form of innovation, but the question of how to best engage in successful entrepreneurial activity is beyond the remit of this chapter. Furthermore, the overall value created by entrepreneurial activities need not be interpreted exclusively in terms of monetary profit. Social and environmental values can be added to the bottom line, but economic profit remains a necessary element of the value created by an activity that is to be called entrepreneurial in this chapter. To say that entrepreneurial activity "creates" value means that the term circumscribes innovative actions that start or trigger a chain of economic surplus value creation. Non-economic forms of entrepreneurship are not covered by the concept as it is used in this chapter.

It makes more sense to define the adjective "entrepreneurial" than to focus on the entrepreneur as a figure. When I refer to the entrepreneur I mean an activity captured in an ideal type or role rather than a "being." I mean a person reduced to a specific activity and driven by a specific motivation. Real owners, farmers, artisans, investors, traders, bankers, managers and so on are entrepreneurial if they engage in certain activities, but reduced to their own specific ideal-typical activities and motivations as farmers, artisans, employees and so on, they are not entrepreneurs. I also hold that individuals and teams can carry out entrepreneurial activity.

Conceptually, entrepreneurial activity is to be distinguished from trading or investing (capitalist). The ideal-type entrepreneur risks own resources, as might traders and investors, but at the same time as investing in a business enterprise, entrepreneurs increase the value of invested resources by efforts of their own. Entrepreneurs do not only invest and wait for the value of their assets to increase by market dynamics, i.e., the activity of others. Nor does the entrepreneur make a living out of a contractually guaranteed rent. Entrepreneurs as such are proactive in their organizational enterprise and their income stems from an uncertain profit. The ideal-typical entrepreneur is also to be distinguished from the employee, including the manager. The latter contributes to the creation of value and might have an entrepreneurial attitude and engage in "intrapreneurial" activities. But the employee depends on a productive infrastructure and organizational setup offering employment. This productive infrastructure is created by person-related entrepreneurial activity at some point. Furthermore, the employee does not risk resources.

He or she brings the resources of time and labor to the enterprise of the entrepreneur on the basis of a contractual guarantee of compensation. In sum, in this chapter I understand entrepreneurial activity as effort-driven creation of net economic value by individuals or teams risking their own resources. Note that the own resources of the entrepreneur can be ideas and labor only. Capital can be borrowed or invested as equity by others. In that case the entrepreneur simply faces more costs and a risk of change of capital costs. But strictly speaking, an entrepreneur can borrow all the start-up capital, she or he is ideal-typically distinct from the capitalist.

Some historical remarks can help clarify the definition put forward. There is a joke about U.S. President Bush saying to French President Chirac: "Jack, you French know nothing about the free market economy, you don't even have your own word for entrepreneur." The word is of course French and can be traced back to the 13th century.[1] But indeed, in its early history the word did not specifically apply to a risk-bearing person engaging in economic value creation. An entrepreneur was somebody who undertook something constructive within given parameters, somebody who operated at the margins or outside the law to make profit, or the adventurous leader of a military expedition exploring or seizing targets of colonial conquest (Vérin, 2011). Richard Cantillon ([1755] 2010) gave the term "entrepreneur" a more consistent meaning. Usually textbooks report a half-truth of what Cantillon meant by entrepreneur and report that according to him, an entrepreneur is somebody who buys something at a certain price in order to sell it at a higher price later on, while bearing the full risks of investment (Filion, 2011: 43). But in the passage usually referred to, Cantillon only talks about the merchant entrepreneur. Overall, Cantillon (2010: I, ch. 13) speaks of "farmer-entrepreneurs," "merchant-entrepreneurs," "artisan-entrepreneurs," each time specifying the activity of value creation that is entrepreneurial about these occupations and the economic uncertainty that characterizes the activities as opposed to drawing a contractually guaranteed salary or rent (Cantillon, 2010: I, ch. 13). According to Cantillon (2015: 43) some entrepreneurs have no capital and only invest labor, others invest both. The bottom line is that the entrepreneur does something with resources and makes them productive or more productive. The poor self-employed entrepreneur is thus covered by Cantillon's conceptualization; the mere capitalist is not an entrepreneur.

As Jean-Baptiste Say further elaborated more or less a century later, specifically entrepreneurial is what certain people do in between the buying and selling of goods. It is the risky, innovative and proactive creation of added value that characterizes entrepreneurial activity; in addition to mere owning, managing, trading, merchandizing or investing (Say, [1815] 1841: 361–382). As specific entrepreneurial activities Say mentions "the application of acquired knowledge to the creation of a product for human consumption" by provision of "labour" and "necessary funds." The entrepreneur is called upon to estimate the importance and probable amount of demand, and the means of its production. She or he must contract labor, buy raw materials, find consumers and so on. It may be noted that the 1880 English translation of Say's *Traité* translates the French "entrepreneur" with "master-agent" and "adventurer" whereby the latter term is used the most (Say, [1880] 1971: 329–332).

Joseph Schumpeter mainly followed Cantillon's and Say's conceptualization of the entrepreneur as risk-bearing value-adder. But famously, Schumpeter exposed the idea that only entrepreneurial activity causes endogenous economic development. This means that entrepreneurial activity is to be distinguished from profit making without creating economic development. Such action contributes merely to what Schumpeter called the "circular flow" of a merely stationary economy repeating the same cycles of production, distribution and consumption of the same goods. The ideal-typical house-, farm, or shop-owner ("Wirt") adjusts to given conditions and makes no profit beyond the covering of costs, his own salary included; s/he leaves no surplus value for the economy (Schumpeter, [1911] 2006: 11, 46). Where there are such owners as self-employed artisans, farmers, merchants and consultants who risk their own resources there can still be economic non-development. There can even be growth of the individual shopkeeper's income without economic development because the static economy in which it operates in a merely adaptive mode is a zero-sum game (ibid.: 45). Entrepreneurial activities, on the other hand, are the root cause of economic development because they consist in offering new types of products, applying new methods and timelines of production, expanding sales to new customers, using new materials, putting into place new organizational forms of enterprise (ibid.: 159). Part of the surplus value so produced are also higher payouts for labor and higher rents on investments for means of production (ibid.: 282). As Schumpeter points out, it would be a mistake to presume that innovative productive action is only present in modern industrial societies. The real economies of pastoralists, indigenous peoples and modern societies are all characterized by some degree of entrepreneurial activity. In modern society entrepreneurial activity exists in more accelerated and accentuated forms (ibid.: 171).

The Schumpeterian notion of entrepreneurship draws the line between economic development and circular flow. The entrepreneur is the energetic "Man of Action" (ibid.: 132) who brings about economic development from within the economy where otherwise there is mere adaptation, stagnation or decline. People, including capitalists, who do not energetically engage in innovative economic activities do not fit the concept of entrepreneur in the strict sense of the term. Schumpeter offers the most clear and distinct concept of entrepreneurial action. However, his account is embedded in a text that is entirely about his theory of economic development. The latter in turn is based on the two abstractions of circular flow on one side and developmental dynamics on the other. In theory the distinction makes sense and it clarifies the specific role of entrepreneurial activity in the system. But from a mere conceptual point of view it suffices to identify entrepreneurial activity as offering new types of products, applying new methods and timelines of production, expanding sales to new customers, using new materials, putting into place new organizational forms of enterprise. The claim that entrepreneurial action causes economic development need not be a necessary element of the definition of "entrepreneurial." A combination of entrepreneurship and development can be observed in many recent UN-related documents on entrepreneurship.[2] They promote entrepreneurship as the cause of development, ideally sustainable development. I neither refute nor adopt this theory. But I contend that the concept of entrepreneurship can be defined without recurring to the overarching notion of development. Besides offering a more parsimonious definition that comes unattached to a theory that carries a heavy burden of proof and that implies contested concepts such as development (Sen, 1988), the non-developmental concept of entrepreneurship I propose has the advantage that when identifying entrepreneurial rights of actors we will not need to make a judgment whether these actors cause development. All action engaging in activities such as offering new types of products, applying new methods and timelines of production, expanding sales to new customers, using new materials, putting into place new organizational forms of economic value creation while risking own resources is entrepreneurial. That is all we need to say in view of the topic of this chapter.

The distinction between the proactive business owner and the entrepreneur is also problematic (Morris, 1998: 2). If the proactive business owner does what it takes for her or his business to remain profitable over time, the activities that are responsible for this result might fall under the definition of entrepreneurial. Entrepreneurial activities are by definition innovative but entrepreneurs engage in them contextually and we do not need to embed these actions in a diagnosis of development to identify entrepreneurial activities in order to be called entrepreneurial. They might just sustain opportunities over time. This might or might not imply development in any of the possible, and in any event controversial, meanings of the term. It might imply large-scale disruptive change that can be interpreted as economic development, but it might also imply small-scale contextual and gradual economic growth in specific life-worlds without the need to interpret this change as development and distinguish it from non-development.

Another way of conceptualizing entrepreneurial activity in a more parsimonious way than Schumpeter is by tying the notion to the concept of productive assets. An activity can be called entrepreneurial if it converts organizational structures and things into productive assets, or if it increases the productivity of assets. Things, tangible and intangible, are not productive independently of the actor that uses them and independently of the environment of supply and demand in which they are used. The same is true for organizational structures of persons. Productivity is not an intrinsic property of things or organizations; it supervenes on them. They are transformed into productive assets by activities including a wide range of organizational actions. I therefore define as specifically entrepreneurial the range of activities that transform things and organizations of persons into productive or more productive assets by whatever it takes to do so in given circumstances. According to John Rawls only personal property has the status of a basic right and he thinks that personal property is not property in means of production (Rawls, 1999: 53). Rawls did not consider the possibility that something could be personal property and a productive asset at the same time simply by the activity of the person. This is obviously a blind spot and not plausible. But something else is important here as well. We again see that entrepreneurial activity is not reducible to the acquisition, use and sale of property. Entrepreneurial activity includes also the transformation of groups of persons into productive teams and organizations. Unless one wants to allow property of humans, the person-related dimension of entrepreneurial activity of value creation cannot be conceptualized in terms of property, be it personal, private or collective.

3. Entrepreneurial Rights

The analysis of entrepreneurial activities has shown that we are dealing with a bundle of person-related and object-related activities that create economic value. As such this bundle forms a special category that is not simply reducible to and protected by property rights. This will be further substantiated in this section. Two further preliminary comments frame this section. First, talking about economic liberties or freedoms, as done abundantly in the literature, is too narrow a scope when dealing with basic economic rights or entrepreneurial rights. The components of these rights include freedoms but are not restricted to freedom. Hence, I always talk about entrepreneurial rights and not only about entrepreneurial freedoms. Second, in this chapter I am mainly interested in identifying and justifying core entrepreneurial rights. A larger bundle of rights that entrepreneurs share with non-entrepreneurs, such as property rights, will also be identified circumstantially but not specifically discussed. In order to give the term "entrepreneurial rights" added value, I want to point to what is specific about this term and to what distinguishes entrepreneurial rights from rights that are already covered by other concepts. Let me therefore proceed by exclusion of rights that are not exclusively entrepreneurial but part of a broader range of rights entrepreneurs would also need to be protected by. In a further step, I will then try to identify the core entrepreneurial rights.

First, activities of self-preservation and subsistence are not covered by the concept of entrepreneurial activities because they do not include the element of creation of net surplus value. The entrepreneurial activity creates a surplus beyond what is necessary for subsistence and survival. Entrepreneurial rights are thus to be conceptually distinguished from the right to subsistence and to activities securing self-preservation. There is a meaningful distinction to be made between opportunity-driven and necessity-driven entrepreneurship (McMullen et al., 2008). But if individuals engage in an entrepreneurial activity they aim at creating a surplus beyond what is needed for their self-preservation. The right to subsistence, be it understood as claim-right or freedom, does not protect these activities; it covers mere decent survival not an activity aiming at profit.

Second, entrepreneurial activity needs to be distinguished from mere trading and investing. The rights to trade or transfer property are part of a larger bundle of property rights that entrepreneurs share with other types of actors and that are not specific to the entrepreneurial activity. Since entrepreneurial activity is more than just mere trading or investing as has been shown in the previous section, the rights to transfer and trade one's own property do not protect the specific realm of entrepreneurship but a much broader range of activities that the entrepreneur also engages in but not exclusively. Although entrepreneurs need to be protected by property rights, entrepreneurial rights are not entirely reducible to property rights in the core meaning of the term.

Third, core labor rights such as the freedom from slavery, the freedom from forced labor, the freedom to engage in the labor relation, the right to decent compensation, decent working conditions or to collective bargaining need to be distinguished from entrepreneurial rights. The core labor rights do not protect the specifically entrepreneurial offering of new types of products, applying new methods and timelines of production, expanding sales to new customers, using new materials, putting into place new organizational forms of economic value creation while risking own resources.

What then are entrepreneurial rights in the specific meaning of the term? According to the definition put forward, entrepreneurial rights are rights that protect the sphere of action of effort-driven creation of net economic value by individuals or teams risking the resources of their enterprise. Entrepreneurial rights protect the specific activities that transform things into productive assets.

Hohfeld (Hohfeld, 1917; Wenar, 2005) identified basic formal components of rights as privilege (liberty, freedom), claim (right in the strict sense used by Hohfeld), power and immunity. He identified the opposites of these elements as duty (opposite of privilege), non-claim (opposite of claim; also "no-right"), disability (opposite of power) and liability (opposite of immunity). Hohfeld further clarified that these eight types of formal legal relations (i.e., all elements of rights and their opposites) regard persons (*in personam*) and/or things (*in rem*). The purpose of the following analysis is not a complete inventory of all the formal rights-components of entrepreneurial rights but rather the circumscription of a core meaning.

Entrepreneurial rights are privileges (i.e., liberties or freedoms), but not exclusively. I use the three terms synonymously although they could be further distinguished but that is not necessary here. Liberty is the absence of a duty. *A* has a liberty (privilege) to something if *A* does not have a duty not to do something. To say that *A* has a right to create economic value by proper efforts and by risking own resources, or to say that *A* has the privilege to turn a thing into a productive asset is to say that *A* has no duty not to create economic value in this way. In this case *A* will not be violating any duty not to create economic value if *A* creates economic value. *A*'s right to compete offering products or services, to design and produce new products, to invent and apply new methods of production, to turn things into productive assets, to set up a profit-oriented organization are all examples of entrepreneurial rights as privileges. Privilege-rights single out what their bearer has no duty not to do. Formally, entrepreneurial rights are first and foremost privileges or liberties that are implied in the absence or negation of a corresponding duty not to create economic surplus value with a certain action regarding certain things.

The pertinence of the Hohfeldian analysis for entrepreneurial rights can be illustrated by an example of reducing profit by competition, for example, by *B*'s liberty to produce and sell a certain type of product that *A* is already producing and selling. The liberty of *A* to engage in an entrepreneurial activity does not entail a correlative duty of *B* not to interfere with this activity by competing. If it does, *A*'s right is not a liberty but a claim-right to a profit at the expense of B's liberty to try to earn a profit. *A* has a Hohfeldian liberty to engage in an entrepreneurial activity, he has no claim that puts a duty on *B* not to engage in a similar activity. One can easily undermine entrepreneurial rights by misconceiving the proper relations between liberties as claims. *A*'s entrepreneurial right to try to earn profits does not entail a correlative duty of *B* not to interfere with *A*'s doing so. It only necessarily entails *A*'s not being under a duty not to strive for a profit (Lazarev, 2005). Conceiving *A*'s entrepreneurial right to earn a profit in terms of *B*'s duty not to interfere with *A*'s earning a profit would undermine the idea of equal rights to entrepreneurial activities.

Once the sphere of entrepreneurial liberty is circumscribed by privileges (liberties), claims as a second element of rights come into play. They exist if duties are imposed on others. *A* has a claim that *B* φ (φ stands for an action) if and only if B has a duty to *A* to φ. The rights to be protected against libel, product identification infringement, the misappropriation of trade secrets, bribery are examples of entrepreneurial claim-rights that exist if the state has a duty to protect every person against persons performing actions considered fraudulous or violent. Most claim-rights, especially the ones that we can identify in bundles of entrepreneurial rights, exist on the basis of contracts or constitutions and they depend on the ability of a natural or legal person, mostly the state, to fulfill a duty.

The two further Hohfeldian components of entrepreneurial rights are powers and immunities. *A* has a power if and only if *A* has the ability to alter his or her own or someone else's components of rights. Actions such as commanding, promising, waiving, sentencing, consenting, selling and abandoning are all examples by which a right-holder exercises a power to change his own or someone other's privileges, claims, powers and immunities. A specific legal power is the right to bind oneself and others by contract or any form of mutually binding agreement, but not all such contracts are specifically and exclusively entrepreneurial in nature. If the entrepreneurial activity is not specifically restricted to buying and selling or even distinct from these aspects, as I hold, we cannot say that the right to enter into contracts of exchange of goods is a specific entrepreneurial power. Normal law-abiding citizens, traders and merchants and so on use the same powers. It is what the entrepreneur does with goods between buying and selling that is specifically entrepreneurial as an activity that creates value.

The specific entrepreneurial act is thus to combine contractual relations of exchange of goods and services in such a manner as to create a value-enhancing dynamic. It is the serial organizational combination of legal powers that is distinctly entrepreneurial, not the individual contract of exchanges of goods and services. One could identify the entrepreneurial powers as norm-creating powers that establish a profit-oriented informal or formal organization and that are applicable within the organizational structure of the private enterprise. The power to contract factors of production and to appoint status and hierarchical order in an organizational structure in the entrepreneurial enterprise is specifically entrepreneurial, because it presupposes an activity that has created enough surpluses to finance paid labor and it is part of an organizational design that is set up to create more economic surplus value after payback of labor and capital costs. Entrepreneurial rights include norm-creating powers (MacCormick and Raz, 1972: 82). It is fair to say that any meaningful bundle of entrepreneurial rights will contain powers to enter into private contracts of exchange that allow for a value-enhancing activity whereby the right to contract labor and to organize status and hierarchy alongside with defining procedure are fundamental.

If *A lacks* the ability to alter *B*'s Hohfeldian components, then B has an immunity vis-à-vis *A*. In other words, *B* has an immunity *if and only if A* lacks the ability to alter *B*'s privileges, claims and powers. The right not to be imposed the duty to perform religious practices by the state is an immunity that every citizen has vis-à-vis the state. The right to remain silent in order not to incriminate oneself is an immunity vis-à-vis the state.

In every one of these instances there exists a domain in which actors lack a power to alter a privilege, claim or power of an actor. The immunity against liability with more than the total value of assets in a bankruptcy or liquidation procedure is an example of an entrepreneurial immunity. Entrepreneurs should be liable with the assets of their enterprise but not with more than these assets. Strictly speaking, they can start from zero with credit, as Schumpeter holds, and in the case of failure they should not fall lower than zero. In other words, in the event of failure an actor can be discharged as debtor, provided the assets are liquidated. Lenders giving out credits of a value beyond the value of collateral assets or without them do this at their own risk.

This conceptual and formal analysis allows for some substantive inferences on what entrepreneurial rights cannot be. Entrepreneurial rights do not protect the resources that entrepreneurs risk in their endeavors, as this would undermine the concept. Entrepreneurs are liable with the assets of their enterprise. But entrepreneurial immunities can put a limit on the liability, e.g., not to go beyond 100 percent of the actual value of business assets at the time of bankruptcy, basically allowing every bankrupt entrepreneur a fresh start and placing a responsibility on creditors and customers and a shared responsibility of transparency on both creditors and debtors. Entrepreneurial rights cannot protect profit margins or market shares entrepreneurs have acquired against competition, as this would discriminate others in their entrepreneurial liberties. Entrepreneurial rights protect a sphere of entrepreneurial action and decision-making, they do not protect profit margins or the market value of property. They do not guarantee a positive outcome of entrepreneurial activity.

Table 6.1 **Core Hohfeldian Components of Entrepreneurial Rights**

Components of Entrepreneurial Rights	*Core Content*
Entrepreneurial liberty	to transforming things into productive assets; to increase the productivity of assets; to earn a profit from free exchange; to associate with entrepreneurial partners
Entrepreneurial claim	to be protected against fraud and extortion (forced trade, libeling, product falsification, misappropriation of trade secrets, bribery, etc.)
Entrepreneurial power	to formalize activities and pool assets in a firm; to contract and command human resources and material factors of production
Entrepreneurial immunity	against liabilities after liquidation of assets

The bearers of the Hohfeldian components of entrepreneurial rights are human persons. Since they have the freedom to associate and form groups of partners and teams pursuing a profit-seeking activity, it seems correct to infer that humans can claim entrepreneurial rights also in partnerships and teams, i.e., collectively. The team is best defined as a strong unit of commitment and performance of all members together, whereas the partnership or group includes a pooling of resources for some activities, but also independent resources and activities of members apart. It seems that teams become increasingly important for entrepreneurship, but this is not an important point for the subject matter of this chapter (Schjoedt and Kraus, 2011). For our purposes it suffices to say that individuals, partnerships and teams are the potential bearers of entrepreneurial rights. If one of the legal powers of entrepreneurs is to formalize a business enterprise as a firm with legal personhood, the question that follows is to what extent the firm becomes a bearer of entrepreneurial rights. In most legal systems, legal persons (private and public) are attributed legal capacity. But not all basic rights are attributable to non-human persons and I will come back to this point in section 5 that deals with the question whether entrepreneurial rights are basic rights.

4. The Justification of Entrepreneurial Rights

In the literature on economic freedoms as basic rights one method of argumentation tries to show that economic freedoms are intrinsic to normative agency and autonomy. At least in one tenet of the argument the main reflection is that a basic right is a liberty that is necessary for the adequate development and full exercise of the moral powers of the person.[3] In this chapter I will not pursue this argument although I think it is correct. Rather, I pursue a relational account in favor of entrepreneurial rights based on the duty of assistance. The argument presented is based on the conceptual implication that if *A* has a non-promissory pro tanto duty to φ-ing (perform an action) vis-à-vis *B*, then *A* also holds the necessary correlative rights concerning φ-ing vis-à-vis *B*, and vice versa for *B* towards *A*. These rights are constrained by overriding conflicting rights and the do-no-harm principle. *A*'s duty to rescue *B* does not give *A* the right to kill four people if that would be necessary to rescue *B*. But within a certain circumscription *A*'s duty to rescue *B* gives her certain rights that she needs to have in order to fulfill her duty.

Note that this implies the idea that if a person has a right, another person has a corresponding duty. It does not imply Sieghart's (1985: 43) general implication from a duty of *A* to a right of *B*, which is doubtful, especially in the case of imperfect duties of charity and benevolence towards everyone (Mill, 1989: 21). What I presuppose is that in a situation in which *A* holds a non-promissory pro tanto duty towards *B* to φ-ing, for instance *A* encounters a specific person *B* in life-threatening or fundamental material need and is thereby under a duty to assist *B*, *A* also holds the rights that are necessary to fulfill the duty in a morally acceptable manner. If *A* sees *B* drown in *B*'s pool across the fence, *A*'s duty to rescue implies *A*'s right to trespass into *B*'s garden without permission. This can be generalized: any person who is or becomes a duty bearer of assistance acquires certain rights that are necessary to provide the assistance and that override *secondary* conflicting rights of others imposing prohibitions. *B* has to grant to *A* that her duty to rescue him implies *A*'s right to trespass onto his private sphere and vice versa.

The way in which the rescue ought to be carried out depends on circumstances. If *A* is not a swimmer, *A* is under no duty to jump into the water to rescue *B*. In this case *A* is under a duty to use a rescue device and if this is not possible to call for help. In general, *A* has a duty to follow a list of measures in order of efficacy regarding her task to rescue *B* given her abilities and means. This implies that *A* has the right to acquire the abilities and means necessary to rescue. If *B* expects *A* to rescue him from the pool in case of need, *B* needs to grant to *A* the right to try to learn how to swim and a right to any other ability and means necessary to perform the duty without harm to others. We thus see that *A* is not necessarily under a duty to learn how to swim given other possibilities to fulfill the duty to rescue and given that not all people are able to learn how to swim or are afraid to swim. But *A* is under a duty to apply any of the possible measures of rescue and *A* certainly has the right to try to learn how to swim. Accordingly, following the logic that any right of a person implies some corresponding duty of another person, *B* has the duty to respect this right, e.g., *A*'s right to learn how to swim. It would not be adequate to state that *A* has the duty to trespass onto *B*'s private sphere just because she has the duty to rescue. If *A* is not a swimmer and has no rescue device she will need to call for help elsewhere. There is no duty to trespass, whereas there is a duty to rescue and a right to trespass. The point is that the duty implies certain secondary rights circumscribed by the duty.

Now, let us presuppose that in a relation of persons *A* and *B*, *A* has a moral duty of assistance towards *B* in case *B* is incapable of providing for her basic needs, and *B* has a moral duty of assistance towards *A* if *A* is incapable of providing for his basic needs. By a positive duty of assistance I mean such things as a duty to rescue, a duty to provide fundamental help in need, e.g., helping a blind person cross the street, and a duty to provide life-saving economic resources to the point where a person again is able to provide for herself. Unlike systems that consider "bad Samaritans" as legitimate non-doers, I presuppose a moral world where *A* and *B* have a moral duty to assist. If *B* is in need, *A*'s non-compliance with the duty to assist is considered as cause of harm by omission. In the legal world we find examples of both, systems with a strong duty to assist and rescue and systems that do not enforce such a duty. But that is not our concern here; I presuppose a society that accepts the duty to assist.

For the sake of argument but also out of conceptual necessity I further assume that *A* and *B* cannot simply rely on abundant goods to be taken from the commons. In such a case of natural abundance the duty to assist with the provision of resources would become obsolete. In the context presupposed here, *A* and B thus need to produce in order to consume. Furthermore, this act of production cannot simply consist in the creation of fiat money, because fiat money is not a resource, it's a symbol for a resource claim (Cheneval, 2016). The same is true for the creation of any kind of mere "bubble" that does not represent true economic value. If the mere creation of money or "bubbles" could solve problems of scarcity, again the situation of need of assistance would not occur. This means that the duty of assistance can be discharged if and only if economic surplus value is produced.

In a society of *A* and *B*, if *A* and *B* only rely on the assistance of the other, they will not only not be able to get any assistance themselves, but they will also never be able to fulfill their duty of assistance. If they only grant to each other the right to provide for themselves (right to livelihood), the same holds true. If *B* thinks he has a moral claim to *A*'s assistance in case of material need, *B* has to grant to *A* the freedom to produce a surplus without violating more important rights, with which *A* can assist *B* in case of need, or which a state could tax in order to grant the assistance, and vice versa; just like *B* needs to grant to *A* the right to learn how to swim or to acquire any other ability and means necessary for his rescue in the example stated above. The duty of assistance of *A* thus implies the duty of *B* to grant to *A* the right to produce an economic surplus. In the first part of this chapter, I have identified the production of an economic surplus as the core of entrepreneurial activity. Applied to the given example the duty of assistance of *A* implies the right to an entrepreneurial activity of *A* and vice versa.

However, the argument developed so far is still incomplete. Granted, there is a need to create an economic surplus in order to provide for people in need of assistance; but *A* and *B* could be considered to be under a duty to form a cooperative endeavor to produce everything as a team and share all the fruits of their production. As Schumpeter has conceded, the state could be conceived as a collective, single entrepreneur or we could assume a setting of market socialism in which everybody is part of productive collectives but not an entrepreneurial individual. The duty of assistance alone does not account for an individual entrepreneurial right to engage in the production of an economic surplus.

The response to this objection is the following. The option to provide assistance collectively and only collectively becomes problematic if one presupposes a prohibition of forced labor, i.e., freedom of occupation. *A* might not want to work in the same team with *B* because *B* is lazy, inefficient or has totally different goals and values and vice versa. In this case, freedom of occupation justifies *A*'s or *B*'s choice to provide for themselves. *A* and *B* just need to discharge their duty of assistance towards each other in case of need and if they dispose of a surplus. Hence the argument in its most simple terms runs as follows: the entrepreneurial right to freely engage in the production of an economic surplus is justified as a fundamental right if one presupposes the duty of assistance and freedom of occupation.

This combined justification of entrepreneurial rights holds under reasonably favorable conditions. There are contingent circumstances in which the duty of assistance and freedom of occupation can conflict. Imagine a situation of a small isolated group in extreme scarcity where only a collective team effort is sufficient for the survival of everybody. Strictly speaking, in this case both the duty to assist and the freedom of occupation are void, because the team effort only guarantees survival and no assistance is offered to a needy person who cannot participate in the team effort. Still, there is a case conceivable in which a group needs a collective effort of everybody to survive and assist one additional needy member. In that case the duty of assistance trumps freedom of occupation. So obviously, my justification of entrepreneurial rights holds for reasonably favorable circumstances, not for all possible circumstances. But this is equally true for core labor rights or social claim-rights. Nobody in the hunter group under threat of survival can claim a right to decent working conditions or a two-weeks paid holiday.

Note that freedom of occupation also implies the right to be an employee rather than an entrepreneur. But the duty of assistance can be discharged only if somebody creates a surplus and the surplus is only created by entrepreneurial activity. Workers can contribute to the creation of surplus if employment is created by entrepreneurship. A generalized right to entrepreneurship is thus justified.

There are two important corollaries to the argument that I would like to mention. First, we see that the justification of entrepreneurial rights via the duty of assistance justifies the creation of surplus value for the economy. The ideal-typical entrepreneur thus has a justification to make profit within the constraints we have circumscribed and constantly reinvest profit into the value-creating enterprise. The practice that is justified is rather in line with what Max Weber called "inner-worldly asceticism" (Weber, 1978: §11). In other words, on the basis of my justification the entrepreneur has no specific right to take capital out of the enterprise for private consumption beyond her or his livelihood; nor does the state have the right to tax the enterprise to waste money on pleasures of a particular group. It must be for assistance. I am not saying there are no other justifications possible, but my argument highlights the inner-worldly ascetic and genuinely relational dimension of entrepreneurship and its consequences for the state.

A second corollary to this argument is that the whole Hohfeldian bundle of entrepreneurial rights mentioned in the above section of this chapter needs to be protected in a socio-liberal society because otherwise the creation of an economic surplus is not protected. Individual rights to fundamental protections against negative externalities, fraud and extortion, for which there exist other justifications beyond the remit of this chapter would be violated as well. It is clear that the concrete design of this Hohfeldian bundle of rights depends on concrete circumstances and is open to variation.

5. Entrepreneurial Rights as Basic Rights

A society that recognizes freedom of occupation as a basic right and that expects its members to discharge positive duties of assistance directly or via the state needs to grant entrepreneurial rights. I interpret any social security system guaranteeing a social minimum as an institutionalization of the duty of assistance broadly conceived. This happens with the goal to not leave the compliance of the duty to assist with a social minimum to the hazard of who happens to be around to help. The question whether entrepreneurial rights are basic rights depends on the status one is willing to grant to the duty of assistance and to freedom of occupation. In many countries both are upheld as basic. Such societies need to grant a fundamental status to entrepreneurial rights. For countries with further-reaching positive economic rights this can be affirmed even more emphatically.

As far as the question regarding the positive human rights status of entrepreneurial rights is concerned, the right to freely choose one's employment is enshrined in Article 23/1 of the Universal Declaration of Human Rights and in the International Covenant on Economic, Social and Cultural Rights in Part III, Article 6. Freedom of occupation is a codified human right. The duty of assistance, the second component of our argument in favor of entrepreneurial rights, is prominent in Rawlsian political philosophy as a fundamental duty of peoples towards each other in a non-liberal world of international relations. Within liberal peoples principles of distributive justice complement this duty. But both, the duty of assistance and further-reaching measures of redistribution, presuppose the creation of economic value.

Liberal societies are characterized by strong duties of redistribution, i.e., assistance and further-reaching economic help. The right to entrepreneurship is thus a basic right in any liberal society. Things are different in a scenario of global distributive justice. If one holds that the human individual *A* has a duty of assistance towards *B*, even if *A* and *B* belong to different peoples, and if one holds that freedom of occupation is a human right, then the entrepreneurial right to freely create economic value is a human right on the basis of the argument presented above.

Basic rights are rights that any legitimate political authority necessarily needs to guarantee and that limit the scope of any legitimate political authority (Platz, 2014: 25). I take it from this definition that some basic rights can extend to legal persons. A second point seems important as well. While human rights are exclusively attributable to humans, the question remains open if rights that are only attributed to legal persons can be basic rights. Take the right of limited liability of firms. This would mean that legal persons could claim basic rights while human persons could not claim the same rights. This seems counter-intuitive. I cannot go to the bottom of this question but presuppose that basic rights can in principle be attributed to the entrepreneurial partnerships or collectives if these rights are also attributable to human persons pursuing an entrepreneurial activity on their own. The rights to create an economic surplus and to limited liability for instance are applicable to human individuals and teams and therefore eligible as basic right. But they are not basic rights that apply to formalized entrepreneurial teams (firms) and not to individuals. The right to choose and exercise an occupation, on the other hand, is an example of a human right in the sense that it is a power that only applies to human persons and their agency. Teams cannot substitute for or override this individual human choice.

In its Article 27/2 the Swiss Constitution holds that economic freedom ("Wirtschaftsfreiheit") is composed of the human rights to a free choice of occupation and the freedom to pursue a private economic activity which includes the entrepreneurial right ("Unternehmensrecht") to make economic decisions without the interference of the state. This is a basic right that all residents in Switzerland can claim and it is tied to freedom of movement in Switzerland and the guarantee of property rights. I mention this to show that what I am proposing, namely to interpret entrepreneurial rights as basic rights with proper analytical qualifications, is actually something that is already the case in existing legal orders.

6. Conclusion

In the general debate on economic and social rights different human rights claims are made to a right to education, to assistance, to subsistence, to economic development, to a sustained livelihood, to a welfare minimum, to a basic income, to decent labor and so on. What this chapter shows is that these positive social rights imply a basic right to entrepreneurship. Basic rights to subsistence, health care and basic education are positive social claim-rights and they are codified human rights and codified basic rights. International and domestic law systems have gone beyond the point to consider positive social rights as aspirational goals only. The realization of positive economic rights depends on the condition that not everybody claims them but rather that people have a corresponding right to a profit-seeking economic activity. From a behavioral point of view the formal right is of course not enough, it is also necessary that a sizable group of people actually seize the opportunity to contribute to the creation of value that makes it possible to guarantee positive social rights. But empirical reality shows that the entrepreneurial activity is something people massively engage in under most circumstances if given the right to do so.

From the point of view of their realization, positive economic claim-rights are not generalizable as duty-less. They cannot be guaranteed if everybody is an addressee and the reciprocity of the mutual assurance of assistance in case of need is void if no right is offered on the contributing side. In the most abstract terms I hold that for assistance to be demanded as duty the right to the free creation of economic value of individuals and/or teams is necessary. The core entrepreneurial right to a free economic activity of value creation is therefore a basic right that needs to be protected not only if one subscribes to a classical liberal but also if one subscribe to high liberal conception of economic rights.

As an afterword I might add that most of the world's poorest people at the bottom of the pyramid massively engage in unprotected activities of economic value creation without disposing of social rights (Prahalad and Hart, 2002; Cho, 2015). Roughly two thirds of all active people in the developing world are entrepreneurial and if we look at gender more women than men are in this situation (Gindling and Newhouse, 2014). Improvement in the facility of doing business notwithstanding (World Bank, 2016), this segment of the global poor are de jure and de facto still very feebly protected in their economic activities vis-à-vis more powerful economic players and the state. In other words, small entrepreneurs and in particular the global poor are at least doubly wronged. Their activity of value creation is not properly protected and the value they create is not sufficiently channeled into the production of public goods and to socio-economic rights which protect them if they are no longer able to engage in their value-creating activities.

Notes

1 Cnrtl.fr. (2018). *ENTREPRENEUR: Etymologie de ENTREPRENEUR*. [online] Available at: www.cnrtl.fr/etymologie/entrepreneur [Accessed 17 Dec. 2018].

2 See UN Resolution 67/202 adopted by the General Assembly on 21 December 2012: Entrepreneurship for Development; Report of the Secretary General, Entrepreneurship for Development (Accessed 18 August 2014).

3 Critical Rawls, 1971: 42, 43, 82; 1991: 228, 232, 298, 335, 338, 363; 2001: 114. Rawls claims that only two economic liberties are basic rights. First, that is the liberty to hold personal property; second, the freedom of choice of economic occupation. Some authors have refuted Rawls and argued for a full bundle of economic freedoms as basic rights challenging his interpretation of necessity and adequacy (Platz, 2014: 28 ff). The free choice of occupation is connected to the right to be a self-governing entrepreneur as opposed to just being an employee choosing one form of employment over another (Tomasi, 2012: 74 ff). The choice of occupation implies rights to self-occupation that in turn implies the right to sell, trade and contract labor. As Tomasi points

out, if the state starts limiting these options it deprives people of the possibility to be authors of their own lives (Tomasi, 2012: 77). Furthermore, it is meaningless, even contradictory to statute a right to choose one's employment if the right to employ and to create options of employment is not guaranteed. If there is only one employer, the state as one big firm, the choice options to create occupational opportunities are severely limited and, following Rawls's condition, there is no adequate protection of the capacity to develop the moral powers of individuals.

References

Cantillon R (2010) *An Essay on Economic Theory. An English Translation of Richard Cantillon's Essai Sur La Nature Du Commerce En Général*, C Saucier (trans). Auburn, Ala: Ludwig von Mises Institute.

Cantillon R (2015) [1755] *Essai Sur La Nature Du Commerce En Général*. Paris: Institut Coppet.

Cheneval F (2016) *Es werde Geld. Schweizer Monat* 1037: 28–31.

Cho Y (2015) *Entrepreneurship for the Poor in Developing Countries*. IZA World of Labor.

Filion LJ (2011) Defining the Entrepreneur. In: Dana LP (ed) *World Encyclopedia of Entrepreneurship*. Cheltenham, UK: Edward Elgar, pp. 41–52.

Gindling TH and Newhouse D (2014) Self-Employment in the Developing World. *World Development* 56 (April): 313–331.

Hohfeld WN (1917) Fundamental Legal Conceptions as Applied in Judicial Reasoning. *The Yale Law Journal* 26(8): 710–770.

Lazarev N (2005) Hohfeld's Analysis of Rights: An Essential Approach to a Conceptual and Practical Understanding of the Nature of Rights. *Murdoch University Electronic Journal of Law* 12(1).

MacCormick N and Raz J (1972) Voluntary Obligations and Normative Powers. *Proceedings of the Aristotelian Society* 46: 50–102.

McMullen, JS, Bagby DR and Palich LE (2008) Economic Freedom and the Motivation to Engage in Entrepreneurial Action. *Entrepreneurship Theory and Practice* 32(5): 875–895.

Mill, JS (1989). *On Liberty*. London: Walter Scott.

Morris MH (1998) *Entrepreneurial Intensity: Sustainable Advantages for Individuals, Organizations, and Societies*. Westport, CN: Quorum.

Platz JV (2014) Are Economic Liberties Basic Rights? *Politics, Philosophy & Economics* 13(1): 23–44.

Prahalad CK and Hart S (2002) The Fortune at the Bottom of the Pyramid. *Strategy+Business* 26.

Rawls J (1971) *Theory of Justice*. Cambridge, MA: Harvard University Press.

Rawls J (1991) *Political Liberalism*. New York: Columbia University Press.

Rawls J (1999) *A Theory of Justice*, revised ed. Cambridge, MA: Harvard University Press.

Rawls J (2001) *Justice as Fairness. A Restatement*, Erin Kelly (ed.). Cambridge: Harvard University Press.

Rawls J (2007) *Lectures on the History of Political Philosophy*, Freeman SR (ed). Cambridge: The Belknap Press of Harvard University Press.

Say JB (1841) *Traité d'économie Politique Ou Simple Exposition de La Manière Dont Se Forment, Se Distribuent et Se Consomment Les Richesses*. Osnabrück: O. Zeller.

Say JB (1880) [1819] *A Treatise on Political Economy: Or the Production, Distribution and Consumption of Wealth*, translated by CR Prinsep, 4th ed. Philadelphia: Claxton, Remsen & Haffelfinger.

Schjoedt L and Kraus S (2011) Teams. In: Dana LP (ed) *World Encyclopedia of Entrepreneurship*. Cheltenham, UK: Edward Elgar, pp. 426–33.

Schumpeter JA (2006) [1911] *Theorie der wirtschaftlichen Entwicklung*, Röpke J and Stiller O (eds) Nachdr. der 1. Aufl. von 1912. Berlin: Duncker & Humblot.

Sen A (1988) The Concept of Development. In: Chenery H and Srinivasan TN (eds) *Handbook of Development Economics* (Vo1:9–26). Handbooks in Economics 9. Amsterdam: North-Holland Publishing Company.

Sieghart P (1985) *The Lawful Rights of Mankind: An Introduction to the International Legal Code of Human Rights*. Oxford: Oxford University Press.

Tomasi J (2012) *Free Market Fairness*. Princeton: Princeton University Press.

Vérin H (2011) *Entrepreneurs, entreprise. Histoire d'une idée*. Paris: Classiques Garnier.

Weber M (1978) *Economy and Society: An Outline of Interpretive Sociology*. G Roth and Wittich C (eds). Berkeley: University of California Press.

Wenar L (2005) The Nature of Rights. *Philosophy & Public Affairs* 33(3): 223–252. https://doi.org/10.1111/j.1088-4963.2005.00032.x.

Wenar L (2013) The Nature of Claim-Rights. *Ethics* 123(2): 202–229.

World Bank (2016) *Doing Business 2017: Equal Opportunity for All*. Doing Business.

7 International Law, Public Reason, and Productive Rights

Fernando R. Tesón

1. Introduction

With one important exception, international law does not generally protect economic liberties. By economic liberties I mean private property rights and freedom of contract, including the individual right to trade. The exception is the global trade system, which encourages gradual lowering of tariffs and thus promotes freer international trade. This system has spawned globalization, which has dramatically fostered growth and, as a result, lifted millions out of poverty.[1] The rules of the WTO, however, address governments, not individuals. They do not recognize a right to trade to anyone, but instead place limits on protectionist legislation. More important, even if we could say that international law encourages *inter-state* capitalism (to an extent, given the protectionist exceptions embedded in the WTO system), it has remained largely silent about *domestic* capitalism. In international trade circles people talk about *nations*' trading. There is little attention in those circles to any right of *individuals* to engage in trade, domestic or international.[2] Moreover, international instruments repeatedly affirm the right of "peoples" to choose their own economic system.[3] This translates into the power of states to curtail or suppress private property and freedom of contract if they judge that such action is required by the national welfare or the public good. Following Bas van der Vossen and Jason Brennan, in the rest of this chapter I will call these economic liberties (property, contract and trade) *productive rights* (van der Vossen and Brennan, 2018). From an economic standpoint, productive rights are entirely derived from the right to private property. Freedom of contract, freedom of use, freedom of investment and freedom to trade are all incidents of property (Honoré, 1961).

A quick review of international and comparative law shows the low status of productive rights. International law protects relatively robust productive rights in only two situations, both involving foreigners (Kriebaum and Reinisch, 2009). First, customary law protects expropriation of *foreign* property. Generally speaking, such expropriation must be nondiscriminatory, for a public purpose and carry adequate compensation.

Second, many states have entered into bilateral investment agreements that protect the investment of their nationals in the territory of the other party. Here, too, those treaties protect only the foreign investor. Neither customary law nor bilateral investment treaties protect *national* owners and investors. The law of human rights, which is supposed to protect nationals, is notoriously weak on productive rights. The Universal Declaration of Human Rights (UDHR) recognizes in its Article 17 the right to own property "alone or in association with others."[4] Yet, whatever one's view about the legal status of the UDHR, this rule has not prevented states from denying property rights altogether. To my knowledge no one, not even governments of capitalist states, has argued that socialist systems, which literally contradict Article 17 of the UDHR, violate international law for that reason. The International Covenant on Civil and Political Rights, widely regarded as a sort of global bill of rights, does not include the right of property, of any kind. The European Convention on Fundamental Rights and Freedoms does include a protection of private property in Protocol 1.[5] But the case law of the European Court of Human Rights applying this provision shows that the Court has only declared illegal the most egregious instances of governmental theft.[6] The very wording of Protocol 1 suggests the weakness of the right to property. Section 2 proclaims that "States may control the use of property in accordance with the general interest." It is well established that "control" includes all kinds of dispossession, including confiscation.[7] No other right in the convention has a comparable low threshold against state interference.

National constitutions do not fare much better. Many constitutions contain a provision that protects land owners against governmental expropriation, such as the takings clause in the United States Constitution. But in fact capitalist nations protect private property mostly in their legislation and in the common law, not in their constitutions. Two examples will suffice. In the United States the takings clause protects land owners, but not capital owners. The government cannot take my house without paying me compensation. But if I sell my house and put the money in the bank, nothing prevents the government from taxing me at 100 percent, thus effectively taking all my assets without compensation (Epstein, 1988). And in my native country, Argentina, the constitutional takings clause has been completely nullified by a mix of anti-property Supreme Court jurisprudence and congressional delegation of economic powers to the President ("*decretos de necesidad y urgencia*").[8] In use of these powers, the Kirchner government expropriated all private retirement accounts (Moffett, 2008). For the rest, many national constitutions treat productive rights, explicitly or implicitly, as the Mexican Constitution does: "The property of all land and water within national territory is originally owned by the Nation, who has the right to transfer this ownership to particulars. Hence, private property is a privilege created by the Nation." That private property is a privilege and not a right means, of course, that the government may revoke it at any time and for virtually any reason. The numerous instances of government expropriation of citizens' property (as opposed to foreign property) have gone virtually unopposed in the media and public opinion, which, following the common understanding in international law, has bought into the idea that such expropriations are deemed to be for the common good and do not violate the owners' rights.[9]

After WWII, victorious nations designed international law in this economically agnostic way for one simple reason: one of them, the Soviet Union, had socialist institutions that did not protect productive rights. To prevent conflict, world leaders sought to create a mechanism of collective security that would be *agnostic*[10] between capitalism and socialism, that is, a system that would not be biased for or against either of these two economic conceptions. In this way, the system created by the UN Charter appeared tolerant: nations should not impose their economic views on other nations. Peaceful coexistence, it was thought, required tolerating diverse forms of economic organization. Choosing between capitalism and socialism is, on this view, a central prerogative of sovereignty.

I argue against this view in three steps. First, I lay down the facts about the role of productive markets in economic growth and poverty alleviation. As an empirical matter, the view that suppression of markets is conducive to prosperity and poverty alleviation is false. Second, I show that liberal tolerance cannot possibly apply to economic beliefs because these beliefs are empirical, not normative. Empirical beliefs are either true or false, and international law should promote, and rest upon, true empirical views. Therefore, international law should *not* be agnostic between capitalism and market-suppressing socialism. Finally, the idea that nations or peoples or states choose economic systems is obscure and thus problematic as a centerpiece of international law and ethics.

2. The Role of Productive Rights in Economic Growth and Poverty Alleviation

The economic literature speaks in one voice about the role of markets in creating prosperity and alleviating poverty. This role is undeniable both for domestic and international markets and is consistent with various views about the extent of wealth redistribution. Domestically, regardless of the presence or absence of protection of productive rights in national constitutions, the correlation between the recognition of productive rights and national wealth, including poverty reduction, is very strong. Internationally, the same correlation holds: the gradual opening of markets has caused a dramatic reduction of global poverty in the last hundred years or so. This point is independent of whether or not successful nations have implemented redistributive policies. As Acemoglu and Robinson show in their path-breaking study, successful nations have established *inclusive* institutions, that is, institutions that enable positive-sum social interactions. In contrast, unsuccessful nations have established *extractive* institutions, that is, institutions that enable mostly zero-sum social interactions (Acemoglu and Robinson, 2013). The recognition of productive rights is the centerpiece of inclusive institutions. Successful nations have varying degrees of governmental intervention in markets. Surely some of them are justified, some are not. But all those nations have robust capitalist markets.

The economic theory that supports the superiority of capitalist markets over alternative arrangements like socialism is straightforward. As Harold Demsetz famously argued, property rights allow people to internalize costs and benefits of their economic activity (Demsetz, 1967). Acemoglu and Robinson underscore the same point: "Economic institutions

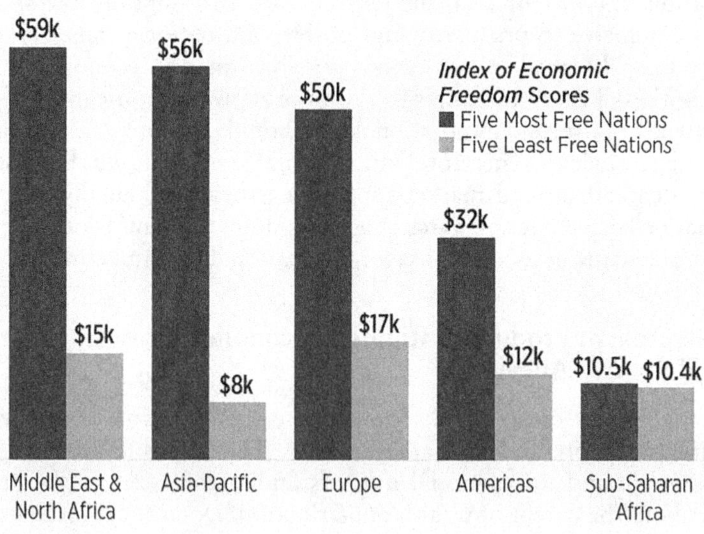

Figure 7.1 Nations with more economic freedom have stronger economies
Source: Tyrell, 2018

foster economic activity, productivity growth, and economic prosperity. Secure property rights are central, since only those with such rights will be willing to invest and increase productivity" (Acemoglu and Robinson, 2013: 75).

What theory predicts empirical studies confirm (Simon Fraser Institute, 2018). Nations that recognize productive rights outperform those who don't along many indicators. Figure 7.1 shows a typical chart (but the data are available at multiple sources).

The specialized literature concurs (Barro and Sala-i-Martin, 2003; Berggren, 2003; Easton and Walker, 1997; Gwartney, 2009; Gwartney et al., 1999; De Haan and Sturm, 2000; McCloskey, 2006, 2010, 2016). I believe that, whatever other criticisms socialists may have of capitalist markets, the empirical matter is settled. Even Marxist philosophers such as G A Cohen concede that capitalism generates wealth, and that the socialist objections to capitalism are purely normative (Cohen, 2009). It follows that *any* political view sincerely committed to human flourishing, and in particular to uplifting the poor, should endorse robust markets. Classical liberals, libertarians and liberal egalitarians all should be united in their support for productive rights.

The issue gets confused in academic and political debates because egalitarians and classic liberals disagree on the nature and extent of *corrections* to the market. Thus, the real debate, one consistent with sound economics, is between defenders of social democracy, on one hand, and defenders of more laissez-faire arrangements, on the other. In contrast, the debate between capitalism and socialism presupposed by international lawyers is obsolete. The idea that successful social democracies like Canada, Sweden and Denmark are socialist societies is a myth fostered by a nostalgic reluctance to bury socialism once and for all. Those societies are thoroughly capitalist, not socialist. They protect productive rights even more than the United States, which in the popular imagination is the archetype of laissez-faire (Heritage, 2018).

What about human rights advocates? If they sincerely cared about the poor and human welfare, they would enthusiastically endorse productive rights. Unfortunately, this is not so. Mainstream human rights advocates are at best indifferent to productive rights, and at worst they openly reject them. Phillip Alston, for example, has angrily denounced attempts by German scholar Ernst-Ulrich Petersmann to incorporate a right to trade to the list of human rights recognized by international law (Alston, 2002). Most of Alston's argument is irrelevant to my purpose here, however. Alston (correctly in my view) denies that *positive* international law recognizes a right to trade. I am not concerned here with positive international law, however; as I indicated earlier, I am critical of international law *precisely* because it fails to recognize productive rights.

Alston, however, goes beyond positive law in two ways. He apparently disagrees with the economic foundation of productive rights, and he thinks that Petersmann's and my own reading of Immanuel Kant's work is flawed and that Kant's work cannot be cited in support of productive rights. I believe Alston is wrong on both counts (although whether or not Kant's work supports productive rights is immaterial, as the arguments in their favor are substantive, not exegetic). On the economic front, Alston gives no argument to deny the findings summarized in the previous section demonstrating the correlation between productive rights and prosperity, including poverty alleviation. He simply makes *ad hominem* attacks against F A Hayek, Milton Friedman and Randy Barnett without showing why these writers are wrong in defending productive rights. He thinks it self-evident that any sane human rights advocate should reject free markets. His is a glaring example of the economic illiteracy that plagues human rights scholarship and activism.

I am not exactly sure why the human rights community is hostile to productive rights, but I venture three reasons. The first reason is historical. Human rights advocates have traditionally shown sympathy for democratic socialism, for the idea that socialist societies are fine as long as they protect civil and political rights, and they may be even superior in protecting socio-economic rights such as the rights to education, food, shelter and health care. The modern human rights movement sees itself (perhaps proudly) as the child of both socialism and political liberalism. Economic liberalism is not part of that equation. The second reason is that human rights advocates may believe that productive rights clash with socio-economic rights. Governments must tax extensively to secure socio-economic rights. This means, they think, that productive rights must yield to the requirements of wealth redistribution which in turn is needed to protect socio-economic rights. Third, human rights advocates distrust big corporations for a variety of reasons. They regard these corporations as perpetrators of private oppression of various sorts, from abusing their bargaining power to influencing politics to polluting the environment with impunity. The surge and power of these corporations stems precisely from an excessive protection of productive rights, so protecting the weak and protecting the environment requires a *curtailment* of productive rights—the opposite of what I argue in this chapter.

These three arguments are questionable. That socialism had a historical influence on the law of human rights is irrelevant for judging the issue at hand. The evidence on the abject failure of socialism is now in, and the international community should be able to use the best empirical evidence available to make sure the human rights norms help, not hinder, people's lives. That evidence is a reason to *eradicate* socialism's influence on the law of human rights.

The second argument is more interesting. It is undoubtedly true that securing food, shelter, clothing, education and health care often requires collecting resources through taxation. But the optimal combination of productive rights and tax policy is open to question. Suppose that the law of human rights or the precepts of justice require a certain level of enjoyment of socio-economic rights. Call it SER—the ethically or legally required level of enjoyment of those goods. Accepting this does not commit us to endorsing vast coercive redistribution of wealth. It commits us to achieving SER. This can be done through a variety of means, the selection of which will be *entirely* dictated by empirical considerations. Sometimes SER will be achieved through a largely laissez-faire institutional scheme; some other times (more often perhaps) SER may be secured by a mix of robust markets and a safety net for the poor established through taxation. The point is that there is no requirement that SER be realized only, or even mostly, by wealth transfers. Market mechanisms may do the greatest (if not all) part of the job. And crucially, in either case, economic growth is a necessary condition of achieving SER. Free markets grow the economy. Indeed, the evidence suggests that the poor have not improved through wealth redistribution but by the recognition of their right to participate in the market as producers as consumers. As Deirdre McCloskey writes: "It is growth from exchange-tested betterment, not compelled or voluntary charity, that solves the problem of poverty."[11] To think that access to economic goods is made possible *only* by taxing the rich is to endorse a primitive conception of society: that all social interactions are zero-sum interactions, so we need to take from those who have plenty in order to give to those who have little. This may be necessary in some cases, but all the evidence indicates that capitalist transactions in liberalized markets do the greatest part in generating prosperity and, consequently, in alleviating poverty. If free markets are the best tool to secure the goods protected by socio-economic rights, then international law must endorse capitalism. At the very least, human rights advocates must concede that robust markets are a precondition of the realization of socio-economic rights.

The third argument, that productive rights enable unjust domination by private actors, is important, as it is prompted by real-life instances of egregious corporate misconduct. But in a way it misses the point. All the instances of corporate abuse that human rights advocates cite involve complicity of corporations with governments and are thus far removed from the liberal foundations of productive rights.[12] This is yet another instance where advocates target private corporations (justifiedly so) but often let the main culprits, the colluding governments, off the hook. Productive rights are at their best under market rules that are fair and clearly defined. The government should not pick winners or losers but allow producers, consumers and workers to compete freely. The abuse by corporations is the direct result of government intervention in the market. It is a sign of decay of the human rights movement, originally born to curb state power, that instead of calling for less state involvement in the economy (an involvement that is at the root of these corporate abuses), it increasingly calls for more state power, more regulations, more opportunities for governmental collusion with special interests and consequently more invasion of freedom and decrease in prosperity. Human rights advocates once talked truth to power. Today, they are largely the allies of power.

3. The Scope of Liberal Tolerance

The facts, then, are well established. Productive rights are instrumental to prosperity and poverty alleviation. What argument could there be, then, for international law's economic agnosticism? Maybe the following. In a world where different states (peoples, nations) endorse and pursue different conceptions of the good it is wrong for liberal states to impose liberal values on illiberal states (Rawls, 1999). According to John Rawls, as long as illiberal states are decent they remain members in good standing of the international community. This reasoning presumably applies *a fortiori* to economic regimes.[13] It is for each state to choose its economic system as it sees fit. Some states have capitalist economies, others have socialist economies and yet others have mixed economies. All of them should tolerate the others, and international law should not unduly favor one economic system over another. Rawls thus extends to international relations a central idea in his late work: reasonable pluralism (Rawls, 1991). International principles, he thinks, must cohere with the hard fact of reasonable pluralism. Different societies disagree about the conception of the good. Philosophical liberalism is but one such conception, and for that reason it cannot sustain a global theory of justice. Many societies around the globe sincerely endorse illiberal conceptions of the good, and liberal foreign policy, as well as the principles of international law, must acknowledge this fact. Prominent among these illiberal views is the denial of private property and freedom of contract—of productive rights. Given that persons in different societies have different political conceptions, it follows that societies *must* respect one another (provided they meet certain minimal conditions.) Liberal tolerance here does not merely mean that liberal societies are not entitled to interfere with (much less invade!) illiberal societies. Liberal tolerance does not even merely mean that liberal societies must accommodate illiberal ones for obvious reasons of peaceful coexistence. Liberal tolerance means something stronger: liberal leaders must *respect, and cooperate with*, decent illiberal societies. These illiberal regimes, Rawls thinks, must be treated as free and equal members of the international community. These illiberal conceptions are reasonable and thus decent enough to warrant respect. Liberal and decent illiberal societies share a common public reason anchored in their adherence to minimal moral values and mutual tolerance. On this view, called public-reason liberalism, just as individuals have different conceptions of the good and the state should remain neutral among them, so nations have different conceptions of the good and the international system should remain neutral among them.

This argument fails. Economic beliefs are *empirical* beliefs and thus they are true or false. They cannot be optionally dependent on a conception of the good. On Rawls's own view, the objects of liberal tolerance are illiberal reasonable comprehensive theories of the good. International public reason encompasses both liberal and illiberal comprehensive doctrines as long as they are reasonable. But then, liberal tolerance applies in principle to *normative* beliefs, not to *empirical* beliefs. Any theory of global justice must be consistent with the best empirical theories available. False empirical beliefs are not and cannot be the proper objects of tolerance and respect. Since socialism embodies false empirical beliefs it cannot count as a reasonable conception of the good. In light of the facts presented in the previous section, socialism is unreasonable. If most people in a society believe that the Earth is flat, then that is not a conception of the good that deserves respect. It is a mistaken empirical belief, and as such it is unreasonable. The fact that many people have false beliefs adds nothing to the plausibility of those beliefs, no more than the reverse. Whatever plausibility illiberal views may have will result from the reasons marshalled in their support, not from the fact that many people hold them. In light of the findings discussed in the previous section, those who endorse the suppression of productive rights are in error, just as those who deny climate science are in error.[14]

Economic beliefs are *not* normative beliefs. Say there is a debate within a society about whether or not Ricardian trade theory is sound. The government then submits the issue to popular vote. The referendum yields, by a slim majority, that Ricardian theory is false and that protectionist laws benefit most people in the country. Would then public-reason liberals say that such erroneous belief is part of the country's conception of the good? Would they say, for example, "Burma's conception of the good rejects Ricardian trade theory"? This is absurd. A majority rejecting Ricardian theory is no more entitled to respect than a referendum that says that the earth is flat.[15]

Climate change provides an interesting example. If (as I think) reliable environmental science supports the view that the Earth's climate is changing due to human activity, then a national referendum holding otherwise has zero value and cannot in good conscience be the basis of public policy. Scientific questions are decided by the scientific method, not by vote. Different nations may disagree on what *policies* to adopt given the scientific facts about climate, since those policies involve normative questions (such as what weight to give to the welfare of future generations). But nations (or peoples) are not entitled to determine their own climate facts as part of their conception of the good.

Or suppose that the World Health Organization is trying to address an epidemic in a region. The medical treatment is well known, and the WHO has garnered the pharmaceuticals to address the epidemic. One of the affected governments, however, bans the medications on the grounds that their use violates the national tradition of healing with magic rituals. Perhaps there is nothing the WHO or anyone else can do to get this government to accept the introduction of the drugs, but surely such tradition is unworthy of respect because it relies on a false medical theory. It sounds hollow (nay, ridiculous) to say that this nation is entitled to seek its own way, and in doing so, allow its patients to die. International norms concerning epidemics should promote true medical principles. It cannot have a clause that says that nations are free to address epidemics any way they see fit, even if those ways will predictably kill many.

As against this, writers invoke the principle of state sovereignty. If a nation chooses socialism it has to be respected because it is a sovereign choice, even if we think it is mistaken. This argument is as weak to deny productive rights as it is to deny civil and political rights. Perhaps the argument assumes that civil and political rights are morally required, while productive rights are not, that recognizing them or not is a mere matter of economic policy. On this view, a government that protects civil and political rights but socializes the economy is simply choosing a different economic path. But this begs the question against productive rights. If, as we saw, the evidence shows that productive rights are essential for prosperity, poverty alleviation and the pursuit of personal projects, then the sovereignty objection collapses because we have powerful reasons to protect productive rights, just as we have powerful reasons to protect civil and political rights. Just as oppressing women and minorities is no longer a matter of governmental choice, so adopting policies that immiserate people should no longer be a matter of governmental choice.

I said that reasonable disagreement applies *in principle* only to normative beliefs and not to empirical beliefs. The qualification is necessary to account for reasonable empirical disagreements. Some, maybe many, empirical theories are controversial. Experts disagree about the optimal tax policy, or about the best level of intellectual property protection, or about the causes of crime. In these cases, different people in different societies will have reasonable empirical disagreements, although those disagreements do not stem from different conceptions of the good but from the fact that the matter is controversial, unsettled, among experts who resort to the scientific method. Some critics of capitalism may say that the correlation between free markets and economic growth is controversial, but this, as we saw, cannot be seriously maintained in light of the massive evidence to the contrary. Denying the role of markets in the alleviation of global poverty is like denying that the earth is warming up due to human activity. The correlation between markets and growth is perhaps the *least* controversial economic proposition today. Denying it is unreasonable.

Think about what economic agnostics claim: governments are entitled, as a matter of sovereignty, to suppress markets, even if it is obvious to anyone who has impartially studied the issue that markets are a necessary condition for national and global growth, and, for that reason, of worthy social goals such as alleviating poverty and providing decent systems of health, education and the like. The relevant controversy is about *market corrections*, not about the benefits that markets provide. It makes sense for international law to be agnostic about the nature and extent of corrections to the market. But to say that international law should be neutral among economic beliefs is like saying that international law should be neutral among medicine and witchcraft, that the scientific method has not decided the question and hence remains controversial. The international law of human rights, which ended international law's traditional agnosticism towards traditional civil and political liberties, should incorporate productive rights to its list. Just as the international law of human rights encourages, to a degree, domestic *political* liberalization, so it should encourage domestic *economic* liberalization. International law should not enable ruling elites who implement economic systems that impoverish their populations. At present, international law allows governments to dispossess their subjects at will, while simultaneously placing limits on how much those governments may enact protectionist tariffs. The result is that a government will abide by international law if it massively *steals* from its subjects while trading with the outside world under the relatively liberal rules of the international trade system.

Defenders of international law's economic agnosticism may try a *deliberative* move. They may claim that citizens are entitled to make policy judgments democratically, even if those judgments are erroneous. On this view, deliberative democracy has moral priority over truth, as it were. The reason why outsiders should respect democratically chosen socialist systems, then, is not that socialism is true or good. Rather, we must respect the choice because it is a democratic choice. Not doing so would disrespect voting citizens and their political autonomy. But of course, this means that political deliberation will often be truth-insensitive (Pincione and Tesón, 2006). To address this problem, Thomas Christiano has argued that political deliberation must rely on "a kind of filter that separates out theories that have some substantial support within the expert community from those that do not. Beyond this the expert community seems to permit a wide variety of theoretical approaches to be used by politicians and ordinary citizens" (Christiano, 2012).

This deliberative move has some plausibility, then, only if the democratically enacted empirical doctrines are genuinely controversial. For example, the causes of crime in any society are genuinely controversial. Citizens may decide democratically to enact policies that rely on one of these controversial causes, perhaps as an experiment. Portugal has tried decriminalizing drugs; the United States has tried harsher laws; other countries may focus on the economic roots of crime and so on. Because experts genuinely disagree about the causes of crime, all these democratic choices are entitled to respect, at least provisionally, even if they turn out to be wrong. Conversely (to return to an earlier example) suppose citizens in a nation afflicted by an epidemic vote to prohibit the introduction of the drug that predictably will cure the epidemic. This is an unreasonable undemocratic choice that does not deserve respect. It cannot be saved by claiming that it is part of a comprehensive religious doctrine that recommends witchcraft as a remedy to disease. This is particularly true of democratic choices that harm many people precisely because those choices rest on false empirical beliefs. In this sense, the democratic choice to suppress markets is in the same category as the democratic choice to use witchcraft. Just as a democratic choice to oppress a minority deserves no respect, so a democratic choice to immiserate people deserves no respect. Christiano tries to avoid this conclusion by suggesting that expert opinion is divided enough on economic matters that citizens are allowed to adopt different economic policies that pick one of the controverted economic theories. This may be true, as I suggested, of the extent of market corrections in an otherwise market-based economy. It is not true of the view that markets are essential for prosperity. I read Christiano as worrying about the former, not the latter. If so, on Christiano's own view, political deliberation does not salvage socialism. A majoritarian decision to suppress markets is not entitled to respect. In Christiano's own terms, it fails to harness expert deliberation with political deliberation in a way that advances the interests of all.

(In passing: I'm not suggesting here any concrete remedy to force reasonable choices on governments or populations who have chosen unwisely. I make the milder point that *international law* should not be agnostic among economic doctrines but promote true ones.)

4. Can Collective Entities Choose Economic Systems?

There is another reason to challenge the economic agnosticism of international law. Whatever the merits of public-reason liberalism when applied to individuals, its extension to nations or peoples is problematic. Simply put, the idea that *states* (peoples, nations) choose an economic system is questionable. Many people think that just as individual autonomy is a value, so group autonomy is a value; just as persons pursue individual projects, so groups pursue collective projects; just as persons seek the private good, so groups seek the collective good. That pursuit by collective entities of the collective good may consist, it is thought, of embracing a socialist project, or a capitalist project, or something in between. This analogy, however, does not hold in a straightforward way. This is because the reasons to respect individual autonomy do not apply to group autonomy. Unlike an individual choice, a group choice (assuming it is discernible) is mediated by *coercion*. Consider the two real-life possibilities. In a dictatorship, the group's choice is the dictator's choice. No political theory I know would say that the dictator's choice must be respected because it is the people's choice. In a democracy, the majority decides and, presumably, this is the people's choice. But, here again, the majority has imposed its choice, backed by public force, to the minority. My point here is not that such choice ought or ought not be respected. My point is that the group choice, even in the more benign case of a democracy, is conceptually dissimilar to an individual choice. Groups do not have minds, or autonomy, or rationality. Only individuals do. It follows that the kinds of reasons to respect group choices are essentially different from the kinds of reasons to respect individual choices. Groups are collections of individuals where some cooperate but others dominate, exploit and prey on others. When an individual makes economic decisions (how to invest, spend, gift) she acts freely (with the usual caveats and exceptions). When a government devises a plan for society it coercively enrolls others in that plan, whether that plan is shared by many or few. This surely deserves a scrutiny that is not captured by simply saying that the nation chose its economic system.

To be sure, recent research suggests that groups may have ends, interests or projects that are not entirely reducible to individual ends, interests or projects (Pettit and List, 2011). But it does not follow that rulers can legitimately impose those ends at gunpoint on the dissenters within the group. Consider the earlier example of the Argentine government's expropriation of private retirement accounts. Perhaps under a group-agency analysis we can say that this dispossession was the will of the collective. But, even if true, that does not resolve the question of whether the collective (supposedly represented by the government) is morally *entitled* to dispossess individuals in this way. Even if it possible to make sense of the notion of a group's preferences as something different from the members' preferences, that says nothing about whether the group leaders are *justified* in imposing the group's will on the members.

My own view is that the realization of human ends, including those that can be realized collectively, should in the last analysis be the result of voluntary interaction among free individuals. There are no non-consensual goods for collectives, nations or tribes (over and above the goods of persons who constitute the collectivity) that group leaders can permissibly enforce. My claim is normative, not conceptual: the only morally valuable projects are (1) individual projects and (2) voluntary group projects. But I don't need that strong position to defend the point under discussion. All I claim here is that the fact that group agency is an intelligible concept says nothing about (i) the permissibility of political coercion by group leaders, or (ii) the permissibility of foreign interference with the group's goals. One reason for this is that the moral worth of collective choices cannot be cashed out in terms of autonomy, dignity or rationality. It follows that those group choices must be evaluated on their merits, and not on the purported value of the choosing itself.

I conclude that the idea of a nation, a state or a people choosing an economic system is muddled and, for that reason, it cannot be a centerpiece of international law and ethics. It rests on anthropomorphic conceptions of the state. These conceptions may have been useful in the past for various reasons, but they ring fragile and unconvincing. The truth is that persons make economic decisions and governments try to regulate those. Sometimes that regulation is morally defensible, sometimes it isn't. But it is dubious that societies choose economic systems. Some groups within those societies impose those choices on other groups. If so, there is no reason to respect policies that rely on empirically false economic doctrines. Those policies are unreasonable. We have all kinds of reasons to value individual choices. We lack similar reasons to value the attempt by some in a group to impose on others limitations on their freedoms, economic or otherwise.

5. Concluding Remarks

Well-founded and well-tested empirical considerations support the thesis of this chapter that the international system can no longer remain agnostic between capitalism, on one hand, and market-suppressing systems, on the other. The evidence for the superiority of markets for attaining valuable goals, in particular the alleviation of poverty, is massive. Current international law is outdated and unjust. It smacks of a primitive world of sovereign monarchs with ample power to oppress and dispossess their subjects. A modernized international law, one in accordance with the best empirical and normative theories available, cannot countenance national systems that immiserate their populations. Just as international law evolved from an exclusively ruler-centric system to one that, to a significant extent, recognizes and protects civil and political rights, so it must take the next step and promote and guarantee productive rights.

It is worth noting that this flaw in international law dovetails with another flaw in international law. The international system primarily protects rulers, not individuals. Under the guise of tolerance, international law enables rulers to increase their power by dispossessing their subjects. Governments, even good ones, like to have that power for a host of reasons. These include not only the possibility of personal enrichment, but also the opportunity to reward the special interests who help them remain in power, with or without elections. Any international law reform concerned with *persons* and not with rulers would take a hard look at the way the rules are currently designed. An international system that focuses on human flourishing *and* relies on the best normative and empirical theories and evidence available will surely recognize and protect productive rights.

Notes

1 The World Trade Organization materials can be found at its website: www.wto.org/english/docs_e/legal_e/legal_e.htm
2 Among legal scholars, Ernst-Ulrich Petersmann is the exception. See Petersmann, 2002.
3 See, *inter alia*, Article 1, International Covenant on Civil and Political Rights.
4 Universal Declaration on Human Rights, at www.un.org/en/universal-declaration-human-rights/ (accessed 20 November 2018).
5 European Convention on Human Rights and Fundamental Freedoms, at www.echr.coe.int/Documents/Convention_ENG.pdf
6 As examples, consider the outrageous behavior of the Italian government in *Beyeler v. Italy*, 5 January 2000, at http://hudoc.echr.coe.int/eng?i=001-58832, declared unlawful by the Court; and the Court's validation of Bulgaria's expropriation of part of the applicants' retirements in *Valkov and Others v. Bulgaria*, 25 October 1911, at http://hudoc.echr.coe.int/eng?i=001-107157.
7 See the summary at www.coe.int/en/web/echr-toolkit/protocole-1
8 A cursory examination of the vast dispossession perpetrated by successive governments in Argentina suffices to show that Article 17 of the Argentine Constitution is virtually dead letter. For a full examination of the issue, see Elías, 2014.
9 For a chart of the risk of expropriation by country, see www.theglobaleconomy.com/rankings/Expropriation_risk/ (accessed 21 November 2018).
10 I say "agnostic," not "impartial," to underscore that I'm addressing a different problem from the one addressed by Steven Ratner (Ratner, 2005). Ratner is concerned with the justification of differential duties within the international system. I offer here an external moral criticism of international law's economic agnosticism.
11 McCloskey, "Growth, not Forced Equality, Saves the Poor," *New York Times*, 26 December 2016, at www.nytimes.com/2016/12/23/business/growth-not-forced-equality-saves-the-poor.html. Mc Closkey's massive trilogy, cited above, provides definitive evidence that increasingly liberalized markets have improved humankind for at least 300 years. It is not possible to argue any longer that the role of markets in poverty alleviation is controversial.
12 For example, the facts in the *Kiobel* case disclosed brutal behavior of the Nigerian government, who violently repressed people in order to protect the corporation's interests. *Kiobel v. Royal Dutch Petroleum Co.*, 133 S. Ct. 1659 (2013).
13 One would expect that Rawls would expressly recommend toleration of socialism and other market-suppressing doctrines, since refusing to do so would amount, on his view, to imposing economic liberalism on illiberal decent peoples. But, to be fair, Rawls does not say this—at least not with any clarity. To him, international public reason covers political, moral and religious doctrines. Economic doctrines do not fall into these categories. Yet, given Rawls's general hostility to laissez-faire ideas, I suspect that he would reject the thesis of this chapter and recommend tolerating socialism. I don't think he would be entitled to do so, given his assertion in *Theory of Justice* that parties in the original position know "the principles of economic theory" and general theories and facts about human society (Rawls, 1971: 137–138). If, as the evidence shows, economic growth is a necessary condition to lift people out of poverty, and if capitalism, but not socialism, does precisely this, then the international system cannot be agnostic between capitalism and socialism on the grounds that socialism is a comprehensive theory of the good deserving of respect.

14 Gerald Gaus makes the important point that a system of private property reduces significantly the burdens of public justification (Gaus, 2011). This is why he thinks public reason supports a strong system of property rights.
15 For an argument of why protectionism is inconsistent with *any* reasonable theory of justice, see Tesón, 2011.

References

Acemoglu D and Robinson J (2013) *Why Nations Fail: The Origins of Power, Prosperity, and Poverty*. New York: Crown Business.

Alston P (2002) Resisting the Merger and Acquisition of Human Rights by Trade Law: A Reply to Petersmann. *European Journal of International Law* 13: 815–844.

Barro RJ and Sala-i-Martin XI (2003) *Economic Growth*, 2nd ed. Cambridge MA: MIT Press.

Berggren N (2003) The Benefits of Economic Freedom: A Survey. *The Independent Review* 8(2): 193–211.

Christiano T (2012) Rational Deliberation Among Experts and Citizens. In: Parkinson J and Mansbridge J (eds) *Deliberative Systems*. Cambridge: Cambridge University Press.

Cohen GA (2009) *Why Not Socialism?* Princeton: Princeton University Press.

De Haan J and Sturm JE (2000) On the Relationship Between Economic Freedom and Economic Growth. *European Journal of Political Economy* 16: 215–241.

Demsetz H (1967) Toward a Theory of Property Rights. *American Economic Review* 57: 347–359.

Easton, ST and Walker MA (1997) Income, Growth, and Economic Freedom. *The American Economic Review* 87: 328–332.

Elías, JS (2014) *The Constitutional Protection of Property Rights in Argentina: A Reappraisal of the Doctrine of Economic Emergency*. PhD Thesis, Yale Law School.

Epstein R (1988) *Private Property and the Power of Eminent Domain*. Cambridge MA: Harvard University Press.

Gaus G (2011) *The Order of Public Reason: A Theory of Freedom and Morality in a Diverse and Bounded*. Cambridge: Cambridge University Press.

Gwartney JD (2009) Institutions, Economic Freedom, and Cross-Country Differences in Performance. *Southern Economic Journal* 75: 937–956.

Gwartney JD, Lawson RA and Holcombe RG (1999) Economic Freedom and the Environment for Economic Growth. *Journal of Institutional and Theoretical Economics* 155: 643–663.

Heritage Organization (2018) 2018 Index of Economic Freedoms. Available at: www.heritage.org/index/ranking (accessed 3 December 2018).

Honoré T (1961) Ownership. In: Guest AG (ed) *Oxford Essays in Jurisprudence*. Oxford: Oxford University Press, pp. 107–147.

Kriebaum U and Reinisch A (2009) Property, Right to, International. *Max Planck Encyclopedia of Public International Law*. Online version.

McCloskey DN (2006) *Bourgeois Virtues: Ethics for an Age of Commerce*. Chicago: University of Chicago Press.

McCloskey DN (2010) *Bourgeois Dignity: Why Economics Can't Explain the Modern World*. Chicago: University of Chicago Press.

McCloskey DN (2016) *Bourgeois Equality: How Ideas, Not Capital or Institutions, Enriched the World*. Chicago: University of Chicago Press.

Moffett M (2008) Argentine Makes Grab for Pensions Amid Crisis. *Wall Street Journal*, 22 October.

Petersmann EU (2002) Time for a United Nations "Global Compact" for Integrating Human Rights into the Law of Worldwide Organizations: Lessons from European Integration. *European Journal of International Law* 13: 621–650.

Pettit P and List C (2011) *Group Agency*. Oxford: Oxford University Press.

Pincione G and Tesón FR (2006) *Rational Choice and Democratic Deliberation: A Theory of Discourse Failure*. Cambridge: Cambridge University Press.

Ratner S (2005) Is International Law Impartial? *Legal Theory* 11: 39–74.

Rawls J (1971) *A Theory of Justice*. Cambridge MA: Harvard University Press.

Rawls J (1991) *Political Liberalism*. New York: Columbia University Press.

Rawls J (1999) *The Law of Peoples*. Cambridge MA: Harvard University Press.

Simon Fraser Institute (2018) Economic Freedom of the World. Available at: www.fraserinstitute.org/studies/economic-freedom-of-the-world-2018-annual-report (accessed 20 November 2018).

Tesón FR (2011) Why Free Trade Is Required by Justice. *Social Philosophy & Policy* 29: 126–153.

Tyrell P (2018) These 3 Charts Show the Importance of Economic Freedom. Available at: www.heritage.org/international-economies/commentary/these-3-charts-show-the-importance-economic-freedom (accessed 1 December 2018).

Van der Vossen B and Brennan J (2018) *In Defense of Openness: Why Global Freedom Is the Humane Solution to Global Poverty*. New York: Oxford University Press.

Part III

Economic Liberties as Human Rights

8 Making a Living

The Human Right to Livelihood

Amanda R. Greene

1. Introduction[1]

In 1981 the Bombay Municipal Corporation initiated plans to evict pavement dwellers from public highways. The targets for eviction were occupying pavements designated as public thoroughfares because they could not find affordable housing after having migrated from rural areas to seek employment. Eleven of these occupants petitioned for a review of their case by the Indian Supreme Court in 1985, just before the eviction. The court held that the pavement dwellers were not entitled to squat on public lands. But it also held that their expulsion would violate their right to livelihood, since it would prevent them from accessing nearby employment, without which they would not be able to provide for their own basic needs. So although the court upheld the eviction, it also required that the Bombay Municipal Corporation identify alternative housing that would allow the pavement dwellers to continue earning a living in the city. The court held that preserving their access to a livelihood was a necessary element of their right to life (Olga Telis & Ors v. Bombay Municipal Council).[2]

There has been relatively little philosophical analysis of the judgment underlying this ruling, namely, that there is a human right to livelihood. In what follows I take several steps towards a defense of this judgment. I understand a livelihood to be the ability to reliably generate personal income that is sufficient for providing for one's own material well-being.[3] In my view, this requires conditions that go beyond what is covered by other economic rights claims—like freedom of occupation, the right to work or the right to personal property. Therefore, the claim that there is a human right to livelihood requires its own defense.

I will formulate my arguments in a way that fits the account of human rights advanced by Joseph Raz. This account begins with an understanding of a right as something that connects interests with duties. The justification of a distinctively human right then proceeds through three stages of analysis.[4] First, a moral right is justified in virtue of some human interest, provided that the interest is sufficiently important to hold others to have duties, and provided that the interest can be served or protected by those duties. Second, a moral right qualifies as a *constitutional* right, only if the interests at stake can be effectively protected through legal processes. And then third, a constitutional right qualifies as a *human* right, only if it is appropriate for it to be enforced through international human rights law—that is, a system of social practices whose distinguishing feature is setting boundaries on state sovereignty.[5]

My argument follows this three-stage justificatory sequence. Much of the work involves showing how having a livelihood contributes to important elements of well-being. I argue that it contributes to individual well-being through providing a sense of (i) control over resource inflow, (ii) "social contribution" esteem and (iii) self-provision (§2). In addition to these direct contributions, I argue, the right to livelihood contributes indirectly to well-being through the collective good of the free market (§3). Then I argue that these aspects of well-being are sufficiently important to hold that others have duties corresponding to them (§4). Finally, I argue that access to a livelihood meets Raz's criteria for being a human right, because the protection of the right to livelihood is an area in which states are not immune from international accountability on grounds of their sovereignty (§5).

2. How Livelihood Contributes to Well-Being

On Raz's definition, "X has a right if X can have rights, and, other things being equal, an aspect of X's wellbeing (his interest) is a sufficient reason for holding some other person(s) to be under a duty" (Raz, 1986: 166). And thus "to assert that an individual has a right," for Raz, is to say that "an aspect of his wellbeing is a ground for a duty on another person" (180). In this account Raz is assigning rights a unique position in the normative landscape. They have a distinct role in practical thinking—in essence, "grounding requirements for action in the interests of other beings" (180)—and so they must be justified in those terms.[6] This means that if we are to accept some putative rights claim, the interests protected by the putative right must be sufficiently important to justify us in holding others duty bound with respect to them.

But then how do we show that some aspect of individual well-being is important enough to generate duties for other people? Simply put, we need to identify some credible grounds for regarding those aspects of well-being as significant ones, and then show that these grounds are not defeated by conflicting reasons (Raz, 1986: 182).[7] And we also have to present a plausible specification of the duties that address the interests at stake in the right. If we want to show that there is a right to *livelihood*, then, we will need to explain why the right-holder's interest in a livelihood is sufficiently important to regard others as having duties corresponding to it. My strategy for explaining these grounds begins by describing the ways in which having a livelihood contributes to well-being. Having a livelihood contributes to well-being because it addresses three fundamental human interests: control over how we secure resources, social contribution esteem and a sense of self-provision. I will take these in turn.

2.1 Control Over Resource Inflow

It matters for our well-being that we have some control over our "resource inflow," i.e., the means through which we secure our resources. The level of control in question is more than economic *security*, but less than full economic *independence*. Economic security implies reliable access to adequate material resources. Of course this matters to our well-being and merits protection. But the way in which this security is achieved—specifically: our ability to have some sort of control over the process—also matters to our well-being. Amartya Sen describes this as the difference between a culmination outcome and a comprehensive outcome (Sen, 1997). For Sen, the latter is a function of how the outcome came about—especially whether it involved some exercise of agency—which is something that matters to an agent beyond the mere value of the outcome.

Having some control over resource inflow does not imply full economic independence.[8] Even for the very wealthy, resource inflow depends on other actors and external conditions. It is affected by changes in property values, taxation and interest rates, in the short term, as well as political stability, trade agreements and the mitigation of environmental threats, in the longer term. However, having a resource inflow that is dependent on these kinds of factors is not, in itself, injurious to someone's well-being. We should distinguish two questions: whether we economically depend on other people and things, and how we *relate* to our (inevitable) dependence. It matters for our well-being that we are able to exercise some agency in respect to this dependence. Wealth is straightforwardly useful for this, and this is one reason why the affluent seek to maintain their wealth. It puts them in a position to choose the mixture of economic dependencies that suits them. When we are able to influence our resource inflow, then we can make trade-offs between different goods that matter to us, such as prestige and leisure.[9] This affords us an important arena in which to match our day-to-day activities with our values and goals in life. And the importance of this matching is not negated by the fact that it can never be perfect, nor by the fact that some people have more scope for attaining it than others.

The importance of control over resource inflow applies to our entire lifespan, including the selection and pursuit of a livelihood. For instance, it matters that we have some ability to decide how much training we are willing to undergo in order to earn more or do more specialized work. Having control over resource inflow across a lifetime means having some ability to preserve or enhance our earning potential, so that we can bear various risks and plan for the future. It also means having some way to transfer earnings into savings and wealth which can then be used as a future income stream, for example, in various forms of self-insurance for retirement or disability.

Granted, one may doubt that having a livelihood is enough to ensure that a person exercises control over her resource inflow, given that income level is always partly determined by extraneous factors. But while it is true that labor is not the sole determiner of income levels, a person with a livelihood still has some power to intentionally act in ways that translate her time and talents into income.[10] She can calculate that this job or product has a price in her social context, and invest her time and energy in a way that—in combination with other predictable factors—leads to acquiring additional income. In other words, a person with a livelihood can increase her resources *according to* the time and energy she devotes to income-generating activities. Relatedly, when we have a livelihood we can *see* that our resources increase according to our income-generating activities. This means that our pool of discretionary resources is something we can deliberately and reflectively manage, at least to some degree. When a person has a livelihood, she can intentionally pursue and attain economic security through her own conscious efforts, and this ability to partly govern her resource situation is a significant contributor to her well-being.

2.2 *Social Contribution Esteem*

Livelihood matters for our well-being in another way. Paid work can provide a unique form of esteem—what I call *social contribution esteem*. I will explain this first by contrasting it with some related ideas. For one thing, social contribution esteem differs from having a vocation. A vocation is an activity one identifies with, which corresponds to one's sense of purpose or "fit," or sense of what makes life meaningful (Muirhead, 2004), and which figures centrally in how one organizes one's time and labor. Even starving artists—bereft of work, paid or unpaid—speak with pride about honing their craft over time. In short, a vocational commitment to an activity, even if unpaid, has positive effects on people's well-being and their sense of identity and self-respect (Veltman, 2016).

But enjoying social contribution esteem is not the same thing as deriving satisfaction from a vocation. Our work may be something that we personally identify with and value, but it also matters to us that our work is valued and recognized by our community. Compare the internal sense of a job well done that is enjoyed by a person chopping wood for his own fire, with the socially reinforced sense of a job well done that is enjoyed by someone who chops wood for the whole neighborhood. Kimberley Brownlee describes this as being a "social contributor," that is, having the sort of status that goes along with contributing to the well-being of other specific individuals (Brownlee, 2016).

Being recognized as a social contributor in this way conduces to our well-being, and paid work is a vital means to this recognition. Granted, certain forms of unpaid work are socially esteemed. But paid work offers a special kind of affirmation that one is a social contributor. As Adam Smith famously observed, "it is not to the pity or compassion of the butcher, but to his self-interest that we address ourselves."[11] In addressing ourselves to the self-interest of others, we put ourselves in a position to be recognized as someone who contributes something of value to them, by their lights. Paid work has this significance in part because it involves an accumulation of people's free spending choices. When we have a livelihood we make a product or provide a service that others freely pay for. In the social valuation of other people's work, as much as in any other context, actions speak louder than words. The customer or client who buys your wares, in the absence of any obligation or coercion, indicates a recognition of the value you can generate. And this recognition is determinate and measurable.

Other liberal theorists make similar points, albeit using different frameworks. For instance, some sympathetic critics of Rawls argue that paid work is an important source of social recognition, and therefore a necessary aspect of the realization of justice. They say that when individuals are not able to earn payment for goods and services, this undermines their two moral powers (Nickel, 2000) or their capacity for self-authorship (Tomasi, 2012). Others argue that without paid work, people lack what Rawls calls primary goods, or all-purpose means. The primary goods that relate to paid work include the fair value of political liberties (O'Neill, 2012: 83–89), holding jobs that involve authority, complexity and responsibility (Arnold, 2012: 99–103) and social recognition (Gheaus and Herzog, 2016: 78–79).[12] The thing that all of these authors agree about, with differing points of emphasis, is that paid work contributes to people's sense of themselves as being worth something to others, and that this esteem is vital to people's interests.[13]

Someone might doubt that market-based income furnishes us with social contribution esteem, and I want to address a few possible sources of resistance. First, someone might doubt that payments are meaningful signals of positive valuation. But this seems unduly skeptical. Suppose the deli owner believes that the long queue at lunchtime shows that his sandwiches are tasty enough to brighten the day of busy workers. Why think that he is confused or mistaken to believe that customers value his products? Even if he runs the only deli for miles around, it still says something that others are willing to pay for his sandwiches rather than packing their own. It is reasonable for him, as it is for many others, to consider spending a decent proxy for positive evaluation. An imperfect signal can still convey a great deal.

A different kind of skeptic might argue that esteem cannot arise from evaluations that are merely subjective, because people are often mistaken about what is good for them. People's spending choices do not correspond with well-being enhancement, the skeptic might think, and therefore we should not regard these choices as a proxy for genuine social value. But this misconstrues my point. Our evaluations and decisions often fail to advance our well-being—most notably in our choice of lovers, friends and pastimes. There are many reasons not to equate spending decisions with objective social value.[14] However, spending decisions are a fair proxy for whether people *believe* something is valuable. They indicate the perceived value to others of what we do, thereby furnishing us with the basis for being viewed by others as a contributor.[15]

Another possible source of resistance to the notion of social contribution esteem comes from those who doubt there is the right kind of connection between the product and the producer. When a person buys mass-produced clothing, so the critic might say, this does not mean that he values the lowly paid laborers who produced the clothing. And so, the critic might conclude, a buyer's appreciation of my product cannot meaningfully translate into appreciating me, the producer. But while it is true that purchasers generally value the product itself, rather than the laborer who produced it, that observation is compatible with my point. In fact, it is precisely because the appreciation is tied to the product, as distinct from the worker, that the worker is entitled to derive the sort of esteem that I am talking about. Consider an anonymized competition for a prize, or the blind review of a journal article. The maker is especially satisfied to be recognized for excellence when their identity is unknown. So the appreciation that furnishes the basis for esteem need not involve any knowledge of or concern for the identity of the producer.

Still, one might worry that esteem cannot attach to the producer if the product or service is not appreciated by the buyer for the right reasons, or appreciated on the basis of the values that drive the producer. Otherwise, one might think, the worker risks feeling alienated whenever they deviate from their ideal of excellent work in order to turn a profit. But again, this misconstrues my point. I grant that there is a tension in any form of productive activity that is aimed at appealing to others' interests. If I am a baker, I cannot merely seek to bake the best possible bread according to my highly refined judgment. I must also think about the cost. And yet, there is a kind of satisfaction that derives from producing bread that others recognize—in light of their alternatives—as worth buying. To produce in this way is to make a different sort of social contribution, but it is still one for which we can be esteemed. Those who operate in the world of enterprise normally connect social contribution with the generation of profit, as evidenced by their frequent talk of solving problems, meeting a need or creating value. They feel proud when they perform well enough to make an honest profit making things that people choose to buy, and it seems implausible to see this pride as simply misplaced or delusional. It is more plausible to see it as an instance of the enjoyment of social contribution esteem, which contributes to our well-being by giving us a sense that what we do is valued by others. (I return to this below, in 2.4–2.5.)

2.3 Providing for Oneself

The esteem that comes with being a valued social contributor is one thing, but it also matters to us that we can have the kind of self-reflective esteem that comes with looking after ourselves and our immediate dependents. Our use of expressions like "earning my keep" or "living within my means" suggests that we want to be able to see ourselves (truthfully) as capable of self-provision. And in order to see ourselves this way, we need some control over how our needs get met. There must be a cognizable connection—one that is mediated by our agency—between our efforts and income, on one hand, and the satisfaction of our needs, on the other hand. When such a connection obtains, it allows us to experience the dignity of self-reliance, because we have met our material needs through intentional, productive agency.[16] So this is another way in which having a livelihood contributes to well-being: it allows us to intentionally manage how we translate activity into needs-provision, thereby allowing us to see ourselves as a self-providing agent.

I am highlighting the relation between self-provision and *well-being*, but others have also emphasized its moral importance. For instance, in Zofia Stemplowska and Kimberley Brownlee's defense of a human right to financial inclusion, they identify an important connection between people's agency and their access to savings and credit.[17] The significance of self-provision is also recognized in debates about distributive justice, going back to early discussions of Rawls. Margaret Holmgren says that "the opportunity to progress by our own efforts is a fundamental interest in life" (Holmgren, 1986: 274), and on this basis she argues that contractors in Rawls's original position would choose "a principle of distribution which would ensure that they would each have this opportunity" (275). Plenty of philosophers working on distributive justice in the wake of Rawls allow that something like a sense of self-provision is important for its *instrumental* role in securing self-authorship, personal responsibility (Dworkin, 2000) and equal citizenship (Satz, 2010). But a sense of self-provision has a non-instrumental significance as well. It is important to our well-being in part because we have the fundamental interest that Holmgren identifies, in having a chance to progress by our own efforts. When we are not in a position to progress through our own effort, we feel shame and stigma. And so, because of this, a feeling of self-provision is crucial to our subjective sense of honor and dignity.[18]

For simplicity, I have been using the term *self-provision* to refer to providing for oneself as well as one's dependents. But I want to emphasize the importance of the latter. Consider the case of giving gifts to one's spouse or one's children on special occasions, like birthdays or holidays. If a person lacks any control over how his resources are used to satisfy his own needs and desires, then he cannot divert resources that would be spent on him in order to buy surprise presents for his children. Parents who are entirely financially dependent on the state are less able to make trade-offs between satisfying their own desires and the desires of their children. In essence, they are impaired in their ability to exhibit generosity with regard to resources.[19] We need a greater degree of control than this—both over the resources which are used to provide for our needs, and the needs of others in our household—in order to have the sense that we are supporting ourselves, in the special sense that conduces to our well-being.

2.4 Unearned Income Support

I have identified three aspects of well-being that the right to livelihood serves: control over resource inflow, social contribution esteem and a sense of self-provision. Articulating these goods raises the question: why can income from public coffers not deliver the same result, perhaps even with a greater sense of security and dignity? I think that market-based income is superior to publicly financed income in delivering these goods—sufficiently superior, in my view, to merit protection as a right. In large-scale societies, there are essentially two alternatives to market-based income: publicly funded (unearned) income support—which I will discuss in this subsection—and publicly funded (earned) income—which I will discuss in the next one.

Someone may doubt that earned income is better than welfare benefits or other forms of unearned incomes, especially if the former is unpredictable and precarious. While it is impossible to say that earned income is better in every respect and every circumstance, it is plausible that earned income is generally superior in providing social contribution esteem and a sense of self-provision. When it is clear to everyone that an income supplement is based on need, the recipient cannot attain contribution esteem. If the recipient were *not* seen as lacking the ability to support themselves, there would be no basis for publicly financed supplemental income.[20]

Someone might nevertheless say that need-based income provides a valuable form of social recognition. I accept this point, but I resist the idea that it can serve as a basis for social recognition as a contributor.[21] Children receive social recognition, but they are not expected to be contributors, nor do they feel shame when they are not. Welfare benefits normally require you to periodically supplicate a bureaucrat with a performance of your human neediness in order to secure income.[22] Whether you get access to income, in that setting, depends on public officials' recognizing your worthiness as an object of public charity. Being viewed this way can be deeply alienating and objectifying. By contrast, having a livelihood allows you to be recognized as a contributing member of society without having your personal worth as a human being evaluated. It enables you to see your income as arising from the unforced recognition by others of the value of what you can provide. Notice that, in this dynamic, the buyer is not recognizing *you* as valuable, but that something you *provide* is valuable. This detaches the social worth judgment from the person, and transfers it onto their labor or products. Only then can the resulting income be viewed as a signal of social contribution, and only then can it serve as a source of social contribution esteem.

For similar reasons, unearned income support offers less of a sense of self-provision than market-based income. What would it mean for a person to derive a sense of self-provision from income support when it is not tied to any work they perform or goods that they provide? It might be argued that the person receiving income support could be required to engage in various civic activities, such that they contribute in some way to the social order. But then in those circumstances they effectively become public employees. Granted, in some cases, governments create "fake jobs" as a mechanism for the ongoing delivery of income support. In these cases, recipients are required to show up, and to clock in and out, for jobs that are superfluous—that is to say, the tasks specified in the job description manifestly do not need to be done. The person cannot lose the job for poor performance, but only for poor attendance. So there is a nominal connection between having a job and receiving income, but the connection is not based on performing the elements of the job. Under these arrangements, then, the income that arises from the employment bears no relationship to the value of the work being performed. It is simply a way for the government to operationalize a program of income transfers without it appearing that the income is "for nothing." The fact that this connection is broken—and is recognized as broken by most people—makes it more like unearned income. As such, it has little to offer by way of social contribution esteem and a sense of self-provision.

2.5 Market Income

This brings me to the second contrast case, that of government employment. I understand a system of government employment as one in which (i) the state is by far the dominant employer, and (ii) salaries are financed through taxation. (Hence I am excluding a mixed system of government and private employment, such as health care in the U.S.) I think that market income is superior to government employment in providing control over resource inflow, social contribution esteem and a sense of self-provision. This superiority is due to two features of government employment, namely, reduced discretion and the politicization of salaries.

The first point of contrast has to do with the control and discretion available in market employment. No doubt government employment can provide many of the goods of work, including a sense of meaning and dignity. But when the government is a *de facto* monopoly employer, crowding out alternative employers for a given job, this situation reduces the scope for individual control over resource inflow, for instance, in salary negotiations. This is partly because market-based income provides a wider range of options. For instance, the feasibility of exiting a particular buyer-seller relationship is likely to be greater in an open market. And the introduction of alternative buyers and sellers in the future is also likely to be greater in a market (provided there is no regulatory capture by industry). So far as this is the case, a system of market-based income furnishes us with a greater range of options in terms of our economic dependencies. Our dependencies may be diffuse or concentrated, according to our determination. What accounts for the fact that those dependencies we choose, taken together, enable us to earn a living is that they are connected through the intentional action of a single individual. Therefore, our individual agency plays a role in assembling our particular set of dependencies, including determining their relative concentration.

This comparatively greater range of options has a further benefit: more discretion over the execution of livelihood activities. If one fails to provide a quality product to one's customer, then one may lose that customer, without losing one's entire business. This is not true when the buyer is the state; the stakes are much higher, thereby decreasing the scope and incentive for experimentation and improvement. And so there is a different sort of dependency on "paying customers" when one has discretion over which customers or clients one engages in commerce with, as opposed to only being able to sell one's medical or educational services to the state. In sum, the lower stakes when the transactions are individualistic and atomized allows for individuals to exercise more discretion over the terms of their economic security, because they have more room for experimentation and improvement.

Notice that this is more than the simple value of control: it reflects the satisfaction of being able to exercise discretion according to one's expertise—whether one be a midwife, plumber or engineer. To the degree that professions are brought largely under government employment, this discretion is reduced. For example, a teacher who is employed in a state school becomes a functionary of the state, and is thereby obliged to modify her methods and approach to teaching to accommodate this role as a civil servant. Due to the terms of her contract, there are constraints on her ability to experiment with different modes of teaching to see if they improve student learning. She also cannot hone her craft as a *livelihood*, because she will not earn more money if she does a better job at teaching students than her peers. So the ability to exercise control and discretion over *the way* in which one's efforts lead to more or less income is present in a different way. The diffusion of dependencies and increased scope for craft-like discretion requires a greater exercise of agency in the generation of income, thereby creating a more robust sense of self-provision.

The second distinguishing feature of government employment is the politicization of salaries. When the government is the dominant employer of teachers and doctors, the determination of their salaries reflects a different set of considerations—in essence, the vicissitudes of politics—than if it were set on the market. The fact that public budgetary decisions should not be taken as reflecting the valuations of a society at-large has been amply demonstrated by public choice economics. Two findings matter for our purposes.[23] First, the results of legislation do not correspond to the preferences of the median voter.[24] Second, even when the legislative will does a decent job reflecting popular valuations, it is easily distorted by the political dynamics of a bureaucracy.[25] Thus there is a double divergence: the divergence between the valuations of voters and legislative decisions, and the divergence between legislative decisions and bureaucratic discretion. This puts considerable distance between the salary of a teacher or railway worker and the perceived value of their contribution by wider society. The gap is distorted by politics in ways that make it harder for a worker to see their salary as reflecting their perceived social contribution.

Market income better furnishes us with social contribution esteem, then, because the determination of payment is closer to the perceived value of what is provided. In a market, income results from payment for service based on perceived quality, rather than electoral politics, lobbying or the government bureaucrat's incentives.[26] On the market, you normally increase your income not by applying political pressure, but by making better widgets, working longer hours or working more efficiently. In other words, you intentionally set out to increase your income through engaging in activities that others regard as valuable. This better aligns the *fact* of income with the *recognition* of the value of the product or service by those receiving it. This alignment is weakened when the employer is the public-at-large. In that case, those who control the budget must be persuaded to continue paying you, even though they are only distantly related to the beneficiaries of your services, and their incentives all run in another direction. You are more likely to feel that your work is a valuable contribution when conditions are such that there is a perceptible link between the quality or quantity of work and the resulting income, which allows for a certain self-satisfaction in translating your effort into income.[27] In sum, then, earned income better delivers the goods of paid work, and thus more effectively conduces to our well-being, when it derives from a market system.

3. The Significance of Livelihood

So far I have argued that a right to livelihood serves the individual well-being of the right-holder. But there is another potential defense of the right to livelihood that can be spelled out in terms of collective goods. Raz says that his account requires "that a right be justified by the service it does to the interest of the right-holder," while allowing that "the value placed on that interest may derive from its usefulness to others" (Raz, 1986: 247). He illustrates this by describing the nature of a journalist's right to protect his sources:

> The journalist's interest is served by the right. But it would not deserve our respect . . . but for the fact that through protecting his interest one serves the interest of all in the free circulation of information which is of public interest.
>
> (247–248)

As the example suggests, some rights receive their justification indirectly through an appeal to collective goods, that is, benefits to the public from which no one can be excluded. Can a right to livelihood be defended via this route? I think it can. In order to show this, first I need to clarify the connection between rights, autonomy and collective goods. According to Raz, there is no right to autonomy *per se*. Rather,

> Personal autonomy . . . serves to justify and to reinforce various derivative rights which defend and promote limited aspects of personal autonomy. But in itself, in its full generality, it transcends what any individual has a right to.
>
> (247)

Autonomy is not something you have a right to directly, for Raz. Rather, it is an overarching ideal that specific rights serve to defend and promote. So individual rights can (and should) be upheld in the service of this ideal, and authority can be exercised in upholding these rights. But respect for a person's rights is not simply *identical* to the person's having autonomy. Rather, individual rights are justified indirectly, insofar as they are means for securing collective goods which *enable* people to be autonomous. And the free market should be counted among these collective goods, according to Raz—provided that it is understood in relation to an appropriate normative backdrop.[28] In particular, Raz wants to remind us of the shared assumptions about the proper limits of market activity that have guided and conditioned the emergence of market institutions in liberal societies (252). If we understand the function of market institutions in light of those assumptions, he says, then we can recognize the free market as "a normative social institution"—not just an alibi for ruthless competition, or a hyper-prioritization of individual liberty, but rather "a network of practices and conventions relating to the conduct of negotiations, the communication of information, the avoidance of actions in restraint of trade, etc." When the free market is understood in those terms, Raz says, we can see its existence as a collective good.

> It benefits all who are subject to it and none of them can be excluded. The right to economic freedom, or the right to freedom of contract, does not exist in opposition to collective goods. Far from its purpose being to curtail the pursuit of collective goods, it presupposes and depends for its value on the existence of at least one collective good: the free market.
>
> (252–253)

Thus we have a picture on which certain individual rights (e.g., relating to property, or freedom of contract) serve as a means for securing a particular collective good (the free market), which then helps particular individuals to live autonomously. What remains to be specified is the mechanism through which the free market as a collective good enables our autonomy. Raz's proposal—though it is not fleshed out in great detail—is that the market fortifies cultural norms that are important for well-being (256). On my reading, what Raz calls "the free market" strengthens the customs and practices that assign cultural significance to personal responsibility, thereby promoting active civil relations, and avoiding widespread, passive dependence on government.[29]

3.1 Right to Take Responsibility

In order to provide some support for Raz's view of the free market, and its role in enabling autonomy as a collective good, I want to discuss a real-world case that bears out some key aspects of his view.[30] In the Cape York region of Australia, isolated indigenous communities currently live on their ancestral lands in a government-run economy. In 1965 they became legally entitled to equal wages, which rapidly accelerated the decline of indigenous employment in the region (Ergas, 2014). Over time publicly financed support has grown from individual unemployment benefits into permanent income transfer arrangements, along with state delivery of goods and services. This has led to a situation in which the members of the community have little incentive to find work in the "real economy."[31] They also do not have ready access to the economic opportunities available in wider Australian society. Moreover, the provision of income, housing and education with limited participation from the community has had corrosive effects on social norms. Children do not attend school, substance abuse (and child abuse) is rampant and the incarceration rate is over 20 percent.

A leader within one of these indigenous communities, Noel Pearson, has been campaigning for welfare reform for several decades. In a policy paper written in response to the devastating dependence on welfare that he witnessed in his community, Pearson argues that full service provision by the government takes away from communities a sense of responsibility—personally and communally—for their ongoing well-being and development (Pearson, 1999).[32] He argues that his people can only regain a sense of responsibility if the government respects their "right to take responsibility." He argues that this requires enabling participation in the market economy in which other Australians participate, noting that the current arrangement of systematic income transfers—interspersed with a few "fake jobs"—disincentivizes individuals from the pursuit of a livelihood.

According to Pearson, the right to take responsibility includes the opportunity to take risks and bear the consequences, without being disincentivized through permanent and widespread reliance on government service provision. While he draws on the agency-oriented approach outlined in *Development as Freedom* (Sen, 1999), Pearson's argument is distinctive because it incorporates an account of the devastating *communal* effects of being insulated from access to a free market. He says:

> Apart from depriving people of a real income, unemployment has other more serious effects that cannot be ameliorated, and indeed may be exacerbated, by long-term income support. These effects include psychological harm, loss of work motivation, skill and self-confidence, an increase in sickness, and disruption of family and social life. Indeed, chronic unemployment of whole groups of people or geographic regions leads to social exclusion, loss of self-reliance and self-confidence, and damage to psychological and physical health.
>
> (Pearson, 2005: 5)

The discussion of these problems leads to Pearson's key conjecture, which is that economic engagement is essential to both individual well-being *and* communal well-being.

> To get at issues of agency, self-esteem and identity, full engagement in the real economy is necessary. It is a fair opportunity to engage in one's own livelihood that underpins skill, pride, purpose, a sense of achievement and fulfilment, dignity and hope. If these latent benefits of work were not vitally important, then passive welfare would not be the social problem it is. Finally, it is chiefly by working that parents convey the message to their children that opportunity exists for the taking, ensuring that attitudes of defeat are not inherited across generations. . . . As more members of a community become dependent on passive welfare, the adverse effect on a community seems to increase exponentially.
>
> (2005: 5)[33]

The circumstances that Pearson describes serve to illustrate the sort of collective degradation and demoralization that occurs when individuals in a community are systematically unable to pursue livelihoods. As such, the illustration lends support to the idea that the interest in livelihood is worth protecting due to its role in securing an important collective good.[34] Other illustrations could be given of the way in which access to a free market is an important collective good because of its relationship to the ideal of autonomy, for example, the aspiring actor who does low-paid contract work, or someone in an abusive relationship who is able to gradually escape by covertly engaging in the "gig economy." But in general I do not think it is too difficult to see why a free market—provided that it is enmeshed with other public goods—forms an important part of a healthy public culture.[35]

4. From Interest to Duties

In previous sections I have put forward two complementary ways of understanding how having a livelihood serves important human interests. But of course not everything that people have an important interest in is the object of a right.[36] Rights correlate with duties. The fact that I have an interest in something, *x*, does not automatically entail that others have a duty to secure *x* for me (Raz, 2010a: 36). In order to bridge this gap, Raz says, what is needed is "an argument which relies on the special character of the value that the right provides" (36).[37] In particular, Raz says that interests give rise to rights just in those cases where they give other people reasons for action; that is

> Only where one's interest is a reason for another to behave in a way which protects or promotes it, and only when this reason has the peremptory character of a duty, and . . . only when the duty is for conduct which makes a significant difference for the promotion or protection of that interest. . .
>
> (Raz, 1986: 183)

Raz qualifies this formulation by acknowledging that there may be other grounds for not holding people to be subject to a duty in relation to other people's interests.

> Where the conflicting considerations altogether defeat the interests of the would-be right-holder, or when they weaken their force and no one could justifiably be held to be obligated on account of those interests, then there is no right.
>
> (184)

So, Raz gives us three conditions that must be met in order for an interest to give rise to a right: (1) the interest is sufficiently strong to hold that others have a duty; (2) the conduct required by the duty makes a significant difference for the interest; and (3) conflicting factors do not defeat the duty. It *is not* a requirement under this account that we can give a precise specification of what the duties in question are. Raz says that we can know that a right exists "without knowing who is bound by duties based on it or what precisely are these duties" (1986: 184). For example, he thinks that the duties related to the right to education are indeterminate, and in some sense unpredictable (185). So it is not necessary to exactly specify the correlative duties for the right to livelihood in order to develop a Razian defense of it. On the other hand, it is useful to have an indicative sketch of those duties, especially if we are going to say that the duties should be enshrined in constitutional and international law.

The duties related to livelihood can be categorized as either duties of *restraint*, or duties of *promotion*. Some of these duties fall on employers, in my view, and others fall on governments. One kind of duty of restraint is avoiding unnecessary restrictions on trade. An example of this kind of action is superfluous licensing regimes, like those that make it illegal for beauticians to sell their services without paying a registration fee to the government. Granted, the public has an interest in independently verifying the beautician's qualifications. But this can be equally well served by private or professional accreditation bodies. So a government licensing regime in this context unnecessarily constrains trade—indeed, one might argue that it is a form of rent-seeking. Duties of restraint also include allowing individuals to contract and sell their labor on their own terms, provided there is no workplace violence or abuse. For instance, our interest in livelihood requires the government to allow employment in temporary contracts without holidays or maximum hours restrictions. (I will come to countervailing considerations below.) Some duties of restraint related to livelihood also apply to employers, such as refraining from driving wages down when the profits are well above the cost of capital (Rangan, 2015).

The duties of promotion associated with a right to livelihood apply to both governments and businesses. For businesses, they include fostering the long-term well-being of workers—for example, by providing access to paid leave and skills upgrades, so that their earning potential does not necessarily fall through exploitation. For governments, duties of promotion include taking reasonable steps to provide economic opportunities, including things like access to markets, access to credit and access to employers. People must be able to access a reasonable range of buyers and employers in order to sell their goods at whatever price and on whatever terms they choose. Similarly, individuals must be able to access a range of sellers and laborers in order to have some control over how their needs are met. Individuals should also have access to financial products that enable them to take risks, such as loans, insurance and investments (Stemplowska and Brownlee, 2015). The duties of promotion that fall on governments are therefore likely to include lowering taxes and tariffs, countering anti-competitive behavior, fostering foreign direct investment and enacting policies that promote economic growth.

Obviously, a government cannot singlehandedly guarantee widespread prosperity through flourishing markets. No one is obliged to do the impossible, as the Roman jurists say. But governments are uniquely positioned relative to the interests at stake. Government regulation of the economy makes a difference to people's livelihood, and thus it makes a difference to the related interests (one of Raz's provisions). Part of the reason that governments have a duty to promote economic opportunity for their citizens is that they are especially well positioned to do so.

4.1 Defeating Duties

The interests that would be protected through a formal recognition of the kind of duties outlined above are weighty. Certainly, they are similarly weighty to other interests that are protected under the aegis of human rights, for instance, interests in freedom of conscience, legal due process or an adequate standard of living. One who accepts this conclusion may still be reluctant to formally enshrine these kinds of duties, though. If recognizing the duties that correspond with a right to livelihood would make it impossible to impose sensible, measured and welfare-promoting regulations upon industry practices and labor markets, then so much the worse for the right to livelihood. However, this unwelcome implication need not follow. To recognize a rights claim is not to insist that the correlative duties can never be overridden by other considerations.[38]

Consider one way in which a government's duty to refrain from interfering with the terms of contract between workers and employers might be overridden. Suppose that the government could enact regulations requiring pension contributions or parental leave, thereby securing an important collective good, namely, the provision of a range of options for managing economic vulnerability. In certain contexts, securing this good through carefully engineered regulation is an aim that overrides the otherwise-applicable duty not to interfere in labor contracts. But at the same time, this conflicting consideration does not totally negate the relevant duty. Providing options for managing economic vulnerability is a worthy aim, but it does not follow that every labor contract should include pension provisions (e.g., freelance contracts), and it certainly does not give the government a license to interfere in labor contracts in whatever way it pleases. In short, we can recognize a *bone fide* right to livelihood, without adopting the implausible view that the government's correlative duties of restraint always eclipse every other concern.

Of course, not just *any* good can override the duties associated with a right to livelihood. Some argue that the collective good of a standardized national curriculum outweighs the livelihood interest of teachers that wish to contract with pupils voluntarily. But it is questionable whether placing the curriculum under the control of a national government is a collective good that is necessary for autonomy, and so it is not clear that this defeats the duties that protect teachers' livelihoods. To take another example, some argue that individuals should be protected from precarious employment by outlawing employment for fixed periods, e.g., in university teaching contracts. But it is unclear that eliminating the risk of loss and insecurity for every individual is a collective good that is sufficient to outweigh the protection of livelihood. I cannot offer a complete analysis of how we should resolve the thorny issues that arise in these sorts of conflicts, but the examples are enough to indicate how a Razian theory of rights allows us to see the right to livelihood as something that is not a source of infinitely stringent duties, while at the same time, something that is not easily outweighed.

5. Constitutional Right

Having furnished a Razian defense of the right to livelihood as a right *per se*, I now turn to the question of whether it ought to be considered a legal or constitutional right. Not every moral right is a legal right. On Raz's picture, this is because of contingent facts about the availability of fair and effective political institutions to enforce them. However, when rights pertain to the maintenance of the background political culture, then constitutional courts often *are* an appropriate enforcement mechanism. It is "usually perceived to be advisable to protect the stability of the basic political culture," Raz says, "by institutional arrangements which isolate it to some extent from the pressures of day to day politics" (Raz, 1986: 260). This implies that rights are suitable for constitutional protection when their justification pertains to collective goods that constitute part of the background political culture. He explains as follows.

> At least some constitutional rights are primarily means of formal or informal institutional protection of collective goods. They protect these collective goods inasmuch as damage to them is caused by harming the interests of identifiable individuals. . . . Where harming an individual seriously jeopardizes the maintenance of a public good, that harm is also a cause of a harm to the community. Therefore, there is in such cases an adequate instrumental justification for holding others to be subject to duties to refrain from such harm.
>
> (258)

The enforcement of these rights can be entrusted the judiciary, Raz says, since the "natural area of operation," for courts, is "dealing with disputes in which an individual has a special standing, and which relate to a limited, self-contained set of facts" (258–259). Insofar as the right to livelihood mirrors other rights that Raz thinks merit constitutional protection through the judiciary, like freedom of expression, his argument applies similarly. So constitutional courts seem like a suitable institutional mechanism for protecting the right to livelihood.[39] In sum, the right to livelihood meets all of Raz's conditions for being a constitutional right: it secures collective goods, which form part of the background culture, and it pertains to disputes in which individuals have a special standing.

5.1 Human Rights and Sovereignty

Can the right to livelihood be understood as a *human* right, under Raz's framework? Raz understands human rights as the subset of constitutional rights which "set limits to the sovereignty of states, in that their actual or anticipated violation is a (defeasible) reason for taking action against the violator in the international arena" (Raz, 2010b: 328).[40] Although a state's sovereign status does not license it to perform any action whatsoever, this status does mark off a sphere of protection for the state against external interference.[41] It entitles the state to say to outsiders, "whether or not I (the state) am guilty of wrongful action is none of your business" (328). The function of human rights claims, then, is to disable this "none of your business" defense.

Is livelihood inside or outside of the domain in which a state can refuse accountability by saying "none of your business"? Sometimes governments actively prevent their citizens from attaining livelihoods in order to maintain their tight grip on control, by maintaining a centralized, oligarchic economy. I consider this to be an egregious abuse of power, one that can lead to immense, widespread and preventable suffering. The "none of your business" defense seems about as intuitively satisfying, in this case, as it does when it is used to resist international sanctions or diplomatic pressure aimed at securing children's right to basic education, or the right to adequate health care.

Whether a state's sovereign status can be overridden in an attempt to remedy these failings depends on "the possibility of morally sound interference by others" (331).[42] When it comes to the right to livelihood, then, the question of whether it can be understood as a human right partly hinges on the question of whether there are mechanisms of international governance that would allow "morally sound" intervention in order to promote or secure it. The current system of international institutions seems at least as capable of sound intervention in this domain as it is in other domains that are recognized as human rights. For instance, bringing pressure to bear on the right to livelihood of West Bank Palestinians is at least as appropriate as bringing pressure to bear for the sake of their religious freedom.

Furthermore, there is another sort of consideration that emerges when we consider Raz's emphasis on the *point* of the human rights movement.

He credits human rights practice with two morally significant achievements in the last half-century. First is that it affirms individual worth through providing meaningful opportunities for ordinary people to stand up for other ordinary people. Second, it provides a counterweight to the concentration of power at the global level. He says,

> One of the most important transformations brought about by the pursuit of human rights has been the empowerment of ordinary people, and the emergence of a powerful network of non-governmental as well as treaty-based institutions pressurizing states and corporations in the name of individual rights. The human rights movement launched a new channel of political action, which continues to be a major corrective to the concentration of power in governmental and corporate hands.
>
> (Raz, 2010a: 41)

Given that the concentration of power in governmental and corporate hands is a major obstacle to people having a livelihood, it is important that people have an avenue to contest that concentration, in the form of human rights advocacy. It also appears that ordinary people find advocacy and support for the pursuit of livelihoods in developing countries appealing.[43] Thus recognizing a human right to livelihood enhances the morally worthwhile features of human rights practice that Raz identifies.

6. Conclusion

A remark commonly attributed to Warren Buffett is that he wanted his children to inherit enough money that they could do anything, but not so much that they could do nothing. Even the very wealthy share the commonplace intuition that making a living is an important part of people's well-being. I have argued that making a living is important enough that it merits recognition as a right. And using Raz's framework, I have argued that further conditions obtain which make the right to livelihood a distinctively human right.

The key feature of a right to livelihood is agency: resources for self-provision are attained *through* one's efforts, in a way that one can see is a result of one's efforts. Someone who has a livelihood experiences first-hand a causal relationship between her efforts, her income and the satisfaction of her needs. When a person has some degree of control over how her needs are met, she can feel that she is providing for herself. Because this complex of causal relationships connects a person's agency to her material status, thereby delivering a sense of contribution esteem and self-provision, it allows a person to experience a form of dignity. Other recognized economic rights do not necessarily secure these ends. The right to freedom of occupation does not address the connection between income and meeting one's needs. The right to an adequate standard of living (Article 25 UDHR) does not address the dignity of living within one's means. The right to employment without discrimination and at favorable remuneration (Article 23) does not address the difference between market-based income and publicly financed income, including welfare "fake jobs." The right to social security or basic income (Article 25) does not address the well-being gains that come from earned income. Finally, there is "the right to work." The right to livelihood as I have characterized it captures what matters about meaningful work, while going further in order to connect it to contribution esteem and self-provision.[44] Therefore, the right to livelihood is distinct from other economic rights that are enshrined in existing treaties and conventions.

This investigation of livelihood, in my view, has revealed some shortcomings in the idea of economic rights in general. Discussions of economic rights often proceed on the assumption that economic rights correspond to the freedom from poverty and deprivation. Consider this recent comment on livelihood from Louka Katseli, Greece's former Minister for Labor and Social Security:

> To me socialism is about the human right to employment and livelihood. It is about the right to basic needs and services. Economic democracy is another point. For instance, a heavily indebted person hardly has the power to negotiate with the bank, a consumer cannot negotiate with the supermarket. Power is asymmetric. People should have the power to bargain collectively if only to ensure their social rights.[45]

Politicians are not the only ones to speak in terms that reduce economic rights to economic security. For example, in their introductory essay to *Economic Rights: Conceptual, Measurement, and Policy Issues*, Hertel and Minkler say that "economic rights require that each and every person secures the resources necessary for a minimally decent life" (Hertel and Minkler, 2007: 3). Everyone agrees that deprivation is bad, but this claim neglects that there are better and worse ways for people to avoid deprivation. Income transfers and comprehensive government provision of services to a community have the potential to be socially corrosive and individually demoralizing. If all needs are met and all services delivered by the government, what room is there for making a living? The importance of livelihood has not been given enough emphasis in theorizing about the right to economic security—either in formulating its justification or in outlining its scope.

Moreover, economic rights are sometimes interpreted in ways that *conflict* with the right to livelihood. For example, Article 24 of UDHR declares a right to paid holidays, which is likely to reduce employment opportunities. Some philosophers argue that when individuals are legally permitted to undertake particular forms of economic risk, this undermines justice (Baderin, 2017). And some legal theorists argue that precarious forms of employment violate human rights (Mantouvalou, 2012). If the case for a right to livelihood is sound, these conclusions are premature. Prohibitions on financial risk and precarious employment can create serious threats to the right to livelihood, thereby complicating the idea of a human right to economic security. A proper consideration of the right to livelihood—which I have begun to undertake here, building on elements from Raz—calls for revision, or at any rate greater care, in our thinking about other economic rights.

Notes

1 For helpful feedback and discussion, I would like to thank Kimberley Brownlee, Chiara Cordelli, Adam Etinson, Anca Gheaus, Lisa Herzog, Tom Parr, Julie Rose, Robert Mark Simpson and participants in the Zurich conference held in preparation for this volume. For valuable editorial advice, I would like to thank Jahel Queralt, Bas van der Vossen and an anonymous referee. I wish to acknowledge that I was employed by Cape York Institute for Policy and Leadership for a few months in 2003, an organization founded by Noel Pearson, the Aboriginal activist whose views on Australian welfare reform are discussed in the chapter.

2 In 1999 the Bangladeshi Supreme Court drew on this precedent to condemn the expulsion of slum dwellers by authorities, on the basis that the expulsion violated their right to livelihood (Ask v. Government of Bangladesh).

3 This roughly follows the definition proposed by the Red Cross: "a means of making a living" which encompasses "people's capabilities, assets, income and activities required to secure the necessities of life" (IFRC, 2017).

4 My description is drawn from Raz's statement that human rights "normally derive from three layers of argument: First, some individual interest often combined with showing how social conditions require its satisfaction in certain ways (for example, via various forms of instruction) establishing an individual moral right. . . . The second layer shows that under some conditions states are to be held duty bound to respect or promote the interest (or the rights) of individuals identified in the first part of the argument. . . . The final layer shows that they [states] do not enjoy immunity from interference regarding these matters. If all parts of the argument succeed then we have established that a human right exists" (Raz, 2010b: 336).

5 Raz considers it a virtue of his account that rights depend on contingent facts about political institutions. Although this contingency implies that the status of the right depends on the practice in which it is embedded, it is not a form of moral relativism (Raz et al., 2003). To highlight the dependence on contingent social facts, he calls his account a political conception of human rights. For Raz, a political conception is manifest in all accounts that take their task to be "(a) to establish the essential features which contemporary human rights practices attributes to the rights it acknowledges to be human rights; and (b) to identify the moral standards which qualify anything to be so acknowledged" (Raz, "Human Rights Without Foundations," 2010b: 327). In contrast, he says that non-political conceptions lack "a convincing argument why human rights practice should conform to their theories" (327–328).

6 Raz's conceptual framework shares some features with the Wittgensteinian approach to rights that is developed in Anscombe, 1978.

7 I am paraphrasing the following technical specification: "An interest is sufficient to build a right on if and only if there is a sound argument of which the conclusion is that a certain right exists and among its non-redundant premisses is a statement of some interest of the right-holder, the other premises supplying grounds for attributing to it the required importance, or for holding it to be relevant to a particular person or class of persons so that they rather than others are obligated to the right-holder. These premisses must be sufficient by themselves to entail that if there are no contrary considerations then the individuals concerned have the right. To these premises one needs to add others stating or establishing that these grounds are not altogether defeated by conflicting reasons. Together they establish the existence of the right" (Raz, 1986: 181–182).

8 In my opinion, escaping all forms of economic dependence is not a coherent goal. In general, freedom from any kind of dependence is not a realistic goal, contra List and Valentini (List and Valentini, 2016). This is one reason why freedom is an ill-fitting term in discussions of economic justice. For a discussion of how indeterminacy and inconsistency in the concept of "freedom" is manifest in debates about economic liberty, see Gourevitch, 2015.

9 For a defense of the significance of making trade-offs between income and free time, see Rose, 2016.

10 I mean this in a straightforward way, which is consistent with acknowledging that social factors affect people's ability to translate effort into income. Acknowledging this does not force us to endorse either a Lockean or Marxian theory of labor.

11 In Vol 1, Book 1, ch. 2 of *Wealth of Nations*, originally published in 1776 (Smith, 1981: 26–27).

12 For instance, Martin O'Neill argues that if we redistribute only *ex post*, we risk creating a permanent economic elite, who hold all the power. Only when individuals have economic agency can they experience full self-respect, he argues. "Only by making sure that the structure of the economy is such as to broadly disperse control over productive resources," he says, "can we ensure that all citizens are able to have this 'lively sense' of their own agency, and in doing so to head off the possibilities of harmful inequalities of power and status" (O'Neill, 2012: 89). The reference to "lively sense" comes from Rawls, 2001: 59.

13 Of course, Rawls intended "social bases of self-respect" to apply well beyond the economic sphere, but it at least included economic activity. This is in contrast to someone like Michael Walzer, who sees the economic and political sphere as separable—and indeed, things that *ought* to be separate—in terms of the social standing that they distribute (Walzer, 1983). A critique of both views can be found in Anderson, 1995.

14 The most radical version of this sort of critique is the Marxian distinction between use value and exchange value (Marx, 1977).

15 Gheaus and Herzog discuss "social contribution" as one of the goods of work, but they deliberately divorce it from the income-generating element of work. They also appear to be focused on objective social contribution, whereas I focus on perceived social contribution (Gheaus and Herzog, 2016: 75–76). Theorists influenced by Hegel have also argued that work is a critical source of social recognition (Honneth, 1995; Hasan, 2015; Jütten, 2017).

16 It is worth noting that a key feature of alienated labor, for Marx, is that reproducing oneself (meeting one's material needs) must go through the intentional action of another (Wood, 1999).

17 Brownlee and Stemplowska draw an analogy between the human right to education and the human right to financial inclusion. They say that this right includes "having access to legitimate, appropriately designed financial

services such as a bank account, saving facilities, and borrowing facilities on reasonable terms"; and all of these provisions, they say, "expand persons' opportunities to shape their own lives" (Stemplowska and Brownlee, 2015: 48).

18 Among liberal theorists, Dworkin seems to be the most concerned with the idea of personal responsibility. However, as Debra Satz argues, it is not clear how that value is to be balanced against equality, the other fixed point in his value system (Satz, 2010: 68–75).

19 Aristotle makes the point in terms of private property. He says, "It is very pleasant to help one's friends, guests, or companions, and do them favors, as one can if one has property of one's own. But those who. . . [abolish] private property exclude these pleasures. They also [hinder] the virtues of temperance . . . and generosity. . ., since one cannot show oneself to be generous, nor perform any generous action" (*Pol. 1263b5-11)* (Aristotle, 1997, 33).

20 Income support is frequently offered on the condition that recipients prove that they are unable to find suitable employment. This condition reinforces the sense that if they had a job, they would not "need" income support. These sorts of conditional income transfers cannot plausibly be regarded as arising from a social contribution.

21 The distinction between contribution esteem and other forms of esteem helps address the worry about adequately including the young, elderly and disabled. I thank Chiara Cordelli and Anca Gheaus for pressing me to clarify this point.

22 A vivid dramatization of how being put in this position erodes one's self-respect can be found in the film, *I, Daniel Blake* (Loach, 2016).

23 Though I cannot address it here, further skepticism arises from noteworthy arguments that "the will of the people" can be informed (Lippmann, 1922), rational (Schumpeter, 1976) or coherent (Arrow, 1951).

24 As James Buchanan says: "median-voter models break down . . . even with simple budgetary allocation problems, when more than one dimension is introduced. If voters, or members of a committee, consider simultaneously several issues or dimensions, such as, say, spending on education and spending on police, the cyclical majority problem returns. And, related to this return, the multiplicity of dimensions allows for vote trading and logrolling" (Buchanan, 1984: 18).

25 Buchanan explains, "Recent developments in public choice theory have demonstrated the limits of legislative control over the discretionary powers of the bureaucracy. Modern government is complex and many-sided, so much so that it would be impossible for legislatures to make more than a tiny fraction of all genuine policy decisions. Discretionary power must be granted to bureaucrats over wide ranges of decisions. Further, the bureaucracy can manipulate the agenda for legislative action for the purpose of securing outcomes favorable to its own interests" (Buchanan, 1984: 19).

26 I have drawn a sharp contrast generically in order to highlight the point, but in some domains the contrast is less sharp.

27 I expect this argument is defeated when the job is to hold an office related to the administration of law. Holding an office involves the exercise of public authority and includes prosecutors and probation officers, though not prison janitors. For an examination of whether such roles must be publicly performed, see Harel, 2014.

28 He laments that liberals have sometimes failed to recognize this dependence: "[In the liberal tradition] many rights were advocated and fought for in the name of individual freedom. But this was done against a social background

which secured collective goods without which those individual rights would not have served their avowed purpose. Unfortunately, the existence of these collective goods was such a natural background that its contribution to securing the very ends which were supposed to be served by the rights was obscured, and all too often went unnoticed" (Raz, 1986: 251).

29 Many things can be meant by norms that assign significance to personal responsibility—it need not entail objective claims of moral desert. For example, it is compatible with broadly Rawlsian ideas of institutional desert or institutional merit (Herzog, 2017).

30 For further development of a Razian account of market legitimacy, see Greene, 2019.

31 Attempts have been made to engage in the "real economy." For instance, some communities have agreed to arrangements in which they receive dividends from the extractive industries that they permit to operate on their land. But normally they do not receive sustained employment opportunities, skills training or a share in ownership and governance. These dividends are unearned income, so they effectively function like the income transfers that would be delivered by the government through a welfare program.

32 As is clear to anyone reading the full paper, Pearson is at pains to acknowledge the causal role of past injustices. He emphasizes that his analysis does not absolve the unjust actors or reduce the pressure on continued efforts to rectify them, for example, through land rights (for which Pearson is a staunch advocate).

33 Pearson has been criticized for using the capability approach, both by theorists operating in the liberal tradition who wish to disavow Pearson, e.g., Johnson et al., 2016, and by critics of liberalism who hope to show that Pearson's ideas demonstrate just how misguided the liberal framework is, e.g., Bulloch and Fogarty, 2016. I lack space to address the criticisms here, but I think they often neglect the bigger picture, which is Pearson's emphasis on the erosion of traditional forms of taking responsibility for material provision (both individually and collectively).

34 Though it remains controversial, Pearson's emphasis on the neglect of livelihood opportunities has gained some acceptance as part of the explanation for deep problems in indigenous Australian communities. A 2012 newspaper article in *The Australian* reports: "[State] Premier Jay Weatherill, a former Aboriginal affairs minister, yesterday said the government's policies had 'robbed people of the autonomy and dignity that is necessary for them to be successful in their lives'. Premier Weatherill said, 'I think, in many respects, a number of things that we have done have robbed people of their dignity and capacity, and created an unfortunate dependence on government'. He said he agreed with Attorney-General John Rau. . . [that] the 'very mode of intervention' was a cause of the problems plaguing indigenous communities. 'Successive governments, state and federal, at least since 1967 have been chucking money and bureaucracy at Aboriginal communities across this country', Mr. Rau said. . . 'I can't help but feel that if you had to strip everything away, the fact that Aboriginal people, for whatever reason, have not been encouraged or enabled to have a sense of their own self-determination as individuals. But rather (they) have through no fault of their own largely been characterised as clients of a government agency, whatever it might be, is in some respects one of the causes of the problem we are looking at now'" (Owen, 2012).

35 It is important to acknowledge the hazards of cultural norms that overemphasize personal responsibility to the exclusion of all other relevant factors that determine economic status. These can lead to damaging discourse

and behaviors—for instance, the endorsement of unfair inequalities, "poor shaming" and so on.

36 On this point, the Razian approach has an advantage over other frameworks of political morality that emphasize agency and freedom—for instance, the capabilities approach as outlined by Amartya Sen and Martha Nussbaum (Robeyns, 2016). In my view, the capability approach lacks a clear and compelling account of rights and legitimate authority. However, it remains appealing as a philosophical theory of human development, suitable for economists and policy makers.

37 For an alternative way of proceeding on the basis of human needs and desires, see the approach to rights in Liao, 2015; Wenar, 2005.

38 As Raz says, if considerations against requiring an action defeat the right-based reasons for requiring that action on some occasions only, then the right-based reasons create a duty which is sometimes defeated (1986: 184).

39 The institutional adequacy of courts is further supported by the fact that they have protected the right to livelihood in the past (Olga Telis & Ors v. Bombay Municipal Council).

40 On the whole, it seems that Raz considers human rights to be a subset of constitutional rights. He says, "Individuals have human rights only when the conditions are appropriate for governments to have the duties to protect the interests which the right protects" (Raz, 2010b: 335).

41 Notice that "violators" of human rights need not be states, and violations need not be such that they justify *armed* intervention (Raz, 2010b: 328).

42 To elaborate, it depends on "who is in a position to assert the limitations of sovereignty" (Raz, 2010b: 330), and "the relatively fixed limitations on the possibility of justified interference by international organizations and by other states in the affairs of even an offending state" (331).

43 Witness the popularity of Kiva, an organization that facilitates charitable sponsorship of entrepreneurial financial products for the poor.

44 To my knowledge, there has been only one scholarly paper published specifically on the "right to livelihood," by Indian legal theorist Kamala Sankaran. She advocates redefining the "right to work" in terms of a "right to livelihood," given that a significant portion of jobs in developing countries are informal self-employment, without social security. I think she is right to observe the shortcomings of a rights discourse that mainly reflects the working conditions in developed countries, where social security is provided through contractual employment. But she draws unwarranted conclusions from it, in my opinion. She thinks a broader right to livelihood would include, for example, "the right to obtain state largesse in the form of subsidies to set up one's own business" (Sankaran, 2012: 87). It seems that her primary concern is to provide a "safety net" against loss of income if one is not able to access markets or employers. It is unfortunate that she does not connect the value of a livelihood to the sorts of considerations that I have presented.

45 Katseli made this comment during an interview published in the *Dhaka Tribune* (Ahmed, 2014).

Legal Cases

Ain o Salish Kandra (ASK) v. Government of Bangladesh (1999) 19 BLD (Supreme Court of Bangladesh).

Olga Telis & Ors v. Bombay Municipal Council (1985) 2 Supp SCR, [1986] AIR SC 180 (Supreme Court of India).

References

Ahmed T (2014) "To Me Socialism Is about the Human Right to Livelihood": An Interview with Louka Katseli. *Dhaka Tribune*. 23 November. Available at: http://archive.dhakatribune.com/long-form/2014/nov/23/%E2%80%98-me-socialism-about-human-right-livelihood%E2%80%99.

Anderson E (1995) *Value in Ethics and Economics*. Cambridge, MA: Harvard University Press.

Anscombe GEM (1978) On the Source of the Authority of the State. *Ratio* 20(1): 1–28.

Aristotle (1997) *Politics* (CDC Reeve trans.). Indianapolis: Hackett Publishing.

Arnold S (2012) The Difference Principle at Work. *Journal of Political Philosophy* 20(1): 94–118.

Arrow, K (1951) *Social Choice and Individual Values*. New York: Wiley.

Baderin A (2017) Risk and Relationship. Available at: https://ecpr.eu/Events/PaperDetails.aspx?PaperID=35267&EventID=96.

Brownlee K (2016) I—The Lonely Heart Breaks: On the Right to Be a Social Contributor. *Aristotelian Society Supplementary Volume* 90(1): 27–48.

Buchanan JM (1984) Politics Without Romance: A Sketch of Positive Public Choice Theory and Its Normative Implications. In: Buchanan JM and Tollison R (eds) *The Theory of Public Choice—II*. Ann Arbor: University of Michigan Press, pp. 11–22.

Bulloch H and Fogarty W (2016) Freeing the "Aboriginal Individual": Deconstructing "Development as Freedom" in Remote Indigenous Australia. *Social Analysis* 60(3): 76–94.

Dworkin R (2000) *Sovereign Virtue: The Theory and Practice of Equality*. Cambridge, MA: Harvard University Press.

Ergas H (2014) Unweaving Welfare Dependency Not Easy. *The Australian*, 31 August. Available at: http://at.theaustralian.com.au/link/af03ca13ed8fbc49c3e71c9d8dc828d6?domain=theaustralian.com.au.

Gheaus A and Herzog L (2016) The Goods of Work (Other Than Money!). *Journal of Social Philosophy* 47(1): 70–89.

Gourevitch A (2015) Liberty and Its Economies. *Politics, Philosophy & Economics* 14(4): 365–390.

Greene, AR (2019) When Are Markets Illegitimate? *Social Philosophy and Policy* (forthcoming).

Harel A (2014) *Why Law Matters*. Oxford: Oxford University Press.

Hasan R (2015) Rawls on Meaningful Work and Freedom. *Social Theory and Practice* 41(3): 477–504.

Hertel S and Minkler L (2007) Economic Rights: The Terrain. In: *Economic Rights: Conceptual, Measurement, and Policy Issues*. Cambridge University Press, pp. 1–35.

Herzog L (2017) Can Incomes in Financial Markets Be Deserved? A Justice-Based Critique. In: *Just Financial Markets? Finance in a Just Society*. Oxford: Oxford University Press, pp. 103–121.

Holmgren M (1986) Justifying Desert Claims: Desert and Opportunity. *The Journal of Value Inquiry* 20(4): 265–278.

Honneth A (1995) *The Struggle for Recognition: The Moral Grammar of Social Conflicts*. Cambridge, MA: Polity Press.

IFRC (2017) "What Is a Livelihood?" International Federation of Red Cross and Red Crescent Societies. Available at: http://media.ifrc.org/ifrc-pages/ifrc-responsive-footer/.

Johnson M, Brigg M and Graham M (2016) Pearson and Responsibility: (Mis) Understanding the Capabilities Approach. *Australian Journal of Politics & History* 62(2): 251–267.

Jütten T (2017) Dignity, Esteem, and Social Contribution: A Recognition-Theoretical View. *Journal of Political Philosophy* 25 (3): 259–80.

Liao SM (2015) Human Rights as Fundamental Conditions for a Good Life. In: Liao SM, Renzo M and Cruft R (eds) *The Philosophical Foundations of Human Rights*. Oxford: Oxford University Press, pp. 79–100.

Lippmann W (1922) *Public Opinion*. New York: Harcourt, Brace.

List C and Valentini L (2016) Freedom as Independence. *Ethics* 126(4): 1043–1074.

Loach K (2016) *I, Daniel Blake*. Film.

Mantouvalou V (2012) Human Rights for Precarious Workers: The Legislative Precariousness of Domestic Labor. *Comparative Labor Law and Policy Journal* 34: 133–166.

Marx K (1977) *Capital: A Critique of Political Economy*. Vintage Books.

Muirhead R (2004) *Just Work*. Cambridge, MA: Harvard University Press.

Nickel J (2000) Economic Liberties. In: Davion V and Wolf C (eds) *The Idea of Political Liberalism: Essays on Rawls*. New York: Rowman & Littlefield, pp. 155–176.

O'Neill M (2012) Free (and Fair) Markets without Capitalism. In: Williamson T and O'Neill M (eds) *Property-Owning Democracy: Rawls and Beyond*. John Wiley & Sons, pp. 75–100.

Owen M (2012) Handouts "Scourge of Self-Rule." 14 May. Available at: http://at.theaustralian.com.au/link/35981cbb8cd7fb681aa2e1f2ba4c215a?domain=theaustralian.com.au.

Pearson N (1999) *Our Right to Take Responsibility*. Cairns: Cape York Institute for Policy and Leadership.

Pearson N (2005) The Cape York Agenda. *Speech to the National Press Club of Australia*, 30. Available at: http://capeyorkpartnership.org.au/wp-content/uploads/2014/files/4-The-Cape-York-Agenda_National-Press-Club.pdf.

Rangan S (2015) *Performance and Progress: Essays on Capitalism, Business, and Society*. Oxford: Oxford University Press.

Rawls, J 2001. *Justice as Fairness: A Restatement*. Edited by Erin Kelly. Cambridge, MA: Harvard University Belknap Press.

Raz J (1986) *The Morality of Freedom*. Oxford University Press.

Raz J (2010a) Human Rights in the Emerging World Order." *Transnational Legal Theory* 1: 31–48.

Raz J (2010b) Human Rights Without Foundations. In: Tasioulas J and Besson S (eds) *The Philosophy of International Law*. Oxford: Oxford University Press, pp. 321–338.

Raz J, Korsgaard CM, Pippin RB and Williams BAO (2003) *The Practice of Value*. Oxford University Press.

Robeyns I (2016) The Capability Approach. In: Zalta EN (ed) *The Stanford Encyclopedia of Philosophy*, Winter. Metaphysics Research Lab, Stanford

University. Available at: https://plato.stanford.edu/archives/win2016/entries/capability-approach/.

Rose JL (2016) *Free Time*. Princeton University Press.

Sankaran K (2012) The Human Right to Livelihood: Recognizing the Right to Be Human. *Comparative Labor Law & Policy Journal* 34: 81–94.

Satz D (2010) *Why Some Things Should Not Be for Sale*. Oxford University Press.

Schumpeter, JA. 1976. *Capitalism, Socialism, and Democracy*. 5th ed. London: Allen and Unwin.

Sen A (1997) Maximization and the Act of Choice. *Econometrica* 65(4): 745–779.

Sen A (1999) *Development as Freedom*. Oxford University Press.

Smith A (1981) *An Inquiry into the Nature and Causes of the Wealth of Nations*. Todd, WB (ed) Liberty Fund.

Stemplowska Z and Brownlee K (2015) Financial Inclusion, Education, and Human Rights. In: Sorell T and Cabrera L (eds) *Microfinance, Rights and Global Justice*. Cambridge University Press, pp. 47–62.

Tomasi J (2012) *Free Market Fairness*. Princeton University Press.

Veltman A (2016) *Meaningful Work*. Oxford University Press.

Walzer M (1983) *Spheres of Justice: A Defense of Pluralism and Equality*. Basic Books.

Wenar L (2005) The Nature of Rights. *Philosophy & Public Affairs* 33(3): 223–252.

Wood AW (1999) *Karl Marx*. Taylor & Francis.

9 The Right to Own the Means of Production

Christopher Freiman and John Thrasher

Liberals of all stripes agree that core civil liberties such as freedom of speech and assembly are "basic" in the sense that the protection of those rights takes priority over other political goals. John Rawls (1958, 1999) enshrines this idea into his theory of justice when he assigns his first principle lexicographic priority over his second (distributive) principle. However important distributive justice is, Rawls and other liberals believe that basic civil and political liberties should not be sacrificed in its name.

There is, however, debate about which liberties and rights should be considered basic. In particular, there is robust disagreement about the status of what are often called "economic liberties" such as the right to own "productive private property" or property used for economic production. Sometimes this is called "capital" or "productive resources," but those terms are both too narrow and too vague to capture what is at stake in this debate. By "productive private property," we mean a right to own what Marxists used to call the "means of production," or what contemporary economists would call "factors of production." This includes fixed, financial, intellectual capital as well as skills (human capital). This right goes beyond what is sometimes called "personal property," that is, the right to own property for non-productive purposes.

At first blush, there is no obvious reason why the ownership and use of "productive private property" should or should not be considered basic. Using Samuel Freeman's (2001) influential taxonomy, what he calls "classical liberals" endorse some right to productive private property as basic, while what he calls "high liberals" do not. Chief among the second category is Rawls (1999: 54), who asserts that "the right to own certain kinds of property (e.g., means of production) [is] not basic" even though the right to own personal property for private use *is* basic. New wave classical liberals (Lomasky, 1990; Schmidtz, 2006; Tomasi, 2012a; Gaus, 2011) argue, *pace* Rawls, that capitalism, perhaps with a robust welfare state, requires the institutionalization of rights to private productive property and that those rights should be considered basic. Perhaps the most explicit defense of this idea is John Tomasi's (2012a, 2012b) fusion of classical and high liberalism. High liberals remain unconvinced. They argue that a basic right to productive private property would, among other things, allow too much inequality and decrease the effective value of the other basic liberties (Freeman, 2011, 2012; Melenovsky and Bernstein, 2015; Platz, 2014).

In this chapter, we argue that there is an individual right to own the means of production. This right is neither a basic liberty in the Rawlsian sense nor a basic human right, but is instead an implication of two other rights that all liberals recognize as basic and that are also protected as basic human rights: the right to personal property and the right of occupational choice. The right to own the means of production (i.e., productive private property), although not itself a basic liberty or human right, should be protected under the aegis of the basic liberties and human rights since it is a direct implication of other, uncontroversial rights.

The right to own productive private property is, we argue, analogous to the right to work as a motivational speaker or as a preacher in a specific church. The right to work as a motivational speaker is not specifically enumerated on the standard list of basic human rights, but its protection is implied by two liberties that *are* on the list, namely the right to occupational choice and freedom of speech. Similarly, the right to be a preacher is not specifically protected, but it is indirectly protected by other basic liberties, e.g., the right to freedom of speech, religion and occupational choice. To deny someone the right to be either a motivational speaker or a preacher would be a serious breach of their basic liberties, even though the specific liberty interfered with is not basic in itself. The same, we argue, is true of the ownership of productive private property.

Our argumentative strategy has the dual goals of showing why the right to own the means of production should be a protected "basic" liberty within liberal societies and why that right should also be considered a basic human right that should be respected internationally. Both of these claims are controversial. Liberals have insisted that there is a meaningful distinction between personal, non-productive property and "capital" or productive property. We argue that this distinction is untenable and that, even if it were tenable, the right to own productive property is an implication of robust protection of the right to personal property and other basic rights. All liberals, high or Classical, should embrace a right to (at least some) private ownership of the means of production on pain of their liberal credentials. Once this claim is established, however, we can extend it internationally by utilizing the same strategy. While the debate over what should be considered a human right is more contentious than the debate over basic liberties, insofar as certain basic human rights are respected, we argue that a human right to productive property follows.

We begin by discussing how political liberals have specified the basic liberties (§1). Then we present our argument that rights to personal property and occupational choice imply a right to own productive private property (§2). We contend that the right to own productive private property is, at a minimum, *presumptively* protected as a specification of one's basic liberties, such that the burden of justification rests with those who claim otherwise. We then review the most promising attempts to meet this burden and find them wanting (§3–4). Next, we argue that the right to own productive private property ought to be considered a specification of our *human* rights as enumerated by the Universal Declaration of Human Rights (§5). We conclude by emphasizing that protecting the right to own productive private property under the aegis of the basic liberties does not imply an *unlimited* right to own productive private property. Rather, the implication of our argument is that the right to own productive private property may be limited only for the sake of basic liberties and not for other political aims (§6).

1. Property and the Basic Liberties

The basic liberties play a crucial role in all liberal theories of justice. Rawls (1999: 179) accords them pride of place by giving them lexical priority over the difference principle and the principle of fair equality of opportunity. If liberties associated with the right to freedom of speech or religion, for instance, somehow got in the way of achieving fair equality of opportunity, this would not justify restricting freedom of speech or religion. This idea reflects the list of basic liberties codified in various declarations of rights including in the U.S. Constitution. Although the interpretation of these rights changes from time to time, any law or policy that may interfere with these basic rights typically requires additional scrutiny. Outside of the United States, we can also see the codification of many basic liberties in Universal Declaration of Human Rights (UDHR) and its many related covenants and accords.

Despite the recognition that *some* protection of basic rights is essential to a just society, there is significant disagreement about what rights should be considered basic. For Rawls, what distinguishes a basic from a non-basic right is whether it secures the conditions necessary for the equal, adequate development of the two "moral powers" of everyone in a given society. In brief, the basic rights are those essential to securing the social conditions necessary for the equal, adequate development of a sense of justice (a conception of the right) and the ability to devise and rationally pursue a conception of the good (a conception of the good). The rights that Rawls enumerates are basic because they express the fundamental respect for all members of society as free and equal moral persons (1999: 157–158).

One need not be a Rawlsian to see the appeal of this argument in defense of recognizing the priority of basic liberties in a liberal regime. Citizens need to be secure in the fact that the political system is publicly committed, through the recognition of rights that solidify every person's basic standing as a citizen deserving of equal treatment in the public sphere. As Freeman (1990) argues, the political recognition of equal basic rights is a shared pre-commitment between citizens and the government to the protection of those rights. Gillian Hadfield and Stephen Macedo (2012) make a related argument in the context of justice more generally that public reason acts as a coordinating commitment mechanism for the law, though there is considerable disagreement about the stability of this approach (Kogelmann and Stich, 2016; Thrasher and Vallier, 2015, 2018).

Rawls is very clear that there is no basic right to own and use private property beyond a limited right to *personal* property. For instance, in *Political Liberalism*, he argues that:

> Among the basic liberties of the person is the right to hold and to have the exclusive use of personal property. The role of this liberty is to allow a sufficient material basis for a sense of personal independence and self-respect, both of which are essential for the development and exercise of the two moral powers.
>
> (1996: 298)

However, Rawls distinguishes a right to *personal* property from a more extensive right to the own the "means of production" and a right to contract. In *A Theory of Justice*, Rawls (1999: 54) argues that these rights do not rise to the level of protection accorded to the other basic liberties:

> The right to own certain kinds of property (e.g., means of production) and freedom of contract as understood by the doctrine of laissez-faire are not basic; and so they are not protected by the priority of the first principle.

Thus, *personal* property, the right to own the types of things that one uses privately in everyday life, is protected as a basic liberty but *productive* property, the right to own the "means of production," is not. Rawls worries that protecting private ownership rights over productive property would threaten the fair value of the political liberties and disallow the redistribution needed to substantiate the worth of citizens' liberties with a robust social minimum.[1]

More recently, Freeman has extended and clarified the claim that productive property rights should not be included in the list of basic rights (2001, 2012, 2018b, 2018a). He argues that the basic rights must be both fundamental and inalienable and that an unrestricted right of contract would, in principle, allow individuals to contractually alienate some of their basic rights (2001: 109–110). The right to freedom of contract and the related right of productive property are in tension with the other basic liberties according to Freeman, which is good reason to think that they are not basic.

2. A Basic Right to Own Productive Private Property

The right to own personal property and the right to occupational choice—rights that all liberals already recognize as basic—imply a right to own productive private property. On our view, the right to own productive private property is simply one *specification* of the rights of personal property and occupational choice. By analogy, the right to work as a motivational speaker is protected under the umbrella of the basic liberties because it is one specification of the rights of free speech and occupational choice. Although the right to work as a motivational speaker is not itself found on anyone's list of basic liberties, it's protected in virtue of being a particular instantiation of rights that *are* on everyone's list. We argue that the same point holds for the right to own productive property generally.

We introduce four examples to illustrate our point. To be clear: at this stage, we're only making a *prima facie* case for the claim that the right to own personal property and the right to occupational choice imply a right to own the means of production. There might be special reasons that defeat the case for counting productive private property as a specification of these basic liberties generally or in certain cases. We consider general defeaters in the next two sections. For now, we intend to show that a right to productive private property as a specification of one's basic liberties can be constructed using only those theoretical materials provided by Rawls and other high liberals. We take this argument to shift the burden of justification to those who would deny this right to explain why the right to productive private property should not be respected.

We begin with a real-world case: using your car to drive for a ride-share company like Uber or Lyft. Your right to drive for the company is protected as an exercise of your right of occupational choice. Your right to use your car as you see fit is protected in virtue of your car's status as your personal property. Your passengers' rights over their personal property entitle them to spend some on a ride in your car. Each part of the transaction is protected by a basic liberty and these transactions result in your car becoming productive property. Thus, your right to own productive private property—in this case, your car—is protected in virtue of your right to own personal property and your right to occupational choice.

The point generalizes. In the knowledge and sharing economy, the distinction between consumption and productive technology has blurred considerably. In the age of AirBnB, anyone who has living space can be a landlord, even with a property that they occupy but do not own. The most powerful productive technologies of the last several decades (personal computers and the internet) are widely available and can be used as both personal and productive property. For instance, a laptop is both a consumer good and powerful piece of productive capital. It can be used to play games and stream videos, but it can also be used to create software or in online publishing. Consumer, personal computers have more computing power than all of the computers that were used to put men on the moon and online publishing or streaming allows one's ideas to reach more people than would have been possible with a radio or broadcast license in previous decades. At first blush, it looks strange that the trivial uses of one's personal property are protected by basic liberties, but the more consequential and valuable uses are not.

This is good evidence that the distinction between *personal* and *productive* property is not a meaningful one. Virtually all personal property can also have a productive component. Restrictions on productive property are not, therefore, restrictions on rights to certain kinds of things, but restrictions on certain kinds of actions or exchanges, namely using various objects, knowledge, or actions in various ways. Although this is not the main thrust of our argument here, recognizing that the distinction between *personal* and *productive* property is illusory redirects the debate from what categories of property basic rights should protect to what interpersonal rights (e.g., to contract, exchange, gift) should be protected.

Our second example is one used by John Tomasi *in Free Market Fairness*:

> Imagine a college dropout named Amy who has an entry-level job as a pet groomer. Dreaming of owning a business of her own, Amy saves her money, builds a sterling credit rating, wins a bank loan, and finally opens her own pet shop (Amy's Pup-in-the-Tub). What does it mean to Amy to walk into her own shop each morning or, when leaving after a particularly long day, to look back and read her name up on the sign.
>
> (2012a: 66)

In this (real-life) example, Amy uses her wages (her personal property) to start a business, at which point she becomes self-employed (an exercise of occupational choice). If Amy has the right to dispose of her personal property as she sees fit and the right to choose her occupation, then she has at least *prima facie* right to employ herself at a business funded by her personal property.

Next, consider a case from Nozick (1974: 163) designed to show that a stable "socialist society would have to forbid capitalist acts between consenting adults." He imagines a fully functioning socialist utopia where no one has a right to productive property and all other holdings are equalized. In this society, he presents a thought experiment of what could happen:

> I melt down some of my personal possessions (under D1 [full equality]) and build a machine out of the material. I offer you, and others,

> a philosophy lecture once a week in exchange for your cranking the handle on my machine, whose products I exchange for yet other things, and so on. (The raw materials used by the machine are given to me by others who possess them under D1, in exchange for hearing lectures.) Each person might participate to gain things over and above their allotment under D1. Some persons even might want to leave their job in socialist industry and work full time in this private sector.
> (Nozick, 1974: 163)

Here Nozick presses an argument similar to ours. He says that a right to productive property of at least some of the means of production would exist in an egalitarian socialist society so long as that society did not forbid people to use their personal resources for productive ends. To put the point in our terms, Nozick's right to melt down his possessions is protected by his basic liberty to dispose of his personal property. What's more, the basic liberty of occupational choice protects both Nozick's right to lecture and his listeners' right to crank the handle on the machine made from Nozick's melted-down possessions.

Notice, though, that Nozick is now the owner of *productive* private property, ownership that arose entirely from the exercise of two basic liberties. Crucially, these are two liberties that are considered basic by all liberals, not simply Nozickian entitlement theorists. One implication of the argument is that a society would have to deny a right to personal property, occupational freedom or the combination of the two to prevent the simple move from the rightful ownership of personal property to productive property. None of these options should be attractive to liberals of any type.

Now for an original case, which we call *Barter*. Suppose Rick owns a knife and a bowl of soup as his personal property. Morty owns a spoon and a potato as his personal property. Rick's liberty to use his knife to stir the soup is protected. Why? First, his right to the knife and the soup falls into the protected category of personal property. Second, his right to employ his labor to stir the soup with the knife is protected by his right to occupational choice. Similarly, Morty's liberty to use his spoon to peel his potato is protected because his right to the spoon and the potato falls into the protected category of personal property. Moreover, his right to occupy himself by peeling the potato with the spoon is protected by his right to occupational choice.

So far, so good. But notice the inefficiency of the arrangement. It makes more sense to stir soup with a spoon and peel a potato with a knife. So, Rick gets a bright idea. Rick will agree to let Morty use his knife (Rick's personal property) so that Morty can peel (Morty's occupational choice) Morty's potato (Morty's personal property). In exchange, Morty agrees to let Rick use Morty's spoon (Morty's personal property) so that Rick can stir (Rick's occupational choice) his soup (Rick's personal property). See Table 9.1.

Rick and Morty are both better off after *Barter*. The key question is this: if the actions in the first case (Before *Barter*) are protected as

Table 9.1 Barter

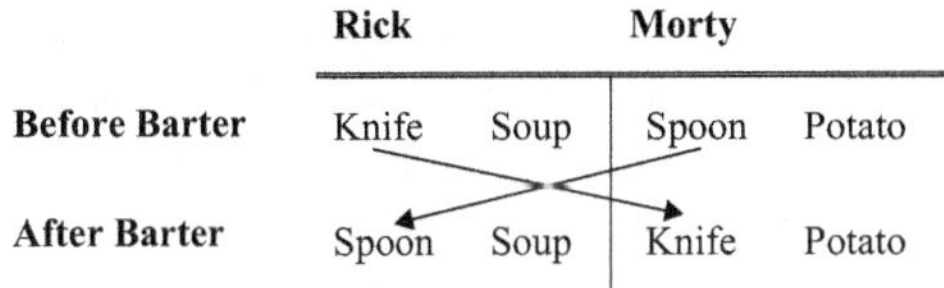

	Rick		Morty	
Before Barter	Knife	Soup	Spoon	Potato
After Barter	Spoon	Soup	Knife	Potato

exercises of the basic liberties, why not the actions in the second case (After *Barter*)? Both cases can be described wholly in terms of people exercising (i) their rights of disposal over their personal property and (ii) their rights to choose how they occupy themselves. Thus, the second case, like the first, is presumptively protected as an exercise of the participants' basic liberties. But note: in the second case, Rick's knife becomes *productive* property. In essence, Rick rents out his knife to Morty in exchange for a fee—the use of Morty's spoon. This is an instance of barter rather than a cash transaction, but the principle is no different than if Rick rents out his knife to Morty in exchange for $5. High liberals, then, need to offer a reason why the protections afforded in the first case are stronger than those in the second case. In virtue of what feature of the second case did some morally crucial transformation take place?

One might think that once Rick uses his knife to help Morty peel his potato, it mutates from *personal* property into *productive* property, which isn't protected. But this reply begs the question. The question is *why* this transformation into productive property results in lesser protection.

Consider an analogy. If one uses a dinner plate as a Frisbee, one could claim that it mutates from personal property to *athletic* property, which isn't protected. The question remains, however: *why* isn't the right to athletic property protected in virtue of being a particular specification of the right to personal property? If no other change in the world has occurred except using your plate for a game rather than for holding your dinner, why would the rights that protect your use of personal property not be protected when it becomes *athletic* property?

The point generalizes. We may use our personal property for musical, athletic entertainment, scientific, religious, philanthropic, social purposes, and more. *Prima facie*, all of these uses are protected. So why not *productive* uses? This argument challenges those who think that the protection of productive property is non-basic to explain in a non-question-begging way what is special about productive purposes that renders them immune from the protection they would otherwise receive. We consider several such arguments in the next section.

3. Property and the Political Liberties

One objection to our argument is that it moves too quickly. While the right to personal property protects many uses of one's personal property, it doesn't protect all of them. Protecting a right to personal property doesn't mean that you have *unlimited* rights to use your personal property as you see fit. You can't, for instance, use your knife to sever your neighbor's foot, or your laptop to engage in murder for hire. In addition, there may be very good reasons for thinking that some things shouldn't be protected as personal property, for instance, nuclear weapons or other humans. The reason that owning these particular items is not protected is not, however, because we lack a basic right to own personal property. Instead, it is because there is something specifically wrong about owning other people and with the private ownership of nuclear weapons. The *prima facie* basic right to personal property can be overridden or erased in cases of where the ownership in question is illegitimate (e.g., slavery) or where there is unacceptable risk involved (e.g., owning nuclear weapons). There are many other similar restrictions on what is, nevertheless, a basic right. The same, we argue, holds for a right to productive property. A right to productive property is a *prima facie* protection that can be overridden in specific cases, given appropriate scrutiny.

One reason to be suspicious of a right to productive property might be that there is something about this right that is inherently dangerous to a democratic or liberal society. Rawls and high liberals argue that the unlimited accumulation of productive property will produce excessive economic inequalities and that these economic inequalities will, in turn, produce political inequalities (Rawls, 2001: 138). Chris Melenovsky and Justin Bernstein share this concern. They argue that:

> Without the power to regulate economic policy, there is no adequate way to protect the fair value of the political liberties. Specifically, in a society that protected free market rights and therefore did not regulate various forms of economic activity, there could be no guarantee that public deliberation would adequately represent the interests of all groups. Without such a guarantee and the protection of fair value of the political liberties, such a system would undermine the social conditions for the full and informed exercise of a sense of justice.
> (2015: 24)

Let's call the idea that a protection of basic rights to productive property would undermine the fair value of political liberties the *political inequality* objection.

We have two replies. First, Rawls acknowledges that basic liberties can conflict. For example, he argues that the principle of equality of political opportunity justifies restrictions on campaign financing and political advertising, restrictions that count as restrictions on freedom of the press and speech (2001: 149). Yet, this conflict does not imply that freedoms of the press and speech are not basic liberties. Rather, it shows that we may find ourselves in the unfortunate position of having to make trade-offs between basic liberties (Rawls, 2001: 149). Jeppe von Platz makes a similar argument. He notes that the objection would work only if the right to productive private property trumped all other rights, implying a right to completely unregulated market activity. But the defender of productive private property is not committed to this further claim (Platz, 2014: 38). So, showing that protecting productive private property may dim the prospects for political equality does not show that productive private property ought not be protected as a specification of basic liberties.

Second, it's simply not clear that the right to productive private property *is* inconsistent with the fair value of the political liberties. John Tomasi's response to the political inequality objection, for instance, isn't adequately addressed by his critics. Melenovosky and Bernstein (2015: 64, fn 53) write:

> Tomasi aims to respond to these arguments [the political inequality objection] by arguing that a government that protects economic privileges better protects the fair value of the political liberties than a government that does not. . . . Yet, this view ignores the way moneyed interests would not only influence the legislatures but also regulators and judges.

Pace Melenovoksy and Bernstein, Tomasi's point is that moneyed interests would have significantly less incentive and power to influence those with political power in his favored regime. The prizes of regulatory capture and rent-seeking—things like tariffs, subsidies, the power of eminent domain, occupational licensing requirements and so forth—are largely taken off the table in a market liberal society precisely because they are inconsistent with the robust free market liberties the regime is designed to protect.

What's more, if one follows Rawls in evaluating institutions within the context of ideal theory whereby citizens strictly comply with the principles of justice, then citizens won't use their productive private property to capture political power in the first place. As has been noted elsewhere, Rawls's (2001: 148) worry "that those with greater wealth and position usually control political life and enact legislation and social policies that advance their interests" is simply inapplicable in ideal conditions.[2] In ideal conditions, the rich comply with the principles of justice—including respecting the fair value of the political liberties—*by hypothesis*, and thus will refrain from using their economic advantages to acquire unequal political power. Therefore, insofar as he is consistently carrying out his stated aim of *ideal* theorizing, Rawls cannot exclude the right to productive private property from his list of basic liberties on the grounds of the political inequality objection.

On the other hand, in non-ideal theory, where individuals do not strictly comply with the demands of justice, it is an open, empirical question whether protecting the right to own productive private property as a basic liberty would increase political inequalities.[3] It is unclear how real the danger of those with productive property corrupting the democratic system is. There is evidence that private interests currently have a significant impact on political actors in the current American political system (Gilens and Page, 2014; Bartels, 2016). This evidence is complicated, however, by other evidence that economic interests are not closely linked to political values and voting behavior.[4] In fact, the most recent evidence on the relationship between democracy, redistribution and inequality show understanding this relationship is extremely complicated (Acemoglu et al., 2015). In any case, whatever the evidence from market societies on the influence of money on politics, the evidence of corruption in societies that do not explicitly defend a right to own productive property is unequivocal. In states where there is no right to private ownership of the means of production, all basic economic questions are fundamentally political. To argue that a solution to the problem of political capture by economic interests is to cede all economic decisions to the political system is merely to institutionalize the problem that originally motivated us. Indeed, it is the move from political control of all economic rights to private, impersonal control of those rights that distinguishes the open, inclusive institutions of developed societies from the rest (North et al., 2009; Acemoglu and Robinson, 2012).

Again, our argument here is not that the more private the ownership of the means of production the better, only that there is a right to at least *some* private ownership. The exact mix will depend on any number of specifics in a given society. All of this is to suggest that the argument from inequality in wealth in a market society to political inequality is complex and may even go in the opposite direction of what Rawls, Freeman and others suggest. On both conceptual and empirical grounds, the political inequality objection is not a plausible reason for holding productive property right to be non-basic.

4. The Moral Powers Objection

Next, let's consider the objection that productive private property shouldn't be regarded as a basic liberty because it doesn't relate to the two moral powers in the right way. For Rawls, basic liberties are those that guarantee the conditions necessary for the adequate development and exercise of citizens' moral powers. The defense of the basic liberties is not meant to ensure that *all* possibilities for exercising the moral powers are defended. Thus, one could argue that a state can guarantee the conditions necessary for the adequate development and exercise of the moral powers without according productive private property rights the protection due to the basic liberties. Call this the *moral powers objection.*

We have two replies. First, the inclusion of productive private property in the set of (the specifications of) basic liberties simply follows from the inclusion of its component parts in that set. Rawlsians and high liberals themselves acknowledge that discretionary control over one's personal property (e.g., to use one's car) is needed "to allow a sufficient material basis for a sense of personal independence and self-respect, both of which are essential for the development and exercise of the two moral powers" (1996: 298). They also recognize that the right of occupational choice (e.g., to choose to work as a chauffeur) is included in the conditions necessary for the adequate development and exercise of the moral powers (Rawls, 2001: 61). Thus, the right to choose an occupation that makes use of one's personal property (e.g., to work as an Uber driver) should also be included in the conditions necessary for the adequate development and exercise of the moral powers. To belabor our analogy, if the rights of free speech and occupational choice must be protected to guarantee the conditions necessary for the adequate development and exercise of the moral powers, then the right to occupy oneself by making motivational speeches should also be included in the conditions necessary for the adequate development and exercise of the moral powers.

Second, the most restrictive interpretation of the moral powers objection proves too much. If a particular specification of a basic liberty is protected as basic only insofar as it is necessary for the adequate development and exercise of the moral powers, then the list of rights assigned special protection will be implausibly sparse. Think back to the person who decides to throw their dinner plate—their personal property—to a friend as part of a game of catch. You could now reclassify the plate as an instance of "Frisbee property," just as you can reclassify an Uber driver's car as an instance of "productive property" once it is used to earn income. Notice, however, that protecting citizens' right to Frisbee property is not necessary for the adequate development and exercise of their moral powers. A state that protects the right to own personal property—*except* when using that property as a Frisbee—still guarantees the conditions necessary for the adequate development and exercise of the moral powers.

High liberals, then, face a dilemma: either the use of one's plate as Frisbee property receives special protection as a specification of the basic liberty of personal property ownership or it does not. Suppose one opts for the first horn of the dilemma. Perhaps you think that we should prefer a more expansive interpretation of the basic liberties, all else equal, or perhaps that the presumption is always against restricting the scope of a basic liberty. In any case, the crucial point is that this horn of the dilemma implies that particular instantiations of the basic liberties (e.g., using one's personal property as a Frisbee) receive special protection even when they are not necessary, considered in isolation, for the adequate development and exercise of the moral powers. But now one may not reject our claim that productive private property is protected under the aegis of personal property and occupational choice on the grounds that this particular instantiation of the two basic liberties is not necessary, when considered in isolation, for the adequate development and exercise of the moral powers.

On the other hand, you could opt for the second horn of the dilemma and assert that the use of one's plate as Frisbee property does *not* receive special protection as a specification of the basic liberty of personal property ownership because it is not necessary for the adequate development and exercise of the moral powers. This move would enable high liberals to deny productive private property ownership special protection on the same grounds.

The theoretical costs of this move, however, exceed the benefits. Consider that the right to use one's personal property is nothing over and above the right to use it as Frisbee property, theatrical property, scientific property, transportation property and so on. Taken one by one, it's probably the case that almost *none* of these particular instantiations of personal property are *necessary* for the adequate development and exercise of the moral powers. Thus, if special protection is due only to those particular instantiations of personal property that *are* necessary for the adequate development and exercise of the moral powers, then it's true that the right to productive private property is in jeopardy—but so are *most* instantiations of personal property (Flanigan, 2017: 6).

Of course, high liberals could simply bite the bullet here and assert that the use of one's personal property for the purposes of playing Frisbee is *not* protected, and neither are all of the other uses that aren't needed for the adequate development and exercise of the moral powers. This is the position that Katy Wells (2016) takes. But this move has radical implications since a similar argument could be deployed against *all* liberties liberals consider basic (Flanigan, 2017). Citizens may use their freedom of speech to chat about who should win the NBA's Most Valuable Player award, their freedom of assembly to become inebriated with strangers, and their personal property to play Pokémon Go. But these uses of liberties are not necessary for the adequate development and exercise of the moral powers. Thus, opting for the second horn of the dilemma takes the high liberal in the direction of a society that is not recognizably liberal.

Another reason why the right to own productive private property might differ from some of the other specifications of basic liberties discussed above is that protecting productive private property ownership threatens the worth of other basic liberties. Freeman (2007: 58, 2011: 30–35) worries that protecting a right to productive property liberties will leave some citizens without the material resources they need to live independent lives. If the state may not tax inheritance, regulate wages or working conditions and so on, Freeman seems to believe that society's poorest will be poorer than they need to be. As Platz notes, however, Freeman's objection "slips between liberty and the worth of liberty and overlooks how economic liberties would belong in a scheme of basic rights . . . the scheme of basic rights is determined independently of considerations of the worth of this scheme" (2014: 37–38). The basic liberties are meant to be both independent of and lexically prior to the considerations related to the second principle. It is no good using arguments drawn from economic consequences that would result from the inclusion of certain liberties when we are drawing up that initial list of liberties. We can't look "downstream" to the second principle of justice to determine which liberties the first principle ought to protect (Thrasher, 2019).

In support of this claim, consider that protecting other basic liberties may conflict—at least in principle—with the realization of an adequate social minimum or fair equality of opportunity. Take the following case. The right to work as an Amish farmer is not itself a basic liberty; however, it is, like the right to productive private property, one particular specification of basic liberties—specifically, religious freedom and occupational choice. Suppose, then, that the country's most economically productive members decide *en masse* to exercise their right to work as Amish farmers. They quit their jobs as doctors, entrepreneurs and research scientists to live a simple life in Pennsylvania Dutch Country. The result is a sharp drop in economic production, a drop that prevents the country's poorest citizens from enjoying an adequate supply of material resources. This should not, however, affect the freedom to work as an Amish farmer because its protection is lexically prior to considerations of distributive justice. The point generalizes to the exercise of other basic liberties—people's decisions to work or retire, to emigrate and to raise a family may have dramatic adverse effects on their society's ability to satisfy the requirements of distributive justice.

5. A Human Right to Own the Means of Production

We have argued that there is a right to own private productive property—to own the means of production—protected by basic rights that all liberals accept. We have defended that right against the most plausible objections. The question remains, however, whether this right to own private productive property is specific to liberal societies or whether we should think that there is a general human right to own productive property. Although there is considerable debate about the theoretical basis of human rights, we believe the strategy we employed above will work equally well in the context of human rights. The right to own and use productive property is not itself a human right, but it is a specification of other human rights and, as such, should be given strong protection in the international community.

One initial objection to this strategy might be that while the Rawlsian "basic liberties" approach is widely used in a domestic context, it is controversial how far the Rawlsian approach can and should be extended beyond borders. Human rights theorists have, in any case, tended looked elsewhere for foundations. Our aim is not to wade into this muddy territory, but instead to merely assert that whatever one's justification for human rights—be it political or moral, welfare- or agency-based—the implication is the same. Our claim is, as above, a conditional one. Insofar as certain rights affirmed, an implication of those rights is a further right to own and use the means of production. Our further claim is that the rights that imply a right to productive property are, in fact, affirmed in the major human rights documents. If one wishes to resist the implication of our argument, those rights will need to be denied. Lest there is any misunderstanding, it is worth repeating again here that affirming the existence of a right to own the means of production only means that no society can justly outlaw all private ownership or productive property, the exact specification of the right, however, will depend on other facts and rights in a given society.

There is considerable diversity and disagreement about what should count as the most basic or fundamental human rights. While there is broad agreement that certain crimes such as genocide, torture and extra-judicial killing are clear violations of basic human rights, there is less consensus when it comes to so-called social and economic rights, including the right to own productive property. One central defense of property is in Article 17 of the Universal Declaration of Human Rights (UDHR), which states:

> **Article 17** Everyone has the right to own property alone as well as in association with others. No one shall be arbitrarily deprived of his property.

This protection for property doesn't clearly specify whether it is productive or merely "personal" property that is protected and it also allows that "collective" ownership of property is consistent with this right. Yet our earlier argumentative strategy works equally well here: pairing the right to own personal property with another right specified by the UDHR—the right to "free choice of employment" protected in Article 23—yields a right to productive property ownership.

One problem with this argument is that the later International Covenant on Civil and Political Rights (ICCPR) and the International Covenant on Economic, Social and Cultural Rights (ICESCR) seemed to reject the earlier defense of, at least some, right to property in the UDHR (Sprankling, 2013). This was largely due to disputes between the democratic and communist states who controlled the main coalitions that developed and ratified these documents. Since the end of communism, however, the anti-property position has become less prominent in the actual practice of human rights even though it still exists in many of the major human rights covenants and treaties (Alvarez, 2017).

If our argument is correct that the protection of a right to own the means of production is implied by other core human rights (namely, to occupational choice and personal property), one implication is that societies that do not respect such a right are always violating an important human right. That is, all socialist or other authoritarian orders that outlaw the private ownership of means of production are always violating human rights. This implies that it is impossible for a society to appropriately respect other fundamental human rights—i.e., to personal property and occupational choice—while not respecting a right to privately own the means of production. This may be a bridge too far for many, but we need to be clear about the modality of the claim. Again, we are arguing only that some private ownership of the means of production must be allowed, not that public or social ownership is illegitimate. It is a violation of basic human rights, on our view, to outlaw the private ownership of the means of production as command socialist systems do, but there are a range of possibilities from full private ownership to full public ownership that would potentially be legitimate.

6. Conclusion

In closing, let us emphasize that our argument is not that citizens have an *unrestricted* right to own productive private property. Rather, our argument is that the right to own productive property or "the means of production" is a specification of other basic rights. As we have suggested, it is possible to resist our conclusion by arguing that neither the right to personal property nor the right of occupational choice (or both) is a basic liberty. We think the theoretical costs of this move exceed the benefits. It's hard to see how you can pursue your own good in your own way when your decision about how to use your toothbrush or your labor is subject to state approval. But we won't press this point here. We claim only that there is a strong *prima facie* case to a right to own the means of production in both liberal thought and existing human rights doctrine.

Notes

1 For a detailed discussion of this point, see Edmundson, 2017: ch. 1.

2 For arguments that Rawls's concern about political inequality is inapplicable in ideal theory, see, e.g., Jason Brennan, 2014: 62 and Christopher Freiman, 2012, 2017: ch. 3.

3 The question may also be stated in terms of relative stability. Maybe the system that robustly protects productive property rights will be less stable relative to one that does not and, hence, we should prefer systems that do not ensure basic rights to productive property. But, this question basically turns on the same assumptions that we make in ideal theory.

4 For three very different takes on why and how the idea that economic interests directly determine or can explain voter behavior, see Brennan and Lomasky, 1997; Caplan, 2011; Achen and Bartels, 2016. For a discussion of the relationship between representative "vote-trading," corruption and public reason, see Thrasher, 2016.

References

Acemoglu D, Naidu S, Restrepo P and Robinson JA (2015) Democracy, Redistribution, and Inequality. In: Atkinson AB and Bourguignon F (eds) *Handbook of Income Distribution* (Vol. 2:1885–1966). Handbook of Income Distribution. Amsterdam: Elsevier.

Acemoglu D and Robinson J (2012) *Why Nations Fail: The Origins of Power, Prosperity, and Poverty*. New York: Random House.

Achen CH and Bartels LM (2016) *Democracy for Realists: Why Elections Do Not Produce Responsive Government*. Princeton: Princeton University Press.

Alvarez JE (2017) The Human Right of Property. *University of Miami Law Review* 72: 580–705.

Bartels LM (2016) *Unequal Democracy: The Political Economy of the New Gilded Age—Second Edition*. Princeton: Princeton University Press.

Brennan G and Lomasky L (1997) *Democracy and Decision: The Pure Theory of Electoral Preference*. New York: Cambridge University Press.

Brennan J (2014) *Why Not Capitalism?* 1st ed. New York and London: Routledge.

Caplan B (2011) *The Myth of the Rational Voter: Why Democracies Choose Bad Policies*. Princeton: Princeton University Press.

Edmundson WA (2017) *John Rawls: Reticent Socialist*. New York: Cambridge University Press.

Flanigan J (2017) All Liberty Is Basic. *Res Publica* 24(4): 455–474.

Freeman S (1990) Constitutional Democracy and the Legitimacy of Judicial Review. *Law and Philosophy* 9(4): 327–370.

Freeman S (2001) Illiberal Libertarians: Why Libertarianism Is Not a Liberal View. *Philosophy and Public Affairs* 30(2): 105–151.

Freeman S (2007) *Rawls*. New York: Taylor & Francis.

Freeman S (2011) Capitalism in the Classical and High Liberal Traditions. *Social Philosophy and Policy* 28(2): 19–55.

Freeman S (2012) Can Economic Liberties Be Basic Liberties? Bleeding Heart Libertarians. 13 June. Available at: http://bleedingheartlibertarians.com/2012/06/can-economic-liberties-be-basic-liberties/.

Freeman S (2018a) *Individual Freedom and Laissez-Faire Rights and Liberties*. Unpublished Manuscript.

Freeman S (2018b) Liberal and Illiberal Libertarianism. In: Brennan J, Van Der Vossen B and Schmidtz D (eds) *The Routledge Handbook of Libertarianism*. New York: Routledge, pp. 108–125.

Freiman C (2012) Equal Political Liberties. *Pacific Philosophical Quarterly* 93(2): 158–174.

Freiman C (2017) *Unequivocal Justice*. New York: Routledge.

Gaus G (2011) *The Order of Public Reason: A Theory of Freedom and Morality in a Diverse and Bounded World*. New York: Cambridge University Press.

Gilens M and Page BI (2014) Testing Theories of American Politics: Elites, Interest Groups, and Average Citizens. *Perspectives on Politics* 12(3): 564–581.

Hadfield GK and Macedo S (2012) Rational Reasonableness: Toward a Positive Theory of Public Reason. *The Law & Ethics of Human Rights* 6(1): 7–46.

Kogelmann B and Stich S (2016) When Public Reason Fails Us: Convergence Discourse as Blood Oath. *American Political Science Review* 110(4): 717–730.

Lomasky L (1990) *Persons, Rights, and the Moral Community*. New York: Oxford University Press.

Melenovsky CM and Bernstein J (2015) Why Free Market Rights Are Not Basic Liberties. *The Journal of Value Inquiry* 49(1–2): 47–67.

North DC, Wallis JJ and Weingast BR (2009) *Violence and Social Orders: A Conceptual Framework for Interpreting Recorded Human History*. New York: Cambridge University Press.

Nozick R (1974) *Anarchy, State, and Utopia*. New York: Basic Books.

Platz J von (2014) Are Economic Liberties Basic Rights? *Politics, Philosophy & Economics* 13(1): 23–44.

Rawls J (1958) Justice as Fairness. *The Philosophical Review* 67(2): 164–194.

Rawls J (1996) *Political Liberalism*. Paperback. New York: Columbia University Press.

Rawls J (1999) *A Theory of Justice*, revised. Cambridge, MA: Belknap Press.

Rawls J (2001) *Justice as Fairness: A Restatement*, Kelly E (ed) Cambridge, MA: Harvard University Press.

Schmidtz D (2006) *The Elements of Justice*. Cambridge: Cambridge University Press.

Sprankling JG (2013) The Global Right to Property. *Columbia Journal of Transnational Law* 52: 464–505.

Thrasher J (2016) The Ethics of Legislative Vote Trading. *Political Studies* 64(3): 614–629.

Thrasher J (2019) Constructivism, Representation, and Stability: Path-Dependence in Public Reason Theories of Justice. *Synthese* 196(1): 429–445.

Thrasher J and Vallier K (2015) The Fragility of Consensus. *European Journal of Philosophy* 23(4): 933–954.

Thrasher J and Vallier K (2018) Political Stability in the Open Society. *American Journal of Political Science* 62(2): 398–409.

Tomasi J (2012a) *Free Market Fairness*. Princeton: Princeton University Press.

Tomasi J (2012b) Democratic Legitimacy and Economic Liberty. *Social Philosophy and Policy* 29(1): 50–80.

Wells K (2016) The Right to Personal Property. *Politics, Philosophy & Economics* 15(4): 358–378.

10 A Claim to Own Productive Property

Nien-hê Hsieh[1]

Economic liberties are largely absent from the International Bill of Human Rights (1996).[2] Yet freedoms to choose one's occupation, to own productive property and to capitalize on economic opportunities all play a crucial role in enabling individuals to lead their lives. This has led scholars to ask whether economic liberties should qualify as human rights (Cheneval, 2006). In this chapter, I take up this question, and examine the case for including among the list of human rights a right to own productive property. I argue that proponents of recognizing a human right to own productive property can avoid objections raised against their case if the right is understood not merely as a liberty to acquire productive property, but as a claim to a certain amount of property. That amount is what is required at the household and enterprise levels to ensure an adequate standard of living as specified by the other human rights in the Bill of Human Rights.

Whether proponents of recognizing economic liberties as human rights are amenable to this line of thought, however, is a question. The case for recognizing economic liberties as human rights is largely associated with libertarian or classical liberal traditions, which emphasize the freedoms associated with economic activity. On the approach to recognizing a human right to own productive property outlined in this chapter, a state would be in violation of its human rights obligations if it did not help ensure that citizens in fact own a certain share of productive property. Ensuring that citizens have an adequate share of productive property, however, may require limiting the exercise of economic liberties associated with commercial activity and the accumulation of capital.[3]

For purposes of this chapter, productive property is understood in fairly broad terms. This is to accommodate the variety of economic regimes found around the world, different levels of economic prosperity and types of economic activity to which the Bill of Human Rights is meant to apply. For example, what counts as ownership of productive property in an economy comprising small household farms—say, owning a plot of land and farming equipment—is different from what counts as ownership of productive property in a highly industrialized economy comprising large publicly-traded corporations in which individuals own shares. Despite these differences, a central feature is that productive property allows owners not to have to rely solely on wage labor to achieve the relevant standard of living through economic activity. It is this feature, I argue, that gives ownership of productive property a role to play in the realization of the ideals associated with human rights.

Understood as such, it may be pointed out that almost any property owned privately by an individual would count as productive property. For example, a homeowner may rent a room in her house to earn an income, or an art collector may put up her collection as collateral to borrow money from the bank to start a business. Accordingly, it may be asked what distinguishes productive property from other forms of property and whether the human right in question is better understood as a right to own an adequate amount of property.[4]

Without denying that physical and financial assets can serve multiple functions in their owners' lives, the rationale for using the term "productive" is to focus attention on the need for individuals to engage in some form of economic production to earn a livelihood and the role that those assets play in shaping the nature of their owners' engagement. Just as economic liberties refer to liberties that can be exercised in the context of economic activity, the idea of productive property refers to property used in the context of the production of goods and services which can be sold in return for remuneration. To be certain, there are circumstances in which some individuals may not need to engage in economically productive activity, because of transfers from others, and there may be assets that individuals could simply sell for their livelihood without involving what we would commonly refer to as production, such as an art collection. Nonetheless, it is difficult to imagine a society—at least given current technologies—in which a significant number of individuals would not need to be engaged in some form of economic production to ensure an adequate livelihood for all members of society. Given this feature of contemporary life, there is reason to focus explicitly on a right in relation to property used in economically productive activity.

While fundamentally a work of normative theory, this chapter draws inspiration from the history of the drafting of the Universal Declaration of Human Rights during which a right along the lines above was initially proposed for inclusion. In the draft drawn up by the Inter-American Juridical Committee and submitted by the delegation from Chile, one finds the following statement regarding a right to property: (1) "Every person has the right to own property"; and (2) "The state has the duty to co-operate in assisting the individual to attain a minimum standard of private ownership of property based upon the essential material needs of a decent life, looking to the maintenance of the dignity of the human person and the sanctity of home life." This statement is said to have influenced John P. Humphrey, Director of the United Nations Secretariat's

Division on Human Rights, who included the following in his first draft of the Declaration: (1) "Everyone has a right to own personal property"; (2) "His right to share in the ownership of industrial, commercial and other profit-making enterprises is governed by the law of the State within which the enterprises are situated"; (3) "The State may regulate the acquisition and use of private property and determine those things that are susceptible of private appropriation"; and (4) "No one shall be deprived of his property without just compensation" (Morsink, 1999: 140).[5] During the drafting process, however, in part "not to tip the scales in the Declaration toward either capitalism or socialism as a way of organizing a national economy," the right to ownership of property was eventually formulated as it now reads in Article 17. Article 17 states: (1) "Everyone has the right to own property alone as well as in association with others," and (2) "No one shall be arbitrarily deprived of his property" (Morsink, 1999: 142).

The chapter proceeds as follows. In the first section, I motivate the focus on ownership of productive property when taking up the question of whether economic liberties ought to count as human rights. In the second section, I summarize a series of objections to including economic liberties among the list of human rights. In the third section, I outline a way for proponents of recognizing a right to own productive property as a human right to avoid these objections, but this involves understanding the right as a claim to own a certain amount of productive property and not merely as a liberty or privilege. The section begins by calling attention to a distinction made between two approaches to arguing that a right counts as a *human* right—what Joseph Raz refers to as "traditional" and "political" (2010).[6] Roughly, the former approach grounds rights in interests or features of human beings that are important to individuals' lives (e.g., freedom from physical harm), whereas the latter looks to features of existing human rights practice. One feature of existing human rights practice is what Allen Buchanan terms "status egalitarianism," which is the idea that "what is at stake is not distributive equality (equality in the distribution of resources or opportunities or outcomes), but something more basic, namely, a notion of equal standing" (2013: 30). Drawing inspiration from the rallying cry during the U.S. Civil War that freed slaves were owed "forty acres and a mule," I explore the role that ownership of productive property plays in realizing the ideal of status egalitarianism. The fourth section addresses objections that may be raised against this account. The fifth section concludes.

1. Economic Liberties as Human Rights: A Focus on Ownership

This section begins by providing a brief overview of the way in which economic liberties have been defined in the philosophical literature. The section then motivates the focus on debating a right to ownership of productive property for inclusion among the list of human rights. In the debate over whether economic liberties qualify as human rights, a common starting point is the work of James Nickel (2000, 2007). Drawing on one schema put forward by Nickel (2000), Jeppe von Platz and John Tomasi identify four sets of economic rights (2015: 264). These concern (1) working (e.g., "to employ one's body, time, and mind in productive activities of one's choice"); (2) transacting (e.g., "to buy and sell goods, to save and invest, to start, run, and close a commercial enterprise"); (3) owning property (e.g., "acquisition, holding, and transfer of property"); and (4) using property (e.g., "to use, consume, destroy, or otherwise do as one pleases"). Tomasi goes one step further to simplify Nickel's fourfold schema (2012a: 54). According to Tomasi's simplified schema:

> The economic liberties of working protect the freedom of individuals to labor and to use labor in productive activities. As Nickel puts it: "This is the liberty to employ one's body and time in productive activity that one has chosen or accepted, and under arrangements that one has chosen or accepted." The other main categories of economic liberty that Nickel describes—those of transacting, holding, and using—can be subsumed under our category of ownership. Thus, the liberty of transacting allows individuals to engage in free economic activity: "This is the freedom to manage one's economic affairs at the individual and household levels and on larger scales as well."

This schema follows the contemporary human rights regime in distinguishing between rights in working and rights in ownership, thereby providing a framework to examine the extent to which economic liberties as theorized are recognized as human rights in practice.

The International Bill of Human Rights enumerates a number of freedoms regarding work. The Universal Declaration of Human Rights, for example, includes:

- Article 4: No one shall be held in slavery or servitude; slavery and the slave trade shall be prohibited in all their forms.
- Article 23: (1) Everyone has the right to work, to free choice of employment, to just and favorable conditions of work and to protection against unemployment. (2) Everyone, without any discrimination, has the right to equal pay for equal work. (3) Everyone who works has the right to just and favorable remuneration ensuring for himself and his family an existence worthy of human dignity, and supplemented, if necessary, by other means of social protection. (4) Everyone has the right to form and to join trade unions for the protection of his interests.

- Article 24: Everyone has the right to rest and leisure, including reasonable limitation of working hours and periodic holidays with pay.

These rights are further underscored and elaborated in the International Covenant on Civil and Political Rights and the International Covenant on Economic, Social and Cultural Rights. The latter covenant, for example, directs states to provide "technical and vocational guidance and training programmes" among the various provisions to ensure the free choice of employment (Article 6), and that state parties ensure an "equal opportunity for everyone to be promoted in his employment to an appropriate higher level, subject to no considerations other than those of seniority and competence" (Article 7). Apart from a right to participate in the management and governance of economic enterprises in which an individual works—what is often referred to as a right to workplace democracy—in its scope and specificity, the International Bill of Human Rights encompasses many of the rights that defenders of worker rights have argued for in the moral and political philosophy literature (Hsieh, 2008, 2012b).

Consider now economic liberties with regard to the second category in Tomasi's schema: ownership of productive property. On this, the Universal Declaration of Human Rights specifies the following:

- Article 17: (1) Everyone has the right to own property alone as well as in association with others. (2) No one shall be arbitrarily deprived of his property.

In contrast to rights in relation to work, the International Bill of Human Rights is much less specific in the case of ownership of property. Furthermore, Article 17 does not readily encompass economic liberties in practice. In the case of work, assuming that individuals are free to not exercise their rights—for example, to forgo safety in exchange for greater remuneration—then the rights enumerated in the International Bill of Human Rights (e.g., Article 6 of the Covenant on Economic, Social and Cultural Rights) encompass economic liberties at work as conceptualized above. However, in the case of property, while Article 17 does not explicitly rule out property rights at the household and enterprise levels, it also does not guarantee their inclusion. Moreover, the International Bill of Human Rights does not provide guidance with regard to what is required of the state to help individuals realize rights to ownership as it does in the case of rights of working. Accordingly, in taking up the question of whether economic liberties ought to count as human rights, the focus in this chapter is on rights concerning ownership of productive property—that is, "the freedom to manage one's economic affairs at the individual and household levels and on larger scales as well."

2. Objections to Ownership of Productive Property as a Human Right

In this section, I outline two objections for including among the list of human rights an explicit right to ownership of productive property along with associated rights to transact and dispose of it at the household and enterprise levels. As part of this discussion, I include objections raised against arguments for including a right to own productive property among the "basic rights" as defined by John Rawls (2001). Although the "basic rights" are not the same as human rights, it is instructive to canvas these objections as they can be deployed by those who object to including a right to own productive property among the list of human rights.

The first objection is what I term the *individualist objection*. The individualist objection is that human rights are justified by the intrinsic value of certain features or interests of individuals and are rights independently of whether they are recognized by others, whereas most property rights are justified largely by the value of the overall property system and require recognition by others to qualify as rights.

Rowan Cruft articulates an objection along these lines (2006, 2010). Cruft uses a right against torture as an example. "My right not to be tortured," writes Cruft, "is justified by the intrinsic importance of my not being tortured, considered independently of the value to others of my not being tortured" (2010: 142–143). Consider now an individual's property rights, such as rights regarding ownership of real property. On many views, ownership of real property is justified by the intrinsic value of certain features or interests of individuals, such as shelter, privacy or self-expression. However, in contrast to the right not to be tortured, justification of the right cannot proceed independently of its value to others, according to Cruft. While it may be plausible to justify a right to ownership of real property for a poor individual on its own, for example, this is not plausible for wealthier individuals with respect to the sorts of houses they may own. In the case of wealthier individuals, property rights protect aspects about their lives that are not sufficiently important to justify property rights on their own. Cruft argues that "most particular property rights of particular people . . . are justified by the value of the whole property system of which they are a part, rather than by their specific value independent of the system as a whole" (2010: 143).

A further feature of the right not to be tortured is that "even if my right not to be tortured goes wholly unrecognized, and will never be recognized by anyone in the future, it still seems to be valuable and justified . . . the right gives me a specific kind of status, a status that is valuable for me to have even when it fails to secure any results in the world" (Cruft, 2010: 144). According to Cruft, the right against torture is "recognition-independent" (2010: 143). Consider again the right to ownership of real property. Cruft asks us to imagine a scenario in which we have received a house in bequest from our parents after which a civil war breaks out. No one else remembers the bequest, no restitution or compensation is provided and others are in fact living in the house. Under this scenario, Cruft doubts we have property rights in the house, "even though [we] would have held such rights if they had been recognized." Property rights are "recognition-dependent" (143).

I now turn to a second objection against recognizing ownership rights in productive property as human rights. Call this the *necessity objection*. This objection follows from a debate about the status of economic liberties in John Rawls's account of justice. In Rawls's account of justice, "basic rights" are those rights and liberties specified by the first principle of justice and protected by the constitution. While Rawls includes a right to personal property among the basic rights, he excludes rights to ownership of natural resources and productive property, whether individually or collectively (2001: 114).[7] John Tomasi argues that on Rawls's account, the list of basic rights ought to include the full range of economic liberties, including rights to the ownership of productive property (2012a, 2012b, 2014).

On Rawls's account, what he terms "basic rights" are rights required for the adequate development and exercise of the two moral powers—a sense of justice and the capacity for a conception of the good—or for securing any of the liberties required for the development and exercise of these moral powers (Rawls, 2001). Of particular interest for purposes of this discussion is the second moral power, which is "the capacity to have, to revise, and rationally to pursue a conception of the good" (Rawls, 2001: 18–19). Rawls writes that "one ground" for including a right to personal property among the basic rights "is to allow a sufficient material basis for personal independence and a sense of self-respect, both of which are essential for the adequate development and exercise of the moral powers." He continues, "having this right and being able effectively to exercise it is one of the social bases of self-respect" (2001: 114). The social bases of self-respect are "those aspects of basic institutions normally essential if citizens are to have a lively sense of their worth as persons and to be able to advance their ends with self-confidence" (2001: 59).

Tomasi argues that on this account, the full range of economic liberties also ought to be counted as basic rights. He writes, "societies that protect the private ownership of productive property as a basic right increase the range of projects, and the forms of economic relationships, that are valuable to citizens . . . broaden the evaluative horizons of citizens . . . [and] make it possible for citizens with diverse values and interests to more fully develop and exercise the powers they have as responsible self-authors" (2012b: 78–79). According to Tomasi, a society that restricts the economic liberties, "diminishes the capacity of citizens to become fully responsible and independent agents . . . [so that] the moral powers of citizens can be exercised and developed in only a stunted way" (2012b: 81).

Jeppe von Platz objects that Tomasi adopts a "maximizing modality" in his interpretation of the relationship between the moral powers and basic rights—that is, what qualifies a liberty as a basic right is that the liberty is required for "the full or maximum development of the two moral powers"—whereas Rawls follows a "satisficing modality" (von Platz, 2014: 32). As von Platz points out, Rawls explicitly rejects the idea of maximizing the two powers. Rawls writes, "We cannot maximize the development and exercise of the two moral powers at once. And how could we maximize the development of either power by itself? . . . [W]e have no notion of the maximum development of these powers" (Rawls, 1996: 333). Instead, "the basic liberties are the protections necessary for reaching the threshold of an adequate, the 'minimum requisite degree' of development and exercise of the two moral powers" (von Platz, 2014: 32).

Katy Wells goes one step further. She interprets the basic right to property in Rawls's account as "a right to privately own or a right to be eligible to privately own housing and personal items" (2016: 359). Wells argues that Rawls's account does not contain within it the resources to justify such a right either with respect to housing or with respect to personal items. In the case of housing, Wells argues that the various values meant to be realized by a basic right to housing—including self-respect, the development of identity or agency, personal independence, privacy—can be just as readily realized under a regime in which the state owns all housing and citizens either rent from the state or a regime in which those who cannot afford to own housing are assigned free accommodation. For example, one argument for the private ownership of housing is that as tenants, citizens may be exposed to checks by the state as their landlord "to ensure that they were behaving appropriately in their homes" (2016: 365). The argument continues that "this kind of behaviour might be self-respect undermining for citizens because it would reflect back at them the judgement that they were not capable of inhabiting the property in the appropriate manner" (2016: 365). Wells responds that "the extent to which the landlord can interfere with and regulate their tenants is, itself, subject to regulation" and "there is no reason why, in the state-ownership scenario, such regulation would not also exist (and be subject to democratic oversight by citizens), to ensure that the relationship between the state and citizen remains respectful by preventing severe interference" (2016: 366). Wells argues that the objections she raises extend to the case for personal items.

The objections raised by von Platz (2014) and Wells (2016) can be generalized to apply to a certain approach to arguing that a right to own productive property qualifies as a human right. Consider, for example, appeals to the value of autonomy (Cheneval, 2006: 12–13) or "a claim to lead one's life" (Nickel, 2007: 126–129) as grounds for including economic liberties among the list of human rights. Similar to Tomasi's line of argument, the approach is to argue that some important feature that is valuable for individuals—e.g., autonomy or the ability to lead one's life—cannot be adequately realized without a right to own productive property on the part of individuals.

What the objections raised by von Platz (2014) and Wells (2016) remind us is that even if protection of economic liberties promotes autonomy or enables individuals to lead their lives, there are two further questions that are likely to be pressed by skeptics of counting economic liberties as human rights. The first is whether there are other ways to realize the relevant values that do not involve recognizing economic liberties as human rights, as in the example of rental versus ownership rights. The second is to specify the degree to which the relevant value, such as autonomy, needs to be realized or protected, and whether the economic liberties under consideration are required. Taken together, these questions point to the second objection that may be raised against counting economic liberties among human rights, which is that only a limited subset of economic liberties, if any, are required to protect the sorts of interests or features—e.g., autonomy—that are commonly invoked to defend property rights as human rights.

3. A Political Account: Property Ownership and Status Egalitarianism

In this section, I introduce a distinction drawn by Joseph Raz between two ways to argue that a right qualifies as a human right: a "traditional" approach and a "political" approach (2010). I argue that one way that proponents of recognizing economic liberties as human rights can avoid the individualist and necessity objections is to adopt a political approach to arguing that a right qualifies as a human right.

One approach to arguing that a right qualifies as a human right to argue that the right protects or promotes an interest or feature of human beings that is valuable in some important and essential way to human life. Consider, for example, Article 5 of the Universal Declaration of Human Rights—"no one shall be subject to torture or to cruel, inhuman or degrading treatment of punishment." Although scholars may debate what is the wrong in torture—say, as opposed to inflicting physical harm (e.g., Sussman, 2005)—that human beings have a fundamental interest in not being tortured is difficult to deny. A right against being tortured thus counts as a human right along the lines articulated above by Cruft. Under this approach, human rights are often counted among the most basic and important moral rights. Raz labels this approach to human rights "traditional," counting among its proponents scholars such as Alan Gewirth and James Griffin (Raz, 2010: 323–327). This approach is also prevalent in contemporary scholarship on business and human rights (e.g., Arnold, 2010, 2013, 2016).[8]

Recall now the individualist and necessity objections. According to the individualist objection, property rights protect aspects about the lives of individuals that are not sufficiently important to justify property rights on their own. It is only by appealing to the value of the property rights system as a whole that property rights can be justified as human rights. The necessity objection presses proponents for recognizing economic liberties as human rights to defend why a right to own productive property is required for the realization of some important value to individuals, such as autonomy or leading their life. Both objections are objections that are made against arguments that appeal to an interest or feature of human beings that is valuable in some important and essential way to human life—that is, the traditional approach to arguing that a right qualifies as a human right.

There is, however, another approach that is available for those who seek to make the case for recognizing economic liberties as human rights. This is what Raz terms the "political" approach and is the approach he defends for theorizing about human rights (2010).[9] Among the various objections he raises against traditional accounts, one is that they fail to "illuminate or to criticize the existing human rights practice" (Raz, 2010: 324). Raz argues that the task of a theory of human rights is not to argue directly from some moral theory, but rather "(a) to establish the essential features which contemporary human rights practice attributes to the rights it acknowledges to be human rights; and (b) to identify the moral standards which qualify anything to be so acknowledged" (2010: 327). Human rights, on this approach, are not merely antecedent moral rights given legal expression. They are both moral and institutional in nature (Zanghellini, 2017: 30).[10]

Given that contemporary human rights practice does not fully recognize economic liberties as human rights, it may be thought that following a political approach—one that looks to contemporary practice—is self-defeating. To be clear, a political approach is not meant to be an interpretive analysis of existing human rights law in relation to economic liberties. Instead, the aim is to take seriously the idea of human rights as understood in the context of contemporary practice and to make sense of the case for including economic liberties among human rights in the light of the values and ideals associated with human rights practice.

If we look to the contemporary practice of human rights, one key ideal it is said to embody is what Allen Buchanan terms "status egalitarianism" (2013). Status egalitarianism is the idea that "what is at stake is not distributive equality (equality in the distribution of resources or opportunities or outcomes), but something more basic, namely, a notion of equal standing" (Buchanan, 2013: 30). It involves (1) universal ascription of rights; (2) equality of rights; (3) the state obligation to make all citizens' rights effective; (4) equality before the law; and (5) rights against discrimination on the basis of race or gender. As understood in this chapter, the ideal of status egalitarianism—the notion that all human beings have equal standing—is reflected in the very idea of a human rights regime (e.g., the universal ascription of rights) as well as in the content of specific rights (e.g., a right against discrimination as specified in Article 7 of the Universal Declaration of Human Rights). I also take it that the ideal helps in determining whether a right ought to be recognized as a human right insofar as the ideal would be further realized by recognizing such a right. With this in mind, I turn to consider the ways in which acknowledging a right to own productive property at the household and enterprise levels as a human right relates to this ideal of equal standing.

During the United States Civil War, "forty acres and a mule" became a rallying cry for what freed slaves were owed. This was in contrast to schemes under which freed slaves were to be hired as wage laborers and at liberty to acquire property. The call was to redistribute land to freed slaves and to ensure protection of their rights of ownership.[11] One way to understand this call is in terms of the interconnectedness of the social, economic and legal status of individuals who were until then legally considered the property of others. On this interpretation, it was not enough that the freed slaves were no longer considered property. Rather, their status as equal citizens depended on owning productive property. Extending to the freed slaves the right to own productive property was a matter of acknowledging their dignity along the lines of what Jeremy Waldron has proposed: "an upwards equalization of rank, so that we now try to accord to every human being something of the dignity, rank, and expectation of respect that was formerly accorded to nobility" (2012: 33). As Waldron writes, this is the idea of "dignity as nobility for the common man" (2012: 22). Generalizing from this interpretation, a right to ownership of an adequate share of productive property is associated with an upwards equalization of rank or social standing.

At first, it may be thought that a more plausible interpretation of the call for "forty acres and a mule" is in terms of ensuring the freedom of the newly freed slaves as opposed to their standing or status. "Freedom," as described by Garrison Frazier, a minister and freed slave, "is taking us from under the yoke of bondage and placing us where we could reap the fruit of our own labor, and take care of ourselves." It is "to have land, and turn and till it by our labor . . . and we can soon maintain ourselves" (Fishkin and Forbath, 2017: 82). On this view, the value associated with the ownership of productive property lies in granting an individual independence from others. Understood in terms of contemporary political philosophy, this view follows along the lines of Philip Pettit's republican conception of freedom as non-domination, according to which an individual is free insofar as she is not subject to the capacity for arbitrary interference by another agent in the choices that the individual is in a position to make (Pettit, 1997: 22). On this view, the right to ownership of productive property is grounded in its role in ensuring the value of freedom as non-dominance. Understood as such, the argument for recognizing the right to own productive property as a human right is not dissimilar from the traditionalist arguments discussed above that look to considerations such as autonomy or a claim to lead one's life.

At the same time, even if we were to grant the centrality of freedom to understanding the force of this call, there is an important sense in which conceptualizing freedom in terms of non-dominance moves us beyond grounding a right to ownership of productive property exclusively in considerations that relate to how an individual leads her life. In contrast to freedom as self-mastery (positive liberty) and freedom as the absence of interference by others (negative liberty), freedom as non-domination involves a claim about an individual's standing in relation to others. This is not to deny that we can say something about an individual's standing in relation to others when she is said to enjoy positive or negative liberty. Self-mastery would not be possible if she were dominated by others, and she would not be free by the standard of negative liberty if she were subject to the domination of others. However, in neither case is her relation to others central to the relevant conception of freedom. To see this, consider the distinction between negative liberty and freedom as non-domination. If freedom as non-domination were simply being free from domination, then it is difficult to understand what distinguishes it from negative liberty. What helps to distinguish the sense in which an individual is free from domination is that there is, in fact, a threat of domination by another. Her freedom involves not merely the absence of domination, but protection from what could otherwise be arbitrary interference in her life by others. In other words, unlike in the case of positive liberty or negative liberty, the full significance of the sense in which an individual is free with respect to non-domination cannot be grasped without taking into consideration her standing in relation to others. What matters is that she is not only free from constraint, but that she stands in relation to another individual who is not in a position to dominate her. Once we acknowledge this dimension of freedom afforded by the ownership of productive property, we return to the role played by a right to own productive property in ensuring the equal standing among individuals.

For the right to own productive property to play this role, there is reason to doubt that a right to acquire property is adequate on its own. At a minimum, it seems what is required is a right to actual ownership of productive property that enables its owner to engage in economically productive activity to earn an adequate livelihood not based exclusively on wage labor. By an adequate standard of living we can look to Article 25 of the Universal Declaration of Human Rights:

- Article 25: (1) Everyone has the right to a standard of living adequate for the health and well-being of himself and of his family, including food, clothing, housing and medical care and necessary social

> services, and the right to security in the event of unemployment, sickness, disability, widowhood, old age or other lack of livelihood in circumstances beyond his control. (2) Motherhood and childhood are entitled to special care and assistance. All children, whether born in or out of wedlock, shall enjoy the same social protection.

The reason for emphasizing the need to own a sufficient amount of productive property to avoid having to rely solely on wage labor to achieve an adequate standard of living is that wage labor opens up the possibility of arbitrary interference by employers in the lives of employees such that employees are no longer free from domination (Hsieh, 2005, 2012a). What form productive property takes is likely to depend on the nature of the economy. In industrialized societies, ownership of productive property may take the form of shares in large publicly traded for-profit corporations or sole proprietorship in a neighborhood store. In largely agrarian societies, productive property may take the form of land and farm animals—that is, "forty acres and a mule."[12]

4. Objections and Ownership in Practice

In this section, I address objections that may be raised against the account above and in doing so try to make more concrete what a right to own productive property involves in practice. Two natural objections to consider are the individualist and necessity objections raised against traditional approaches to arguing that a right to own productive property is a human right.

In response to the individualist objection, the point of the political approach to theorizing about human rights is that human rights need not be grounded mainly in the intrinsic value of certain features or interests of individuals. That is, the political approach to theorizing about human rights takes a different view on what it means for a right to qualify as a human right. Accordingly, that a right to own productive property is grounded in the role such a right plays in realizing ideals associated with the overall practice of human rights need not count against recognizing it as a human right. While one may disagree with adopting a political approach to theorizing about human rights, if one does adopt such an approach, the individualist objection loses its force.

In contrast, in the case of the necessity objection, there is a version that cannot be so easily set aside for the account put forward in the previous section. There are two parts to this objection. The first is that more needs to be said about why status egalitarianism requires an upward equalization of status rather than a lowering. Put another way, it may be asked why not simply deny everyone the right to own productive property as a way to equalize their standing. The second is to ask why the appropriate level of standing cannot be realized just as well under a system that guaranteed an adequate standard of living without involving ownership of productive property, say along the lines of a system that guaranteed a basic income. In what follows, I outline how a proponent of recognizing a right to own productive property as a human right may respond if adopting the approach put forward in the previous section.

In response to the first part of the objection, it may help to recall that at the core of the contemporary human rights regime is the concept of dignity. Recall that the preamble to the Universal Declaration of Human Rights opens by stating that "recognition of the inherent dignity and of the equal and inalienable rights of all members of the human family is the foundation of freedom, justice and peace in the world," and that the International Covenant on Civil and Political Rights and the International Covenant on Economic, Social and Cultural Rights both make clear that "these rights derive from the inherent dignity of the human person." Status egalitarianism then is not simply about equal status or standing, but rather entails a specific kind of status or standing that reflects the inherent dignity of every human being. Dignity thus sets an absolute standard, and the International Bill of Human Rights lays out what that standard is. Part of that standard includes an adequate standard of living as defined in Article 25, and insofar as the ownership of productive property is required to achieve that standard consistent with ensuring freedom from domination, then the ideal of status egalitarianism cannot be realized by simply "levelling down."

This brings us to the second part of the objection, which is to ask why the relevant status of individuals could not be equalized under an economic regime that did not involve private ownership of productive property. For example, it may be asked why a system in which all citizens are guaranteed a basic income does not secure the independence required to realize the ideal of status egalitarianism. In response, I raise three points to consider.

One point concerns the role that ownership of productive property plays in enabling access to credit.[13] Thus far, the value of ownership of productive property has been framed in terms of reducing an individual's reliance on wage labor, thereby protecting her against arbitrary interference by others. In contemporary economies, however, property plays another important role, which is to serve as collateral for obtaining credit. For an individual who does not own any property, securing credit is likely to involve relinquishing some portion of her projected future income stream. At the extreme, this raises a concern about becoming an indentured servant, a concern that connects directly to a conception of freedom as non-domination. Property, however, is alienable. In response, it may be asked why a guaranteed stream of income would not serve to allay this concern if used as collateral. This leads to a second point.

To continue with the above example, consider a system in which all individuals are guaranteed a basic income from the state that is adequate to meet the relevant standard of living. Under such a system, it seems reasonable to assume that individuals stand in relation to one another in a way that avoids the sort of domination with which we are concerned. However, this status is dependent on receiving an income from the state. An individual's ability to maintain her status relies in large part on a claim against the state. In contrast, when an individual owns productive property, her ability to maintain her status is as much about asserting her rights against other individuals. Insofar as status egalitarianism is about the standing of individuals in relation to one another, there is a sense in which exercising a right to own productive property reflects this ideal more fully. In response, it may be objected that a regime of private property rights relies just as much on recognition by the state as does a system in which a basic income is guaranteed, which brings us to a third point that may be raised.

The third point concerns another key feature of contemporary human rights practice, which is the idea that there are limits on state sovereignty. According to Raz, a key feature of contemporary practice is that human rights "set limits to the sovereignty of states, in that their actual or anticipated violation is a (defeasible) reason for taking action against the violator in the international arena, even when—in cases not involving violation of either human rights or the commission of other offences—the action would not be permissible, or normatively available on the grounds that it would infringe the sovereignty of the state" (2010: 328). Once we acknowledge this feature of contemporary human rights practice, we can distinguish between the two ways to ensure economic independence discussed thus far. If economic independence is enabled by provision of income by the state, it is the failure of the provision of those benefits that sanctions intervention by other sovereign states who then are required to provide those benefits. In contrast, if economic independence is enabled by private ownership of productive property, then the intervention by other sovereign states is to protect ownership of productive property rather than to provide for an adequate standard of living. Intervention of the latter sort is much more direct, it seems, and in keeping with the ideal of limits on state sovereignty. To the extent that these points represent plausible responses to a version of the necessity objection, then there is reason not to reject the case put forward in this chapter for recognizing a right to ownership of productive property as a human right.

5. Conclusion

In his account of prison life in Siberia *Notes from a Dead House*, Fedor Dostoevsky writes, "Money is minted freedom and therefore, for a man completely deprived of freedom, it is ten times dearer" (2016 [1862]: 18).[14] For many, this sentiment rings true. The statement captures the sense in which having money can help give an individual freedom by removing constraints or providing her with resources to increase her options. In this light, it is not difficult to understand why scholars have argued that the list of human rights—a collective expression of what are some of the most fundamental freedoms—ought to include a right to the ownership of productive property. Ownership of productive property removes constraints and provides resources that increase an individual's options. Furthermore, the activity itself of acquiring, developing and disposing of productive property, say through the operation of private enterprise, can contribute significantly to the sense in which individuals are authors of their own lives.

What I have tried to demonstrate in this chapter is that including a right to own productive property among the list of human rights is not so straightforward. If a right to own productive property is to qualify as a human right, there is reason to hold it is not simply the liberty to accumulate and dispose of productive property, but rather the claim to a certain amount of productive property. On this account, states fail to meet their human rights obligations if they do not assist individuals in acquiring and maintaining a share of productive property at the household and enterprise levels that ensures an adequate standard of living as specified by other human rights. The thought is that acknowledging such a right best realizes an important ideal embodied in the contemporary human rights regime, which is the ideal that all individuals—all members of the human family—ought to be able to stand in equal relation to one another. To close, it will help to note that this too is an ideal that finds expression in what Dostoevsky writes, for it is largely at the hands of other human beings that individuals are completely deprived of their freedom.

Notes

1 An early draft of this chapter was first presented at the workshop "Economic Liberties and Human Rights" held at the Center for Ethics of the University of Zurich. For the invitation to participate, I thank Francis Cheneval, Jahel Queralt and Bas van Der Vossen. I am grateful for their guidance and patience in revising this chapter and for the helpful comments of an anonymous referee. I also thank participants in the workshop as well as participants in the Harvard Human Rights Colloquium for many helpful questions and suggestions. For first-rate research assistance, I thank Victor Wu. Harvard Business School provided funding for this research. All errors remain my own.

2 This consists of the Universal Declaration of Human Rights (1948), the International Covenant on Civil and Political Rights (1966a) and the International Covenant on Economic, Social, and Cultural Rights (1966b).

3 Under some circumstances, the resulting economic regime may look like what John Rawls labels a property-owning democracy, which is one that ensures "the widespread ownership of productive assets and human capital (that is, education and trained skills) at the beginning of each period, all this against a background of fair equality of opportunity" (2001: 139). For a defense of property-owning democracy on grounds similar to those put forward in this chapter for a right to own productive property, see Thomas, 2016. The idea of a human right to

ownership of productive property, however, is not limited to property-owning democracy. I thank an anonymous referee for raising this point.

4 I thank the editors for pressing me to clarify these points.

5 Through his archival work, Morsink makes the case that it was not the influence of the communist countries for the presence of social, economic and cultural rights in the Universal Declaration of Human Rights as is commonly held, but rather the tradition of Latin American socialism (Morsink, 1999: 130–156). For discussion about the broader contribution of Latin America to international law, see Lorca, 2006, 2017.

6 For a helpful overview, see Cruft et al., 2015.

7 For one discussion of what this means for arguing about the rights of workers within a Rawlsian framework, see Hsieh, 2005.

8 Denis Arnold, for example, writes, "agentic accounts of human rights provide an appropriately deep foundation for corporate human rights obligations, particularly when limited in scope to basic rights such as liberty, physical security, and subsistence" (2016: 9–10). For an overview of the business ethics literature on human rights, see Brenkert, 2016 and Wettstein, 2012. Elsewhere, I have argued against adopting a traditional approach to theorizing about business responsibilities for human rights in favor of a political approach (Hsieh, 2015, 2017). The rationale, in part, is that much of the literature on business and human rights aims to incorporate features associated with contemporary human rights practice—e.g., the permissibility of state intervention to ensure their enforcement—into our understanding of the responsibilities of business enterprises. The thought is that what makes the idea of human rights compelling is that they are not merely moral rights, but rights that carry with them institutional recognition. That is what makes appeal to the idea of human rights so compelling in the first place.

9 For a legal positivist line of criticism of human rights as moral rights, see Macklem, 2015; Lorca, 2017. According to this line of criticism, human rights acquire normative validity from within the legal order, which is to "monitor the structure and operation of the international legal order . . . because human rights are an instrument to do 'justice to the actual international legal order in which we live' " (Lorca, 2017: 472).

10 For a helpful discussion of the relation of Raz's view on human rights to his overall account of rights, see Zanghellini, 2017. Zanghellini explains, "being grounded in a fundamental moral concern is not the *watershed* between human rights and other rights; it is the fact that human rights justify interference with state sovereignty that sets them apart from other rights. But what morally justifies such interference is largely a function of changeable features of international politics" (30).

11 On the Reconstruction period after the Civil War, see Foner, 2014. For a history of the ideology that informed this call, see Foner, 1995.

12 For a contemporary statement of what "forty acres and a mule" may entail, see Amar, 1990.

13 For discussions on a right to credit and to access financial services more generally, see Meyer, 2018; Queralt, 2016.

14 For one account of the relationship of freedom and money, see Cohen, 2011.

References

Amar AR (1990) Forty Acres and a Mule—A Republican Theory of Minimal Entitlements. *Harvard Journal of Law & Public Policy* 13: 37–43.

Arnold D (2010) Transnational Corporations and the Duty to Respect Basic Human Rights. *Business Ethics Quarterly* 20(3): 371–399.

Arnold D (2013) Global Justice and International Business. *Business Ethics Quarterly* 32(1): 125–143.

Arnold D (2016) Corporations and Human Rights Obligations. *Business and Human Rights Journal* 1(2): 255–275.

Brenkert G (2016) Business Ethics and Human Rights. *Business and Human Rights Journal* 1(2): 277–306.

Buchanan A (2013) *The Heart of Human Rights*. New York: Oxford University Press.

Cheneval F (2006) Property Rights as Human Rights. In: De Soto H and Cheneval F (eds) *Realizing Property Rights*. Zurich: Rüffer & Rub.

Cohen GA (2011) *On the Currency of Egalitarian Justice, and Other Essays in Political Philosophy*, Otsuka M (ed). Princeton: Princeton University Press.

Cruft R (2006) Against Individualistic Justification of Property Rights. *Utilitas* 18(2): 154–172.

Cruft R (2010) Are Property Rights Ever Basic Human Rights? *British Journal of Politics & International Relations* 12(1): 142–154.

Cruft R, Liao SM and Renzo M (2015) The Philosophical Foundations of Human Rights: An Overview. In: Cruft R Liao SM and Renzo M (eds) *Philosophical Foundations of Human Rights*. Oxford: Oxford University Press.

Dostoevsky F (2016 [1862]) *Notes from a Dead House*, Pevear R and Volokhonsky L (trans) New York: Vintage.

Fishkin J and Forbath W (2017) Wealth, Commonwealth, and the Constitution of Opportunity. In: Knight J and Schwartzberg M (eds) *Wealth* (NOMOS LVIII). New York: New York University Press.

Foner E (1995 [1970]) *Free Soil, Free Labor, Free Men: The Ideology of the Republican Party Before the Civil War*. New York: Oxford University Press.

Foner E (2014 [1988]) *Reconstruction: America's Unfinished Revolution, 1863–1877*, updated ed. New York: Harper Collins.

Hsieh N (2005) Rawlsian Justice and Workplace Republicanism. *Social Theory and Practice* 31(1): 115–142.

Hsieh N (2008) Justice in Production. *Journal of Political Philosophy* 16(1): 72–100.

Hsieh N (2012a) Work, Ownership, and Productive Enfranchisement. In: O'Neill M and Williamson T (eds) *Property Owning Democracy: Rawls and Beyond*. Malden: Wiley-Blackwell.

Hsieh N (2012b) Work. In: Gaus GF and D'Agostino F (eds) *The Routledge Companion to Social and Political Philosophy*. London: Routledge.

Hsieh N (2015) Should Business Have Human Rights Obligations? *Journal of Human Rights* 14(2): 218–236.

Hsieh N (2017) Business Responsibilities for Human Rights. *Business and Human Rights Journal* 2(2): 297–309.

Lorca AB (2006) International Law in Latin America or Latin American International Law? Rise, Fall, and Retrieval of a Tradition of Legal Thinking and Political Imagination. *Harvard International Law Journal* 47(1): 283–305.

Lorca AB (2017) Human Rights in International Law? The Forgotten Origins of Human Rights in Latin America. *University of Toronto Law Journal* 67(4): 465–495.

Macklem P (2015) *The Sovereignty of Human Rights*. Oxford: Oxford University Press.

Meyer M (2018) The Right to Credit. *Journal of Political Philosophy* 26(3): 304–326.

Morsink J (1999) *The Universal Declaration of Human Rights Origins, Drafting, and Intent*. Philadelphia: University of Pennsylvania Press.

Nickel J (2000) Economic Liberties. In: Davion V and Wolf C (eds) *The Idea of a Political Liberalism: Essays on Rawls*. Lanham: Rowman & Littlefield, pp. 155–175.

Nickel J (2007) *Making Sense of Human Rights: Philosophical Reflections on the Universal Declaration of Human Rights*, 2nd ed. Berkeley: University of California Press.

Pettit P (1997) *Republicanism: A Theory of Freedom and Government*. Oxford: Oxford University Press.

Queralt J (2016) A Human Right to Financial Inclusion. In: Gaisbauer H and Schweiger G (eds) *Ethical Issued in Poverty Alleviation*. Amsterdam: Springer.

Rawls J (1996) *Political Liberalism: Second Paperback Edition*. New York: Columbia University Press.

Rawls J (2001) *Justice as Fairness: A Restatement*. Kelly E (ed). Cambridge: Belknap Press.

Raz J (2010) Human Rights Without Foundations. In: Besson S and Tasioulas J (eds) *The Philosophy of International Law*. Oxford: Oxford University Press, pp. 321–337.

Sussman D (2005) What's Wrong with Torture? *Philosophy and Public Affairs* 33(1): 1–33.

Thomas A (2016) *Republic of Equals: Predistribution and Property-Owning Democracy*. Oxford: Oxford University Press.

Tomasi J (2012a) Democratic Legitimacy and Economic Liberty. *Social Philosophy and Policy* 29(1): 50–80.

Tomasi J (2012b) *Free Market Fairness*. Princeton: Princeton University Press.

Tomasi J (2014) Democratic Capitalism: A Reply to Critics. *Critical Review* 26(3–4): 439–471.

United Nations (1948) Universal Declaration of Human Rights.

United Nations (1966a) International Covenant on Civil and Political Rights.

United Nations (1966b) International Covenant on Economic, Social and Cultural Rights.

United Nations (1996) Fact Sheet No.2 (Rev.1), The International Bill of Human Rights. Available at: www.ohchr.org/Documents/Publications/FactSheet2Rev.1en.pdf.

Von Platz J (2014) Are Economic Liberties Basic Rights? *Politics, Philosophy & Economics* 13(1): 23–44.

Von Platz J and Tomasi J (2015) Liberalism and Economic Liberty. In: Wall S (ed) *The Cambridge Companion to Liberalism*. New York: Cambridge University Press, pp. 261–281.

Waldron J (2012) *Dignity, Rank, & Rights*. Oxford: Oxford University Press.

Wells K (2016) The Right to Personal Property. *Politics, Philosophy & Economics* 15(4): 358–378.

Wettstein F (2012) CSR and the Debate on Business and Human Rights: Bridging the Great Divide. *Business Ethics Quarterly* 22(4): 739–770.

Zanghellini A (2017) Raz on Rights: Human Rights, Fundamental Rights, and Balancing. *Ratio Juris* 30(1): 25–40.

11 Creativity, Economic Freedom and Human Rights

Robert Cooter and Benjamin Chen

1. Introduction

A capability "of central importance to human life" is "being able to use imagination and thought" (Nussbaum, 1997: 286–287). "[F]reedom is prized and praised as the existence of the conditions in which creative activity is possible" (Garnett, 1960: 27). Contemporary human rights documents promote creativity by guaranteeing freedom. The International Covenant on Economic, Social and Cultural Rights, for instance, commits signatories to "respect the freedom indispensable for . . . creative activity." These documents tend to emphasize the arts. For example, a European Union Agency for Fundamental Rights report suggests that by "recogni[zing] and protecti[ng] . . . the right to be creative, unpredictable, confronting, subversive, beautiful and ugly[,]" "[h]uman rights can facilitate the creation of spaces for artists and art to engage and flourish" (European Union Agency for Fundamental Rights, 2017: 6). "Human rights," it continues, "provide the protection needed to break out of dogma, opening up possibilities for new thinking, which are often foregrounded in art."[1] Similarly, a United Nations resolution directs states to "ensure that persons with disabilities have the opportunity to utilize their creative, artistic and intellectual potential" through "dance, music, literature, theatre, plastic arts, painting and sculpture."[2]

Although the human rights discourse on creativity focuses on the arts, most people express themselves through their labor. They spend more hours working than dancing, painting or making music, and they are more invested in their jobs than their art. For many individuals, work is a calling while art is a hobby. Criticism for uninspired marketing or a poor line of code can cut deeper than a clumsy dance step, a drab still life or a botched chord. By extolling the arts and overlooking work, legal documents diminish the importance of creativity and distort the relevant human rights.

Why has human rights law minimized the importance of economic creativity? Biblically, "painful toil" was Adam's curse for disobeying God: "In the sweat of thy face shalt thou eat bread, till thou return unto the ground" (Genesis 3:19, King James Version). Likewise, the liberal tradition dismissed economic life as "barren soil for the development of individuality" (Tomasi, 2012: 30). In recent decades, however, a technological revolution has transformed the nature of production. Robots are performing mundane tasks for humans. Companies thrive by innovating, and firms prize creative employees over diligent ones. The internet has re-configured economic relationships. Our understanding of economic liberties needs to catch up to economic changes. A transformed economy requires a new understanding of economic freedom based on the value of human creativity. We sketch this understanding of economic freedom and explain why it is a human right, not merely good policy.

2. Defining Economic Creativity

Human activity is consciously directed towards some end. As Karl Marx observed,

> [a] spider conducts operations which resemble those of the weaver, and a bee would put many a human architect to shame by the construction of its honeycomb cells. But what distinguishes the worst architect from the best of bees is that the architect builds the cell in his mind before he constructs it in wax. At the end of every labour process, a result emerges which had been conceived by the worker at the beginning, hence already existed ideally. Man not only effects a change of form in the materials of nature; he also realizes [*verwirklicht*] his own purpose in those materials. And this is a purpose he is conscious of, it determines the mode of his activity with the rigidity of a law, and he must subordinate his will to it.
>
> (Marx, 1994: 274)

The ability to conceive *and* execute, and thereby act purposefully, differentiates humans from other animals. It also allows for creativity.[3] Creativity involves an exertion that rises above routine or recall. It demands an element of originality, but not an entirely original thought that has never been entertained by humankind (Csikszentmihalyi, 1996: 27). Besides novelty, creativity also "achieves something" (Grant, 2012: 278). An aspect of creativity is excellence appropriate to the activity in question (Grant, 2012: 278–279). "[W]hether a product is creative constitutively depends on the judgements of a field of experts using the appropriate standards of the historically conditioned domain of activity" (Gaut, 2010: 1037). In short, creativity can be understood as "a socially recognized achievement in which there are novel products" (Barron and Harrington, 1981: 442).

Applied in the economic domain, creativity involves the invention of new products, processes and forms organizational forms, as well as the modification of familiar ones. But novelty is not sufficient. To qualify as economically creative, an innovation must fulfill human needs at a cost commensurate to its benefits. The introduction of an ingenious good or service—say one-hour delivery of online shopping by drone—is not economically creative unless it has a realistic chance of financial success. In contrast, lobbying an electorally vulnerable legislator for an exclusive license to operate a casino may bring financial success, but it is not economically creative (in economic terms, it is merely "rent seeking"). "[A]lertness to possibly new worthwhile goals and to possibly newly available resources" is the "*entrepreneurial* element" that renders human action "active, creative, and human rather than . . . passive, automatic, and mechanical" (Kirzner, 1973: 35). Economic creativity is exemplified by the entrepreneur who discovers a superior product or an underserved market, and founds a company to bring his or her insight to fruition. It may also be exhibited by firms, whether they are small or large, fledgling or established, and by consumers who tweak off-the-shelf appliances to fit their own uses.[4]

3. The Value of Economic Creativity

Humans flourish by exercising creativity, so much so that some philosophers identify one with the other (Garnett, 1960: 26). Conversely, they condemn the suppression of creativity as human stultification. Adam Smith, while praising divided labor, lamented its effect on laborers:

> The man whose whole working life is spent in performing a few simple operations . . . has no occasion to exert his understanding, or to exercise his invention finding out expedients for removing difficulties which never occur. He naturally loses, therefore, the habit of such exertion and generally becomes as stupid and ignorant as it is possible for a human creature to become. . . . But in every improved and civilized society, this is the state into which the labouring poor, that is the great body of the people, must necessarily fall, unless government takes some pain to prevent it.[5]
>
> (Smith, 2003: 987)

More trenchantly, Karl Marx denounced the "enslaving subordination of the individual to the division of labor" as the "antithesis of mental and physical labor" (Marx, 1994: 321). For Marx, labor should express one's individuality; it should be a "free manifestation of life" (Marx, 1994: 53). The industrial economy, however, reduces people to cogs in a wheel. Machines extinguish the skill and ingenuity of the craftsmen, rendering "labor . . . external to the laborer" (Marx, 1994: 61). Work is no longer "the satisfaction of a need, but only a means to *satisfy* other needs" (Marx, 1994: 62). Alienated from his activity, the laborer "feels miserable and unhappy, develops no free physical and mental energy but mortifies his flesh and ruins his mind" (Marx, 1994: 62). Both Smith and Marx, therefore, see the capitalist mode of production as "a Faustian bargain whereby the wealth of nations necessitates the impoverishment of individuals" (Murphy, 1993: 11).

But such a trade-off does not hold true in the post-industrial economy where profits are reaped through innovation (Fagerberg and Verspagen, 2002). Computers have altered the nature of production. Before WWII, the best computers executed computations at a speed ten to a hundred times faster than the hand (Nordhaus, 2007: 142). In 1960, machines existed that outpaced manual computation by a million times (ibid.: 143). This disparity widened even more dramatically in the decades that followed. By 2006, a century and a half of technological progress had succeeded in reducing the price of computation by a factor of seven trillion (ibid.).

The cheap availability of computing power transformed the economy. Because machines excel at the rigid implementation of rule-bound procedures, they took on routine tasks previously performed by humans, a theme that has prevailed since the Industrial Revolution (Autor et al., 2003: 1284). This phenomenon is likely to continue (Frey and Osborne, 2017). Yet non-routine tasks, "[t]asks demanding flexibility, creativity, generalized problem-solving, and complex communications" resist algorithmic solutions (Autor et al., 2003: 1284). Consequently, many jobs today combine machines and minds, thereby enriching the possibilities of human imagination.[6] Jobs today demand more spontaneity and skill than in the 1970s (ibid.; Spitz-Oener, 2006). The revolution is not merely happening on the factory floor and at office desks. Technology has inspired alternatives to traditional organizational forms. One contemporary observer quipped,

> Uber, the world's largest taxi company, owns no vehicles. Facebook, the world's most popular media owner, creates no content. Alibaba, the most valuable retailer, has no inventory. And Airbnb, the world's largest accommodation provider, owns no real estate.
>
> (Goodwin, 2015)

The internet has incubated virtual markets where individuals trade goods, services and ideas. Markets once jealously guarded by corporate hegemons who dominated the channels of distribution are today accessible to the most modest of start-ups. Online applications not only match buyers and sellers but also evaluate them—community reputation substitutes for managerial supervision in disciplining behavior. These trends erode the contribution of physical capital and corporate bureaucracy to profitability. Companies, large or small, are increasingly under pressure to innovate to stay ahead.

Thus, instead of penalizing creativity, the market now rewards it. Firms encourage their employees to think out of the box rather than toeing the line. The *Harvard Business Review* runs articles teaching captains of industry how to "manage for creativity" (Amabile and Khaire, 2008; Carucci, 2017; Florida and Goodnight, 2005; Hill et al., 2014). Nations seek to foster creativity in their citizens to advance their competitiveness. The European Union declared 2009 "European Year of Creativity and Innovation[,]" "to raise awareness of the importance of creativity and innovation for personal, social and economic development" (European Commission, 2009).

4. Economic Freedom as a Human Right

Economic creativity has intrinsic and instrumental value. It is intrinsically valuable as an expression of human freedom and an aspect of human flourishing. People who have a choice prefer creative tasks to uncreative toil.[7] It is instrumentally valuable because it improves the human condition by supplying better goods to more people at a lower cost. Promoting economic creativity is therefore good policy. But does the value of economic creativity ground a human right to economic freedom?

This chapter adopts a naturalist conception of human rights: human rights are the moral rights that we have in virtue of being human (Gewirth, 1978: 64; Simmons, 2001: 185; Tasioulas, 2007: 77). These moral claims may be justified as concomitants of human status or because they defend fundamental human interests.[8] Either way, we understand human rights to be animated by notions of human agency.[9]

> Human life is different from the life of other animals. We human beings have a conception of ourselves and of our past and future. We reflect and assess. We form pictures of what a good life would be. . . . And we try to realize these pictures. This is what we mean by a distinctively human existence. . . . And we value our status as human beings especially highly, even more highly than even our own happiness.
>
> (Griffin, 2008: 32)

Human rights therefore protect and promote our personhood. Following this reasoning, a person has a human right to make informed and unforced choices (right to autonomy). She has a human right to adequate resources and capabilities for realizing those choices (right to minimum provision). And she has a human right to be free from external interference in her pursuit of a worthwhile life (right to liberty) (Griffin, 2008: 33).[10]

The most general and abstract human rights are universal in the sense that they always belong to everyone. They are invariant by place and time because they are based on human nature, not culture. However, many of the rights announced in international legal documents vary by place and time. Take, for example, the right to education articulated in the Universal Declaration. "The right appears to lack universality for it exists only where the social and political organisation of a country makes it appropriate to hold the state to have a duty to provide education" (Raz, 2010b: 335). Moreover, it is not timeless because cave dwellers in the Stone Age could not have understood, much less asserted, the distinctions that the Universal Declaration makes between various stages and kinds of education (Raz, 2010a: 40). Hence, the right to education "cannot be grounded in our humanity alone" (Raz, 2010a: 40). Opponents therefore accuse a naturalistic approach to human rights of being so unmoored from the practice of human rights "as to be irrelevant to it" (Raz, 2010b: 323).

Naturalistic theories of human rights can, however, be understood in a way that accommodates many positively established human rights. Distinguish between basic and applied human rights (Griffin, 2008: 50; Wellman, 2010: 41). Basic rights are rights that are grounded in ultimate moral reasons. Applied rights, in contrast, are rights derived from other rights: they may be a special case or a necessary condition for the satisfaction of more basic rights, or they may facilitate or help secure the enjoyment of those rights (Wellman, 2010: 48–50). An applied right may be derived from more than one basic right. The distinction between basic and applied rights alleviates the tension between the idea that human rights are rights persons have by virtue of their humanity and the observation that many of the human rights we recognize are embedded in specific socio-historical circumstances. The basic human rights are pre-institutional and ahistorical. The applied human rights typically are not. For example, freedom of the press is contingent on technological and institutional features of modern society. But freedom of the press may be derived from freedom of expression (Griffin, 2008: 50). Freedom of expression may, in turn, be derived from autonomy. Thus, while freedom of the press is contextual, it is grounded in basic rights that are universal and timeless.

Like freedom of the press, economic freedom should be regarded as an applied right. Human rights primarily safeguard human agency. No matter where they are born, most people spend the majority of their time making a living. As a result, they tend to define themselves not by their hobbies, but by their occupations. There is little to be said for spending one's days on a factory floor cutting wire for pins. However, repetitive and mindless tasks are increasingly undertaken by machines, not humans. More than ever, individuals enjoy opportunities for creativity in performing and structuring their work. Economic life has emerged as our biggest canvas for self-authorship. One's efforts in securing the necessities and conveniences of life are today articulations of one's individuality. The right to economic freedom therefore derives from a basic right to liberty.[11]

Moreover, a right to economic freedom may be derived from the basic right to minimum provision (Griffin, 2008). Guaranteeing everyone the means necessary for acting meaningfully on their choices requires a degree of abundance. Yet, the gains from dividing labor more finely are subject to diminishing returns. Wealth cannot increase perpetually by the law of division of labor. To produce more, economies must innovate. The rise in global living standards over the last few decades has been sustained by breakthroughs in technology and evolution in organizational forms.[12] To illustrate:

> Washing machines have saved mountains of time . . . a mid 1940s study by the US Rural Electrification Authority reports that, with the introduction of the electric washing machine and electric iron, the time required for washing a 38 lb load of laundry was reduced by a factor of nearly 6 (from 4 hours to 41 minutes) and the time taken to iron it by a factor of more than 2.5 (from 4.5 hours to 1.75 hours). Piped water has meant that women do not have to spend hours fetching water (for which, according to the United Nations Development Program, up to two hours per day are spent in some developing countries). Vacuum cleaners have enabled us to clean our houses more thoroughly in a fraction of the time that was needed in the old days, when we had to do it with broom and rags. Gas/electric kitchen stoves and central heating have vastly reduced the time needed for collecting firewood, making fires, keeping the fires alive, and cleaning after them for heating and cooking purposes.
>
> (Chang, 2010: 34–35)[13]

Creativity in economic life makes our lives more comfortable. It also multiplies the resources and capabilities we have to pursue our own visions of the good life. Because economic freedom unleashes creativity, it is implied by a basic right to minimum provision.

A moral human right to economic freedom is a *pro tanto* reason for establishing a corresponding legal human right.[14] But not all moral claims ought to be legally enforceable, as we discuss later in detail. Also, it may be a mistake to think that the content of legal human rights must mirror that of moral human rights. As Allen Buchanan argues, "neither the interests nor the autonomy, nor any other feature of any particular individual is of sufficient moral importance to justify the ascription of the extensive and expensive duties that are correlates of many legal rights, whether domestic or international" (Buchanan, 2013: 63–64). "To put the point bluntly: No matter who you are, you are not important enough to justify a set of duties that correlate with the panoply of legal rights." On his view, while some legal human rights may, in fact, be grounded in pre-existing moral rights, most legal human rights have to be defended by their contribution to "the interests and autonomy of large numbers of people" (Buchanan, 2013: 63–64).

We are sympathetic to this perspective on legal human rights. Take, for example, the right to free speech. This is a well-established right that is recognized in both national and international law. The Universal Declaration of Human Rights affirms everyone's "right to freedom of opinion and expression." "[T]his right includes freedom to hold opinions without interference and to seek, receive and impart information and ideas through any media and regardless of frontiers."[15] The First Amendment of the United States Constitution forbids the legislature from "abridging the freedom of speech, or of the press." But freedom of expression does not serve only to affirm human status or a person's interest in communicating his or her own ideas or beliefs. It is also the foundation for a vibrant and robust democracy. "The right of citizens to inquire, to hear, to speak, and to use information to reach consensus," the Supreme Court of the United States has explained, "is a precondition to enlightened self-government and a necessary means to protect it."[16] Hence, the guarantees of freedom of speech and freedom of the press " 'ha[ve] [their] fullest and most urgent application' to speech uttered during a campaign for political office."[17]

American constitutional law also makes a distinction between traditional public forums, designated forums and non-public forums. Because public streets and parks "have immemorially been held in trust for the use of the public and, time out of mind, have been used for purposes of assembly, communicating thoughts between citizens, and discussing public questions," content-based restrictions applying to such traditional public fora are subject to more exacting scrutiny.[18] The burdens imposed by a legal human right to free expression on legitimate state objectives are justified not solely by reference to the speaker's liberty, but also by the significance of public discourse for democratic self-government (Buchanan, 2013: 62).

Similarly, the intrinsic value of economic creativity, standing alone, may not establish a legal human right to economic freedom. But creativity in the economic domain betters our material condition. The market values goods by how much people desire them. People mostly desire things that are good for them, although not always. By anticipating and responding to such desires, creative economic activity fuels economic growth, enhances our standard of living and fosters human agency. Because economic freedom *enables* economic creativity and thereby contributes to "the interests and autonomy of large numbers of people," we should recognize it as a legal human right.

5. Legalizing Economic Freedom

We come finally to the question of how to implement a human right to economic freedom. Law can be supranational or national,[19] constitutional or non-constitutional. In addition, a right enshrined in a national constitution or a human rights charter may or may not entitle the right-holder to a remedy at law. If the right may be vindicated in court, then it is justiciable; otherwise, it is aspirational. Between justiciable and aspirational rights are rights that are declared to be "principles" or "state directives." These principles or state directives do not give rise to legal claims, but they may be invoked to interpret ambiguous legislation. The legal form a right to economic freedom ought to take depends, among other things, on the institutions and actors who should be responsible for explicating it. This is because hardly any right is absolute, and the contours of a right are determined by the best interpretation of its grounds.

It is instructive to reprise, in this context, Dworkin's distinction between abstract rights and concrete rights (Dworkin, 2013: 119). An abstract right is a general political aim that does not, by itself, tell us how it is to be resolved or reconciled against other political aims. A concrete right, on the other hand, is more precise and represents a compromise or an accommodation between competing political aims.

Consider, once again, freedom of speech. While Article 19 of the International Covenant on Civil and Political Rights emphatically declares that "[e]veryone shall have the right to hold opinions without interference" and "the right to freedom of expression," it also qualifies that these rights may be circumscribed "[f]or respect of the rights and reputations of others" and or for the maintenance of "national security," "public order" or "public health or morals."[20] Yet an abstract commitment to free speech tells us nothing about whether, say, citizens protesting an abortion clinic must keep a minimum distance from the facility.[21] Whether free speech encompasses a concrete right to approach abortion clinics to deliver a pro-life message is a question whose answer must draw on an understanding of the value of free speech, its paramount importance for both the individual and society and the media and fora of speech in contemporary life.

Likewise, to ascertain the concrete rights that flow from an abstract right to economic freedom, one must appreciate the value of economic freedom, its significance for human flourishing and the nature of the modern economy. Agreement on the terms of a contract argues for its enforcement. Though people do not read everything they sign, the law usually ascribes consent to a party who fails to object to a later-disputed term.[22] Doing so lowers the transaction costs of making legally enforceable commitments. But contracts may also inhibit economic freedom and impair its value.

To illustrate, garden leave clauses proliferate in employment contracts in the United Kingdom. These provisions require a departing employee to remain in the employer's service for a period of time without any of their usual duties or responsibilities. Employees may also be excluded from the workplace while on garden leave. Gardening leave hinders the mobility of employees. No statutory provision in the United Kingdom addresses the permissibility of garden leave. Judges have developed the law in this area by expounding the principles of freedom of contract and the freedom to compete. Though the English common law has retreated from its ancient hostility to even the faintest restraint on trade,[23] it remains suspicious of garden leave clauses because they may result in "compulsory sterilization" and the "atrophy of skills."[24] As one of the lord justices explained in *Provident Financial Group v. Hayward* [1989] ICR 160 (CA):

> The employee has a concern to work and a concern to exercise his skills. That has been recognised in some circumstances concerned with artists and singers who depend on publicity, but it applies equally . . . to skilled workmen and even to chartered accountants.

British courts have thus refused to compel employees to be idle in the absence of a legitimate business purpose, such as the protection of a trade secret, preservation of confidential information[25] and the retention of goodwill or customer connections.[26] By elaborating on the business reasons that qualify as legitimate, judges implicitly balance the intrinsic and instrumental value of creativity and articulate concrete rights from the abstract right to economic freedom.

Because an abstract right has to be rendered concrete for it to have practical consequences, legalization of a right to economic freedom implicates questions of institutional competence, capacity and pedigree. By positing a right that is constitutional *and* justiciable, a polity designates its judiciary as the prime expositor of the right.[27] In contrast, tagging a constitutional right as aspirational preserves the legislature's authority to construe and implement it. Should economic freedom be justiciable or aspirational? There is no general answer. Any proposed solution must take into account the realities of the global order as well as a society's history and circumstances. However, acknowledging a legal human right to economic freedom means—at a minimum—that the right has normative legal force. It can be invoked in defending existing statutory schemes or advocating for legislative reform. Affirmation of an abstract right to economic freedom allows for more concrete rights to be hammered out through legal and political contestation in the domestic and international arena.

6. Conclusion

Human rights documents associate creativity almost exclusively with the arts. But individuals today have far greater opportunities to exhibit creativity in their economic lives. The transformation from the industrial to the innovation economy has reconciled productivity and creativity. Far from being antithetical to productivity, creativity now enhances it. Thus, creativity has intrinsic value for the individual who exercises it and instrumental value for those who benefit from its fruits. Because economic freedom enables creative activity, we should recognize it as a legal human right. Legalization of an abstract right to economic freedom involves complex questions of institutional design. But no matter how the abstract right is legalized, the concrete rights flowing from it have to be explicated by reference to what gives economic freedom its value—releasing human creativity.

Notes

1 Philosophers have expressed similar sentiments. For example, James Griffin asserts that to be "free from interference in the pursuit of our major ends," "[w]e must be free to . . . create works of art" (Griffin, 2008: 193).

2 This is Rule 10 of the Standard Rules on the Equalization of Opportunities for Persons With Disabilities adopted by the United Nations General Assembly on 20 December 1993.

3 The same physical act can be creative or uncreative, depending on the actor's relationship to it. Consider an artist who designs a life-sized LEGO® statue and assembles it from many small LEGO® blocks. For the artist, the task of assembling the statue is tedious but creative because the effort embodies his original artistic vision. The same task becomes tedious and mundane if carried out by a hired hand.

4 Von Hippel (2017) refers to this as "free innovation." As Samuelson, 2016: 564 exclaims, "[n]ever before in human history has it been more possible for tens of millions of people around the world to express themselves in creative ways, including by tinkering with existing artifacts and sharing the fruits of their creativity with others."

5 Hsieh, 2008 refers to these kinds of argument as "formative arguments."

6 Acemoglu, 2002: 8 observes that "[a]lthough the consensus is now broad, the idea that technological advances favor more skilled workers is a twentieth century phenomenon."

7 John Stuart Mill called it "an unquestionable fact that those who are equally acquainted with, and equally capable of appreciating and enjoying, both, do give a most marked preference to the manner of existence which employs their higher faculties" (Mill, 2001: 9).

8 The function of a right, under the will theory, is to grant the right-holder discretion over the conduct of another and thereby define domains where the right-holder is a small-scale sovereign (Hart, 1982: 183). In contrast, the function of a right, under the interest theory, is to benefit for the right-holder. The will and the interest theories differ, for example, about the kinds of things the bearer of rights and the susceptibility of rights to consequentialist reasoning. We do not pass on these long-standing debates here. Suffice it to say that an individual's interest does not extend only to her well-being but may also encompass the ability to make genuine and informed choices (Sen, 1984, 1985; Satz, 2003).

9 Alan Gewirth (1978) derived a human right to the necessary conditions for successful agency, namely freedom and well-being, by starting from the premise that rational agents act voluntarily and purposefully. Though Gewirth and Griffin have human agency at the heart of their respective theories, Gewirth, unlike Griffin, sought to elaborate an account that is logically implied by the idea of human rights itself.

10 These rights give rise to both negative and positive duties, that is, duties to forbear as well as duties to act. It might be suggested that rights entailing positive duties are inchoate until institutions are in place to elaborate their correlative duties. Arguing for an asymmetry between universal liberty and welfare rights, Onora O'Neill writes that "[i]f it is not in principle clear where claims should be lodged, appeals to supposed universal rights to goods or services, including welfare, are mainly rhetoric, which proclaim 'manifesto' rights against unspecified others" (O'Neill, 1996: 132). But we agree with John Tasioulas that a right can be established although its "duties [are not] being precisely specified or allocated to particular agents" (Tasioulas, 2007: 92).

11 This is not to suggest that economic freedom is purely negative in nature. It may, for example, support a right to education and a right to credit because education and credit are necessary to creativity in the modern economy. See also the related discussion in footnote 11.

12 Economists use a measure called Total Factor Productivity (TFP) as a proxy for innovation. TFP captures the amount of economic growth not attributable to physical and human capital accumulation. Christenson et al. (1980) estimated TFP's contribution to the increase in Gross Domestic Product in France, Germany, Italy, Japan, the United Kingdom and the United States between 1947 to 1973 at 55 percent, 56 percent, 64 percent, 42 percent, 52 percent and 33 percent, respectively.

13 As an additional data point, consider that in 1965, women in the United States spent an average of 22.61 hours per week on chores like meal preparation and cleanup, doing laundry, ironing, dusting, vacuuming, indoor household cleaning, and indoor design and. maintenance (Aguiar and Hurst, 2007: 976). In 2003, the time spent on such non-market production declined to 13.23 hours per week, representing a decrease of over 40 percent.

14 Joel Feinberg, for instance, calls the identity between "*A* has a moral right to do (have or be) *X*" and "*A ought* to have a *legal* right to *X*" the "there ought to be a law" theory of moral rights and believes that it appears to "provide a sensible interpretation of moral rights talk" (Feinberg, 2003: 43).

15 This right is also recognized in Article 19 of the International Covenant on Civil and Political Rights, Article 9 of the African Charter on Human and Peoples' Rights, Article 13 of the American Convention on Human Rights and Article 10 of the European Convention on Human Rights.

16 *Citizens United v. FEC*, 558 U.S. 310, 339 (2010).

17 *Id.*

18 *Pleasant Grove City v. Summum*, 555 U.S. 460, 460–461 (2009).

19 The violation of a supranational legal human right gives other state and non-state actors reasons for condemning and perhaps, intervening in, a state's domestic policies.

20 Similarly, Article 10 of the European Convention on Human Rights affirms "the right to freedom of expression," but clarifies that it may be limited "in the interests of national security, territorial integrity or public safety, for the prevention of disorder or crime, for the protection of health or morals, for the protection of the reputation or rights of others, for preventing the disclosure of information received in confidence, or for maintaining the authority and impartiality of the judiciary."

21 For the United States Supreme Court's attempts at answering this question, see *Hill v. Colorado*, 502 U.S. 703 (2000) and *McCullen v. Coakley*, 134 S. Ct. 2518 (2014). In the United States, government regulation of speech is permissible if it is "justified without reference to the content of the regulated speech," "narrowly tailored to serve a significant governmental interest" and "leave[s] open ample alternative channels for communication of the

information." The *McCullen* court held that a Massachusetts statute excluding individuals from a 35-feet buffer zone around reproductive health care facilities flunked this test because it " burden[ed] substantially more speech than necessary to achieve the Commonwealth's asserted interests" in public safety.

22 See, for example, *ProCD, Inc. v. Zeidenberg*, 86 F.3d 1447 (7th Cir. 1996).

23 See *Dyer's Case* (1414) 2 Hen. V, fol. 5, pl. 26.

24 *Elsevier Ltd v. Munro* [2014] EWHC 2648 (QB).

25 See, for example, *Symbian Ltd v. Christensen* [2001] IRLR 77 (CA).

26 See, for example, *JM Finn & Co Limited v. Holliday* [2013] EWHC 3450 (QB) and *Eurobrokers Ltd v. Rabey* [1995] IRLR 206.

27 In the United States, for instance, the federal judiciary is insulated from politics and revising the Constitution is no easy feat. Consequently, judges have a strong role in explaining and enforcing constitutional rights.

Bibliography

Acemoglu D (2002) Technical Change, Inequality, and the Labor Market. *Journal of Economic Literature* 40(1): 7–72.

Aguiar M and Hurst E (2007) Measuring Trends in Leisure: The Allocation of Time Over Five Decades. *The Quarterly Journal of Economics* 122(3): 969–1006.

Amabile T (1996) *Creativity in Context*. Boulder: Westview.

Amabile T and Khaire M (2008) Creativity and the Role of the Leader. *Harvard Business Review* 86(10): 100–109.

Arneson RJ (1987) Meaningful Work and Market Socialism. *Ethics* 97(3): 517–545.

Arneson RJ (2009) Meaningful Work and Market Socialism Revisited. *Analyse & Krtik* 31(1): 139–151.

Arnold S (2012) The Difference Principle at Work. *The Journal of Political Philosophy* 20(1): 94–118.

Attfield R (1984) Work and the Human Essence. *Journal of Applied Philosophy* 1(1): 141–150.

Autor DH (2014) Skills, Education, and the Rise of Earnings Inequality Among the "other 99 percent." *Science* 344(6186): 843–851.

Autor DH, Levy F and Murnane RJ (2003) The Skill Content of Recent Technological Change: An Empirical Exploration. *The Quarterly Journal of Economics* 118(4): 1279–1333.

Barron F and Harrington DM (1981) Creativity, Intelligence, and Personality. *Annual Review of Psychology* 32: 439–476.

Boden MA (2004) *The Creative Mind: Myths and Mechanisms*, 2nd ed. London: Routledge.

Buchanan A (2013) *The Heart of Human Rights*. New York: Oxford University Press.

Carucci R (2017) How to Nourish Your Team's Creativity. *Harvard Business Review*.

Chang HJ (2010) *23 Things They Don't Tell You About Capitalism*. New York: Bloomsbury Press.

Christenson LR, Cummings D, & Jorgenson D (1980) Economic Growth, 1947–73: An International Comparison. In: Kendrick JW and Vaccara BN (eds), *New Developments in Productivity Measurement*. Chicago: University of Chicago

Press, pp. 595–698.Cruft R, Liao SM and Renzo M (2015) The Philosophical Foundations of Human Rights: An Overview. In: Cruft R, Liao SM and Renzo M (eds), *Philosophical Foundations of Human Rights*. Oxford: Oxford University Press, pp. 1–44.

Csikszentmihalyi M (1996) *Flow and the Psychology of Discovery and Invention*. New York: Harper Collins.

Dworkin R (1985) Liberalism. In: *A Matter of Principle*. Cambridge: Harvard University Press.

Dworkin R (2013) *Taking Rights Seriously*. London: Bloomsbury Academic.

Elster J (1985) *Marking Sense of Marx*. Cambridge: Cambridge University Press.

Elster J (2000) *Ulysses Unbound Studies in Rationality, Precommitment, and Constraints*. Cambridge: Cambridge University Press.

European Commission (2009) Boosting Creativity and Innovation in Europe: Official Launch of the European Year 2009 in Prague. Available at: http://europa.eu/rapid/press-release_IP-09-23_en.pdf (accessed 1 May 2018).

European Union Agency for Fundamental Rights (2017) *Exploring the Connections Between Arts and Human Rights*. Luxembourg: Publications Office of the European Union.

Fagerberg J and Verspagen B (2002) Technology-Gaps, Innovation-Diffusion and Transformation: An Evolutionary Interpretation. *Research Policy* 31: 1291–1304.

Feinberg J (2003) In defense of moral rights. In: *Problems at the Roots of Law: Essays in Legal and Political Theory*. Oxford: Oxford University Press, pp. 37–56.

Finnis J (2011) *Natural Law and Natural Rights*, 2nd ed. Oxford: Oxford University Press.

Florida R and Goodnight J (2005) Managing for Creativity. *Harvard Business Review* 83(7): 124–131.

Frey CB and Osborne MA (2017) The Future of Employment: How Susceptible Are Jobs to Computerisation? *Technological Forecasting & Social Change* 114: 254–280.

Garnett CA (1960) Freedom and Creativity. *Proceedings and Addresses of the American Philosophical Association* 34: 25–39.

Gaut B (2009) Creativity and Skill. In: Krausz M, Dutton D and Bardsley K (eds) *The Idea of Creativity*. Leiden: Brill, pp. 83–104.

Gaut B (2010) The Philosophy of Creativity. *Philosophy Compass* 5(12): 1034–1046.

Gewirth A (1978) *Reason and Morality*. Chicago: University of Chicago Press.

Gini A and Sullivan T (1987) Work: The Process and the Person. *Journal of Business Ethics* 6(8): 649–655.

Goodwin T (2015) The Battle is for the Customer Interface. Available at: https://techcrunch.com/2015/03/03/in-the-age-of-disintermediation-the-battle-is-all-for-the-customer-interface/ (accessed 1 May 2018).

Grant J (2012) The Value of Imaginativeness. *Australasian Journal of Philosophy* 90(2): 275–289.

Griffin J (2008) *On Human Rights*. Oxford: Oxford University Press.

Hart HLA (1982) *Essays on Bentham: Studies in Jurisprudence and Political Theory*. Oxford: Clarendon Press.

Hill LA, Brandeau G, Truelove E and Lineback K (2014) The Inescapable Paradox of Managing Creativity. *Harvard Business Review*.

Hsieh N (2008) Survey Article: Justice in Production. *The Journal of Political Philosophy* 16(1): 72–100.

Katz LF and Murphy KM (1992) Changes in Relative Wages, 1963–1987: Supply and Demand Factors. *The Quarterly Journal of Economics* 107(1): 35–79.

Kieran M (2014) Creativity as a Virtue of Character. In: Paul ES and Kaufman SB (eds) *The Philosophy of Creativity: New Essays*. New York: Oxford University Press, pp. 125–146.

Kirzner IM (1973) *Competition and Entrepreneurship*. Chicago: University of Chicago Press.

Liao SM (2015) Human Rights as Fundamental Conditions for a Good Life. In: R Cruft, MS Liao and M Renzo (eds), *Philosophical Foundations of Human Rights*. Oxford: Oxford University Press, pp. 79–101.

Marx K (1994) *Selected Writings*. Indianapolis and Cambridge: Hackett Publishing Company.

Mill JS (2001) *Utilitarianism and the 1868 Speech on Capital Punishment*, 2nd ed. Indianapolis and Cambridge: Hackett Publishing Company.

Miller RW (2002) Too Much Inequality. *Social Philosophy and Policy* 19(1): 275–313.

Murphy JB (1993) *The Moral Economy of Labor: Aristotelian Themes in Economic Theory*. New Haven: Yale University Press.

Nagel T (1995) Personal Rights and Public Space. *Philosophy & Public Affairs* 24(2): 83–107.

Nordhaus WD (2007) Two Centuries of Productivity Growth in Computing. *Journal of Economic History* 67(1): 128–159.

Nussbaum MC (1997) Capabilities and Human Rights. *Fordham Law Review* 66(2): 273–300.

O'Neill O (1996) *Toward Justice and Virtue: A Constructive Account of Practical Reasoning*. Cambridge: Cambridge University Press.

Rawls J (1971) *A Theory of Justice*. Cambridge, MA: Harvard University Press.

Rawls J (2005) *Political Liberalism*. New York: Columbia University Press.

Raz J (2010a) Human Rights in the Emerging World Order. *Transnational Legal Theory* 1(1): 31–47.

Raz J (2010b) Human Rights Without Foundations. In: Besson S and Tasioulas J (eds) *The Philosophy of International Law*. Oxford: Oxford University Press, pp. 321–338.

Roessler B (2012) Meaningful Work: Arguments from Autonomy. *The Journal of Political Philosophy* 20(1): 71–93.

Samuelson P (2016) Freedom to Tinker. *Theoretical Inquiries in Law* 17(2): 563–600.

Satz D (2003) Child Labor: A Normative Perspective. *The World Bank Economic Review* 17(2): 297–309.

Schwartz A (1982) Meaningful Work. *Ethics* 92(4): 634–646.

Sen A (1985) Well-Being, Agency and Freedom: The Dewey Lectures 1984. *Journal of Philosophy* 82(4): 169–221.

Sen A (2004) Elements of a Theory of Human Rights. *Philosophy and Public Affairs* 32(4): 315–356.

Simmons AJ (2001) *Justification and Legitimacy: Essays on Rights and Obligations*. Cambridge: Cambridge University Press.

Smith A (2003) *The Wealth of Nations*. New York: Bantam Dell.

Spitz-Oener A (2006) Technical Change, Job Tasks, and Rising Educational Demands: Looking Outside the Wage Structure. *Journal of Labor Economics* 24(2): 235–270.

Stigler GJ (1951) The Division of Labor Is Limited by the Extent of the Market. *Journal of Political Economy* 59(3): 185–193.

Tasioulas J (2007) The Moral Reality of Human Rights. In: Pogge T (ed) *Freedom from Poverty as a Human Right: Who Owes What to the Very Poor?* New York: UNESCO and Oxford University Press, pp. 75–102.

Tasioulas J (2012) On the Nature of Human Rights. In: Ernst G and Heilinger J-C (eds) *The Philosophy of Human Rights*. Berlin and Boston: Walter de Gruyter, pp. 17–60.

Tasioulas J (2013) Human Rights, Legitimacy, and International Law. *The American Journal of Jurisprudence* 58(1): 1–25.

Tomasi J (2012) *Free Market Fairness*. Princeton: Princeton University Press.

Van Parijs P (1995) *Real Freedom for All: What (if anything) can Justify Capitalism?* Oxford: Clarendon Press.

Von Hippel E (2017) *Free Innovation*. Cambridge, MA: MIT Press.

Wellman C (2010) *The Moral Dimensions of Human Rights*. Oxford: Oxford University Press.

Wiles E (2006) Aspirational Principles or Enforceable Rights? The Future for Socio-Economic Rights in National Law. *American University International Law Review* 22(1): 35–64.

Part IV

Critical Views

12 Economic Rights as Human Rights

Commodification and Moral Parochialism

Daniel Attas

1. Introduction

The question this chapter addresses is conceptual and normative: given our best understanding of the nature of human rights, and of what their justification might be, should economic rights (which we plausibly have good reason to promote) be considered human rights? In other words, *ought* Economic Rights be codified in international declarations, treaties and conventions pertaining to Human Rights? The question is important for the reason all philosophical questions are important: we should get things clear. If there are practical implications down the way, which there very well may be, that would be an added bonus.

Perhaps the best way to promote some important interests, such as those specified by economic rights, is to entrench them in human rights codes and practice. Human rights discourse enjoys considerable rhetorical force, such that if an interest comes to be taken as a legitimate aim or object of human rights, this already gives it a significant practical advantage. I do not want to outright deny that some economic rights ought to be protected, and that portraying them as human rights may be the most effective way of doing just that. Though I will, towards the end of this chapter, raise some doubts regarding this claim.

I will propose an understanding of human rights as a construct of international law, informed by the deep-seated fact of global cultural pluralism and the concern of establishing a system that recognizes this pluralism, transcends a narrow parochial perspective and thus avoids the accusation of cultural or moral colonialism. Economic rights I understand not as general rights to participate in economic activities such as production and consumption, but the very specific rights to commodify. That is to say, rights to take part in such activities within a distinctive social form by which production and consumption are mediated through exchange. Thus, the two concerns of parochialism and commodification, which I will shortly clarify, will form the axis of my argument. Very briefly, the argument will be that endorsing rights of commodification is incompatible with a genuine concern with parochialism. Hence, I will argue, economic rights should not be considered human rights.

I proceed as follows: In section 2, I present the notion of human rights (HR) and the concern of parochialism to which I believe an adequate theory of HR should be framed as a response. In section 3, I discuss economic rights and the sense in which they take a commodified and narrowly restrictive view of general human practices of production, consumption and economic cooperation. I then present two strategies in HR thought that are precisely framed to take account of the charge of parochialism: section 4 introduces a naturalistic or moral conception of HR; and section 5 introduces a political conception of HR. I then show, in sections 7 and 8, how under each of these views economic rights should not properly be considered human rights. Finally, in section 9, I respond to the more pragmatic-minded activist who, concerned with promoting human well-being, is eager to embrace the idea of economic rights as human rights for practical reasons.

2. Human Rights and Moral Parochialism

Human rights, it is often presumed, are rights possessed by all human beings simply in virtue of their humanity (e.g., Donnelly, 2013: 10; Tasioulas, 2012). Many would agree to this deceptively simple formulation. It implies that all human beings, regardless of religion, race, gender or citizenship possess these rights. Moreover, it binds all countries to respect these rights, regardless of their form of regime, culture or economic development. Furthermore, human rights do not follow from the institutionalization in domestic legal codes, rather they set moral standards that all domestic codes ought to follow and that serve as a basis of criticism if they do not. In this respect, HR appear to be not too dissimilar from moral natural rights. Indeed, much of our understanding of the former is mediated by the tradition of the latter.

But HR, more specifically, have a more recent and concrete origin. Designed as a response to the post–world wars historical situation, they are a principal component of a world order established in that specific context. In this sense, part of the rationale of human rights (unlike natural rights) is the role they play in international law: the contraction of state sovereignty, and the justification of sanctions against countries that fail to abide by these standards. When thought of in this context, their universality is not a substantive aspect of their grounds. It is not that these rights are based on some trait common to all human beings as such that entitles them to these protections. There may indeed be no such grounds. It is merely a formal feature of their claim against all countries, regarding all individuals without any further qualification.

The framing of the Universal Declaration of Human Rights (1948), and the development of subsequent conventions and covenants, were struggling, right from the start with the problem of cultural pluralism. Not all cultures and political ideologies shared the same views regarding the sort of protections that ought to be entrenched in international law. The natural rights tradition, that played a more or less conscious part in the minds of the original framers and ever since, is a specifically Western idea, itself the product of a specifically European history. This plausibly raises the worry, and sometimes the allegation, of cultural or moral parochialism and colonialism. Human rights are viewed as Western liberal values, imposed across all countries mainly due to the superior power, both military and economic, of the West.

The concern of parochialism isn't a mere afterthought in an account of HR. It isn't that after working out a full-blown theory, determining which rights are justified on our developed conception, we need now to measure it against the claim of cultural and ethical pluralism (cf. Buchanan, 2013: 249 ff). Rather, it is that the concern of parochialism informs from the very start the idea of human rights as a central component of a legitimate international legal order. Legitimacy is grounded against a background of reasonable pluralism.

Peoples and cultures differ with respect to what they take to be valuable in a human life, and in ways they deem appropriate to promote such value. If a HR regime is to demand compliance, and to foster such compliance by means of intervention, its legitimacy must be justifiable in the eyes of all cultures and peoples subject to it. The concern of parochialism is that politically and economically more powerful states, mostly in the West, impose their ultimately European values and ways of promotion, perhaps innocently believing their undeniable moral validity. Or worse, that these more powerful states forcefully institutionalize the values and methods that bolster their continual dominance and serve their more mundane commercial and military interests. As I will argue later on, such a suspicion is all the more plausible (and worrisome) in the case of economic rights. In this I am not endorsing moral relativism, or the position that all moral views are equally valid. What I am claiming is that as a matter of political morality, an international coercive structure must respect, at least to some extent, such a plurality by justifying its specific content in terms that all cultures, no matter how diverse, should accept (cf. Nickel, 2007: 168–184).

There are two strategies to take full account of such basic cultural pluralism and to legitimate the specific content of International Human Rights. These underwrite a "moral" and a "political" conception of human rights (cf. Cruft et al., 2015: 4–10): (i) Moral Human Rights (MHR) as based on human nature or dignity, claimed to be common to all humankind, and not on some cultural preference or, even worse, partial interest of the West. This views human rights on an individualistic basis: promoting fundamental human interests of individual persons such as well-being or agency, seen as necessary for dignity. Thus, for example, freedom from discrimination (UDHR Article 2), a right to own property (Article 17) and a right to education (Article 26) are justified on the grounds of the well-being and agency they promote, and the dignity they respect, for the individuals protected by these rights. If the list of recognized human rights truly promotes interests which all human beings as such have, then there is less of a worry that something specifically Western is being illegitimately imposed on cultures and peoples that do not share these values. Their protestations notwithstanding, and the offense they may take to their own culture, it is surely they who unjustifiably crush important human interests that deserve promotion.

(ii) Political Human Rights (PHR) as a necessary component of an institutionalized world order designed to reduce the likelihood of war and strive towards stable peace among all nations, an interest presumably shared by all countries, and not merely the liberal West. This views human rights on a political-social basis: promoting an interest of international society as a whole, such as peace or justice. Thus, the articles previously mentioned, and others in UDHR, are justified on the grounds that protection of these interests (whether or not they can be considered fundamental in any sense, or distinctively human) is necessary or at least contributorily significant for promoting world peace. Individual peoples who do not feel committed to a specific list of rights or do not see it as reflecting their political-moral outlook, and on this basis justify their opposition to some or all human rights, are in a sense missing the point. In their refusal, it is they who unjustifiably fail to take the necessary measures for an evident universal interest in stability and peace.

Both the individualistic grounds of the fundamental interest of human beings in dignity and the political-social grounds of a principal interest of humankind in stability and peace are alluded to in the opening sentence of the preamble to UDHR:

> Whereas recognition of the inherent *dignity* and of the equal and inalienable rights of all members of the human family is the foundation of freedom, *justice and peace in the world.*
>
> (italics added)

One way to understand this is that a test for the just inclusion of specific rights in the list of International Human Rights must relate to the interest that these rights protect, either by showing that it is a fundamental human interest (that it is necessary to protect the individual's dignity) or that it is a means to achieve an important goal of humankind as a whole (that it is necessary to the promotion of world peace). It should be stressed that the individualist-naturalistic and the social-political are two independent strategies. The test for legitimacy need succeed in answering only one. Our question then is "Can Economic Rights, including Labour Rights, and all other rights pertaining to economic roles, be justified on either of these two views?" First I shall take a closer look at the notion of economic rights.

3. Economic Rights and Commodification

It is not uncommon to set apart civil and political rights (such as freedom of movement or freedom of expression) from social-economic rights (such as a right to basic health care or education, or a right to employment). The former are taken to be predominantly negative in character, the latter more positive. Though both must have negative and positive aspects, it is thought that civil and political rights ground mostly duties of non-interference, social and economic rights ground, to a greater extent, duties of provision and have more thoroughly distributive implications. How much should be provided (in terms of education or health care, for example) remains unspecified, since that should surely depend on the economic development and capacities of the different states. Partly for this reason social-economic rights are more controversial, and their inclusion in human rights declarations and conventions are more often challenged. I do not endorse this line of criticism. I mention it here only because I want to make a further distinction within the category of social-economic rights and to separate the social and economic rights that are regularly lumped together. Whatever stand one may take with respect to social rights, the focus here is on economic rights in both their negative and positive aspects. Such rights are not concerned with the direct provision of material benefits although they may indirectly contribute to that too. Rather they relate to, or facilitate, or regulate, our functioning within the economy. That is to say, economic rights specify protections and restrictions that pertain to our roles as producers of goods and services, consumers, investors and so on. Some of what I shall say against taking economic rights as human rights may also count against other non-economic rights, including social rights, but it would not be because they are too vague, too general or positive. Nevertheless, economic rights are sufficiently distinct to warrant dealing with them alone.

One class of economic rights incorporated in HR documents are those that form part of what are referred to as labor rights. These may include freedom of occupation, a right to a just wage, a right to workplace privacy, a right to minimal standards of hygiene and safety on the job, a right against unfair dismissal, a right to organize and bargain collectively and more.[1]

It is perhaps so obvious as not to be worth mention that "work" in these documents refers predominantly, if not exclusively, to wage labor, a right to be *employed*, to organize with fellow *employees* and to be treated fairly within the *employment* relation. No doubt, employment in modern society is a principal means, and often the only means, to a satisfactory standard of living, to social status and to a sense of meaningfulness. Having a paid job indirectly serves some highly significant interests for all human beings. Nevertheless, these rights do not directly refer to any of these advantages. Instead they pertain to the person in her role as employee. Thus, it seems apt in this context to apply the term "economic rights," rather than social (or social-economic) rights, to labor rights.

It is plausible, and perhaps even strictly consistent, to extend the sort of protection afforded to a person with regard to her role as employee also to other roles in the economy. For example, we may think that, given the central role of consumer relations, there is a no less significant interest in guaranteeing the freedom to purchase goods and services provided in the market, under fair terms, that these goods and services be safe, and not marketed on false pretenses, as well as perhaps also to organize under the wings of various consumer advocacy groups and associations. The same would apply to the role of loaner, and also to rights of the corresponding roles of employer, investor, seller and creditor.

Note that economic rights are more specific than rights of inclusion. Basically, they are *rights to commodify under fair terms* such as equal access, non-domination, non-discriminatory conditions, safety and hygiene, free from coercion or deception. To borrow Robert Nozick's (1974: 163) memorable phrase: the rights to engage without force or fraud in "Capitalist acts between consenting adults," under decent conditions and fair return. Labor rights are not simply a right to work, they are rights relating to the *selling* of labor power; consumer rights are not simply a right to consume, they are rights relating to the *buying* of goods and services and so on and so forth.

Commodification is a certain arrangement of economic activities. It is the provision and acquisition of goods and services in return for direct commensurate payment—typically, but perhaps not necessarily, monetary payment. The term is often used pejoratively: the commodification of that which ought not be commodified. Arguably, this may include love, sex, the human body, art, labor, land and so on. But my use of the term is strictly neutral. Thus, it is not an argument against economic rights *per se* that they "commodify" and are therefore objectionable. I don't presume commodification to be necessarily evil. But, I will argue, the fact that economic rights narrow the scope of protections and guarantees to commodified forms of economic activity is grounds for *denying their status as human rights*. Whether it is good or bad to commodify, economic rights pertain to such a practice. They are not merely about working, consuming, cooperating with others. They are about *selling* one's labor power; *buying* goods and services; creating partnerships of *exchange*, for the production, distribution or consumption of goods and services. My argument will hinge on the idea that reasonable peoples and political cultures, with differing ethical views, may have valid reasons to object to full commodification in each and every sphere of economic activity. They may quite reasonably wish to restrict it in various ways. This is sufficient, I believe, to question the status of economic rights (i.e., rights to commodify) as human rights.

4. Moral Human Rights

As I argued in section 2, the idea of HR as an international, universally binding, legal order, is informed by a concern to transcend culturally or ideologically parochial views of what all persons as such are owed. For a legal order such as this, backed by coercive sanctions that encroach an otherwise boundless right of self-determination and state sovereignty, must possess a legitimacy the grounds of which can be acknowledged by all under its claimed jurisdiction. There are two strategies to cope with this concern. One is a *political* view by which human rights and their establishment in international law are designed to promote a collective interest shared by all reasonable states: an interest in world peace. In the next section I shall briefly present this view. Here I present a *moral* view, by which human rights serve to protect individual interests that all humans share: an interest grounded in what is most distinctive about their humanity. There are many forms such a view can take. One prominent example is provided by James Griffin (2008).[2] Beginning from a culturally situated conception of human rights, developed within a certain philosophical tradition, and receiving extensive expression in political declarations and in institutionalized law, Griffin proceeds to investigate what might justify this set of rights and the way we think about them. His aim is to clarify and provide justification for *roughly* those rights taken to be human rights in this tradition.

Rights, and human rights in particular, signal a sort of urgency or a degree of priority within our moral topography. It is for this reason that rights discourse is politically significant and there is a strong pull towards rhetorical expansionism of the concept of human rights. If we can get a particular interest to be recognized as a human right, this might give us a certain advantage in its promotion. So one important prerequisite for such a theory, according to Griffin, is that it should set more or less clear limits on what may be regarded as a human right. We would want such a theory not only to specify some fact about humans that explains why roughly *all* humans and *only* humans have these rights; but also how this fact might explain or justify their having *rights* rather than being the object of some other kind of moral concern.

Griffin suggests that human rights are designed to protect what is most distinctive of our human existence: our status as human beings or our personhood. This personhood centers on what we value especially highly about our lives, sometimes more than our happiness, namely our being normative agents. That is to say, our reflecting, deliberating and forming of a conception of a good life, and our choosing and acting to realize that conception (Griffin, 2008: 32). This is what Griffin calls the normative agency view of the personhood account. All human rights according to this view comprise the highest-level rights to the basic components of agency—viz. autonomy, liberty and a minimum provision of material resources—to the extent required to protect our *capacity* for normative agency, our *exercising* of that capacity, or both. Four criteria can be extracted from this view:

i. HR as providing a moral, pre-institutional, critical standard
ii. The importance or urgency of the interests protected by HR
iii. The interests are possessed by all human beings (regardless of special characteristics, such as gender, race, ethnicity or citizenship)
iv. They apply in all institutional circumstances and at all times—they are timeless in the sense that they are independent of social forms

Why ought HR be codified in international law? Presumably, because doing so will contribute to their codification in domestic law, and their inculcation in a general moral outlook. This in turn will afford them greater protection and as such achieve a morally more perfect world.

Still, given that this view consciously starts from the natural rights tradition, it is not unreasonable to suspect that it espouses a specifically Western view of human nature. How can we respond to such an objection? Why might we believe that in demanding human rights codification in international law, the West isn't simply imposing its own parochial moral standards? Or worse, its own partial interests? What is supposed to appease this worry is precisely the grounding of human rights on interests that *undeniably* relate to all human beings regardless of cultural background or social development.

For example, a right against torture is supposed to be grounded on the interest all human beings have in their autonomy and well-being insofar as these are necessary components of their normative agency. It is this capacity that allows humans to live their lives according to a conception they freely endorse, and that sets them apart from non-human animals. Torture, by means of violence, frustrates this capacity, getting the victims to do what they do not want to do, or worse to live in ways they would not freely choose. It is precisely by diminishing their autonomy or well-being so fundamentally that it interferes with their normative agency that the dignity of victims of torture is compromised. This is so regardless of their religion, customs, political ideology, level of economic development or forms of institutions. The catalogue of human rights, then, should enumerate the various protections of a basic level of material well-being and autonomy insofar as these are necessary for the free exercise and development of normative agency, and accordingly manifest a "recognition of the inherent dignity" humans possess.

5. Political Human Rights

To explain the political or institutionalist approach I start from Rawls's *Law of Peoples* and offer a particular interpretation of the sense in which human rights are justified as intrinsic to a stable international legal system guaranteeing world peace, and not to any conception of human nature or non-political moral doctrine (Cf. Audard, 2006). The point is to overcome the charge of political parochialism: human rights on this view do not follow from some specifically Western liberal ideas, local or regional history, but from what is necessary for a lasting world peace, presumably an interest shared by all (reasonable) peoples.

"World Peace" means stability for the right reasons, that is to say, due to peoples affirming the principles of international order and willingly abiding by them. It is not a mere *modus vivendi*, not a contingent equilibrium of power. The latter would be fragile in the sense that any detected disequilibrium would result in a violent realignment. And the expected dynamics would mean that war would be inevitable. Moreover, it would be a reflection of an order biased towards the interests or the moral and political outlook of the more powerful countries. Thus, if what is being canvased as world peace is a mere *modus vivendi*, we would still be rightly suspicious of liberal Western political-moral colonialism, if not a downright economic opportunism.

The conditions that would enable world peace are to be specified by international law, or the best way to interpret international law is as the conditions that are conducive to world peace. These include (Rawls, 2001: 37): (a) A general respect for state sovereignty in managing its affairs vis-à-vis other states, and autonomy regarding its internal concerns; (b) Just war as only war in self-defense, against aggression by other states, and conducted subject to specified restrictions; (c) Justified intervention (political, economic or military) in cases of grave human rights violations.

It seems quite obvious how a general respect for state sovereignty and autonomy, as well as abiding by principles of *jus ad bellum* and *jus in bello*, may be conducive to world peace. Less obvious is why the protection of human rights is viewed as similarly necessary.

Here are a few thoughts why we might consider them so (Cf. Beitz, 2011: 106):

1. Democracies, due to their internal structure, may be tempted to go to war in case of grave violations of HR, presumably, due to moral outrage (Rawls, 2001: 8). This tight relation between liberal democracies and a law of peoples is explained by the fact that, at least in Rawls's scheme, the law of peoples is an extension of justice as fairness, and applies to how liberal democracies would choose to govern

the relations among them. Decent (non-democratic) societies are also included by a further extension, but the question is posed and the agreement is initially sought from liberal democracies. This is somewhat unfortunate, for thusly framed it could not release us from the strong sense that the idea of human rights as ideologically parochial. If the question of a just and stable world order were asked from the perspective of states of a non-liberal-democratic culture, it is not clear that non-aggression were not sufficient, and that human rights would have to be established too. Presumably such states would not feel the moral urge to apply sanctions and, ultimately when all fails, to go to war against states that systematically violate human rights.

One way to respond to this is to say that the practical point of entry to the idea of world peace is the 200-year observation that democracies don't go to war against each other. The explanation being that democracies' internal structure make it quite unlikely that a democracy would go to war for the sake of honor, conquest or subjugation of other peoples (Rawls, 2001: 51–54). Democracies, unlike monarchies or other authoritarian regimes, are a reflection of the people and not of a group of individuals who have managed to get control of political levers of power. So the long-term bedrock of stable world peace would be that eventually all states would be democracies (or regimes similarly motivated by their internal structure, if there are such regimes). If HR violations, even by non-aggressive nations, stir up democratic sensibilities, this would undermine the long-term quest for world peace.

2. Grave violations of HR will tend to make states internally unstable, and such instability is likely to leak out and spread internationally, at first to neighboring countries but eventually also to geographically remote states. That is to say, civil revolt can rarely be contained within the bounds of the state. Part of the explanation of why this is so is the social and economic globalization to which a law of peoples must adequately respond. For example, global networks of communication spread information and footage of what is happening in the country. Also, international supply of armaments, smuggling of weapons and people across borders, shady businesses identifying a source of high profit, legitimate international businesses attempting to protect their investments—all these create worldwide economic repercussions of domestic violence. Finally, the flight of refugees puts pressure on potential host countries and generates economic hardship and ethnic or racial unrest which may lead to political turmoil, violence and international conflict. Witness recent events in Europe due to mass migration from Syria and Africa.[3]

3. Nation-states and communities of identity—religious, ethnic or racial—rarely correlate, and so HR violations, which tend to occur across such lines, are likely to stir up indignation in extended communities abroad. For example, if Christians are persecuted in a Muslim country, or German speakers in a French-speaking country or Asians in a predominantly white country, this is likely to inflame Christians, German speakers and Asians, respectively, and to pressure their governments to take action against the HR violating country. In other words, grave and unchecked HR violations will tend to provoke indignation worldwide in communities of allegiance, and pressure governments to take progressively stronger action against such violations.
4. HR violations, even if they do not lead to direct confrontation and war, will tend to foster distrust in violators. This seems certainly so by democratic societies that view it as an affront to their moral sensibilities, and by societies with a strong allegiance to the persecuted minorities who may view it as an assault to their own identity. A "peace" hanging on such distrust will be a mere *modus vivendi* achieved for "the wrong reasons," a fragile order rather than a real case of stability.

Perhaps none of this is very persuasive, and there is no clear mechanism by which human rights violations are likely to lead to violent conflict. In that case an international human rights regime, backed by coercive measures, would lack legitimacy. Accordingly, it seems to me, something of this sort must be true if human rights are to be justified on the basis of the aspiration to "justice and peace in the world." HR would then be that protection of interests a violation of which would tend to stir civil unrest and lead to international indignation and increase the risk of war.

6. The Upshot So Far

I have presented in bare outline two views of the idea of human rights as constitutive of a world order informed by the concern to avoid political-moral parochialism. The two views share the following conditions:

1. HR protect individual interests universally, i.e., for all humans across all countries and cultures.
2. HR warrant international enforcement, and therefore require legitimacy.

Moral human rights (MHR) are designed to protect distinctly human *individual* interests, such as their well-being and autonomy, insofar as such protection embodies a recognition of their "inherent dignity." For example, insofar as the interests protected are necessary components of their normative agency. The need to recognize human dignity, and how the interests protected connect to this idea, should be accepted by all, regardless of culture, social form or economic development. International enforcement is not a mere imposing of the moral standards or political-economic interests of the more powerful nations. This view of HR exemplifies a pre-political morality, whereby the political mechanisms of coercion (international or domestic) are seen as means to enforce a more moral outcome. As such, it must be grounded on some view of human nature or of well-being or other interest which humans share. That is the main problem of such a view. For it is doubtful that any interest of this sort exists. And the concern is that if such a ground is allegedly identified, it is in fact a mere cultural or ideological parochialism. The fear is augmented when it is realized that the view is the product of a distinctly European political history and philosophical tradition.

Political human rights may protect individual interests, such as well-being and autonomy, only insofar as such protection promotes a *global social* interest such as stability of the international system or world peace. For example, insofar as the interests when compromised are likely to inflame cross-border hostilities. This view of HR exemplifies a political morality, whereby the political mechanisms of coercion and the use of force are legitimized as a necessary means to the interests of stability and peace that all (reasonable) peoples share—whatever their cultural or moral-political background. However, it seems that only the most blatant violations of human dignity and well-being may have such international destabilizing effects. The problem of this view, then, is that it leads to a rather minimalist list of human rights: much closer to the triad of "life, freedom and the pursuit of happiness" than to the elaborate catalogue of the UDHR and subsequent documents. Anything beyond such minimalism is suspect of being morally parochial.

When we come to think about the question whether economic rights ought to be established as human rights we need to ask the following: could they be considered MHR, i.e., the kinds of rights that protect a significant and distinctively human pre-political interest? Or could they be considered PHR, i.e., the kind of rights the violation of which would endanger world peace (by any of the mechanisms sketched in the previous section)? An affirmative response to either of these questions would be sufficient for us to think that they may be part of a legitimate, non-parochial, world order. In the next two sections I will argue for a negative response.

7. Economic Rights as MHR

The question we are still considering is whether economic rights—that is to say, employee, consumer, investor, entrepreneur (and so on) rights to commodify under fair terms—ought to be recognized as HR. The first way to answer affirmatively is to show that they warrant international enforcement due to their role in underpinning the dignity of human beings on the basis of pre-political interests that should be recognized as such by all cultures and peoples.

An initial difficulty arises from the fact that economic rights depend for their validity on the existence of a wide-ranging institution, a particular way in which economic activity is organized, a mode of production (to borrow a Marxian term). Labor rights, such as a right to work, to fair pay, to decent working conditions, depend in this way on the institution of employment (wage labor). Capital rights similarly depend on a financial system (money, banking, corporations and so on). This creates some tension and raises doubt whether strictly speaking they are rights at all. Arguably, no individual interest can be so significant as to provide conclusive reason to set up a whole particular way of organizing production in society (Raz, 1986: 202 ff).

The problem goes deeper. A central feature of this view, namely its universality and timelessness, seems not to apply to economic rights. Consider the following: one way to ground the universal application of human rights, across peoples, cultures and ideologies, is to ground them on an interest that is distinctly human—that any human would have regardless of any particular way society is organized. This is precisely the view of MHR. Such rights are timeless in the sense that they protect interests that transcend any historically specific conditions. A right to be employed or to a loan are neither a distinctly human interest nor a timeless concern. True enough, employment is a widespread and important means to make a living and to take part in meaningful social interaction in modern capitalist economies. But that doesn't make employment, rather than work or some alternative form of social activity, a human right. Consider how bizarre it would be to think of rights to participate in the very specific forms of interaction typical of some historical era as human rights. Although serfdom may be the central social form of work in a feudal mode of production, it would be odd to say that there was at the time, or should have been, a human right to serfdom, or a human right to a fair corveé or other feudal fee. Even more so would be to think of a human right of enslavement in a society where that would be for many the only realistic option for meaningful social interaction. Employment and wage labor should be viewed for what they are: contingent, historically specific, social form of work, rather than a timeless human mode of production. As such labor rights (that at least implicitly assume employment) should not be viewed as human rights. Similar considerations apply to other economic rights.

To be sure, an individual interest in subsistence, or in provision of all material needs, may ground a right of access to whatever form of provision there happens to exist in society, but there can be no right to take part in the employment relation in particular if such a form of interaction does not exist, and there is no right that government take action to ensure that such forms of interaction do exist. There is, in other words, no right to a historically specific institution, i.e., no right to a capitalist mode of production.

Some have argued that timelessness is not a necessary feature of human rights.[4] But even without these comparisons across times, even within a predominantly capitalist society, there are non-economic ways of engaging in meaningful social activities: political, creative or environmental. As well as other ways of participating economically and making a living. For example, one could be self-employed, or run a small business, or be a member of a cooperative. All these options and their regulation may be covered by some economic rights. But there would be nothing obviously contrary to a distinctly human interest in the fact that a society aim to minimize employment and encourage the formation of cooperatives or "self-employment." Or that a society discouraged participation in the economy altogether, in favor of other, more sustainable forms of social activity. Or that it responded to a clear historical trend of a contracting participation in the economy, not by producing jobs and opportunities for investment, but rather by establishing, funding and maintaining spheres of non-economic meaningful social activities.

None of this, I maintain, is unrealistically utopian. To some degree, it is standard policy in most liberal democracies. Let's examine the interests that may be served by commodification, and some alternatives to commodification. As well as reasons some may hold to resist commodification and prefer the latter. There are three main interests to which commodification (*selling* one's labor, goods or services) may serve: an interest in participating in socially meaningful activity, an interest in provision of material needs, an interest in gaining recognition in the value of one's beneficial activities.

I've already mentioned artistic, political and other activities as socially meaningful non-commodified activities. Another major activity is personal caregiving: raising one's children, assisting one's elderly parents, caring for the ill and the weak. Recent decades have witnessed a marketization of these activities, and concerns have been raised that such commodification may "crowd out" caring feelings. Worries are expressed on both sides of the political spectrum:

> On the left, an abiding suspicion of capitalism leads to a fear that monetization of care will lead to care becoming an impersonal commodity, produced at least cost and sold to the highest bidder. On the other hand, many social conservatives decry paid child care, for example, as in all ways inferior to mother provided care (at least if the mother is married and middle class), and try to demarcate a special protected sphere of "family values."
>
> (Folbre and Nelson, 2000: 130)

Both concerns seem reasonable enough for a democratic government to take steps to restrict economic rights in these domains without being subject to international condemnation. There may be other domains where the same logic applies.[5]

A second interest to which commodification may be instrumental is meeting the material needs we all have. In a market-centered society many of the goods we consume and services we seek most of us get by contracting and paying for them in an open market; and these become affordable to us by similarly contracting our labor and receiving a wage in return. Thus economic rights protect the way in which most of us get access to basic needs and to some sphere of material freedom. But there are other means by which our material needs can be met, and are met. Many basic needs are collectively provided and paid for through taxes. Public health care and public education are cases in point, as are public roads and lighting, personal safety and so on. The provision of health care collectively, for example, brings to the fore the complex relationship between physician and patient: the quality and type of treatment isn't a function of how much or by whom the doctor is paid. On the contrary, we expect it to be what she considers to be the best available treatment. Arguably, decommodifying the relationship increases the likelihood of this being so. Collective provision is also more likely to achieve an equal treatment for all patients, since it will be independent of their ability to pay. To guarantee the highest equal standard for all, it may be necessary to restrict private practice. Perhaps only for doctors practicing in public hospitals, perhaps more widely. At least it is reasonable for democratic governments to enact such economic rights-restricting policies if they view this as the best means to provide health care equally and at a high standard.

Receiving a wage for one's labor is a principal means by which individuals in a market-based economy, and many other economic forms, make a living and acquire the means of subsistence and a sphere of personal material freedom. These are no doubt basic human needs, aspects of one's dignity. But here too there are alternative ways by which subsistence and material freedom can be guaranteed, by *decoupling* work and pay, at least partially. The idea of an unconditional basic income aims to do precisely that. And most welfare benefits, even if not unconditional, are guaranteed pay without work. In a collective community such as a Kibbutz, members do not receive a wage for their work, but they are provided with all their needs and they also receive an allowance, which is independent of the kind or amount of work they are expected to do. An economic right to commodify one's labor may thus be restricted without compromising the basic interest of subsistence and material freedom. At least it would not be unreasonable for governments to enact such decommodifying policies with the aim of better covering of the material interests which supposedly ground economic rights.

Lastly, commodification may be a means to proper social recognition of the value of one's activities. By willingness to pay for the goods one produces or for one's services, recognition of one's valuable contribution is expressed. Though sometimes payment may be more an expression of grudging compulsion, there is no doubt that it can also signify genuine appreciation. But there are other ways in which we can and do express a recognition of value, an appreciation or gratitude. Performers are rewarded with applause, sometimes with standing ovations, or with idolizing comments on their web page; academic writers are cited approvingly; prizes are distributed for outstanding achievements ranging from the Nobel Prize in Medicine to "Store Employee of the Month"; routine mention is made in organizational newsletters or in workplace gatherings of exceptional work, or sometimes of everyone's work, of the team spirit, or of successful attainments of goals; extraordinary gratitude and admiration for a job well done is communicated in letters of appreciation. All these are forms of expressing recognition without pay. Perhaps these are insufficient, perhaps there could in theory be many other ways, perhaps in the world we live in there is no genuine alternative to recognition through pay. But the point is that surely "the world we live in" is culture-specific, and there may be cultures less economically centered, where appreciation is regularly shown in a way that is independent of pay. Indeed, where pay for services rendered may be a form of insult. Moreover, if pay is to be our only means of expressing appreciation, and pay is to be roughly determined by the market, we may worry that differentials in pay do not track, even roughly, differentials in value. We may feel that school teachers or nurses, for example, deserve at least as much gratitude and admiration as brokers or hackers, but that this is hardly reflected in the pay they receive. So, policies that restrict commodification in ways that may reduce the ability to express recognition of value through pay may still allow other forms of recognition that are at least as successful in appropriately expressing social appreciation.

To sum up. Economic rights to commodify protect interests in ways that fall short of being distinctly human, timeless or culture-independent. As such they seem to lack legitimacy for international enforcement. It is a stretch to think that failure to uphold a right to employment, or to commodity quality standards, or to fair interest rates, would justify economic sanctions or international condemnation. It is even less plausible to think that international sanctions are due against a society that chooses to organize in a mode of production that relies mainly on self-employed producers and service providers, or on membership in collective communities; or that is guided by a post-productivist ethos.

8. Economic Rights as PHR

The question we are still considering is whether ER—employee, consumer, investor, entrepreneur (and so on) rights to commodify under fair terms—ought to be recognized as HR. A second way to establish that they do is to show that economic rights warrant international enforcement due to their vital role in enabling stability of a just international order and world peace. The problem is that mechanisms by which violations of rights may provoke war don't appear so compelling when we think of ER. Consider the following:

To justify interventions it would have to be believed that violations of rights such as these would generate moral outrage in democracies. Unlikely as it seems, it will also have to be claimed that such disapproval would urge them to take punitive action. Yet even mere condemnation of such violations in regular diplomatic channels seems rare. Compare this to how democracies do indeed react to violations of political freedoms, such as the right to organize, freedom of expression and freedom of religion, as well as the grave violations of some social rights, denying or not taking action to guarantee sufficient water, food, basic health care and education. All these are clear forms of oppression to which democratic sensibilities may be understandably stirred. But it is taking it too far to see oppression in a system that fails to guarantee employment, or to make loans available, or is criminally lax in enforcing safety standards of consumer products. It is incredible that anyone would consider it seriously oppressive if services provided by government (e.g., health care, education, personal security) are prohibited in the private market, thus restricting occupational choice and entrepreneurial initiatives by decommodifying at least certain aspects of the economy. Even a centrally planned economy, where economic freedoms are meager, needn't be considered oppressive. The question is not whether these are good ideas or even sane policies, it is whether they are oppressive and hence likely to raise moral outrage in democracies that would eventually lead them to take action against such states and endanger stability of the international order.

For similar reasons, it is difficult to see why such violations might stir civil revolt or solidaristic calls to action on the basis of cross-border religious or ethnic allegiances. Or, no matter how disastrous they are thought to be, that they would raise distrust in governments that promote such policies. Compare these to common reactions to the violation of political liberties, life and personal possessions. The issue is ultimately empirical: would such violations jeopardize world stability? Normatively, there are areas where states should reasonably expect to plan and implement policies they regard as the most fitting. Economic structuring and regulation are significantly important for state autonomy and must surely be a central part of what is protected by that idea. If it isn't, what could be?

Not only is it unclear how economic rights might fit with the proposed mechanisms of stability, it seems that the imposition of some of these rights, under some unfavorable circumstances, might have the opposite effect. I am thinking of circumstances where the enforcements of such rights will be detrimental to the interests of the individuals it is supposedly designed to protect. Thus, certain labor standards and regulations, some financial regulations or consumer protection and so on may have an overall negative effect on the standard of living in some developing countries, at least in the short term but often in the longer term too.

Recent decades have witnessed an aggressive promotion of global capitalism. The development blueprint devised by the Washington Consensus, that includes economic liberalization, deregulation, privatization, and budgetary discipline, backed by conditional assistance by the IMF. Many people and governments of the global South, rightly or wrongly, associated this with what they viewed as human rights colonialism and imperialism (Nowak, 2017: 30).[6] Construing rights to commodify as human rights bolsters the validity of such claims. If human rights include rights to employ and be employed, to produce for *sale* and to *buy* in order to consume, then human rights become synonymous with capitalism. And, never too often to stress, such synonymity and compliance is proposed by means of international *sovereignty-diminishing* interventionism.

International insistence on economic rights, and enforcing them by means of political or economic sanctions, may appear like a clear case of moral colonialism. Worse still, insofar as sustaining a right to commodify labor in developing countries will be in the economic interest of investors and consumers of developed countries, this may understandably smack of outright economic opportunism. Similarly for other types of ER. Including economic rights in the grand human rights project thus seems more likely to stir up conflict and instability than to sustain world peace.

9. The Activist's Challenge

The Activist is motivated by the urgency of correcting injustice and alleviating human suffering. She has no time for philosophical niceties. The point is well taken: practical moral concerns take precedence over intellectual pedantry. The Activist is surely right that Economic Rights—Labour, Capital and Consumer Rights—serve important interests and may very well be significant requirements of justice in many societies. Since commodification is the most common way to access means of subsistence, as well as other basic human interests, and for many it is the only way, it is imperative that *equal access* to labor and financial markets, for example, be guaranteed. Moreover, given that the exchange relation is often a scene for many types of abuses, care must be taken to *protect against mistreatment* such as domination, exploitation, deception, manipulation and so on and so forth. Incorporating these concerns in International Law, under the heading of Human Rights, the Activist maintains, is one means of achieving this. Whether such imperatives merit the title of Human Rights is mere quibble. The question the Activist urges us to consider is: would incorporating some economic right in International Law as a human right promote the cause of human development and welfare? An unequivocal "Yes" should be taken as sufficient to justify treating Economic Rights as HR.

There is, no doubt, much to this challenge. Although a lot hangs on the plausible yet largely speculative prediction that institutionalizing economic rights in International Law would indeed have this positive effect. In response I offer the following observations. First, the Activist's position is intellectually dubious. It treats HR as a political tool, not as a certain kind of concern, with some specific justification and method. Of course, the Activist doesn't deny that. It is precisely the point. If there is an effective tool that can make the world better, why refrain from using it merely because it fails some test of conceptual analysis or consistency? But the argument I proposed for denying economic rights HR status is not merely conceptual. It is normative. The Activist's position ignores the question of legitimacy.

Second, although establishing economic rights as HR may appear an effective means for improving the human condition, in the long run it may turn out to be counterproductive. A complaint often made is about the expansionist tendencies of human rights discourse. Rather than the slim catalogue of basic needs, we have an inflation in rights recognized under various conventions as HR. Such further inflation through recognition of economic rights may have the effect of devaluing more urgent rights in the list, impoverishing the kind of claim HR is taken to be, draining it of the political potency it previously possessed (Hopgood, 2013).

Third, there may even be direct and short-term harm in recognizing some economic rights as human rights. For example, equalizing economic regulation across countries, including labor and consumer standards, may act against a trend of the flow of capital to less developed regions. If this is true, then imposing such standards globally, as human rights are intended to do, may worsen all things considered the situation of those the rights are most concerned to benefit. There is also the possibility that, at least for labor standards, unionization and collective bargaining may be a more effective means of improving employment conditions than instituting these as human rights (Mantouvalou, 2012: 160 ff). Perhaps consumer advocacy should follow this model for better results.

Fourth, taking all economic rights as a whole—employee, consumer and loaner, investor and employer and so on—as they arguably should be taken, must generate an array of tensions and inconsistencies. Thus, for example, one way to achieve well-being would be to promote consumer rights by means of relaxing labor regulation (as neoliberal rhetoric proposes); or contrarily to expand labor rights and accept the resulting higher prices for consumer products. Similarly with the capital side of the triad—ought the free exit of capital be restricted in favor of domestic employment? Or on the contrary, ought the right to employment be relaxed so that it would not infringe on the rights of capital? Surely, the proper mix of satisfying our interests as investors, consumers and employees isn't a matter of a neat implementing of universal rights, but at the end of the day an issue to be resolved by political decision that may differ from one society to the next. At bottom, these issues are best resolved by consequence-oriented regulation, rather than deontologically informed rights. Of course, not all conflicts among rights must be settled by consequentialist reasoning. All I am claiming is that these sorts of issues regarding economic structure, goals and priorities most naturally lend themselves to such reasoning.

Finally, there is the worry that the establishment of economic rights as HR may inhibit more radical political-economic reform. Human rights are part of a legal superstructure, maintaining certain economic structures and impeding the development of others. Incorporating employment and capital rights in the catalogue of human rights, backed by international sanctions, legitimizes and reinforces a particular mode of production. One that centers on commodification of labor, of means of production and of means of subsistence. A plausible moral view challenges this way of organizing production, and calls for a decommodification of labor, goods and means of production, as the most morally acceptable way of organizing it. That is to say, the entrenchment of such economic rights, by means of institutionalizing them in a HR regime, would inhibit possible long-term progress towards post-capitalist economic structures. So, it would make such a supposedly human right, which should be the basis of some widely shared moral standard, highly contentious. Indeed, it would appear to be a clear example of moral imperialism.

To sum up. The Activist is fixed on making things better rather than on getting them right. She should reconsider her position: it ignores the question of legitimacy, establishing economic rights as HR may in the long run weaken the political power of human rights more generally, more immediately it may worsen the situation of those it is supposed to protect, more widely it may inhibit some reform that may reasonably be considered progress.

10. Conclusion

Human rights are a principal component of an international legal regime. Backed by international sanctions, in effect, they contract state sovereignty contrary to the *prima facie* principle of national self-determination. Their legitimacy depends on them being appropriately informed by cultural and ideological pluralism, and on defusing the charge of moral parochialism. There are two broad strategies to do this: by invoking an individualist-moral conception of HR and by invoking a social-political conception of HR.

Economic rights are rights to commodify—to *sell* one's labor, to *buy* goods and services and so on—under fair terms. Whether or not there is anything necessarily wrong with commodification, the point is that economic rights, as they are typically construed, restrict the world of production and consumption, to such activities taking place within exchange relations. When this is brought into sharp relief, it becomes quite clear that economic rights are unnecessary to protect either some natural interest shared by all humans, or the stability of a peaceful world order. Thus, commodification defeats both of the above strategies and reintroduces the worry of parochialism and moral colonialism. It is therefore unjustified to include them in the standards of international HR. Even from a mere pragmatic point of view, there are reasons to doubt that establishing economic rights as HR would serve the long-term interest that such rights are presumably designed to promote.

Two points of clarification and emphasis. First, if economic rights were understood more widely as rights to subsistence, to some material freedom, to taking part in meaningful social institutions, then they may very well be human rights. At least, nothing in my argument would suggest otherwise. It is to the commodified construal that I objected. Second, once certain kinds of economic institutions exist (employment, buying and selling of goods and services, investment, etc.), it would be wrong to exclude some from taking part in these. But the wrong is in the *discrimination*, not in the restriction of commodification. Such a wrong is already protected against by the human right against discrimination and is independent of any specifically economic interests one may have.[7]

Notes

1 Article 23 of UDHR states: (1) Everyone has the right to work, to free choice of employment, to just and favorable conditions of work and to protection against unemployment. (2) Everyone, without any discrimination, has the right to equal pay for equal work. (3) Everyone who works has the right to just and favorable remuneration ensuring for himself and his family an existence worthy of human dignity, and supplemented, if necessary, by other means of social protection. (4) Everyone has the right to form and to join trade unions for the protection of his interests.

See also: International Covenant on Economic, Social and Cultural Rights (1966), European Social Charter (1961), ILO Declaration on Fundamental Principles and Rights of Work (1998).

2 Griffin's account is perhaps not the most accepted or influential, but it is one of the clearer and deeper examples of the moral view of human rights.

3 India justified its intervention in East Pakistan (now Bangladesh) in 1971 as a response to what it called 'refugee aggression' that saw as many as 10 million people cross the border into West Bengal (Wheeler, 2000: 61). Tanzanian intervention in Uganda (1979) and Vietnamese intervention in Cambodia (1978) both involved destabilized borders and fears of refugee flows (Ibid., chaps 2–4) as did the flight of Hutu refugees from Rwanda in 1994 that led eventually to a civil war in the Democratic Republic of Congo.

4 Usually by pointing to some rights on the UDHR catalogue that seem to be quite time-specific. This begs the central question of justification and legitimacy.

5 For example, where we hope for work to be done out of a sense of professionalism, the application of aesthetic standards or out of a feeling of communal

responsibility. The quality of the output may depend on these being the underlying motivations. The worry is that commodification may have a corrupting effect on them.

6 That the neoliberal project of imposing capitalism globally has had damaging effects on some developing or newly marketized economies was pointed out early on also by Stiglitz (2002).

7 Thanks to David Enoch, David Heyd, Avner de-Shalit, Stephen Hopgood, Jahel Queralt, Reem Segev, Bas van der Vossen, participants of the Zurich workshop on Economic Liberties and Human Rights, and the Jerusalem Law and Philosophy workshop.

References

Audard C (2006) Cultural Imperialism and "Democratic Peace." In: Martin R and Reidy DA (eds) *Rawls's Law of Peoples: A Realistic Utopia?* Oxford: Blackwell, pp. 59–75.

Beitz CR (2011) *The Idea of Human Rights.* Oxford University Press.

Buchanan A (2013) *The Heart of Human Rights.* Oxford: Oxford University Press.

Cruft R, Liao SM and Renzo M (2015) The Philosophical Foundations of Human Rights: An Overview. In: Cruft R, Liao SM and Renzo M (eds) *Philosophical Foundations of Human Rights.* Oxford: Oxford University Press.

Donnelly J (2013) *Universal Human Rights in Theory and Practice.* London: Cornell University Press.

Folbre N and Nelson JA (2000) For Love or Money—or Both? *The Journal of Economic Perspectives* 14(4): 123–140.

Griffin J (2008) *On Human Rights.* Oxford: Oxford University Press.

Hopgood S (2013) *The Endtimes of Human Rights.* New York: Cornell University Press.

Mantouvalou V (2012) Are Labour Rights Human Rights? *European Labour Law Journal* 3(2): 151–172.

Nickel JW (2007) *Making Sense of Human Rights.* Oxford: Blackwell.

Nowak M (2017) *Human Rights or Global Capitalism: The Limits of Privatization.* Philadelphia, PA: University of Pennsylvania Press.

Nozick R (1974) *Anarchy, State and Utopia.* New York: Basic Books.

Rawls J (2001) *The Law of Peoples: With, the Idea of Public Reason Revisited.* Cambridge, MA: Harvard University Press.

Raz J (1986) *The Morality of Freedom.* Oxford: Clarendon Press.

Stiglitz JE (2002) *Globalization and Its Discontents.* New York: WW Norton.

Tasioulas J (2012) On the Nature of Human Rights. In: Ernst G and Heilinger JC (eds) *The Philosophy of Human Rights: Contemporary Controversies.* Berlin: Walter de Gruyter, pp. 17–59.

United Nations (1948) Universal Declaration of Human Rights.

13 How Fundamental Is the Right to Freedom of Exchange?

Rowan Cruft

1. Introduction

This chapter asks two questions about the moral right to be allowed to engage in free market exchanges. The first question is how important this right is: in particular, when it should prevail in conflicts with other rights. The second question is how context-dependent this right is: how deep in our nature are the interests that make this moral right exist: interests in being unimpeded in exchanging or making gifts, subject to one's recipient's consent. The two questions are related but independent.[1]

Both questions have a bearing on the further issue of whether the right to freedom of exchange is a "human right." I favor what is sometimes called a "naturalistic" or "orthodox" view of human rights as important moral rights held by each human for her own sake—rights that are given legal and institutional form by contemporary human rights practices, but that are not constituted by these practices (despite Beitz's and Buchanan's different claims to this effect), nor are limited to those rights whose violation is permissibly a matter of international concern (despite Rawls's and Raz's versions of this claim).[2] I will not defend my "naturalistic" view of human rights here, nor engage directly with the question of whether freedom of exchange is a human right. Instead, my focus is on the ways in which it is fundamental, as outlined in my first paragraph: how important is this right vis-à-vis others, and how contextually variable is its importance?

The aim is to find the correct place for freedom of exchange in relation to such rights as political participation, freedom of association, health, education, life. My nuanced conclusion will be that in many but not all ways exchange is less fundamental: its existence and importance are rather more dependent on context, and the results of exchanges are systemically overridden by a certain class of rights. But this will turn out to depend on fairly "brute" intuitive claims; further, this result leaves the right nonetheless with real significance as a vitally important right in the modern world—a significance we need both to remember and avoid overstating.

It is worth noting that a defense of freedom of exchange is not necessarily a defense of capitalism, defined as a system in which all means of production are privately owned (and not always as worker-owned cooperatives). An economic system could have many large industries nationally owned or worker-owned yet still respect free market exchanges so long as whatever *is* owned privately (including cooperatives owned by workers) can be voluntarily exchanged subject only (or largely) to consent of owner and recipient. My question is: must what is owned privately generally be voluntarily exchangeable? Would many restrictions on this *themselves* constitute a fundamental injustice or violation of the owner's freedom?

In the next section (§2), I clarify what I mean by the right to freedom of exchange. Then in §3, I run through familiar ways in which free exchange is beneficial. We will see that many of these cases for free markets are instrumental or derivative, where this means that their success depends on context, rather than on value attaching acontextually to freedom of exchange in itself. It thus looks doubtful that free markets ought to have been required *throughout modern history*, nor that alternatives to the free market could never make an acceptable reappearance—unlike, say, norms restricting suffrage or supporting gladiatorial combat: these could not acceptably make a comeback, nor were they ever acceptable in the first place. Further, we will see that many of the reasons in favor of a right to unrestricted free exchange explored in this section are reasons other than the right-holder's own good—and they thus fail to establish this right as one that exists for the right-holder's own sake. This does not make the right unimportant, but marks one significant distinction with some other canonical important rights such as those to education, political participation or absence of torture.

Before looking, in §5, at defenses of free exchange that are both acontextual and "for the right-holder's sake" (defenses focused on the important interest simply in being able to exchange as one wishes, independently of how doing this will serve other goods), I say more in §4 about the relative importance of the right to free exchange. Even if this right's justification is highly dependent on modern conditions, and even if it is not grounded for the right-holder's own sake, it might nonetheless be of great importance, justifying expenditure of many resources (e.g., by constitutionalizing free exchange in order to prevent private and public activities that limit it) that could otherwise be spent on other rights. In this way it would be akin to such local/modern-but-important moral rights as a right to internet access or IVF treatment (though the latter are groundable primarily for the right-holder's own sake), or doctors' or politicians' rights to perform their duties of office (important but modern and only groundable for the sake of others beyond the right-holder). In §4, I outline a limit to exchange's relative importance, but one shared by other central rights such as that to political participation: the rights created by exchanges, like any other rights created by our will independently of whether this serves anyone's well-being, should be subordinated to those rights grounded by how they protect well-being.

§5 then focuses on free exchange's relation to the interest in running one's life as one wishes: an interest that promises to ground the right acontextually, and for the right-holder's own sake. The section argues that the right specifically to individual free exchange is of comparatively low acontextual importance. The argument is driven by fairly untheorized intuition, and I reflect on this fact. My conclusion is that if the driving intuition is correct, then while societies that severely limit free markets are less necessarily guaranteed thereby to violate a fundamental moral right than those restricting suffrage or denying primary education are, nonetheless in the contemporary context such societies are very likely to do so. But this should not mislead us into seeing free markets as acontextually required by human nature.

2. Defining Rights to Freedom of Exchange

My focus is the freedom to buy and sell owned items as one wishes, subject to consent only from oneself and one's co-contractor.[3] In Hohfeldian terms, this freedom is constituted by a power: the power to alter one's own and others' duties and privileges, conditional on the consent of one's co-contractor.[4] To put this precisely, *ownership* of a given item (material or perhaps non-material, as with owned ideas or melodies) constitutes in the paradigm case duties borne by all others, owed to the owner, not to trespass on the item, accompanied by Hohfeldian privileges held by the owner to use the item (where the latter means that the owner owes nobody any duties not to use it). *Transfer* of this item involves the original owner giving up her privilege of use, which is acquired by the recipient, and this involves the transferor placing herself under a new duty, owed to the recipient, not to use the item; transfer also involves "redirecting" everyone else's duties not to use the item, so they are now owed to the recipient rather than the original owner—and hence violation of these duties will now wrong the recipient rather than the original owner. *Exchange* involves transferring one item in return for another, with the relevant Hohfeldian privileges swapped and the duties-not-to-use redirected.[5]

We can distinguish (1) the rights of ownership constituted by others' duties, owed to one, to allow one to use an item from (2) the power to transfer or exchange these rights, as outlined above, and also from (3) further rights protecting the exercise of this power, rights constituted by others' duties owed to one to *allow* one to exercise this power: to allow one to sign contracts that will be binding, not to impede delivery on these contracts nor to prevent communication with potential co-exchangers. By "rights to freedom of exchange" I will mean rights of types (2) and (3).

The structure constituted by rights of types (2) and (3) is frequently encountered: many powers are protected by further rights (claim-rights in Hohfeld's sense) that place others under duties to allow one to exercise these powers. The rights to vote and to marry are examples.

It is standard to point out that ownership in modern societies can vary significantly from the ideal-type sketched earlier (e.g., I might "own" a major work of art but still be compelled to let others view it), and that such variations can often be justified.[6] It is also standard to point out that even canonical or ideal-type ownership and exchange rights have standard limits: limits generated both by the rights of others and by further values such as efficiency (as policed by e.g., anti-trust legislation). Our question about the defensibility of free markets is not a question about such standard limits to the market. It is, rather, the question whether *in the general case* voluntary market exchanges and contracts should be permitted, and if so how far this is necessary given our nature, and how far this is dependent upon modern contextual factors. I focus on cases involving transfer of ownership of objects, and will bracket questions about ownership of the body and sale of services—not because they are unimportant but to keep a manageable topic.

My question for the current chapter is: supposing some ownership rights of type (1) are justified (whether over limited or extensive holdings, and whether as fundamental human rights or as morally justified rights with a lesser status), how important are the reasons to allow *free exchange* between holders of such rights?[7] Do they ground rights to free exchange (in both senses 2 and 3) in a range of contexts, rights that can rarely be justifiably overridden?

3. Freedom of Exchange's Contextual Importance in Securing Other Goods

In one part of his defense of economic liberty, Nickel highlights how freedom to exchange serves our other human rights. Two examples he offers are freedom of religion and freedom of movement:

> Many activities protected by freedom of religion have important economic dimensions. Restricting economic activities in a wholesale way will accordingly restrict freedom of religion. Religious people frequently engage in activities such as (1) buying, renting, or constructing buildings for religious activities; (2) starting and running religious enterprises such as churches, schools, and publishing houses; (3) hiring employees to serve as religious leaders, editors, teachers, office workers, and janitors; (4) soliciting donations for religious causes; (5) saving, managing, and spending the funds coming from donations and the proceeds of religious enterprises; and (6) abandoning work or career to pursue religious study and callings. [. . .]

> There are also strong links to freedom of movement. Key parts of freedom of movement require economic activity. To illustrate this point we can use one particular important type of movement, namely internal or external migration to escape famine, severe poverty, or persecution. At the individual level success in such a migration requires quitting one's job (if any), converting any assets one has to money or things that can be carried or shipped, and buying supplies. If the process of travelling is extended, survival along the way will require finding places to sleep, eat and drink, and work or donations. Substantial restrictions on economic activities can impose restrictions on migration.
>
> (Nickel, 2007: 129–131)

These claims strike me as true and very important, but contingent. The "but" is not meant to be denigrating: *given that freedom to sell assets and buy supplies is essential for movement*, restricting such market freedoms really will be an attack on fundamental freedom of movement. Similarly, *given that freedom to rent a building or solicit donations are essential for certain religious activities*, restricting such market freedoms will again be a real attack on fundamental religious freedom.

Nonetheless, the claims of "essentialness" or "necessity" here are in my view made true by contingencies that are not themselves essential to human societies. It seems possible to engage in freedom of movement or religion without market freedoms, for example, in a society in which travelers can expect free hospitality as they travel,[8] or in a society in which services enabling religious worship are provided "free at point of use" by the state, as health care is in the UK's National Health Service.[9] Now, I am not recommending these alternative ways of securing freedom of movement or religion. I mention them simply to make clear that contingent contextual factors—e.g., the non-existence of the alternatives mentioned—play important work in delivering Nickel's conclusions that market freedoms are needed to secure the other human rights.

The same seems to be true of some of van der Vossen and Brennan's arguments against what we might call the extreme cruelty of protectionism (van der Vossen and Brennan, 2018: 21–25, 61–63). They outline scenarios in which preventing someone from completing an exchange which the parties have entered voluntarily is intuitively unjust, leaving a producer starving because she is unable to exchange. Again, in the modern world protectionist policies often do starve potential producers—but this seems contingent. For example, it is not unimaginable that the starved producers could be fed through other means, perhaps most obviously by state welfare provision.[10]

A further point to note here is that what we might call the traditional "invisible hand" arguments in favor of free markets—those of Hume, Smith and Hayek—do not justify the moral right to engage in free exchange on the basis of what this does for the individual right-holding exchanger.[11] Instead, each person's right to free exchange is justified on the basis of how the system as a whole serves everyone: for example, by allowing you to get what you want that is currently owned by me. Of course my good plays a role in this justification, but its role is not specifically to justify my own right to freedom of exchange. Rather each person's having such a right is justified by how this serves everyone. The benefits I can gain from your exchanging are as essential to the justification of your right as the benefits you gain, on this approach. This is a distinct point from my earlier one just above. It does not show the exchange right's justification to be especially contextually sensitive, but rather shows that a right justified in this way is not grounded specifically for the right-holder's own sake. This need not make the right therefore less important, but it contrasts with, for example, my right not to be tortured or my right to political participation: while the benefits these rights bring to others can be appealed to in order to justify them, such appeal is not *necessary* for their justification; one can alternatively justify them simply by appealing to how they serve the right-holder alone (Cruft, forthcoming: chs. 8–9). By contrast, the "invisible hand" approach makes the benefits to others absolutely central to the justification for my right to freedom of exchange.[12]

Van der Vossen and Brennan are aware of these issues, especially those raised in the paragraph before the last one. They aim to prove that *acontextually*, any limitation on free trade appears intuitively unjust—even if the free exchange was not necessary to secure other important rights. Further, their examples are naturally read as focusing on the good *to the exchanger* of being able to engage in free exchange: "suppose that Jane, after several years of struggling, built a successful business online. And suppose that you prevent the (now) rich Jane's products from being delivered to her customers. It still seems like you are doing something morally wrong" (van der Vossen and Brennan, 2018: 62). Van der Vossen and Brennan think it clear that you wrong Jane; their wider discussion suggests that even *state-based* rather than individual prevention of a voluntary trade would be unjust. This chapter is, in part, prompted by my own uncertainty about how to understand my intuitions in the latter kind of case. Of course my individual prevention of Jane's trade would probably be unjust, at least in a broadly unified market like the United States, organized along free market lines that are broadly justifiable and broadly democratically endorsed. But it is much less clear whether Jane would have been wronged if the voters of another state had denied her market entry. By contrast if these voters had compelled Jane to engage in gladiatorial combat, or if Jane's own local voters had denied her freedom to move within her own state or practice a religion, then I believe our default conclusion should be that this wronged Jane. But I suspect that states can in many contexts permissibly engage in fairly extensive internal market restrictions, and I am unsure whether van der Vossen and Brennan would follow me here: if they did, they would presumably want to say that the default should favor free markets and that some case—whatever it is that establishes exchange rules as rightly a matter for national self-determination and democratic choice—is needed to override this. If a state democratically collectivized its economy, would there be any residual or default sense in which its members should have had a right to engage in free exchange? Is this a right they should have had, the case for which can nonetheless be overridden by certain kinds of collective decisions? Certainly if the collectivization threatened other rights—as in Nickel's examples—then the answer is "yes." But if the collectivization did not threaten other rights, I am simply unsure of my views on the case.

I should make clear that I recognize and endorse van der Vossen and Brennan's defense of the benefits to both parties of any voluntary trade, and I recognize the wider efficiencies of allowing such trades.[13] Furthermore, I endorse van der Vossen and Brennan's sense that individuals choosing on their own to prevent particular voluntary trades by using force would be unjust. But I remain uncertain whether a society's decision to organize itself in a way that restricts free trade must involve any even overridden violation of those restricted, in the way that it would if it decided drastically to restrict movement or religion.

4. The Subordination of the Results of Exchange to Well-Being-Based Rights

An obvious defense of the Hohfeldian power to enter into whatever exchanges one voluntarily chooses—a defense that does not depend on contextual factors to make such a power necessary for other important freedoms—regards the power to exchange as simply part of a natural power to run one's life as one wishes. I think it is this idea that drives the pro-exchange intuitions in Brennan's and van der Vossen's cases: surely Jane can exchange her produce with whomever she chooses, if they agree to it and this has no harmful effects on third parties? Indeed we might add that even certain sorts of harmful effects on third parties should not impede Jane's and her co-contractor's decision to run their lives as they wish: compare decisions to marry or to form friendships (Nozick, 1974: 263). And it looks like it is Jane's interest rather than the interests of others that drives this conclusion, making her right to exchange a right that she holds for her own sake.

Before examining this argument further in §5, I note a limitation it shares with rights to political participation, to marry, to associate. This point depends on the distinction between *duties grounded on the value of what they enjoin*, and *duties we have created (through natural powers) at will independently of the value of what they enjoin*. As Nozick's characterization of market distributions as "unpatterned" makes clear, freely entered exchanges need not serve the well-being of those who exchange, or of anyone else—just as they need serve no further value such as desert or merit (Nozick, 1974: 155–164). Of course often people will agree to an exchange in order to improve their position; but they might also agree on a whim, or make a mistake about what would be an improvement, or agree for the sake of others' well-being at the expense of their own. Allowing free exchange is allowing exchange dependent only (within certain familiar limits) on the *wills* of the two exchangers. There is therefore no guarantee that post-exchange ownership rights will serve the *interests* of the exchangers.

For these reasons, we cannot see any ownership rights that result from free exchanges as groundable in Razian fashion on the interests of the owner—nor, more broadly, on the *good* of the owner (Raz, 1986: 166). Perhaps sometimes my interest in your keeping away from my piano is sufficient to ground your duty to do so, but if this duty is owed to me as a result of a free exchange I entered, there is no guarantee that this is the case. Requiring exchanges to serve recipients' interests would stop them being *free* exchanges that can be entered simply *at will* by transferor and recipient.

This means that a third party's reason to respect distributions of property resulting from free exchanges cannot be respect for the good or well-being of those who end up holding the property. For their good or well-being is not what makes the duties in question (to keep off certain items) owed to the property-holders as their rights. Rather, it is the exchanging parties' *wills* that have generated this result, and they generate this result independently of whether the exchange serves anyone's well-being.

Now, my crucial claim here is that rights or duties that people hold in virtue of their will to hold them are, despite being very important, of lesser priority than rights or duties that exist simply in virtue of a party's well-being or good. Our fundamental human rights fall into the latter category: your duty not to torture me, to allow me freedom of speech and political participation, and I would add to secure me with health care and education, are all *made to exist* primarily by my interest in the relevant goods (in not being tortured, in speaking and participating freely, in health and education). To put this more precisely, my well-being is sufficient to constitute a strong positive case for the existence of the duties which constitute such rights.[14] By contrast, your duty not to trespass on items gained by me through exchange is *made to be owed to me* by my and my exchanger's will—not by my or anyone else's interests. Rights made in this way are of course not unimportant: respect for people's wills (when used in morally acceptable ways) is a basic moral requirement. It encompasses the importance of respecting promissory duties (reflecting will of promisor and recipient), duties of transfer and exchange. But—I contend—respect for people's well-being is also a basic moral requirement, and if the two conflict well-being generally takes priority.

Why do I believe well-being-based duties take priority? This is partly a matter of intuition: promises, contracts and agreements—even "sacred" marriage promises—seem less important in the round than our well-being-based rights. Often, respect for someone's well-being requires respect for their will, but when they genuinely diverge, for example, when a friend asks something of one which would constitute the unjustifiable non-fulfillment of that friend's fundamental well-being-based rights, a good friend should follow the relevant party's well-being rather than her will. (There are of course lots of complications here: it would be terrible to overlook a friend's request to choose to sacrifice him for the sake of his child on the basis that one should serve one's friend's well-being rather than respecting his will—but here I would say that sacrificing the friend for his child as requested *is* better for the friend's well-being: well-being often—but not always—encompasses what one wills and wants.)

These intuitive points will not persuade the opposition, I recognize. A related point to note is that the metaphysics of well-being-based rights is interestingly different to that of rights created at will. The former—rights constituted by duties that exist simply because some aspect of a person's well-being is sufficient to make them exist—are recognition-independent, and in that sense clearly "natural" rights: they exist independently of whether anyone recognizes that they exist. By contrast, rights that exist because we have intentionally exercised a Hohfeldian power to make them exist are obviously not "natural" in the same sense. This is not itself a reason for the former kind of right to have priority over the latter, but it seems consonant with that view. A reverse priority, subordinating the "natural" rights (which exist as violated even in legal systems that do not recognize them, such as systems enshrining discrimination or restricting suffrage) to the rights created by our will (where these might include justified or unjustified legal systems or contracts), would be surprising.

5. The Acontextual Importance to the Right-Holder of Freedom of Exchange?

Even if we accept these points, we might still see free transfer as something that has to be allowed *except when restricting it is necessary to fulfill fundamental well-being-based rights*. And this sounds rather close to something like van der Vossen and Brennan's view: that we can justify restrictions necessary to uphold law and order and welfare services, but the free market, defined by freedom of exchange, should be the default. Further, note that other standard important moral rights protecting the ability to change the normative situation at will—rights to political participation, to marry, to form associations—appear similar: we can justify restricting them for various ends, but freedom to exercise them (freedom of participation, marriage, association) should be the default.[15]

One difference between these rights, I suggest, is that freedom of exchange is more readily overrideable by democratic choice and national self-determination than rights to freedom of participation, association or movement. In the current section, I try to explain my reasons for regarding freedom of exchange as less important and less acontextually central to human life than freedom of political participation, association or movement. The key thought is that when we subtract the contextual factors that happen to make freedom of exchange closely linked to other important rights (i.e., factors like those mentioned by Nickel in §3),[16] it is unclear that what we are left with is of fundamental importance to the right-holder. That is, we should imagine the right to freedom of exchange independently of its relation to health, subsistence, education, religion, political participation, exclusion or corruption, and focus in on it on its own. Seen in this light, it seems to me less important than, say, freedom of movement or freedom to issue promises that do not involve external items, or freedom of political participation or freedom to pursue one's projects. Of course in any real world freedom of exchange will be closely entwined with the latter freedoms, but it seems to me that the main moral importance it has it thereby gains from these other freedoms. By contrast, any one of the latter, taken independently of their linkages to other important rights, still seem fundamentally important to the right-holder in my view. Take political participation: being able to play a part in collective decisions about how we should live strikes me as desperately important, even if one does not exercise this freedom or oneself conceive it as important.[17] Freedom to shape the economic and material context through bilateral decisions involving external goods—that is, freedom of exchange—seems also important, but less so.

What is disheartening for me about this claim (though perhaps heartening for my opposition) is that it is just a claim, reporting a fairly "brute" intuition.[18] Van der Vossen and Brennan report a rival intuition, supported by the Jane example, in the passage quoted at the end of §3 above. Is there more I can say? In other work I develop an argument—not just a brute claim like the one above—for the thesis that the trespassory duties constitutive of property rights or ownership are in many cases morally justifiable only by what they do for the wider community, and not simply by what they do for the individual owner (Cruft, forthcoming: chs. 12–13). Rights to freedom of exchange protect a Hohfeldian power to adjust and change such ownership- or property-constituting duties. Might the fact that freedom of exchange is a power to alter rights that are not themselves grounded by how they serve the right-holder somehow speak in favor of my claim to free exchange's comparatively non-fundamental moral status? I suspect not, for other rights that I have claimed to be more fundamental—including my example of political participation—share the same structure. In a representative (as opposed to direct) democracy, powers of political participation are powers to adjust or change the rights constitutive of the Presidency, or of being a Member of Parliament, say. Political participation powers are (among other things) powers to strip one person of the aforementioned rights and confer them on another. These rights over which one's political participation gives one power are themselves rights grounded not by how they serve the right-holder, but by how they serve the people in general. That is, the President's rights are not morally justifiable for the sake of the individual who is President, but for the sake of the wider public. Rights of political participation are powers to change such community-grounded rights of political office. In this way they are like rights to freedom of exchange.

We seem to have reached the conclusion that there are several rights structurally similar to freedom of exchange: in the current §5, we have just seen that these are rights protecting Hohfeldian powers to alter other rights, the latter sometimes being groundable only by what they do for the wider community beyond the right-holder. From §4, we have seen that the relevant powers are powers the exercise of which will result in a distribution of rights that need not serve or be grounded by the right-holder's interests or well-being, and hence that will be subordinated to rights that are so grounded. Neither point singles out freedom of exchange as structurally special in a way that distinguishes it from, say, political participation or freedom of religion; thus neither point specially supports my intuition that freedom of exchange is a right whose importance is highly context-dependent, and that is not of great importance to the right-holder when considered acontextually in itself. Of course they do not speak against this either, and I would note that many of the oppositional claims made in free exchange's defense tend to draw on contextually contingent aspects of exchange: this is especially clear in the passages from Nickel in §3. Van der Vossen and Brennan's Jane example does more to isolate freedom of exchange from its contextual benefits, but in doing this van der Vossen and Brennan diminish its force: suppose that Jane's trade was prevented by someone who said "we have decided to arrange our economy differently here, Jane; you cannot sell your goods here but you are welcome to join our approach instead, which will require you to give up on individual freedom of exchange and participate instead in democratic control of the marketplace." Is there a sense in which a fundamental interest of Jane's has been overridden in this scenario? I am unsure, and so remain unpersuaded of free exchange's acontextual importance.

Suppose the above is correct—despite the reliance on brute intuition. This does not speak against the importance to each individual of recognizing a right to freedom of exchange *in the context of modern capitalism*. But it should leave us open to alternative possibilities, including possibilities in which individual exchange decisions are subordinated to collective decisions. Imagine an intentional collective democratic decision to limit free exchanges, made by a polity with "natural" Hohfeldian powers of self-determination. The decision might be to limit free exchanges within the society itself, or in relation to external trade. I am unclear why such an intentional collective exercise of Hohfeldian power should be subordinated to any individual decisions to exercise individual Hohfeldian powers constitutive of free exchange. That is, I am unclear why the individual rather than the collective power should be favored when the two conflict. What we have are metaphysically similar powers—powers to create or change duties and rights at will, powers that we are assuming exist recognition-independently even though the duties or rights they create will of course not be recognition-independent—that differ only as borne collectively on the one hand, and individually on the other. In both cases they are powers to create duties *at will*, and hence powers whose creations need not, though they often tend to, serve their exercisers' well-being. It is unclear to me that the individual power must take priority over the collective one.

I am not sure whether van der Vossen and Brennan would disagree, but my sense is that we all *should* disagree if what was being subordinated were individual decisions about movement, religion or participation. Individual interests in such choices are, in my view, sufficiently important to ground rights protecting their exercise largely independently of whether these rights serve others (though of course they often will); this makes such rights exist for the right-holder's sake (Cruft forthcoming, ch. 8). By contrast, my view of free exchange, outlined above, is that my interests in itself in exchanging—interests considered independently of contextually generated important aspects of exchange—are insufficient to ground a very powerful or important right to be unimpeded in such exchanging.

This is not to deny that having control over the ordering of one's life, including Hohfeldian powers to exchange, is very important for the individual's well-being and can thereby ground well-being-based protective rights. But it seems to me that allowing people a range of (restricted) freedoms to make promises, gifts and contracts offers nearly enough of this sort of control even if free exchange is fairly heftily restricted. By contrast, such restricted political participation would not be nearly enough. But requiring *relatively unlimited powers of exchange* is on this view akin to offering free higher education or forbidding people from taking any photographs involving unconsenting strangers: it allows a very high level of protection for an interest (in ordering one's life, being educated, in control over one's body) that does indeed ground well-being-based fundamental rights for one, but it gives a higher level of protection to this interest than such fundamental rights require.

6. Conclusion

As noted, the argument relies at a key point on a brute intuitive claim about the relative unimportance of interests in freedom of exchange vis-à-vis other interests grounding more fundamental rights. Nonetheless, I hope that the additional points made—about the subordination of the results of such exchanges to well-being-based rights (§4), about the structural similarities between freedom of exchange and other rights protecting freedoms (§5) and about the contextual importance of free exchange in the modern world (§3)—have added nuance to how we should understand the brute intuition. I suspect that those who champion freedom of exchange as a fundamental right have been misled by its contextual importance in the modern world. Because a large part of its current importance depends on how exchange delivers goods for parties other than the right-holder as much as for the right-holder, we should be especially wary of taking it to be a fundamental right because the extent to which it is groundable on the right-holder's own good is limited—and I argue elsewhere that our most fundamental rights have to be groundable primarily on the right-holder's good, as rights that exist for the right-holder's sake (Cruft forthcoming, chs. 7–8).[19] Nonetheless, none of this should divert our attention from its great importance in context: as Nickel, Queralt Lange, van der Vossen and Brennan show, in a modern world—especially a capitalist world with limited welfare services—freedom of exchange is essential to the satisfaction of human rights. Where we go wrong is in assuming that this must be true in alternative contexts, or in taking the contexts which make this true not to be justifiably alterable.

Notes

1 Some moral rights only arise in specific modern contexts, such as rights to internet access or IVF treatment, yet within the appropriate context they are extremely important, justifying significant expenditure of resources that would otherwise be spent on other rights. In principle conversely some moral rights could also be comparatively trivial but run very deep, existing throughout history. As it happens, the way the systematic exclusions generated by, say, patriarchy work means that even what would otherwise be trivial, readily overrideable rights borne by all humans through time—e.g., to be treated politely, or not to be interrupted in conversation—rightly become matters of great importance, because a seemingly "minor" individual violation takes on a different appearance within a broader system of exclusion.

2 Beitz, 2009; Buchanan, 2013; Rawls, 1999; Raz, 2010. For a variety of naturalistic accounts, compare the accounts of human rights in Gould, 1988; Griffin, 2008; Nussbaum, 2011: ch. 3; Tasioulas, 2015. Compare also Woods, 2014: ch. 4.

3 Note that "oneself" and one's "co-contractor" here could be individual humans, or collective or corporate parties.

4 For this idea of a power as the ability to alter duties, rights and other normative positions, see Hohfeld, 1964. The notion of "privileges" in my next sentence is also explained there.

5 Penner, 2013: 246–248 points out that talk of "redirection" is misleading if we are strict Hohfeldians; instead, we should see transfer or exchange as

involving the extinction of duties-owed-to-the-former-owner to keep off an item, simultaneous with the new creation of duties-owed-to-the-new-owner to keep off that item. Unlike Penner, I do not see this Hohfeldian redescription as problematic—it looks more like a "distinction without a difference."

6 Honoré, 1961 sketches all the incidents of "full liberal ownership," and notes that most cases of modern ownership do not fully satisfy this ideal type.

7 Note also that even if ownership rights were *unjustified*, there might be strong reasons to allow *free exchange* of such rights if such unjustified rights were inevitably going to persist. Compare Waldron, 2001 on property's "normative resilience": the sense in which we find theft and fraud dishonest even when what is stolen or defrauded are unjustified property rights.

8 Take, for example, the norms at work in Highland Scotland in the 17th century, exploited by the Glencoe massacrers.

9 Note that one can also of course have economic liberty without having freedom of movement or religion.

10 Compare van der Vossen's 2015 focus on the way free exchange serves autonomy: in many cases (but not all—see §5 below) the interests served by such exchange could be served by alternative systems. Perhaps in many alternatives the interests would not be as well served (compare Cheneval's argument, in the current volume, that without free markets societies would not be rich enough to provide welfare provision), but in some they could be sufficiently well served.

11 See Hume, 1978 [1739–40]: Bk III, Pt. II, §II; Smith, 1976 [1776]; Hayek, 1960; see perhaps especially the "invisible hand" argument encapsulated in Smith's much-quoted claim about how free market exchanges harness human selfishness to each party's benefit: "It is not from the benevolence of the butcher, the brewer, or the baker, that we expect our dinner, but from their regard to their own interest. We address ourselves [in market exchange], not to their humanity but to their self-love" (Smith, 1976 [1776]: Bk. I, ch. II, p. 18). Compare Cruft, forthcoming: ch. 13.

12 Compare Hayek's insight that it is not just my rights, but others' rights and my capacity to exchange things in order to make them mine which serve my human interest in getting what I want. For Hayek, this market mechanism serves these wants more efficiently than would direct rights to whatever I want: "The benefits I derive from freedom are [. . .] largely the result of the uses of freedom by others" (1960: 122). This means that the benefits any one person's right to freedom of exchange brings to people beyond that person (benefits through its role as part of an efficient system, for example) are essential and central to the justifiability of that person's right.

13 As illustrated by van der Vossen and Brennan's Vulcans example (2018: 66–69), and thematized by the fundamental theorems of welfare economics and the "invisible hand" arguments referenced at notes 11 and 12 above.

14 See Tasioulas, 2015 and Cruft, forthcoming: ch 8.

15 Thanks to Jahel Queralt and Bas van der Vossen for pressing this hard.

16 Compare also the factors mentioned in Queralt Lange, forthcoming.

17 This is compatible with a participation-focused version of Raz's suggestion that "if I were to choose between living in a society which enjoys freedom of expression [or participation], but not having the right myself, or enjoying the right in a society which does not have it, I would have no hesitation in judging my own personal interest better served by the first option" (1994: 54). This might be true yet it *still* be the case that one's interest in expression or participation can work largely on its own to ground rights (to freedom of expression and participation) for one. See Cruft, forthcoming: ch. 8. By

contrast, it seems to me that one's interest in freedom of exchange seems less likely, acontextually, to be important enough on its own to play a large role in grounding rights for one.

18 In a sense, it simply reports my intuition in favor of the "high liberalism" that Tomasi 2012 criticizes.

19 For the ways in which my right to free exchange is best justifiable for how it serves parties beyond me, see the discussion at §3 and notes 11 and 12 above.

References

Beitz C (2009) *The Idea of Human Rights*. Oxford: Oxford University Press.

Buchanan A (2013) *The Heart of Human Rights*. Oxford: Oxford University Press.

Cruft R (forthcoming) *Human Rights, Ownership, and the Individual*. Oxford: Oxford University Press.

Gould CC (1988) *Rethinking Democracy: Freedom and Social Cooperation in Politics, Economy, and Society*. Cambridge: Cambridge University Press.

Griffin J (2008) *On Human Rights*. Oxford: Clarendon Press.

Hayek FA (1960) *The Constitution of Liberty*. London: Routledge.

Hohfeld WN (1964) *Fundamental Legal Conceptions*, WW Cook (ed). New Haven: Yale University Press (reprinted from *Yale Law Journal* 1913 and 1917).

Honoré AM (1961) Ownership. In: Guest AG (ed) *Oxford Essays in Jurisprudence*. Oxford: Clarendon Press.

Hume D (1978 [1739–40]) *A Treatise of Human Nature*, Selby-Bigge LA and Nidditch PH (eds). Oxford: Clarendon Press.

Nickel JW (2007) *Making Sense of Human Rights*, 2nd ed. Oxford: Blackwell.

Nozick R (1974) *Anarchy, State, and Utopia*. Oxford: Blackwell.

Nussbaum MC (2011) *Creating Capabilities: The Human Development Approach*. Cambridge, MA: Harvard University Press.

Penner JE (2013) On the Very Idea of Transmissible Rights. In: Penner JE and Smith HE (eds) *Philosophical Foundations of Property Law*. Oxford: Oxford University Press.

Queralt Lange J (forthcoming) Protecting the Entrepreneurial Poor: A Human Rights Approach.

Rawls J (1999) *The Law of Peoples with "The Idea of Public Reason Revisited."* Cambridge, MA: Harvard University Press.

Raz J (1986) *The Morality of Freedom*. Oxford: Clarendon Press.

Raz J (1994) Rights and Individual Well-Being. In: *Ethics in the Public Domain*, revised ed. Oxford: Clarendon Press.

Raz J (2010) Human Rights Without Foundations. In: Besson S and Tasioulas J (eds) *The Philosophy of International Law*. Oxford: Oxford University Press.

Smith A (1976 [1776]) *An Inquiry into the Nature and Causes of the Wealth of Nations*, Cannan E (ed). Chicago: University of Chicago Press.

Tasioulas J (2015) On the Foundations of Human Rights. In: Cruft R, Liao SM and Renzo M (eds) *Philosophical Foundations of Human Rights*. Oxford: Oxford University Press, pp. 47–70.

Tomasi J (2012) *Free Market Fairness*. Princeton: Princeton University Press.

Van der Vossen B (2015) Imposing Duties and Original Appropriation. *Journal of Political Philosophy* 23: 64–85.

Van der Vossen B and Brennan J (2018) *In Defense of Openness: Why Global Freedom Is the Humane Solution to Global Poverty*. Oxford: Oxford University Press.

Waldron J (2001) Property, Honesty, and Normative Resilience. In: Munzer SE (ed) *New Essays in the Legal and Political Theory of Property*. Cambridge: Cambridge University Press.

Woods K (2014) *Human Rights*. Basingstoke: Palgrave Macmillan.

Part V

Economic Liberties in Practice

14 Economic Rights of the Informal Self-Employed

Three Urban Cases

Martha Alter Chen

1. Introduction

Fifty years ago, both the informal sector and self-employment were viewed as traditional forms of small-scale economic organization soon to be rendered obsolete by the combined logic of capital accumulation and mass production (Arum and Muller, 2004; Chen, 2012). Contrary to such predictions, both informal employment and self-employment have grown in many countries over recent decades. Today, 61 percent of the global workforce is informally employed and 44 percent is self-employed, more so in developing countries (ILO, 2018). Not all self-employed are informal, notably the professional self-employed. And not all informal workers are self-employed; many are wage-employed. But there is a strong overlap between being self-employed and being informally employed: over 90 percent of all self-employed are informal (UN, 2015) and two thirds of all informal workers are self-employed (ILO, 2018).

The reality of work today defies the norm on which the economic rights of workers are based: namely, a recognizable so-called standard employer-employee relationship. Not only is half of the workforce self-employed but also many employees today are in temporary, short-term and part-time jobs. Indeed, around the world, formal firms, both public and private, are increasingly hiring workers informally, without contributing to their social insurance. Further, many workers today are transnational migrants for whom their citizenship status as well as their status in employment determine whether they have economic rights.

One of the things this volume seeks to address is the fact that limited attention has been paid to the economic rights and freedoms of the self-employed. This chapter interrogates more specifically the economic rights of the self-employed in the urban informal economy. Conventional notions of the self-employed derive largely from the global North. In the global South, compared to the global North, the share of self-employment in both total and urban employment is higher and the nature of self-employment tends to be different. This chapter interrogates the economic rights of the urban self-employed through the lens of three groups of informal workers who constitute a significant share of the urban self-employed in the global South: home-based workers, street vendors and waste pickers.

This chapter has four sections. Section 2 provides an overview of the conceptualization, classification and measurement of self-employment. Section 3 details, as illustrative examples, the employment arrangements and working conditions of three groups of urban informal occupational groups who are largely self-employed and poor: home-based workers, street vendors and waste pickers. Section 4 provides a conceptual framework for considering the economic rights of the informal self-employed, including a typology of economic rights and freedoms and a set of relevant policies and regulations. Section 5 provides a roadmap for realizing the economic rights of the informal self-employed. The chapter ends with some concluding reflections on the way forward towards realizing the economic rights and freedoms of the informal self-employed.

The key messages of this chapter are as follows. Over 60 percent of the global workforce—around 2 billion people—are informally employed (ILO, 2018). Nearly half of the global workforce (44%) and majority of informal workers globally (64%) are self-employed. Most informal self-employed remain poor—cannot work their way out of poverty—due to low earnings and high costs and risks. The *negative forces* which undermine the earnings and increase the costs and risks of the informal self-employed include the following: stigmatization and penalization as "informal" (assumed to be illegal, avoiding regulations and taxation and/or a drag on the economy); inappropriate policies and laws biased in favor of formal firms and workers; lack of access to public services, public space and public procurement; lack of legal and social protections; and lack of representative voice in policy-making and rule-setting processes. The realization of economic rights for the informal self-employed entails addressing these negative forces, including promoting an enabling policy and legal environment. This, in turn, requires that organizations of informal workers are represented in the policy and legal reform process.

2. Self-Employment in Today's Global Economy

2.1 Size and Composition

Recent estimates suggest that, globally, nearly half of *all* workers (44%) are self-employed: more so in low-income developing countries than high-income developed countries; and, among geographical regions, more so in South Asia, Southeast Asia and Sub-Saharan Africa plus Oceana than in Latin America and the Caribbean (UN, 2015). Among *informal workers*, the share of self-employment is higher still: representing 64 percent of informal workers globally and nearly 80 percent of informal workers in low-income countries (ILO, 2018).

Self-employment is heterogeneous: so much so that, unless appropriately disaggregated, the concept tends to conceal more than it reveals. In the past, in the global North, the self-employed were classified largely by occupation: notably, farmers, proprietors and/or self-employed professionals (Blau and Duncan, 1967 for the U.S.; Erikson et al., 1979 for Europe). But these occupational categories fail to capture the full range of self-employed occupations, especially in the global South, including the three groups that are featured in this chapter. Further distinctions among the self-employed include their levels of education and skills and whether they take on a managerial role by hiring or overseeing others. In considering economic rights, another important classification system to disaggregate the self-employed is useful: namely, "status in employment" which refers to the degree of risk and autonomy in different employment arrangements. The status in employment classification has the additional advantage of disaggregating self-employment into four meaningful categories which cut across occupations and skill/education levels and differentiating whether the self-employed hire workers.

According to the 1993 International Classification of Status in Employment (ICSW), used by labor statisticians in collecting and tabulating labor force data, the self-employed include:

- *Employers*: owner operators of informal or formal enterprises who hire others
- *Own account workers*: owner operators in single-person units or family businesses or farms who do not hire others
- *Unpaid contributing family workers*: family workers who work in family businesses or farms without pay
- *Members of producer cooperatives*: members of producer cooperatives, either formal registered or informal non-registered

Among the *informal self-employed* globally, 3 percent are employers, 25 percent are contributing family workers and 70 percent are own account workers (ILO, 2018: Table 1, p. 14). Indeed, among *all workers* globally, 1 percent of women and 3 percent of men are employers, 20 percent of women and 7 percent of men are contributing family workers, and 29 percent of women and 39 percent of men are own account operators (UN, 2015).[1]

Considered another way, over half (51%) of all employers worldwide are informal, 86 percent of own account workers are informal and all contributing family workers are informal (ILO, 2018: Table 1, p. 14).

2.2 *Characteristics and Consequences*

By definition, self-employment involves investment of human (skilled or unskilled labor) and economic capital (fixed assets and working capital) as well as (often) social capital (social networks and contacts): unlike wage employment which involves the "sale" of human capital/labor capacity to an employer. By definition, self-employment also involves engagement with the market and taking on associated risks which, in turn, requires entrepreneurial or at least organizational skills. In some cases, self-employment also involves the recruitment and management of workers (paid and/or unpaid).

Self-employment is often, therefore, associated with entrepreneurship: with risk-taking entrepreneurs trying to grow their business. But most informal self-employed are working poor persons trying to earn a living and to cope with existing risks. They often do not seek to grow their individual business but rather to diversify income sources within the household to be able to be able to feed, clothe and educate their families and to deal with economic shocks (such as the recent global recession), work-related risks and the common core contingencies of illness, disability and death, against which they have limited (if any) protections.

Traditional self-employment, whether in single-person or family units, is often embedded in social relationships: workers (paid or unpaid) are often recruited from networks of family, kinship and community; intra- and inter-firm relationships are often "non-contractual"; household and enterprise accounts are often not separated; and entry into self-employment often involves inheriting a parental business or carrying on the kinship group's line of work. In their introduction to an edited volume of a comparative study in 11 advanced countries of self-employment dynamics and social inequality, Richard Arum and Walter Muller refer to these features as "family-embeddedness" and "intergenerational inheritance" of self-employment (Arum and Muller, 2004). Societies with high levels of family-based social capital—for example, with a large share of extended families with parents living with adult earning children—are more likely to have large shares of family-embedded and inherited self-employment (Arum and Muller, 2004). This is often the case in developing countries but is also the case in some developed countries. Among the 11 advanced developed countries in this comparative research project, which analyzed trends from the early 1980s to the late 1990s, Italy, Japan and Taiwan had relatively high levels of self-employment in traditional non-professional skilled occupations (Arum and Muller, 2004). Further, in Japan and Italy, more than half of self-employment was in occupations that were inherited from parent to child (Arum and Muller, 2004). In the nine other countries in this comparative research project, approximately one-third of self-employment was inherited (Arum and Muller, 2004).

Given its heterogeneity, self-employment has different consequences for different groups of the self-employed. For some, being self-employed means having flexible hours of work and control over how they work; while for others, it means working long hours with little, if any, time for leisure. For some, self-employment means they can choose to work in—or quit—a particular line of work when they like or need to; while for others, it means being, or feeling, trapped in low-earning work with no exit options. For some, self-employment means being able to work—or not work—as they would like or need to; while for others, it means continually searching for customers, buyers, orders and seldom finding enough. Given this heterogeneity of consequences, self-employment is associated with both independence, agency and self-fulfillment on one hand and drudgery, hardship and uncertainty on the other (Hotch, 2000).

Given these differences, it is difficult for the self-employed to come together—or be considered as a class. Among the self-employed, the employers are non-poor, on average, while own account operators and contributing family workers are poor (Chen et al., 2005). Based on its research, data analysis and experience, the WIEGO Network[2] specifies four classes of self-employed, as follows:

- *Entrepreneurs*: employers in incorporated enterprises
- *Professionals*: own-account operators of incorporated enterprises
- *Proto-Entrepreneurs*: employers in unincorporated enterprises (those who run small-scale businesses or workshops; and those who operate as intermediaries putting out work to others)
- *Survivalists*: own-account operators and contributing family workers in unincorporated enterprises

(Chen and Roever, 2016)

The global movement of informal workers, inspired by the Self-Employed Women's Association (SEWA) of India and supported by the WIEGO Network, have made the case that own account workers and contributing family workers should be seen as "workers," not as "entrepreneurs." In so doing, they have challenged key notions of two sets of observers: mainstream economists who equate self-employment with entrepreneurs; and formal trade unionists who equate workers with employees. During the General Discussion on Decent Work and the Informal Economy at the 2002 International Labor Conference, a delegation of informal workers facilitated by the WIEGO Network was able to successfully make the case that own account workers should be included under the Workers Group, not the Employer Group, of the ILO tripartite partners: arguing that most own account operators are poor and invest more labor than capital into their business activities and, thus, should be considered working class, not entrepreneurial. They did so by making the following argument, which was included as clause # 4 in the Conclusions on Decent Work and the Informal Economy:

> Workers in the informal economy include both wage workers and own-account workers. Most own-account workers are as insecure and vulnerable as wage workers and move from one situation to the

> other. Because they lack protection, rights and representation, these workers often remain trapped in poverty.
>
> (ILO, 2002)

To sum up, the heterogeneity within self-employment challenges the notion of who is self-employed. It also challenges the often simplistic debates about what drives or causes informality: notably the debate over whether the self-employed choose to operate informally. But also, more fundamentally, it challenges "the simplistic division between labor and capital" (Khattak, 2002: 38) as own account workers, and the contributing family workers who work alongside them, tend to invest more labor than capital into their informal businesses. They are not only the most marginal and labor-intensive but also the largest groups of self-employed. This chapter focuses on the economic rights of three groups of informal workers who tend to be own account workers or contributing family workers, not employers; who represent a significant share of the urban self-employed in many cities in the global South; and who illustrate the economic disadvantages, including infringement of rights, associated with different types and places of work of urban self-employment.

3. Three Groups of Urban Self-Employed

3.1 Home-Based Workers

Home-based workers produce goods or services for the market from their own homes or adjacent grounds and premises: stitching garments and weaving textiles; making craft products; processing and preparing food items; assembling or packaging electronics, automobile parts and pharmaceutical products; selling goods or providing services (laundry, hair-cutting, beautician services); or doing clerical or professional work, among other activities. Although they remain largely invisible, home-based workers are engaged in many branches of industry and represent a significant share of the urban workforce in many countries, especially in Asia and particularly for women: from 6 percent in urban South Africa to 14 percent in urban India (Chen and Raveendran, 2014: 11; ILO and WIEGO, 2013: 46). Also, in India, 32 percent of the female workforce is home-based (Chen and Raveendran, 2014); and 36 percent of all enterprises are home-based (Government of India, 2016). While home-based work tends to be associated with manufacturing, many home-based workers are in trade—37 percent in South Africa and 23 percent in Buenos Aries (ILO and WIEGO, 2013: 46). In most countries, the majority of home-based workers are self-employed, with a minority being subcontracted workers.

For home-based workers, whose home is also their workplace, housing is an essential productive asset. Inadequate housing is a commonly cited problem by home-based workers. A small house hampers productivity as the home-based worker cannot take bulk work orders because she cannot store raw materials and her work is interrupted by competing needs for the same space of other household members and activities. Poor quality housing often results in raw materials and finished goods being damaged. Monsoon rains force home-based workers to suspend or reduce production, as equipment, raw materials or finished goods get damaged when roofs leak or houses flood; products (e.g., incense sticks) cannot dry due to leaks and humidity; and orders are reduced due to decreased demand and/or difficulties associated with transport during the rains (Chen, 2014).

When the home is also the workplace, basic infrastructure services are essential for the productivity of work, notably electricity but also water and sanitation. The accessibility and cost of public transport is also a key factor for home-based workers who commute to markets on a regular, if not daily, basis to buy raw materials and other supplies, to negotiate orders and to sell finished goods. The distance between the home-based worker's home and the market, contractor or customers she deals with is critical, affecting the cost of transport. When home-based workers are relocated to peripheral areas they often have poor access to public transport and their transport costs rise sharply. A recent study of home-based workers in Ahmedabad (India), Bangkok (Thailand) and Lahore (Pakistan) found that transport accounted for 30 percent of business expenses; and of those who had to pay for transport, one quarter operated at a loss (Chen, 2014).

In sum, home-based workers and their livelihood activities are affected by government policies and practices, notably land allocation, housing policies, basic infrastructure services and public transport. This is because their homes are their workplaces and they have to commute to markets and transport supplies/goods to and from their homes. Legal reforms should support policy interventions that upgrade settlements with large concentrations of home-based workers to ensure they have adequate shelter, water, sanitation and electricity. If and when home-based workers and their families have to be relocated, efforts should be made to ensure the relocation sites have, from the outset, adequate shelter, basic infrastructure, transport services and access to markets.

3.2 Street Vendors

Street vendors offer a range of goods and services from streets and other open public spaces. They represent 4 percent of urban employment in India, between 12 and 24 percent of urban employment in eight African cities, and 15 percent of non-agricultural employment in South Africa (Chen and Raveendran, 2014: 11; Herrera et al., 2012: 95; Wills, 2009: 3). Some street vendors come from castes or communities for whom street vending is a hereditary occupation. Others are migrants or laid-off workers for whom street vending affords low-end but steady employment. Also, many home-based producers of garments, textiles, crafts or cooked food sell their goods in street markets. Street vendors offer working people, and even middle-class consumers, a convenient place to buy goods at low prices; serve as key links in the wider urban distribution system; and enrich the cultural life of cities.

More so than home-based workers, street vendors are directly affected by the regulations and policies of city governments and the practices of city officials. Across most cities worldwide, government policies or practices undermine the ability of street vendors to pursue their livelihoods. Abuse of authority by the police and local officials is the most common complaint; this "includes police harassment, demands for bribes, arbitrary confiscations of merchandise, and physical abuse. These practices tend to take place in urban policy environments that do not define a role for street trade or offer a viable space to accommodate it. In that context, street traders also rank the lack of a fixed and secure workplace and evictions from (or demolitions of) existing workplaces among the most significant negative drivers" (Roever, 2014: 25). A study of street vendors and public space in Ahmedabad found that local leaders collect "protection" money each day, week or month from street vendors in their market areas which they hand over to the police after taking their cuts: the amount paid differs by whether the street vendor sells from the pavement or from a push cart (Brown and Mahadevia, 2012).

Where cities attempt to regulate street vending, the licensing and permitting practices and their associated taxes, fees, tolls and levies have a significant impact on vendors. Most vendors "pay all manner of tolls, levies, and fees—as well as bribes—to use public space" (Roever, 2014: 26). But most street vendors lack urban infrastructure services at their vending sites, including running water and toilets, electricity and waste removal. "Prepared food vendors must cook at home or ferry water to their stalls, street tailors and hairdressers stop working when the power goes out, and market vendors spend time and money organizing ad-hoc waste removal systems where city services fail" (Roever, 2014: 26). The fact that most cities do not consult with street vendors around such practices only compounds the problem.

When they operate without a license, street vendors are considered illegal under most municipal acts or by most municipal officials: leaving them subject to treatment as criminals and to rent-seeking in the granting of licenses. But the license regime for street vending is opaque and repressive. Many cities have inappropriate license ceilings: for instance, in Mumbai, India, when there were an estimated 250,000 street vendors, the municipal corporation arbitrarily fixed a ceiling of only 14,000 licenses and even these were not issued for many years (Bhowmik, 2000). Across India, those without licenses are subject to summary warrants, confiscations and fees under the Indian Penal

Code. In Kolkata, India, street vending without a license is a non-bailable offense (Bhowmik, 2000).

Estimates suggest that, in India, street vendors occupy only 2 percent of urban land but are legally barred from doing so. A 2000 study of street vending in eight cities of India found that only two cities, Bhubaneswar and Imphal, made provisions for street vendors in their city plans (Bhowmik, 2000). The other six cities, Ahmedabad, Bangalore, Delhi, Kolkata, Mumbai and Patna, earmarked spaces in their plans for hospitals, parks, offices, residential colonies, bus and rail terminals but excluded the vendors who naturally congregate around these areas, providing essential goods and services at low costs. Increasingly, cities around the world are allocating public space for large-scale modern retail—malls and shopping arcades—while continuing to neglect small-scale traditional retail.

3.3 Waste Pickers

Around the world, large numbers of people from low-income and disadvantaged communities make a living and create value from waste. Waste pickers collect, sort, recycle and sell materials, reclaiming reusable material for personal use or recyclable materials for use by industries as raw materials or packing materials: helping in the process to reduce carbon emissions. Waste pickers may collect household waste door-to-door or from the curbside; commercial and industrial waste from dumpsters; or litter from streets and urban waterways. Some work on municipal dumps. An estimated 24 million people worldwide, of whom 80 percent are informal, make their living picking waste (ILO and WIEGO, 2013: 37). Waste pickers constitute around 1 percent of urban employment in many countries (ILO and WIEGO, 2013: 48; Vanek et al., 2012).

In many cities in the global South with inadequate solid waste management, solid waste is burned contributing to air pollution, or accumulates on the city's periphery or in landfills. Waste pickers help reduce accumulation of solid waste in the streets, public spaces and urban water resources. In a 2006 study of six cities, more than 70,000 people and their families were responsible for recycling about 3 million tons per year (Scheinberg et al., 2010: 12).[3] In terms of environmental contribution, the study found that in three cities, waste pickers recovered approximately 20 percent of all materials that entered the waste stream (Scheinberg et al., 2010: 15). Recovery of recyclable materials and organic matter leads to the reduction of greenhouse gases and to the mitigation of climate change (Scheinberg et al., 2010). Despite the public service they provide to the city, the environment and the economy, waste pickers often are denied access to waste, or face confiscation of the waste by city authorities or municipal street cleaners. Organizations of waste pickers are rarely allowed to compete alongside private companies for solid waste management contracts.

Despite the public service they provide to the city, the environment and the economy, waste pickers are usually treated as nuisances by authorities and with disdain by the public. They are particularly susceptible to violence by the police. They may face exploitation and intimidation by middlemen, which can affect their earnings. Most crucially, they are negatively impacted by the privatization of municipal solid waste management services, which increases competition for waste and renders the recycling activities of waste pickers invisible or even illegal.

To sum up, all three groups work in so-called non-standard places of work—private homes or public spaces; and are subjected to stigmatization, exclusion or penalization by the state without legal or social protections. Yet each group typifies the need for a specific public resource: public services (home-based workers), public space (street vendors) and public procurement (waste pickers).

4. Economic Rights of the Informal Self-Employed

The debates on whether and how to extend economic rights to workers who are not in the so-called standard employer-employee relationships often center on whether to bring all workers under the rights and forms of regulation and representation designed for formal employees—the so-called standard workers—or whether to devise specific rights and forms of regulation and representation for so-called non-standard workers. Given that half of today's global workforce is self-employed and that self-employed workers need a greater variety of economic rights than waged or salaried workers, the terms of the debate need to be expanded to assess the specific economic rights and forms of regulation and representation of the self-employed, not only non-standard wage workers.

This section lays out a framework for thinking about the economic rights and freedoms of the informal self-employed who are working poor. It begins with a typology of the economic rights and freedoms that the informal self-employed need and want. It then considers what laws and regulations impact on these rights and the role of different actors as both violators and defenders of these rights. The next section discusses how the progressive realization of these rights and freedoms should be promoted. The common economic rights and freedoms that all informal self-employed demand and have struggled for include (a) the right to legal recognition as workers; (b) the right to work and pursue their livelihoods; (c) property rights; (d) commercial rights; (e) the right to access public resources; (f) the right to social protection; and (g) the right to collective representation.

4.1 Core Economic Rights

4.1.1 Legal Recognition

Underpinning the many legal demands raised by different groups of informal workers is a primary demand for legal recognition and status

(Sankaran and Madhav, 2013). This demand for legal recognition has several inter-related dimensions. First, informal workers want to be recognized as being legal, not illegal. Through their legal struggles, they try to highlight that the existing regulatory frameworks force them to operate illegally: if their residential area is zoned for single-use (home-based workers), if not enough licenses are issued (street vendors) or if waste is privatized (waste pickers), these informal workers and their activities are considered illegal. Second, informal workers want to be recognized as economic agents who contribute to the economy, to the city and to society and want to be integrated into local economic development and city plans.

Considered another way, in terms of negative freedoms, the right to legal recognition implies the freedom *from* stigmatization and penalization as being illegal, avoiding regulations and taxation or a drag on the economy which leads, in turn, to being excluded from economic development and urban plans: in brief, the right *not to* be stigmatized and penalized.

4.1.2 *Right to Work*[4]

The "right to work" has been enshrined in several international human rights documents, including the Universal Declaration of Human Rights. This right is enshrined in the constitutions of many countries from Colombia and Mexico to India and Vietnam. While the "right to work" as a human right does not explicitly mention self-employment, it should be interpreted as including both wage work and self-employment. In South Africa, the constitution states that every citizen has the "right to choose their trade" (Republic of South Africa, Chapter 2, 22). The use of the term "trade" reflects the fact that not all persons will gain wage or salaried jobs in South Africa which has quite high rates of unemployment, and that some persons will seek to pursue a trade: that is, to be self-employed.

In Colombia, Article 333 of the Constitution which mandates the "*right to pursue business or trade*," has been used by the Constitutional Court to rule that cooperatives of waste pickers, not just corporations, have the right to compete for municipal solid waste management contracts. In India in 1986, in a case brought by pavement dwellers to resist eviction by the Bombay Municipal Corporation, the Supreme Court ruled that the "right to livelihood," which is a variation on the "right to work," derives from the "right to life" (Article 21 of the Indian Constitution): as no person can live without the means of livelihood and evicting the petitioners from their dwellings would deprive them of their livelihoods (*Olga Tellis v. Bombay Municipal Corporation*, AIR 1986 SC 180).

4.1.3 *Property Rights*

The informal self-employed need to be able to acquire property on fair terms, without being excluded by social or legal norms. They also need to be able to protect their property from expropriation without compensation. In the process of acquiring and protecting their assets, the poor need to be able to settle competing property claims. Also, they need to be able to use their assets as collateral to leverage access to credit and other resources, including basic infrastructure services for their homes which are also often their workplace (especially for women). Hernando de Soto, the Peruvian economist and expert on the informal economy, argues that property rights need to be extended to the working poor in the informal economy if they and their countries are to succeed economically (de Soto, 2000).

While de Soto focused mainly on individual rights to private property, it is important to highlight that the informal self-employed also need collective rights to public property. They need secure use rights, if not ownership rights, to their workplaces which are often in public spaces or in informal settlements, many of which are on public land. Therefore, a comprehensive system of property rights for the self-employed poor should include not just rights to private property but also access to and use of public resources, including public land or public space in urban areas and public forests, pastures and waterways in rural areas, as will be discussed below.

4.1.4 Commercial Rights

The informal self-employed need several levels of commercial rights to be realized in roughly the following sequence:

- *Basic business rights*: right to work, including right to vend; right to a work space (including public land and private residences) and related basic infrastructure services (electricity, water, sanitation)
- *Intermediate business rights*: right to government incentives and support (including procurement, tax holidays, export licensing, export promotion); and right to public infrastructure (transport and communication)
- *Advanced business rights*: legal rules related to limited liability, default, raising capital, transferring the value of the business.[5]

Most of the working poor who are self-employed need basic and intermediate business rights. Few would worry about advanced business rights unless and until their basic and intermediate business rights are taken care of. In return for enjoying business rights, the informal self-employed would need—and are often willing—to comply with regulations. Take, for instance, street vendors—the most visible of self-employed in the urban informal economy. All street vendors need basic and intermediate business rights and the benefits that come with them. However, the regulations that they should be expected to comply with should vary by what they sell, as follows:

- Those who sell fruit and vegetables: need to comply with zoning regulations (provided these are appropriate, not burdensome or exclusionary)
- Those who sell cooked food: need to comply with public health and safety as well as zoning regulations (again, if appropriate)
- Those who sell small domestically produced manufactured goods: need to be regulated to ensure that the goods they sell are not pirated
- Those who sell more valuable imported manufactured goods: need to be regulated to ensure that the goods they sell are not smuggled or pirated

4.1.5 Right of Access to Public Resources

The livelihoods of the informal self-employed depend on access to resources, especially to public resources including public space, public services and public procurement. As noted in Section 2, access to key public resources is essential to the livelihoods of the three groups featured in this chapter: housing in central locations for home-based workers; vending sites in good locations for street vendors, ideally in existing natural markets around transport nodes, public institutions and residential areas; access to waste and solid waste management contracts for waste pickers; basic infrastructure services at their workplaces for home-based workers and street vendors; space to store and sort goods for street vendors and waste pickers. And for all three groups, accessible and affordable public transport is essential. Evictions from established places of work as well as privatization of public resources and services pose major threats to their livelihoods. For urban informal workers, most of these access rights are governed by municipal regulations. Municipalities are responsible for balancing competing users of public resources in regulating who can do what, and where.

4.1.6 Right to Social Protection

All informal workers, both self-employed and waged, want and need social protection because, by definition, they do not enjoy employment-based social protection. The current global commitment to universal health and the growing commitment to universal pensions must include a focus on the informal workforce: both the specific risks that they face as well as the specific barriers they face in gaining access to universal systems of health insurance, health care and pensions (Chen, Lund et al., 2015).

4.1.7 Right to Collective Representation

Most fundamentally, as it will allow them to demand, secure and sustain their economic rights, the informal self-employed, like all workers, want and need the right to organize as well as legal recognition of their organizations and the right to be represented in relevant collective bargaining, policy-making and rule-setting processes.

Collective bargaining is usually understood as taking place between an employer and employees to achieve a collective agreement, primarily around wages and working conditions. (See the International Labour Organization's definition of collective bargaining: *C154: Collective Bargaining Convention, 1981 [No.154].*) Workers in the informal economy, including the self-employed, also engage in forms of collective bargaining through their membership-based organizations. However, their counterparts across the table are often not employers but other stakeholders. Street vendors most often negotiate with local authorities, different municipal departments and with the police regarding harassment, confiscation of goods and evictions. Waste pickers negotiate with local authorities for storage and sorting facilities or, more ambitiously, for the right to bid for solid waste management contracts (Chen, Bonner and Carrré, 2015).

Unlike formal wage or salaried workers whose rights are usually laid down in labor statutes, most informal workers do not have statutory collective bargaining rights. While the right has been acknowledged by the ILO in its 2002 ILO Resolution and Conclusions Concerning Decent Work in the Informal Economy, including for the self-employed, it has not generally been extended to these workers. Most often, negotiations take place in ad hoc meetings—often arising out of a crisis—or in consultative forums without statutory obligation on the part of the authorities, and without enforceable agreements or continuity. While dialogues, consultations or meetings to resolve immediate disputes play a role in enabling informal workers to raise their voices and make gains, ad hoc agreements reached can be easily ignored or undermined. Informal workers need statutory collective bargaining and negotiating rights; and the right to direct representation in the ILO tripartite system (Chen, Bonner and Carré, 2015).

4.2 Relevant Policies, Laws and Regulations

In implementing and protecting these rights for the urban informal self-employed, it becomes necessary to assess which laws, policies and regulations impinge or infringe these rights for the working poor in the informal economy who are self-employed. In working with urban informal self-employed in cities around the world, the WIEGO network has found that the policies and regulations that impinge on the rights of the urban informal self-employed can be broadly categorized as follows: *municipal regulations* that specify who can do what, where; determine access to—and use of—public resources; and balance conflicting needs and uses; *sector-specific regulations* that govern specific sectors (e.g., manufacturing, trade, waste); *commercial regulations* that govern economic transactions and relationships; *macro-economic regulations* and policies that govern taxation, expenditure and investment and, in turn, generate demand.

What follows is a brief summary of how each branch of policy or regulation impinges on the three groups of urban informal self-employed.

4.2.1 Municipal Regulations

In addition to integration into city plans and local economic development, each group of urban informal workers needs municipal governments to guarantee certain specific rights: home-based workers need housing rights and mixed-use zoning of the areas where they live and work; street vendors need licenses (or permits) and secure vending sites, ideally in the natural markets where they have always vended; and waste pickers need access to waste and the right to bid for solid waste management contracts. Underlying all of these sector-specific demands is a common struggle against the tendency of municipal governments to privilege formal commercial enterprises over informal commercial enterprises and the leisure and consumption of the rich over the work and production of the poor.

Overly strict separation of land uses (such as single-use zones) can negatively impact the livelihoods of urban informal self-employed. It is important to promote a balanced mix of uses that fruitfully interact with each other. Most critically, evictions and relocations of homes and other workplaces, especially to the periphery of cities at a distance from markets, contractors and customers, pose a direct threat to the livelihoods of the urban self-employed.

Most self-employed informal workers in urban areas rely on access to public resources for their livelihoods. For example, public land and housing for home-based workers; public space for street vendors; waste for waste pickers; public space/warehouses for sorting and storage for street vendors and waste pickers; basic infrastructure services at their homes for home-based workers and at their natural markets for street vendors; and public transport for all three groups.

The policies and regulations that determine access to public resources and services are often biased against the working poor in the urban informal economy, who are not considered to be productive and are not, therefore, included in most urban plans or local economic development plans. Most critically, privatization of public resources and services often poses a direct threat to the livelihoods of the urban self-employed.

On the other hand, policies, legislation and regulations that seek to protect the sustainable use of public resources and the environment may contribute to protecting livelihoods of the urban informal self-employed. For instance, policy or regulatory choices to protect the environment through composting and recovery of recyclables can protect the livelihoods of a large number of waste pickers. Similarly, policy or regulatory choices to protect public green spaces might also support the livelihoods of street vendors by allowing them to vend around these spaces as part of the cultural landscape. Also, policy or regulatory choices to protect the environment might support home-based production, which leaves less of a carbon footprint than production in workshops and factories.

4.2.2 Sector-Specific Regulations

Regulations that govern specific manufacturing industries should in principle cover home-based workers in those sectors: for example, in India, home-based workers who produce hand-rolled cigarettes (*bidis*) should be entitled to certain protections and benefits mandated in two laws from the 1960s governing the *bidi* industry. Street vendors are impacted by the regulations governing the location, management and fee structure of wholesale markets. Marketing costs at the wholesale markets include market fees, commission fees, loading and unloading charges. How much is incurred by sellers to or buyers from these markets is determined by local multi-stakeholder committees that manage wholesale markets and often differs for sellers/buyers of different goods such as fruits versus vegetables. Also, as noted earlier, waste pickers are directly impacted by whether or not municipal governments decide to privatize solid waste management or retain public responsibility for social waste management.

4.2.3 Commercial Regulations

The informal self-employed do not operate within the bounds of traditional commercial jurisprudence which is premised on formal establishments of a certain size. Therefore, in their legal struggles, many organizations of informal workers turn to the state to be the arbiter and regulator of commercial contracts and relationships. More can, and should, be done to modify and extend commercial regulations and protections to match and cover the various types of informal self-employed.

4.2.4 Macro-Economic Policies

Fluctuating demand and prices are key macro factors that impact directly on the urban informal self-employed (Chen, 2014; Roever, 2014). Ensuring steady markets and reasonable prices for their inputs and products is of critical importance to the informal self-employed. But whether governments or markets should set prices is hotly debated. Other accepted domains of macro-economic regulations and policies—taxation, expenditure and investment—are not particularly sensitive to the specific needs of the informal self-employed (Sankaran and Madhav, 2013). The whole issue of taxation and the informal economy needs to be better understood and addressed: as most informal workers pay taxes and operating fees of various kinds but feel they get little in return from the government (Chen, 2014; Roever, 2014). The informal self-employed who pay value added tax (VAT) on supplies cannot easily claim tax rebates to which they might be entitled if their enterprises were legally incorporated (Valodia, 2012). Further, one important means to increase and stabilize demand for the goods and services of the informal self-employed is government procurement, notably: contracts to supply goods and services to public institutions such as schools or hospitals; and contracts to provide waste management services.

5. Realizing the Economic Rights of the Informal Self-Employed

Realizing the economic rights of the informal self-employed requires not only understanding which laws, policies and regulations impinge on their rights but also addressing how these laws, policies and regulations need to be reformed to protect—not infringe—their rights. This will require reforms of relevant policies and laws, and an approach to formalizing the informal economy which focuses on the economic rights of informal workers, not only on their obligation to register their businesses, pay taxes and comply with regulations. Most fundamentally, it will require that policy-making and rule-setting processes are made more transparent and participatory, inviting organizations of informal workers to the policy table.

More focused attention needs to be paid to which policies, laws and regulations impinge—directly or indirectly, negatively or positively—on workers in each sector of the informal economy. This will require ongoing efforts to ensure that informal workers in all sectors are visible in labor force and other economic statistics and that organizations of informal workers have a voice in relevant policy-making and rule-setting processes. It will also require that informal workers and their activities are recognized and valued as the broad base of the workforce and economy and are incorporated into economic planning at all levels of government. In sum, it requires increasing the Visibility, Voice and Validity of the informal self-employed.

5.1 Making the Legal Case for the Economic Rights of the Informal Self-Employed

In the promotion of economic rights, the rights of wage workers are better understood and covered by ILO conventions and national labor laws than the rights of the self-employed. Of course, the reality of wage employment today is that the employer-employee relationship is often disguised, ambiguous or multi-party: making it hard to identify the employer or duty bearer. But the rights of the self-employed are not well understood or covered: a gap this volume seeks to help fill. The Peruvian economist Hernando de Soto has been the main champion of the economic rights of a more entrepreneurial class of the informal self-employed: whom he refers to as "plucky entrepreneurs" (de Soto, 1989).

The WIEGO Network and the Self-Employed Women's Association of India have together helped build a global movement of the working poor in the informal economy, including national, regional and international networks of domestic workers, home-based workers, street vendors and waste pickers. Between them, these networks have more than 1,000 affiliated organizations in some 90 countries with a combined total of nearly 5 million informal workers as members. Most of the members are self-employed.

Around the world, the organizations of informal workers in this global movement have been fighting for the economic rights of their members, with support from activist lawyers and academics, SEWA and the WIEGO Network. To understand how they have made the case for economic rights, consider the legal arguments used in recent court cases on behalf of street vendors and waste pickers. To defend the rights of these categories of urban informal self-employed, lawyers in India have made the following legal arguments in a set of successful court cases. In the case of street vendors, the lawyers argued that the "*right to vend*" flows from the "right to carry on a trade or business" (Article 19 (1) (g) of the Constitution). In regard to the "*right to vend in public space*," the lawyers acknowledged that the state has the right to regulate use of public space, including streets and roads; but argued that the courts have a right to intervene if the state imposes unreasonable restrictions on the access to public space. In the case of waste pickers, the lawyers argued that the "*right to a healthy life/environment*" which flows from the "*right to life*" (Article 21 of the Constitution) obligates municipalities to undertake waste management; and that municipalities should not ignore waste pickers and their contribution to waste management in planning the waste management system (personal communication, Kamala Sankaran, Professor of Law, Delhi University).

In two recent cases in support of waste pickers in Colombia, the lawyers used the following legal arguments: the "*right to survival*" flows from the "*right to life*" (Article 11 of Constitution) and gives waste pickers the right to pursue waste picking as a livelihood; the "*right to equality*" mandates that waste pickers need preferential treatment or judicial affirmative action in the tendering and bidding process for government contracts to manage waste which are otherwise biased towards private companies; the "*right to pursue business or trade*" (Article 333 of

Constitution) gives the cooperatives of waste pickers, not just corporations, the right to compete in waste recycling markets; and the "*principle of legitimate trust*" was used to argue against sudden changes in policies that acknowledged and permitted waste picking without the provision of alternative sources of livelihood. In these judgments, the Government of Colombia, represented by the relevant local policy-making authority (e.g., mayor's office), was seen as the duty bearer (Chen et al., 2012).

5.2 Policy and Legal Reforms to Support Informal Self-Employed

Realizing economic rights for the informal workforce in general, and the self-employed in particular, requires transforming existing legal and regulatory frameworks. Here are three lessons for future policy and legal reforms that have emerged from the ongoing advocacy and legal struggles of organizations of informal workers in the WIEGO Network.

First, policy and legal reforms for the informal workforce in general, and the self-employed in particular, will require fundamental rethinking regarding regulations and the informal economy. To begin with, there is a common assumption that the informal economy—and those who work in it—are outside the reach of the state or its laws. However, as the evidence presented in this chapter has illustrated, the informal workforce and their activities are not outside the reach of the state or its laws. Rather, most often they are *inside the punitive arm* of the law but *outside the protective arm* of the law.

Second, labor and employment laws have limited salience for the informal self-employed. As noted earlier, most labor and employment laws are premised on an employer-employee relationship and, therefore, are not directly relevant to the self-employed. Moreover, most self-employed are not obliged to comply with labor laws and regulations as so few hire workers. However, the core labor rights of organization and representation are as critical to the self-employed as to the wage-employed.

Third, as detailed in section 3, a wide range of policies, laws and regulations have salience for the informal self-employed: from municipal laws and ordinances to commercial laws to sector-specific policies to macroeconomic policies. What is required to reduce the legal risks and barriers faced by the informal self-employed—and thereby to increase their earnings and productivity—is to assess and monitor the impact of all laws, regulations and policies on their livelihoods and lives. At present, most laws, regulations and policies relating to the functioning of cities and the economy ignore the productive roles and contributions of the working poor, relegating them to the domain of social policies. What the informal self-employed want and need is legal recognition and legal protection as economic actors as well as integration into economic planning at all levels.

Finally, and most fundamentally, the informal self-employed need to be empowered to help shape appropriate policy and legal reforms and need to be represented in the policy and legal reform process. This requires two enabling conditions.

The first is *voice*. The rights to organize and be represented—two core labor rights—are critical to ensuring the economic rights of the informal self-employed. To ensure their economic rights are appropriately framed and properly enforced, the informal self-employed need representative voice in the processes and institutions that determine economic policies and formulate the "rules of the (economic) game." This requires building organizations of informal workers and recruiting informal self-employed into existing trade unions, cooperatives and other worker organizations. This also requires making rule-setting and policy-making institutions more inclusive and ensuring that representatives of the organizations of informal workers have "a seat at the (policy) table."

The second is *visibility*. To capture the attention of policy makers, and inform policy-making, the informal self-employed—and their contributions to the economy—need to be visible in official economic statistics and in relevant policy research. Fortunately, in May 2018, the ILO published the first-ever global estimates of informal employment, rural and urban: its size, composition and characteristics (ILO, 2018).

Increased voice and visibility are the key enabling conditions through which the informal self-employed can gain *validity*—legal recognition and legitimacy—and engage in policy and legal reforms and, thereby, realize their other economic rights.

With increased Voice, Visibility and Validity, the informal self-employed are more likely to be able to advocate effectively for their economic rights, including an enabling policy and regulatory environment. This process is depicted graphically in Figure 14.1.

Where and how has this worked in practice? Consider the case of legal reforms for street vendors. In the late 1990s, SEWA and the National Alliance of Street Vendors of India (NASVI) conducted studies on street vending in seven major cities of India (Bhowmik, 2000). The findings of this study were presented at a large meeting of street vendors in Delhi in

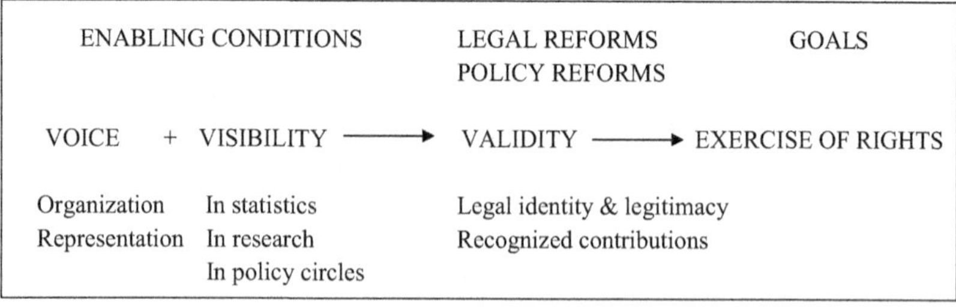

Figure 14.1 Realizing economic rights of the informal self-employed

2001, organized by SEWA and NASVI in collaboration with the Ministry of Urban Development. At this meeting, the government promised to set up a taskforce to draft a national policy on street vending. This policy was approved by the cabinet of India in 2004. The same year, the government set up a National Commission on Enterprises in the Unorganized Sector (NCEUS), which was mandated, among other tasks, to review the national policy on street vendors. A new policy was approved in 2009.

While SEWA and NASVI had advocated for the national policy, they felt that a national policy was not enough, that street vendors also needed legal rights. They argued that street vending was not just an issue of urban policy but rather an issue of the legal right to livelihood (Bhowmik, 2014). They began organizing meetings and demonstrations of street vendors in all their constituencies across India to demand a uniform law to protect the livelihoods of street vendors by regulating street vending in an appropriate and transparent way.

The Street Vendors (Protection of Livelihoods and Regulation of Vending) Act was passed by the Lok Sabha (Lower House of the Parliament of India) in September 2013 and by the Rajya Sabha (Upper House) in February 2014, and received the assent of the President of India in March 2014. The Act aims to provide livelihood rights and social protection to street vendors and to regulate and improve the prevailing license system. "The Act states that no existing street vendor can be displaced until the local authorities conduct a census of street vendors in the concerned urban center. All existing vendors have to be provided with permits for conducting their business and a Town Vending Committee (TVC) will supervise the activities of the vendors. This committee, which will be the main policy making body on street vending, comprises municipal authorities, policy, the health department and other stakeholders. Representatives of street vendors will constitute 40% of its membership and women will comprise 33% of the street vendors' representatives" (Bhowmik, 2014: 1).

The Act came into force on May 1, 2014. NASVI, SEWA and street vendors around the country welcomed this Act as a major victory as it mandates that street vendors should be protected, not just regulated, and specifies clear procedures for regulation and registration, including the local vending committees with street vendor representatives.

6. The Way Forward

Policy and legal reforms in support of the economic rights of the informal workforce in general, and the self-employed in particular, will require transforming the debates and mindsets about the informal economy. So long as the informal self-employed are blamed for being illegal or criminal, for avoiding regulations and taxation, for having low productivity or representing a drag on the economy, they will continue to remain under the punitive, rather than the protective, arm of the law. And yet most of the working poor in the urban informal economy are trying to earn an honest living in a hostile regulatory environment.

What is also needed is a fundamental transformation of the vision of cities to embrace economic diversity—the informal and traditional alongside the formal and modern—and a fundamental transformation of the political economy of cities to reduce the disadvantage of the working poor in the urban informal economy.

Fortunately, many of the economic rights that are of critical importance to the urban informal self-employed are enshrined in the Universal Declaration of Human Rights and in the International Covenant on Economic, Social, and Cultural Rights. More recently, the global community has committed to the UN Sustainable Development Goals, which mandate economic rights of all workers, including the informal workforce, and call for more inclusive economic development and more inclusive cities.

Furthermore, organizations of informal workers, with support from the WIEGO Network, campaigned for key provisions in two other global commitments that are of particular relevance to their economic rights: Recommendation 204 of the International Labor Organization and the New Urban Agenda of the Habitat III summit. Thanks to their efforts, ILO Recommendation 204 recognizes that most informal workers are working poor; that informal livelihoods need to be preserved in the transition; that informal workers need social protection; and that regulated access to public space and natural resources are essential for informal livelihoods. The New Urban Agenda calls for the integration of the informal self-employed and their livelihood activities into urban plans and local economic development planning.

The way forward is to support organizations of informal workers in their ongoing campaigns to translate these global commitments, well captured by the following excerpt from the New Urban Agenda, into local realities:

> We commit to recognize the contribution of the working poor in the informal economy, particularly women, including the unpaid, domestic, and migrant workers to the urban economies, taking into account national circumstances. Their livelihoods, working conditions and income security, legal and social protection, access to skills, assets and other support services, and voice and representation should be enhanced. A progressive transition of workers and economic units to the formal economy will be developed by adopting a balanced approach, combining incentives and compliance measures, while promoting preservation and improvement of existing livelihoods. (UN HABITAT, 2016: 17)

As this chapter has illustrated, understanding and promoting the economic rights and freedoms of the informal self-employed, compared to formal wage-employed, requires assessing and addressing a broader range of laws, policies and regulations. It requires moving beyond labor and employment law to assess and address how a range of macro, micro and sectoral laws, policies and regulations, in their existing forms, infringe and undermine the economic rights and freedoms of the informal self-employed. Most fundamentally, to protect their economic rights and freedoms, the informal self-employed need to be centrally involved—to be collectively represented—in the policy and legal reform process. "Nothing for us, without us" is the motto of the global movement of informal workers.

Notes

1 Few countries collect and fewer still report data on members of producer cooperatives.
2 For more information about the WIEGO Network, see http://wiego.org
3 The six cities included in the study were Cairo, Cluj-Napoca, Lima, Lusaka, Pune, Quezon City.
4 In the United States, several states have adopted laws which guarantee that no person can be compelled, as a condition of employment, to join or not to join, nor to pay dues to a labor union. Regrettably, these laws are called "Right to Work" laws: an unfortunate but deliberate co-option of a term whose original constitutional meaning in most countries was quite different.
5 The Institute of Liberty and Democracy in Peru, founded and directed by Hernando de Soto, focuses a good deal of its attention on developing legal tools to ensure that small businesses enjoy these advanced business rights.

References

Arum R and Muller W (eds) (2004) *The Reemergence of Self-Employment: A Comparative Study of Self-Employment Dynamics and Social Inequality*. Princeton, NJ: Princeton University Press.

Bhowmik SK (2000) *Hawkers and the Urban Informal Sector: A Study of Street Vending in Seven Cities*. Delhi: National Alliance of Street Vendors of India (NASVI).

Bhowmik SK (2014) *Street Vendors in India Get Legal Protection*. Global Labor Column, Number 174. Global Labor University. Available at: http://global-labour-university.org/fileadmin/GLU_Column/papers/no_174_Bhowmik.pdf.

Blau PM and Duncan OD (1967) *The American Occupational Structure*. New York: Free Press.

Brown A, Lyons M and Mahadevia D (2012) *Claiming Urban Space: Street Vending in Ahmedabad*. Working Paper 2: Law, Rights and Regulation in the Informal Economy, ESRC-DFID Research Project. Cardiff, Wales: Cardiff University.

Chen M (2012) *The Informal Economy: Definitions, Theories, & Policies*. WIEGO Working Paper #1. Cambridge, MA: WIEGO. Available at: http://www.wiego.org/sites/default/files/publications/files/Chen_WIEGO_WP1.pdf.

Chen M (2014) *Informal Economy Monitoring Study Sector Report: Home-Based Workers*. Cambridge, MA: WIEGO. Available at: http://wiego.org/sites/wiego.org/files/publications/files/IEMS-Sector-Report-Home-Based-Workers-Full-Report.pdf.

Chen M, Bonner C and Carré F (2015) *Organizing Informal Workers: Benefits, Challenges & Successes*. Background Paper for the UN Human Development Report 2015. New York: UN HDR Office.

Chen M, Bonner C, Chetty M, Fernandez L, Pape K, Parra F, Singh A and Skinner C (2012) *Urban Informal Workers: Representative Voice & Economic Rights*. Background paper for World Development Report 2013. Washington, DC: World Bank.

Chen M, Lund F, Chatterjee M, Thomas S, Tulaphan P and Tangworamongkon C (2015) Universal Health Care for Informal Workers: Lessons from India & Thailand for Overcoming Barriers, Addressing Gender Dimensions. Paper prepared for the Asian Development Bank.

Chen M and Raveendran G (2014) *Urban Employment in India: Recent Trends and Patterns*. WIEGO Working Paper (Statistics) No. 7. Cambridge: WIEGO.

Chen M and Roever S (2016) Enhancing the Productivity of Own Account Enterprises from the Perspective of Women in the Informal Economy. Policy Brief for the UN Secretary General's High Level Panel on Women's Economic Empowerment.

Chen M, Vanek J, Lund F, Heintz J, Jhabvala R and Bonner C (2005) *Progress of the World's Women 2005: Women, Work and Poverty*. New York: UNIFEM.

De Soto H (1989) *The Other Path: The Economic Alternative to Terrorism*. New York: Harper and Row.

De Soto H (2000) *The Mystery of Capital: Why Capitalism Triumphs in the West and Fails Everywhere Else*. New York: Basic Books.

Erikson R, Goldthorpe JH and Portocarcero I (1979) Intergenerational Class Mobility in Three Western European Societies: England, France and Sweden. *British Journal of Sociology* 30: 415–441.

Government of India (2016) Sixth Economic Census. Available at: www.mospi.gov.in/sixth-economic-census.

Herrera J, Kuépié M, Nordman C, Oudin X and Roubaud F (2012) *Informal Sector and Informal Employment: Overview of Data for 11 Cities in 10 Developing Countries*. WIEGO Working Paper 9 (Statistics). Cambridge, MA: WIEGO. Available at: www.wiego.org/sites/wiego.org/files/publications/files/Herrera_WIEGO_WP9.pdf.

Hotch J (2000) Classing the Self-Employed: New Possibilities of Power and Collectivity. In: Gibson-Graham JK, Resnick SA and Wolff RD (eds) *Class and Its Others*. Minneapolis and London: Minnesota University Press.

ILO (2002) *Resolution Concerning Decent Work and the Informal Economy*. Geneva: ILO.

ILO (2018) *Women and Men in the Informal Economy: A Statistical Picture*, 3rd ed. Geneva: ILO.

ILO and WIEGO (2013) *Women and Men in the Informal Economy: A Statistical Picture*, 2nd ed. Geneva: ILO.

Khattak SG (2002) Subcontracted Work and Gender Relations: The Case of Pakistan. In: Balakrishnan R (ed) *The Hidden Assembly Line: Gender Dynamics of*

Subcontracted Work in a Global Economy. Bloomfield, CT: Kumarian Press, pp. 35–61.

Roever S (2014) *Informal Economy Monitoring Study Sector Report: Street Vendors*. Cambridge, MA: WIEGO. Available at: http://wiego.org/sites/wiego.org/files/publications/files/IEMS-Sector-Full-Report-Street-Vendors.pdf.

Sankaran K and Madhav R (2013) *Legal and Policy Tools to Meet Informal Workers Demands: Lessons from India*. WIEGO Legal Brief No. 1. Cambridge, MA: WIEGO. Available at: www.wiego.org/sites/default/files/publications/files/Sankaran-Legal-Policy-Tools-Workers-India-WIEGO-LB1.pdf.

Scheinberg A, Simpson M and Gupt Y (2010) *Economic Aspects of the Informal Sector in Solid Waste Management*. Eschborn, Germany: German Technical Cooperation Agency (Gesellschaft für Technische Zusammenarbeit) and Collaborative Working Group on Solid Waste Management in Low- and Middle-Income Countries.

UN HABITAT (2016) The New Urban Agenda. Habitat III Summit Outcome Document.

United Nations (2015) *The World's Women 2015: Trends and Statistics*. New York: United Nations, Department of Economic and Social Affairs, Statistics Division.

Valodia I (2012) Technical Notes. In: Bali N, Chen M and Kanbur R (eds) *Bridging Perspectives: The Cornell-SEWA-WIEGO Exposure Dialogue Programme on Labour, Informality, and Poverty*. Ahmedabad, India: SEWA Academy.

Vanek J, Chen M and Rayeendran G (2012) *A Guide to Obtaining Data on Types of Informal Workers in Official Statistics*. WIEGO Statistical Brief 8. Cambridge, MA: WIEGO. Available at: www.wiego.org/sites/wiego.org/files/publications/files/Vanek-Guide-Obtaining-Data-Informal-Workers-WIEGO-SB8.pdf.

Wills G (2009) *South Africa's Informal Economy: A Statistical Profile*. WIEGO Working Paper 6 (Statistics). Cambridge, MA: WIEGO. Available at: www.wiego.org/sites/wiego.org/files/publications/files/Wills_WIEGO_WP6.pdf.

15 Addressing Land Rights in the Human Rights Framework

Karol C. Boudreaux

1. Introduction

Over the past 15 years, the idea that secure rights to access, use, manage, benefit from and trade land and other property are an essential foundation for economic growth has become commonplace (Acemoglu and Robinson, 2012; Besley, 1995; Besley and Ghatak, 2009; Deininger and Jin, 2005; Haydaroglu, 2015). More recently, international development experts have argued that secure rights to land are "critical" to achieve the Sustainable Development Goals, particularly Goals 1 (no poverty), 2 (no hunger) and 5 (gender equality) (Cordes and Sachs, 2015). To realize these positive outcomes, secure rights should be available to all members of a society, not just majority groups or elites (Acemoglu et al., 2005; Joireman, 2011). Recognizing that marginalized individuals and groups often lack secure rights to land, which can put them at risk of physical harm, displacement, loss of property and livelihoods, civil society organizations have developed advocacy campaigns to raise awareness of the importance of secure land rights for women, indigenous peoples, ethnic minorities and the poor.[1] Campaigns such as the International Land Coalition's "LandRightsNow!" and the "Kilimanjaro Initiative" shine a light on the physical and social costs people and communities face when their rights to land and the resources found on land are violated.

International development agencies also recognize that by securing the land rights of local people goals related to food security, eliminating poverty, empowering women and addressing climate change can be met (USAID, no date(a)) Recognizing and respecting the land rights of local people and communities is important for development finance institutions (such as the IFC), commercial banks and the private sector as well, which can face significant and costly financial and reputational risks by not attending to the land rights of people affected by their activities. These risks are substantial: a 2012 report found that companies that ignore pre-existing or customary local land rights in their land acquisition process can face costs ranging from a 29-fold increase in operating costs to complete abandonment of a commercial project (The Munden

Project, 2012). More companies are now working to address land rights as a component of their business and human rights commitments. Far from being an obscure issue, the global movement to secure rights to land is gaining traction as more people and institutions come to see these rights as an important "gateway" to other essential human rights and as foundational for human well-being.

This chapter ties concerns associated with rights to access, use, manage, benefit from and trade land to the existing human rights framework. There is limited recognition of land rights under this framework: rural women and indigenous people rights do have some recognized rights to land and decision-making related to land uses. However, land rights are not recognized as universal, though they do support, and are interdependent with, other recognized human rights. This chapter will not present a theoretical argument in favor of universal recognition of land rights. Rather, it offers a practice-based discussion of why land rights and land tenure security matter and why they should play a more prominent role in human rights discussions.

The chapter argues that secure rights to land promote economic and social well-being, help achieve gender equality, enhance decision-making and agency and reduce conflict. Weak or insecure land rights often reflect unequal, discriminatory treatment, contribute to poverty and hunger, frustrate economic and social opportunities and undergird a variety of disputes. Problems are particularly evident for women and for some marginalized groups, such as indigenous people, whose ability to access, use, manage and transfer land is often constrained.

The chapter begins with a discussion of what is meant by land rights and tenure security and identifies common sources of insecure tenure. It then turns to the question of why these rights matter, in a practical sense, exploring the protective and empowering role that secure rights to land can play, particularly for women. Next, the chapter looks at linkages between land rights and human rights and situates land rights within the human rights framework. Finally, the chapter provides some examples of what is working to address and remedy the profound gaps in the formal recognition of land rights. Identifying and implementing solutions to close this gap is essential to provide more people with security over their persons, homes, businesses and environments and with the opportunity to exercise the agency that flows from such security.

2. What Are Land Rights and Tenure Security?

Land rights consist of a bundle of rights that people or entities hold over parcels of land. These rights define how people can access, use, manage, benefit from and transfer land. Land rights, or rights over real property, are a subset of property rights, along with moveable property (such as a television or computer) and intellectual property (such as a patent or copyright). The non-binding Universal Declaration of Human Rights recognizes that "everyone has the right to own property alone as well as in association with others. No one shall be arbitrarily deprived of his property" (Article 17). However, there is only limited recognition of land rights under the current human rights framework. Though rights to land are not currently recognized as a universal human right, land rights are increasingly seen as "an essential element for the realization of many human rights" (UN OHCHR, no date).

Land tenure refers to the relationships that people hold with regard to land—these relationships can be extensively or narrowly defined and they can be articulated and enforced through formal government-provided systems or through customary or traditional, non-state systems. Formal, state-issued land rights may be secure, or they may be insecure (if, for example, a government lacks capacity to enforce rights) and rights held "informally" under customary systems may be quite secure if all actors in the environment respect and enforce these rights. Therefore, while land rights held under a customary governance system may be "informal" they are not necessarily insecure, and they should not necessarily be considered as "illegitimate."

By some estimates, up to 65 percent of the world's land is held under these customary or traditional systems (RRI, 2015). Most of these lands are not formally registered in the names of the individuals, families or authorities who manage them—rather, they are identified as "owned" by the state or by private actors. This means that in many countries two legal systems governing land (and other issues) exist side-by-side, which can create confusion and conflict.

Increasingly, governments "recognize" the rights of customary land holders to use lands they occupy. This recognition may come through provisions of a national constitution or through other laws or policies. In addition, soft international law documents as the Voluntary Guidelines on the Responsible Governance of Tenure of Land, Fisheries and Forests in the Context of National Food Security (the VGGT) call on states to recognize customary rights as "legitimate." Yet, in other cases, customary land rights are not recognized by national law. In this case, people may have informal tenure rather than a formal right to land. Land rights can be held by individuals, groups of individuals, legal entities such as corporations or by governments. In addition, multiple parties can hold rights over the same piece of land. For example, if a farmer sells the right to harvest apples from trees on the farm she owns, the farmer would hold the primary right to land while the apple collector would hold a secondary use right. In many contexts, secondary land use rights, including rights to plant crops, access water and use rangeland or pastures, are critical, especially for women, to maintain livelihoods and support families or communities.

As a bundle of rights, land rights can be relatively thick or quite thin. Someone who has the authority to make decisions about how to use or manage land, who can keep the proceeds from land use, who can exclude others, who can lend/lease or mortgage the land and eventually bequeath or sell the land has a thick bundle of rights. On the other hand, someone who has temporary rights to access land to cross from one area to another has a very thin (but perhaps still quite valuable) bundle of rights. Land rights may be defined by formal legal rules such as those contained in the Anglo-American common law, in state or federal statutes or in civil law codes. Formal rights to land are rarely absolute and are often constrained by regulations that limit the ability of a land owner to take certain actions or that require land owners to behave in certain ways. Examples of regulations that restrict a land owner's freedom to act include prohibitions on draining a wetland on one's land or forbidding a homeowner to change elements of a historic property. Common law practices also impose limits on what land owners can do with their property. For example, under the common law if a land owner unreasonably interferes with the ability of another person to enjoy his or her property the offending land owner will be liable for damages or face an injunction.[2]

Formal land rights are captured in written contracts and documents such as lease agreements or deeds of sale. Geospatial information about the location and size of land holdings is often conveyed in plats or cadastral maps that are registered with government land administration offices and agencies. These documents and records provide information about the location of a piece of land, the land's value, who owns the land and any registered claims against the land. Having validated, up-to-date, accurate and accessible land records makes it easier to transfer property with assurance that the seller has rights to sell the property. This is essential for the smooth functioning of real property markets in the developed world.

Land rights may be secure or insecure—and typically fall along a continuum from very insecure to very secure. By secure land rights we mean that the rights of individuals or groups over a particular parcel of land will be recognized, respected and enforced against wrongful use or appropriation by others. Land rights will be insecure if a rights' holder faces wrongful eviction, is unable to access land and property, if others transfer property without their permission, if others are able enter and use property without their permission and without sanction, or if property is expropriated without timely and just compensation

Insecurity arises for many different reasons. For example, if a government fails to enforce these rights and fails to sanction rights' violators, rights will be insecure. This may happen because governments lack the revenue, the trained professionals or the equipment needed to survey and register rights to land. Governments in developing countries commonly lack accurate maps of land holdings, they may have a very small number of licensed surveyors and other land professionals, they may not have digitized records of land holdings (some still rely on paper records that can be easily lost, manipulated or destroyed), and even if they have digitized land information the system (and information in the system) is often out-of-date. These constraints create bottlenecks, and opportunities for corruption that make it difficult for most citizens to use state land administration services. The costly and cumbersome processes required to formally register and transfer land creates strong disincentives to register property claims. Weaknesses in the state-run formal system mean as much as 70 percent of the world's land is currently undocumented.

In other cases, governments may have professional staff and revenue, but officials ignore or choose not to enforce the rights of some, either because these people have little political power or because officials wish to impose costs on certain groups (as, for example, to punish those who support an opposition group). Additionally, even in cases where governments have staff and revenue, shifting policy priorities may create land rights insecurity. This may occur, for example, if governments prioritize large-scale commercial agricultural development over protection of smallholder land rights. In countries such as Tanzania, Cameroon, Ethiopia and Papua New Guinea, vast tracts of land have been transferred into the lands of investors, creating insecurity on the ground for local women and men who often lose rights and receive little or no compensation in return (Fraser and Mousseau, 2016; Mittal and Fraser, 2018; Oakland Institute, 2015, 2017).

As noted above, in many places land is still held, often communally, under informal customary governance systems. Members of a customary group hold use rights over land based on rules the group has created and that have evolved over time. Customary leaders, such as chiefs or heads of clans, are responsible for allocating land to families within their group (or they may delegate this authority to local headmen, village elders or land priests). They hold land "in trust" for their community and have a fiduciary obligation to group members to manage resources responsibly for future generations. It is these leaders who are responsible for keeping track of who is using land and under what conditions. Individuals or families living under customary land rules cannot sell their rights, but they can trade, lend or bequeath rights (subject to the approval of other community members and/or the leader). If group members violate land use rules, leaders resolve conflicts. Land records under these systems are rarely written down and disputes are normally settled through a mediation process. However, as land values rise and opportunities for personal enrichment present themselves, some leaders disregard their obligations and sell or transfer communal lands to investors without the consent of the group (Chimtom, 2018; Joireman, 2011). The result can be landlessness and homelessness for community members.

The formal statutory legal system in some countries does recognizes the rights of customary land holders to access and use land (Knight, 2010).[3] In such cases, governments may issue "certificates of use rights" to people living in customary areas. This formal sector recognition of the rights to customary land holders may enhance the security of their rights by identifying parcel holders and boundaries. In many countries, however, governments have still not created statutory mechanisms to recognize customary rights and this lack of formal sector recognition can contribute to insecurity and enable outsiders or government actors to more easily take these lands, often for infrastructure or economic development purposes.

Insecurity can also be the result of status, particularly under customary systems, where different group members have different land use rights. In many customary land-holding systems women, for example, often have lower status and may only hold secondary use rights to land and resources. And yet worldwide women provide much, or a majority, of the agricultural labor required to grow food crops. If a woman's formal rights to own and manage land (which exist under international law and in many national legal frameworks) are not recognized by a customary authority, she will have fewer opportunities to make decisions about how to use the land, which crops to plant and whether to lend, mortgage or lease the land, limiting her agency and her ability to pursue entrepreneurial opportunities.

In some customary areas, if a husband dies, a wife may lose her right to remain in the marital home and access the land she needs to grow food. According to one study, in Uganda, as many as 40 percent of widows have experienced an attempt by others (often her husband's family) to forcibly take their marital property; 30 percent of them have lost land through familial "land grabbing"; over 18 percent have had threats made against their lives and more than 30 percent experienced threats against their children (IJM, 2014). Such discriminatory social norms and practices often violate national laws on gender equality and nondiscriminatory treatment as well as international laws and human rights conventions that call on states to provide for equal treatment before the law, including the Convention on the Elimination of all Forms of Discrimination Against Women (CEDAW). Today, equality under the law, equality of opportunity and equality of voice for women are core development objectives. Practitioners are well aware of these problems and a great deal of attention has, over the past decade, been focused on working with customary authorities and government officials to shift norms and change behavior to recognize women's land rights.[4]

In any state-based judicial contest or in formal political/administrative decision-making, rights held under the formal system are typically favored over customary rights that are not recognized under a constitution or other law. As a result, people living under customary systems may have less tenure security (though this is not always the case), they may be at greater risk of displacement, they may have fewer opportunities to legally contract with others to benefit from the land's use and they will be unable to mortgage land (though they may be able to borrow against crops in the ground or against housing or improvements to land). With clearer recognition of their land rights, customary rights' holders could have beneficial opportunities to lease land for agribusiness or another commercial development, provide timber concessions or engage in joint venture conservation or eco-tourism efforts. When these rights are formally recognized, respected and enforced, through, for example, a state-issued certificate of land use, individuals living under customary governance systems can enter into agreements with outsiders to use their land and resources under terms and conditions that local people find beneficial.[5]

While good outcomes are possible for people when rights to land and property are secure, this is the exception, not the rule in much of the world. Recognizing the serious harms that often follow displacements of individuals and communities whose land rights are lost to government development projects or some private investments, in 2012 the international community endorsed soft international law guidance for good land governance: the VGGT. Subsequent soft law guidance incorporates the VGGT by reference—notably, the Principles for Responsible Investment in Agriculture and Food Systems. The African Union has developed "A Framework and Guidelines on Land Policy in Africa" that calls on states to acknowledge the legitimacy of customary (or indigenous) systems, strengthen women's rights to land and enhance access to land through needed land reforms. In this case, women's rights to land are interpreted to supersede rights that exist under customary systems and so customary leaders, and government officials, have an obligation to recognize and respect these rights. Through its Agenda 2063 effort, the African Union is now working with member states to ensure that the amount of land allocated to women is 30 percent at a minimum.

International development agencies and finance institutions have also created guidelines and performance standards for investors and borrowers to protect individuals and communities from losing land rights and to promote "responsible" land-based investing. Private-sector producer associations such as the Roundtable on Sustainable Palm Oil, the Roundtable on Sustainable Biomaterials and the Forest Stewardship Council have made commitments to respect local land rights and conserve landscapes. In addition, several multinational firms, including Coca-Cola, Cargill, Illovo Sugar, Nestlé's, Rabobank and Unilever, have adopted corporate policies designed to limit or eliminate harms associated with violations of local peoples' land rights.[6] At the same time, customary land holders and civil society organizations continue to take action—through protests, litigation and advocacy—to stop land transfers, concessions, infrastructure development and mining and extractive activities when they are not adequately consulted, likely to be harmed and do not directly benefit from the activity. Increasingly, these groups are winning national and international legal cases by focusing attention on the issue of who owns and should control the world's land.

3. Why Do Land Rights Matter?

Land rights matter because land remains a critical economic and social asset for up to 2.5 billion people worldwide. These women and men manage or depend upon small and subsistence farms to feed themselves and their families (FAO, 2018). Farmers need secure rights to their homesteads to ensure rights to privacy and they need secure rights to their fields to protect and hopefully to improve their livelihoods. With more secure land rights, the world's smallholder farmers gain enhanced incentives to invest labor and capital to improve productivity, expanding economic opportunities. With tradeable rights, farmers can also choose to leave rural areas and move to cities, seeking different economic and social opportunities. For the urban poor, having secure rights to housing, a recognized economic and social right, can support their pursuit of other human rights including rights to personal security and privacy. Secure housing often provides space for a home-based business, and it can provide a source of income if all or part of the property is rented out. As with the rural poor, property rights provide the urban poor with a foundation to pursue livelihoods and entrepreneurial opportunities.

For women, it may be especially beneficial to hold secure rights to land and yet, gender equality in terms of the ability to access, use or own land is often denied. In more than half of countries, inequitable laws and customs constrain women's equal rights to land, frustrating equal treatment and gender equality. Addressing this inequitable treatment could have important benefits for women, their children and communities. Research shows that women are more likely to engage in activities that help improve productivity on farms when they have secure land rights. They expend more time and effort on soil conservation and they use more capital to increase productivity (Ali et al., 2011). Productivity improvements can lead to improved food security and higher household income (Hagos and Holden, 2013). With higher incomes, women invest in the health and education of their children, which creates positive future benefits for families and communities. Similarly, when women have improved tenure security in urban areas they increase investments in housing and they build the human capital of family members, particularly children (Radoki, 2014). Research from Nicaragua and Honduras finds that in households where women own more land, expenditures on food and schooling for children increases (Katz and Chamorro, 2002).

Holding secure rights to land and housing enables women to participate in land/property rental markets—generating new economic opportunities. In some cases, more secure rights to land and property may lead to improved access to credit (Menon et al., 2014). The positive impacts of secure land tenure and property rights can empower rights' holders by enabling them to pursue opportunities and fulfill their unique potential (Golla et al., 2011). For example, in Tanzania, women whose land rights were formalized were three times more likely to have off-farm work opportunities. They earned nearly four times more income and were 1.35 times more likely to have individual savings than non-land owners (Peterman, 2011). This is particularly important in rural areas where formal sector employment opportunities are limited. In Nepal, 37 percent of women land owners had the final say on a household decision whereas only 20 percent of non-land owners had the same ability (Santos et al., 2013). Similarly, in Ethiopia, when women's land rights were certified, this led to a 44-percent increase in the likelihood that a wife could decide what crops to grow on the lands she controlled (Bezebih and Holden, 2010). In urban areas of Vietnam, women who held property jointly with husbands felt this provided them with more protection in case of marital conflict, greater equality within the marriage and more decision-making authority and increased scope for engagement in business (World Bank, 2008). One study found that: "urban women perceived extensive gains in their power when they control major assets, are free (or freer) from domestic violence, acquire greater social capital, and have a supportive local opportunity structure" (Radoki, 2014: 14). Combining the ownership and control of economic assets such as land and housing with social capital such as education, or with financial capital such as an income (from farm or off-farm activities), may be particularly important to increase women's household-level decision-making power (Klugman et al., 2014).

In some contexts, secure land rights also matter for health reasons. In Nepal, land is a source of power and status in addition to providing the basis for a large agricultural sector. While women do much of the agricultural work in the country, they have limited land rights. Analyzing survey data from the country's Demographic and Health Survey, one researcher found that the odds that women who own land will have children who are severely underweight is reduced by half compared with non-land owning women (Allendorf, 2007). This outcome is the result of women land owners having larger incomes and resources. The study concludes that land ownership is comparable in its impacts on children's health to women's education or employment. For women, who continue to hold less land than men in many parts of the world and land of lower quality, having secure rights over homesteads and fields would help ensure their equal treatment before the law. It would provide them with expanded entrepreneurial opportunities, increased decision-making authority and enable them to enjoy their human rights to dignity and equal treatment. As research shows, secure land rights also matter to promote greater food security and improved nutrition for women and their children and it contributes to more education and medical care for children. Men enjoy similar benefits from secure land rights but given the greater asset gap between women and men's land holdings, securing land rights for women helps close an asset gap and a rights gap.

Secure land rights also matter because they help reduce conflict between community members and with outsiders. Throughout the world, land is a contentious, sensitive and political (or politicized) issue. In many areas of the world, land is not simply an economic commodity to be managed through impersonal market transactions, it is also a source of power and prestige. People often disagree and fight over who should have this power and control. One example involves transhumant pastoralists and settled farmers, who are often of different ethnic groups and different religions. Under customary governance systems, these groups would commonly (though not always) negotiate trades of property—farmers would provide access to already-harvested fields in exchange for manure and milk from cattle. Violations of the terms of the exchange would be dealt with by elders or other traditional authorities who had authority to create and enforce customary rules.

Rather than recognize and formalize such traditional claims to land, colonial and socialist then post-colonial and post-socialist transition governments instead nationalized most (or all) land, often vesting these rights in the person of the President (or Prime Minister). Customary land rights, which have evolved over the course of centuries or even millennia, have been displaced in many areas by a formal statutory system. And yet, these formal systems often fail to enforce the laws they create, creating potential for a clash between the systems. Across the Sahel and east Africa much of the conflict between farmers and herders is, at its core, about unresolved property conflict (BBC, 2018). As lands for grazing become scarcer, pastoralists fight with each other to access and use the resources they need (Butler and Gates, 2010). They also fight with settled farmers, some of whom may use formal systems to secure rights that previously were allocated through customary systems. Many disputes between community members and with outsiders now escalate into conflict rather than being settled by negotiation.

Conflict also exists between community members and governments. Pastoralists such as the Masaai in Kenya and Tanzania have been forced off land to make room for national parks and conservation areas. Because they often lack formalized rights to the pastures, water sources or migration routes they use, pastoralists are at risk of losing access to these resources. In some countries governments have adopted policies that encourage or require migratory pastoralists to settle in villages. "Villagization" may make it easier for governments to provide education and health care to pastoralist groups, but when pastoralists are settled, governments may find it easier to reallocate land and water to investors, such as large-scale agribusinesses, growing palm oil or sugar cane. Reallocation of customary lands to outsider investors has created many conflicts over the past decade and contributed to outbreaks of violence in Central America, Africa and Southeast Asia.

Land rights also matter to decentralize power and provide some (relatively) safe space in the face of authority. As noted above, governments can punish opponents by violating their land and housing rights. In May 2005 the Zimbabwe government launched Operation Murambatsvina (translated as "Drive out the Rubbish" or "Restore Order"), razing over 90,000 homes and businesses in urban areas and forcibly displacing an estimated 700,000 people. The government claimed that its actions were designed to clear and improve informal settlements, or slums, and address criminal activity in these areas but many questioned this rationale as the targeted areas were opposition strongholds. On the ground, the results were profoundly negative as hundreds of thousands of people lost shelter, income and faced increased food insecurity and negative health impacts. Many of these displaced persons were then forced into the countryside, rather than being allowed to resettle in urban areas (Potts, 2006). These forcible evictions violated international human rights and appeared, in part, to be retaliation against people who voted for the opposition party in March 2005 elections. In addition, by evicting these urban residents, the government could reduce the threat of mass protests in reaction to the country's severe economic crisis (Bratton and Masunungure, 2006). Forced evictions are considered a gross violation of human rights, particularly the right to housing but often, necessarily, they also violate rights people hold to underlying land and other property.

A growing source of land-based conflicts involves local people and investors, both domestic and foreign. Over the past decade, a well-documented global rise in demand for farmlands, pastures and forest resources has led to an increase in land-based investments by national and international commercial agricultural and forestry firms. While some projects have created new economic opportunities for local communities, others have imposed significant costs as local people have lost control over and access to land, suffered violations of human rights and experienced environmental and other social harms (Cordes et al., 2016; Cotula et al., 2009; FAO, 2015; Global Witness, 2013; IFC, 2012; Iff and Joras, 2015; Thoumi, 2017).

Conflicts often involve loss of access to lands with spiritual value, lands used for housing, or to grow food, access water and important forest products. They have involved the large-scale production of palm oil in Indonesia, sugar production in Malawi, plantation agriculture in Mozambique and forestry in Cambodia. To avoid these harms, investors need to understand who has legitimate rights to land. *De jure*, this may be the government, given that the state is the titleholder over most or all land in many countries. In this case, an investor will need to negotiate a concession or leasehold with state officials. However, even when the state formally owns land, people may live on or use land and their land rights should be recognized. According to one estimate, 93 percent of all concessions in emerging markets are inhabited by local people (Alforte et al., 2014). Unfortunately, investors may not be aware that project lands are occupied, and governments may not take the rights and needs of these people into account before issuing concessions. To date, governments have transferred hundreds of thousands of hectares of land to investors for such projects (Dell'Angelo et al., 2017; Rulli et al., 2013).

Investors need to look beyond the formal titles and legal rules to identify if any individuals or groups hold customary, traditional land rights to project areas based on long-term occupancy. If companies fail to identify, consult with and provide benefits to these people, local people may lose lands, water, forests and pastures they depend upon. They may lose access to important cultural or spiritual sites and so lose cultural heritage. Conflicts over who has the rights to make decisions about land uses and who has rights to benefit from activities continue to drive deadly protests. Over the last several years hundreds of women and men have lost their lives defending their traditional, customary or informal rights to land and housing (Chandran, 2017; Global Witness, 2017).

As more businesses, governments and development organizations align policies and practices with the UN Guiding Principles on Business and Human Rights (UNGP), with social safeguard documents such as the IFC's Performance Standards and with institutional and sector-specific safeguards and codes of conduct,[7] the need to address land rights and tenure issues as a part of human rights impact assessments and enhanced due diligence processes also increases (GRI, 2016). If an investment takes place in a context where local discrimination is unwittingly cemented, this may mean that an investor or implementer is complicit in violations that contribute to negative human rights impacts.

For example, if investors are unaware of, or ignore, past actions that violated the legitimate tenure right of women, indigenous people and other vulnerable or marginalized groups and, as a result, only recognize rights held by male heads of household or by government, they may violate rights to equal treatment. If traditional leaders monopolize or effectively shut out participation of community members to personally benefit from a land transaction, this may create costly local grievances and violate rights of local peoples (Cordes et al., 2016). As well, wrongful displacements or poorly managed resettlement efforts can violate rights to livelihoods. Guidance from U.S. law firm Foley Hoag makes this point quite clearly:

> [C]ompanies should not simply rely on government assurances that they have clean title. Even if such title stands up in court (and it may not), companies potentially face years of tension or open conflict

> with neighboring communities. They also could be considered to be complicit in human rights abuses related to population displacement. Ultimately, companies should seek to engage directly with potentially affected traditional land users to negotiate for access to land, and should consider adopting a policy on free, prior, and informed consent.
>
> (Lehr, 2013)

For many reasons then, having secure rights to land and natural resources found on land matters deeply to individuals and groups that hold such rights. Secure rights over land serve multiple goals including equal treatment before the law; increased economic opportunities and investments that contribute to improved livelihoods; improved food security and nutrition; enhanced decision-making authority and agency; and reduced violence and conflict. But how do land rights fit within the broader human rights framework? The next section briefly explores this question.

4. Land Rights and Human Rights

Although the right to hold property is recognized as a human right under the Universal Declaration of Human Rights (Article 17), there is no general "right to land" in the core international human rights conventions. However, the international human rights framework does recognize rights to land for indigenous people and for rural women. This is not to say that secure land rights are important only for these groups. As discussed above, secure land rights are important for virtually all rural people and for many urban dwellers. Providing more women and men with secure rights to access (through inheritance, gift or voluntary exchange), use, manage, benefit from and transfer land rights is a growing concern for civil society, the private sector and many development practitioners and agencies. How governments respond to calls for action on this front, in law and in practice, remains to be seen.

For indigenous people, ILO Convention 169 and the United Nations Declaration on the Rights of Indigenous People (UNDRIP) provide bases for recognizing the land and resource rights (collective and individual) of indigenous peoples. UNDRIP recognizes that indigenous people "have the right to own, use, develop and control the lands, territories and resources that they possess by reason of traditional ownership or other traditional occupation or use, as well as those which they have otherwise acquired" (Article 26). States are required to "give legal recognition and protection to these lands, territories and resources." Having secure rights to live on, manage, exclude others and benefit from land they have traditionally occupied and used is essential to prevent discrimination, promote self-determination, improve economic and social conditions and protect the cultural identity of indigenous people. However, many countries, including Botswana, Costa Rica, Guatemala, India, Kenya, the Philippines and Sweden, among others, continue to provide only limited recognition—or no recognition—for these land rights claims. Through advocacy campaigns and strategic litigation, in some areas these discriminatory practices are changing but the costs are high: as noted above, hundreds of people have been killed defending their lands (Global Witness, 2017).

Although women hold rights to "equal treatment in land and agrarian reforms as well as in land resettlement schemes" and to the "same rights for both spouses in respect of the ownership, acquisition, management, administration, enjoyment and disposition of property" (Articles 14.2 and 16 1 (h)) under the Convention on the Elimination of All Forms of Discrimination Against Women (CEDAW), women continue to face discrimination and unequal treatment when it comes to land and real property. Their land rights are often insecure, and they typically hold less land than men and poorer quality land (FAO, no date(a)). In more than 90 countries, women still do not have equal rights to own land (Arsenault, 2016). Many countries still have gender unequal laws related to the inheritance of property and to division of property upon divorce. To address this gap, the CEDAW Committee has stated that "rural women's rights to land and natural resources are . . . fundamental human rights" (CEDAW General Recommendation No. 34, para. 56).

Discriminatory social norms continue to make it difficult for women to exercise formal, *de jure* rights that they do hold under national and international law. To take just one example, in Tanzania although women have equal rights to inherit land under formal statutory law, the Customary Law Declaration Order of 1969 remains in effect, enabling fathers to pass land to sons only. Having secure rights to land and housing could help women experience more equal economic, social and cultural rights; support livelihoods and improve incomes; increase the amount of food they produce; and, in some contexts, protect them against gender-based or intimate-partner violence (Boudreaux, 2018). As women take on more agricultural work (with men migrating to urban areas and other countries), providing them with secure land rights is critical to support equal treatment, support livelihoods and enhance food security. For these reasons, among others, secure rights to land, even if not formally recognized as a human right, are necessary to exercise a variety of other human rights and may even be an emerging human right (Cordes, 2017).

Beyond international law norms and principles, regional human rights instruments and courts have also provided some protection for land rights. These regional instruments, such as the African Charter on Human and Peoples Rights, which provides for a right to property (Article 14), a right to practice religion (Article 8) and a right to culture (Article 17), have been used to derive a right to land for indigenous and traditional communities. The Inter-American Court of Human Rights has found that the rights of indigenous peoples and other communities to property and the use of land, resources and territories is protected by the American Convention on Human Rights (Article 21). In several cases, the Court has found that these rights were violated by commercial activities such as mining, large-scale ranching or commercial agriculture. As well, national law may provide protection for land rights of individuals, groups and legal entities.

Today the human rights framework is limited to recognizing the land rights of indigenous people and rural women. Yet too often these rights are ignored by governments. And for many poor men or men from vulnerable groups, such as pastoralists, land rights are also insecure. For millions, rights to access, use, manage, benefit from and trade land remains insecure—limiting their ability to expand economic and social opportunities, constraining their decision-making authority and exposing them to discriminatory practices and conflict. While a growing movement among civil society, supported by development agencies and some private sector actors, is raising awareness of the importance of secure land rights, and while more cases are being decided in favor of women, men and groups whose rights are violated, the problems associated with providing more secure land rights are still enormous and the need to raise awareness of land rights as a human rights issue remains. The next section discusses several new efforts to improve policies and adopt technology to address bottlenecks in the land sector and help secure the land rights of people around the world.

5. What Can Be Done to Secure Land Rights?

Many national governments, international organizations, bilateral and multilateral development agencies, civil society organizations and private sector actors have taken steps designed to strengthen land rights. This section presents a sampling of some of the most interesting policy and technology-based developments.

To improve the legal framework related to land rights, governments, civil society and the private sector have come together to develop new guidelines and policies to protect and respect the legitimate land rights of women and men. In 2012, the Committee on World Food Security shepherded the unanimous endorsement of the VGGT. The VGGT represents a broad consensus on the need to improve land governance in support of the realization of the human right to adequate food. The VGGT are seen as a tool that states and the private sector can use to promote sustainable development (and so can work synergistically with the UN SDGs), social stability, housing security, rural development, environmental protection and sustainable social and economic outcomes (FAO, no date(b)). The UN Food and Agriculture Organization (FAO), the international organization that supports implementation of the VGGT, has developed specialized guidance on how to achieve better outcomes on land, provides trainings on the topic and is helping national governments assess and revise their legal frameworks to align with the principles and objectives of the VGGT. International development agencies such as USAID, DFID, GIZ, SIDA and the World Bank also support efforts to implement the VGGT. As noted earlier, the African Union has been quite active in developing guidance for member states on improved land governance. The AU, together with the UN Economic Commission for Africa, supports the Land Policy Initiative which works with member states to support land reform processes such as adapting measures to recognize and secure community land rights, work to secure women's land rights and the land rights of youth and to integrate land rights concerns into national agricultural policies (UNECA, no date).

A stronger legal framework is a necessary, if not sufficient condition, for securing the land rights of those who currently face insecurity. However, in addition to strengthening legal frameworks it is essential to improve the ability of governments to deliver secure rights in a cost-effective and accessible manner. Several technology-focused projects, mostly funded by international development agencies, are working to overcome the administrative bottlenecks that make it costly and time-consuming for women and men to apply for and receive formal documentation of land rights. In Rwanda, the UK's DFID supported a systematic mapping and registration of land rights for all 10.3 million parcels of land in the country. This project, called the Land Tenure Regularisation Programme (LTRSP), supported the Government of Rwanda's efforts to clarify land ownership (conflict over land having been identified as one of the drivers of the 1994 genocide) to reduce social tensions and promote economic growth by increasing land's productivity. The project adopted a low-cost, community-based approach to build local understanding of land rights, train local para-surveyors, identify individual parcels on aerial photographs to create (and then validate) index maps, deliver an updated land registry and improve government capacity to manage land administration services. These land certificates were jointly titled in the names of husbands and (legal) wives to promote more gender equitable outcomes, although the project was criticized for failing to address the claims of women in informal marriages or customary unions. Over 80 percent of titles were provided to couples jointly, 11 percent of titles were provided to women solely and 9 percent to men solely (Gillingham and Buckle, 2014). The Government of Rwanda is now working with Microsoft and a Swiss firm to enhance the security of its land registry by adopting blockchain technology (isiAfrica, 2018).

In Ethiopia, DFID's Land Investment for Transformation (LIFT) project has adopted the Rwanda model and is working with the government to map and provide land certificates for 14 million parcels of land and over 6 million households. This project hopes to improve incomes of the rural poor to promote economic growth. As with Rwanda, women's land rights are a focus issue and the project has a target of ensuring that 70 percent of documents are jointly titled in the names of husbands and wives (Allebachew et al., 2017). These projects demonstrate that with donor support to adapt technology and scale its use, some governments can title lands fairly quickly.

Other international development agencies are also experimenting by combining participatory data collection with technology to capture, record and register land rights. In Tanzania, USAID has piloted and taken to scale an approach that works with local youth, serving as para-surveyors, to map and record land rights using smartphones. The Mobile Application to Secure Tenure (MAST) approach features an open-source mobile application to capture geospatial data in the field (USAID, no date(b)). Para-surveyors walk parcel boundaries with neighbors, collect reference points and ownership information, resolve boundary disputes in the field with the help of local officials, and then store this information in a database that is accessible by the local government. Government land administration officials can then download the information, check data for accuracy and identify any needed corrections. Official documents can be printed based on the information collected in the field. As compared with the standard government process, this method of land registration saves time and is more transparent so may help reduce local conflicts. As with the DFID projects in Rwanda and Ethiopia, this project also focuses on ensuring that women and men understand the rights women hold under the law and work to jointly title land in the names of husbands and wives—in this case, close to 50 percent of parcels are jointly titled. USAID has adapted the technology and it is also being used in Burkina Faso to provide official certificates to land holders.

The Global Land Tenure Network (GLTN)[8] worked with a number of UN agencies, university-based partners and civil society organizations to develop a different open-source technology tool to map and record land rights in formal and customary settings. The Social Tenure Domain Model (STDM) is a pro-poor tool designed to capture geospatial and social/demographic information about land parcels to help communities and governments improve land use planning and help individuals and communities secure their rights to land and housing. The STDM tool has been used in Malawi, Nepal, Uganda and the Palestinian West Bank to help improve the tenure security of smallholder farmers and slum dwellers. Governments can use the STDM tool to build an accurate, accessible and flexible land information database which is an important step in the direction of improved tenure security and expanded economic and social opportunity (Wegen, 2018).

Civil society organizations have also been active in the development of new technology tools to improve transparency in the land sector by strengthening the knowledge base associated with land ownership. The

World Resources Institute manages two important projects: LandMark and Global Forest Watch. LandMark provides a much-needed global platform to identify the location of collectively held indigenous and community lands. Users upload data about land claims to the LandMark site; once claims are validated they are entered onto an interactive map that identifies the boundaries of lands held under customary governance systems or used by these groups. The platform captures national-level data on the percent of a country held by indigenous people and communities and provides indicators on the legal security of these lands, the assets found on them and pressures (e.g., private sector concessions) that create risks for the land (LandMark, no date). Global Forest Watch provides detailed data on the world's forests, the communities that live in them and the threats they face. The platform is interactive, and it provides a mobile application, Forest Watcher, to report and monitor threats to forests, such as destruction of peatlands or deforestation activities (Global Forest Watch, no date). The Rights and Resources Initiative (RRI), a global advocacy alliance, also tracks ownership of forests around the world and reports on changes over time from a quantitative and qualitative perspective (RRI, no date(a)).

At the local or community level many international and national civil society organizations have worked for years to expand the knowledge base around land ownership. They collect tenure information, upgrade slum settlements, certify land holdings, identify the number and quality of government services provided in rural and urban settlement areas, provide para-legal services to local people to defend land rights and work with attorneys to pursue strategic litigation actions. One of the best-known efforts is OpenStreetMap, an online wiki that enables its community of users to upload and edit information to a map of the world, creating a picture of areas that may previously have been "hidden" (OpenStreetMap, no date). Driven by its users, OpenStreetMap has been able to capture information about the conditions in slums, cities, peri-urban and rural areas in extraordinary detail and this information can be used by international agencies and government officials to respond to natural disasters, target development aid and public services and improve land use planning. As a tool for securing land rights, OpenStreetMap can be used to demonstrate settlement or the extent of a land claim.

Slum and Shack Dwellers International (SDI) has developed a participatory, community-driven methodology to collect important local information about slum settlements to support an effort called "Know Your City." To date, SDI affiliates have collected information about 7,712 slum settlements in 12 countries (SDI, no date). This project relies on slum dwellers to gather information including numbers of inhabitants, settlement types, settlements at risk of eviction, number of toilets, schools and number of local savings groups, then shares this information on an interactive platform. The project also identifies community priorities for the services they want. For example, in Adabraka settlement in Accra Ghana, local residents want access to sanitation sewage, improved water drainage, secure land tenure and better housing, in that order (SDI, 2017).

In order to reduce conflicts, RRI has worked extensively with private sector firms to raise awareness of the problems associated with insecure land and resource rights in investment areas or in areas with ongoing operations. The organization has developed a set of Private Sector Risk Analysis Tools that are designed to identify, mitigate or eliminate land tenure risks and reduce conflicts between investors and communities and promote more beneficial outcomes for all parties involved in land-based investments (RRI, no date(b)).

These examples represent a small but illustrative sample of the kinds of innovative policy initiatives and technologies that are being used to recognize, respect and protect the land lights of people around the world. Other interesting technology that can be used to map and record rights and provide enhanced protection against fraudulent transactions include drones, mini or cube satellites and blockchain technology. Each of these technologies has been deployed to enable people to respond more quickly, with more precision and at lower cost to the demand for information on land claims. Meeting this demand is critical to enhancing the tenure security of the world's poor—most of whom still lack documented rights to their land and resources.

6. Conclusion

Today millions of women and men around the world live under conditions of land tenure insecurity—their rights to access, use, manage, benefit from and trade land are not formally recognized by governments and this failure to recognize their claims by issuing some formal documentation of rights puts many at risk of displacement and dispossession. When people lose rights to the land they depend upon for their livelihoods, their shelter, their cultural heritage and their privacy, they face the potential of human rights violations. For women and indigenous peoples, the combination of discriminatory laws and discriminatory social norms and practices compounds these concerns, subjects them to unequal treatment and makes some vulnerable to physical harms including gender-based violence. While land rights are not currently recognized as human rights, there is a growing movement among civil society organizations, development and finance agencies and even the private sector to respect the legitimate land rights of women and men—both as means to achieve positive outcomes such as food security, improved economic opportunity and environmental conversation and to avoid the costly harms associated with land-based conflict. Working collaboratively, and leveraging technology developments, these groups can help close the yawing tenure gap and, in the process, protect the human rights of many of the world's people.

Notes

1 See, for example, Land Rights Now (www.landrightsnow.org); the Kilimanjaro Initiative (www.actionaid.org/sites/files/actionaid/kilimanjaro_bronchure.pdf) and Solid Ground (http://solidgroundcampaign.org/).
2 A land owner would create a private nuisance if, on her land, she emits excessive noise, foul odors, vibrations, excessive light or smoke and these emissions harm neighboring land owners.
3 In Africa, Botswana, Mozambique and Tanzania have adopted this approach.
4 In Tanzania, international development agencies such as USAID and the UK's Department for International Development (DFID) are supporting large-scale land registration, including in areas where social norms discriminate against women. Programs raise awareness of women's legal rights to land at the grassroots level through trainings and workshops and then encourage villagers to register rights either jointly in the names of husbands and wives or, if the household is woman-headed, in the name of the woman head of household.
5 For example, in Namibia the government devolved rights to manage wildlife to local communities, subject to community members forming a voluntary "conservancy." Managing wildlife requires communities to manage their lands to create the conditions for wildlife to thrive and co-exist with livestock and people. Since 1995 over 80 conservancies have been formed by people who jointly negotiate land boundaries, land uses, craft a constitution, manage wildlife, develop benefit plans and then implement plans to protect wildlife. Conservancies hold 19 concessions in national parks and on state lands—expanding economic opportunities in rural areas for their members. In 2016, conservancies generated over $9 million in revenue and provided over 5,100 jobs to local people (NACSO, 2016).
6 See, for example, Nestlé's "No Land Grab Commitment" available at: www.nestle.com/asset-library/documents/library/documents/corporate_social_responsibility/nestle-commitment-land-rights-agriculture.pdf/.
7 For a list of pertinent guidelines and standards in the agribusiness sector see: Agribusiness: Risks and Impacts in Conflict-Affected Areas, at: http://reliefweb.int/sites/reliefweb.int/files/resources/Economy_AgribusinessRisks Impacts_EN_2015.pdf.
8 The GLTN is a partnership of civil society organizations, research institutions and bilateral and multilateral international agencies that work to secure tenure rights and enhance land access. The GLTN is facilitated by UN-Habitat.

References

Acemoglu D, Johnson S and Robinson J (2005) Institutions as a Fundamental Cause of Long-Run Growth. In: Aghion P and Durlauf S (eds) *Handbook of Economic Growth*, 1(A) New York: Elsevier, pp. 385–471.

Acemoglu D and Robinson J (2012) *Why Nations Fail*. New York: Crown Publishing Group, Random House, Inc.

Alforte A, Angan J, Dentith J, Domondon K, Munden L, Murday S and Pradela L (2014) *Communities as Counterparties: Preliminary Review of Concessions and Conflict in Emerging and Frontier Market Concessions*. Washington, DC: Rights and Resources Initiative. Available at: http://rightsandresources.org/wp-content/uploads/Communities-as-Counterparties-FINAL_Oct-21.pdf (accessed 2 July 2018).

Ali DA, Deininger K and Goldstein M (2011) *Environmental and Gender Impacts of Land Regularization in Africa: Pilot Evidence from Rwanda*. Policy Research

Working Paper Series (No. 5765) Washington, DC: The World Bank. Available at: https://openknowledge.worldbank.org/bitstream/handle/10986/18770/WPS6908.pdf?sequence=1&isAllowed=y, (accessed 7 July 2018).

Allebachew M, Leckie J and Smith A (2017) Large-Scale Rural Certification and Administration in Ethiopia: The Challenges of a Decentralized Approach. Paper prepared for presentation at the 2017 World Bank Conference on Land and Poverty, 20–24 March.

Allendorf K (2007) Do Women's Land Rights Promote Empowerment and Child Health in Nepal? *World Development* 35(11): 1975–1988.

Arsenault C (2016) Female Farmers in 90 Nations Face Discriminatory Land Law. *Reuters*, 8 March. Available at: www.reuters.com/article/us-women-land-rights/female-farmers-in-90-nations-face-discriminatory-land-laws-idUSKCN0WA0P6 (accessed 8 July 2018).

Besley T (1995) Property Rights and Investment Incentives: Theory and Evidence from Ghana. *Journal of Political Economy* 103(5): 903–937.

Besley T and Ghatak M (2009) Property Rights and Economic Development. In: Rodrik D and Rosenzweig M (eds) *Handbook of Development Economics* New York: Elsevier, pp. 4525–4595.

Bezebih M and Holden S (2010) *The Role of Land Certification in Reducing Gender Gaps in Productivity in Rural Ethiopia*. Gothenburg, Germany and Washington, DC: EFD/RFF.

Boudreaux K (2018) *Intimate Partner Violence and Land Tenure*. Washington, DC: USAID, Available at: www.land-links.org/research-publication/intimate-partner-violence-land-tenure/ (accessed 7 July 2018).

Bratton M and Masunungure E (2006) Popular Reactions to State Repression: Operation Murambatsvina in Zimbabwe. *African Affairs* 106(422): 21–45.

British Broadcasting Corporation (BBC) (2018) Nigeria's Benue Clashes: Mass Burial After Farmer-Fulani Clashes, 11 January. Available at: www.bbc.com/news/world-africa-42648492 (accessed 7 July 2018).

Butler CK and Gates S (2010) *Communal Violence and Property Rights*. Third Workshop of the Households in Conflict Network. Brighton, UK: Institute of Development Studies. Available at: www.unm.edu/~ckbutler/workingpapers/CVandPR.pdf (accessed 1 July 2018).

Chandran R (2017) Land Rights Defenders Appeal to U.N. to End Violence by States, Corporations. *Reuters*, 22 September. Available at: www.reuters.com/article/us-landrights-violence-un/land-rights-defenders-appeal-to-u-n-to-end-violence-by-states-corporations-idUSKCN1BX1KC (accessed 7 July 2018).

Chimtom NK (2018) Church in Ghana Asks for Action Against "land grabbing." *Crux*, 1 January. Available at: https://cruxnow.com/global-church/2018/01/01/church-ghana-asks-action-land-grabbing/ (accessed 7 July 2018).

Cordes K (2017) Is There a Human Right to Land? *State of the Planet*, 8 November. Available at: http://blogs.ei.columbia.edu/2017/11/08/is-owning-land-a-human-right/ (accessed 8 July 2018).

Cordes K, Johnson L and Szoke-Burke S (2016) *Land Deal Dilemmas: Grievances, Human Rights and Investor Protection*. New York: Columbia Center on Sustainable Development.

Cordes K and Sachs JD (2015) Measuring Land Rights for a Sustainable Future. *Sustainable Development Solutions Network*. Available at: http://unsdsn.org/news/2015/09/22/measuring-land-rights-for-a-sustainable-future/ (accessed 8 July 2018).

Cotula L, Vermeulen S, Leonard R and Keeley J (2009) *Land Grab or Development Opportunity? Agricultural Investment and International Land Deals in Africa*. London and Rome: IIED/FAO/IFAD. Available at: http://pubs.iied.org/12561IIED/?k=vermeulen (accessed 1 July 2018).

Deininger K and Jin S (2005) The Potential of Land Rental Markets in the Process of Economic Development: Evidence from China. *Journal of Development Economics* 78(1): 241–270.

Dell'Angelo J, D'Odorico P and Rulli MC (2017) Threats to Sustainable Development Posed by Land and Water Grabbing. *Current Opinion in Environmental Sustainability* 26–27: 120–128.

Food and Agriculture Organization (FAO) (2015) *Safeguarding Land Tenure Rights in the Context of Agricultural Investment*. Rome: FAO. Available at: www.fao.org/3/a-i4998e.pdf (accessed 7 July 2018).

Food and Agriculture Organization (FAO) (2018) *Innovative Financing, Tapping the Private Sector*, 8 January. Rome: FAO. Available at: www.fao.org/support-to-investment/news/detail/en/c/1068668/ (accessed 6 July 2018).

Food and Agriculture Organization (FAO) (no date(a)) *The Female Face of Farming*. Rome: FAO. Available at: www.fao.org/gender/resources/infographics/the-female-face-of-farming/en/ (accessed 7 July 2018).

Food and Agriculture Organization (FAO) (no date(b)) *Governance of Tenure*. Rome: FAO. Available at: www.fao.org/index.php?id=90972 (accessed 7 July 2018).

Fraser E and Mousseau F (2016) *Backroom Bullying: The Role of the US Government in the Herakles Farms' Land Grab in Cameroon*. Oakland, CA: The Oakland Institute. Available at: www.oaklandinstitute.org/sites/oaklandinstitute.org/files/backroom-bullying-final.pdf (accessed 8 July 2018).

Gillingham P and Buckle F (2014) *Evidence on Demand: Rwanda Land Tenure Regularisation*. London: DFID.

Global Forest Watch (no date) *Forest Monitoring Designed for Action*. Available at: www.globalforestwatch.org/ (accessed 1 July 2018).

Global Reporting Initiative (GRI) (2016) *Land Tenure Rights: The Need for Greater Transparency Among Companies Worldwide*. Amsterdam: GRI. Available at: www.globalreporting.org/resourcelibrary/GRI-G4-Land-Tenure-Rights.pdf (accessed 7 July 2018).

Global Witness (2013) *Rubber Barons: How Vietnamese Companies and International Financiers Are Driving a Land Grabbing Crisis in Cambodia and Laos*. London: Global Witness.

Global Witness (2017) *Defenders of the Earth: Global Killings of Land and Environmental Defenders in 2016*. Washington, DC: Global Witness. Available at: www.globalwitness.org/en/campaigns/environmental-activists/defenders-earth/ (accessed 7 July 2018).

Golla AM, Malhotra A, Nanda P and Mehra R (2011) *Understanding and Measuring Women's Economic Empowerment*. Washington, DC: International Center for Research on Women.

Hagos HG and Holden S (2013) *Links Between Tenure Security and Food Security: Evidence from Ethiopia*. ESSP Working Paper 59. Washington, DC: Ethiopia Development Research Institute and International Food Policy Research Institute.

Haydaroglu C (2015) The Relationship Between Property Rights and Economic Growth: An Analysis of OECD and EU Countries. *DANUBE: Law and Economics Review* 6(4): 217–239.

Iff A and Joras U (2015) *Agribusiness: Risks and Impact in Conflict-Affected Areas*. London: International Alert/Swisspeace.

International Finance Corporation (IFC) (2012) *IFC Performance Standards on Environmental and Social Sustainability*. Washington, DC: IFC.

International Justice Mission (IJM) (2014) *Property Grabbing from Ugandan Widows and the Justice System*. Washington, DC: International Justice Mission. Available at: https://ndigd.nd.edu/assets/172925/property_grabbing_for_ugandan_widows_and_the_justice_system.pdf (accessed 7 July 2018).

isiAfrica (January 3, 2018) Rwanda to Adopt Blockchain Technology for Its Land Registry. isiAfrica. Available at: http://isiafrica.net/rwanda-to-adopt-blockchain-technology-for-its-land-registry/ (accessed 1 July 2018).

Joireman S (2011) *Where There Is No Government: Enforcing Property Rights in Common Law Africa*. Cambridge: Oxford University Press.

Katz E and Chamorro JS (2002) *Gender, Land Rights and the Household Economy in Rural Nicaragua and Honduras*. Madison, WI: CRSP, USAID.

Klugman J, Hanmer L, Twigg S, Hasan T, McCleary-Sills J and Santamaria J (2014) *Voice and Agency: Empowering Women and Girls for Shared Prosperity*. Washington, DC: The World Bank.

Knight RS (2010) *Statutory Recognition of Customary Land Rights in Africa: An Investigation into Best Practices for Lawmaking and Implementation*. FAO Legislative Study 105. Rome: FAO. Available at: www.fao.org/docrep/013/i1945e/i1945e00.pdf (accessed 1 July 2018).

LandMark (no date) What Is LandMark? Available at www.landmarkmap.org/about/ (accessed 1 July 2018).

Lehr A (2013) *Land Tenure Risk: Why It Matters for Companies, Investors, and Communities. Corporate Social Responsibility and the Law*, 8 October. Available at: www.csrandthelaw.com/2013/10/08/land-tenure-risk-why-it-matters-for-companies-investors-and-communities/ (accessed 1 July 2018).

Menon N, van der Meulen Rodgers Y and Nguyen H (2014) Women's Land Rights and Children's Human Capital in Vietnam. *World Development* (54): 18–31.

Mittal A and Fraser E (2018) *Losing the Serengeti: The Maasai Land That Was to Run Forever*. Oakland, CA: The Oakland Institute. Available at: www.oaklandinstitute.org/sites/oaklandinstitute.org/files/losing-the-serengeti.pdf (accessed 8 July 2018).

NACSO (2016) The State of Community Conservation in Namibia: A Review of Communal Conservancies Community Forests and Other CBNRM Initiatives. Windhoek, Namibia: National Association of CBNRM Support Organisations (NACSO). Available at: http://www.nacso.org.na/sites/default/files/State%20of%20Community%20Conservation%20book%20web.pdf (accessed 8 March 2019).

The Munden Project (2012) *The Financial Risks of Insecure Land Tenure: An Investment View*. Washington, DC: RRI. Available at: http://rightsandresources.org/wp-content/uploads/2014/01/doc_5715.pdf (accessed 29 June 2018).

The Oakland Institute (2015) *We Say the Land Is Not Yours: Breaking the Silence Against Forced Displacement in Ethiopia*. Oakland, CA: The Oakland Institute. Available at: www.oaklandinstitute.org/sites/oaklandinstitute.org/files/Breaking%20the%20Silence.pdf (accessed 8 July 2018).

The Oakland Institute (2017) *Taking on the Logging Pirates: Land Defenders in Papua New Guinea Speak Out!* Oakland, CA: The Oakland Institute. Available at:

www.oaklandinstitute.org/sites/oaklandinstitute.org/files/taking-on-logging-pirates-hi.pdf (accessed 8 July 2018).

OpenStreetMap (no date) About. Available at: www.openstreetmap.org/about (accessed 8 July 2018).

Peterman A (2011) Women's Property Rights and Gendered Policies: Implications for Women's Long-Term Welfare in Rural Tanzania. *Journal of Development Studies* 47(1): 1–30.

Potts D (2006) "Restoring Order"? Operation Murambatsvina and the Urban Crisis in Zimbabwe. *Journal of Southern African Studies* 32(2): 273–292.

Radoki C (2014) *Expanding Women's Access to Land and Housing in Urban Areas*. Women's Voice and Agency Research Series No. 8. Washington, DC: The World Bank. Available at: www.worldbank.org/content/dam/Worldbank/document/Gender/Rakodi%202014.%20Expanding%20women's%20access%20to%20land%20and%20housing%20in%20urban%20areas.pdf (accessed 1 July 2018).

Rights and Resources Initiative (2015) *Who Owns the World's Land: A Global Baseline of Formally Recognized Indigenous and Community Lands*. Washington, DC: RRI. Available at: https://rightsandresources.org/wp-content/uploads/GlobalBaseline_web.pdf (accessed 1 July 2018).

Rights and Resources Initiative (no date(a)) *Tenure Data & Tool*. Washington, DC: RRI. Available at: https://rightsandresources.org/en/work-impact/tenure-data-tool/#.W0EmO_ZFw2x (accessed 1 July 2018).

Rights and Resources Initiative (no date(b)) *Private Sector Risk Analysis Tools*. Washington, DC: RRI. Available at: https://rightsandresources.org/en/work-impact/strategic-initiatives/private-sector-risk-analysis/#.W0EonvZFw2x (accessed 1 July 2018).

Rulli MC, Saviori A and D'Odorico P (2013) Global Land and Water Grabbing. *Proceedings of the National Academy of Sciences* 110(3): 892–897. Available at: www.pnas.org/content/110/3/892.short (accessed 8 July 2018).

Santos F, Fletschner D, Savath V and Peterman A (2013) *Can Microplots Contribute to Rural Households' Food Security? Evaluation of a Gender-Sensitive Land Allocation Program in West Bengal, India*. Washington, DC: International Food Policy Research Institute.

SDI (2017) Settlement: Adabraka. *Know Your City*, 5 March. Available at: http://knowyourcity.info/settlement/1846/15080768 (accessed 8 July 2018).

SDI (no date) The Know Your City Campaign. *Know Your City*. Available at: http://knowyourcity.info/explore-our-data/ (accessed 8 July 2018).

Thoumi G (2017) Pepsico and TIAA Face Financial Risks from Agriculture Investments and Supply Chains. *The Chain*, 27 April. Available at: https://chainreactionresearch.com/the-chain-pepsico-and-tiaa-face-financial-risks-from-agriculture-investments-and-supply-chains/ (accessed 1 July 2018).

United Nations. Economic Commission for Africa (no date) About LPI. Addis Ababa: UNECA. Available at: www.uneca.org/alpc/pages/about-lpi (accessed 8 July 2018).

United Nations. Office of the High Commissioner for Human Rights (no date) Land and Human Rights. Available at: www.ohchr.org/EN/Issues/LandAndHR/Pages/LandandHumanRightsIndex.aspx (accessed 2 July 2018).

United States Agency for International Development (USAID) (no date(a)) *Land Tenure Primer*. Available at: https://land-links.org/what-is-land-tenure/land-tenure-primer/ (accessed 3 July 2018).

United States Agency for International Development (USAID (no date(b)) *Mobile Application to Secure Tenure (MAST) Learning Platform*. Washington, DC: USAID. Available at: https://land-links.org/tool-resource/mobile-applications-to-secure-tenure-mast/ (accessed 1 July 2018).

Wegen, WV (2018) *The Necessity of a Modern Cadastral System*. GIM, 19 January. Available at: www.gim-international.com/content/article/the-necessity-of-a-modern-cadastral-system (accessed 7 July 2018).

World Bank (2008) *Analysis of the Impact of Land Tenure Certificates with Both the Names of Wife and Husband in Vietnam: Final Report*. Washington, DC: The World Bank.

Contributors

José E. Alvarez is Herbert and Rose Rubin Professor of International Law at New York University Law School. He is a former president of the American Society of International Law, the previous co-editor-in-chief of the *American Journal of International Law*, and a member of the Institut de Droit International and Council on Foreign Relations. His books include *The Public International Law Regime Governing International Investment* (2011), *The Impact of International Organizations on International Law* (2017) and *International Investment Law* (2017).

Daniel Attas (DPhil, Oxford 1997) is Ahad Ha'am Professor of Philosophy at the Hebrew University of Jerusalem. His research is in moral and political philosophy, including topics such as property, equality and well-being. He is author of *Liberty, Property, and Markets: A Critique of Libertarianism* (Ashgate, 2005). He is currently co-director of the Centre for Moral and Political Philosophy in Jerusalem.

Samantha Besson is Professor of Public International Law and European Law at the University of Fribourg, Switzerland. Her research and publications lie at the intersection of international and European public law and legal theory, and focus on international and European human rights law and theory and on international and European institutional law and theory.

Karol C. Boudreaux is a land lawyer with over 20 years of experience on land and property issues in academia, government and the non-profit sector. She has worked around the world on land rights issues including legal and policy analysis, program design and implementation and proof of concept pilot projects. She is currently Chief of Programs at Landesa, an award-winning international NGO that has worked in over 50 countries to strengthen the land rights of more than 110 million women and men. Karol's JD is from the University of Virginia and her BA is from Douglass College, Rutgers University.

Benjamin Chen is Postdoctoral Research Scholar and Lecturer-in-Law at Columbia Law School. He is an interdisciplinary scholar whose research on law and legal institutions is informed by perspectives drawn from economics, philosophy and political science. He received his JD and PhD in Jurisprudence and Social Policy from the University of California, Berkeley, in 2017. Before joining the law school, Benjamin served as a law clerk on the United States Court of Appeals for the Ninth Circuit.

Martha Alter Chen is Lecturer in Public Policy at the Harvard Kennedy School, an Affiliated Professor at the Harvard Graduate School of Design, and Senior Advisor of the global-research-policy-action network Women in Informal Employment: Globalizing and Organizing (WIEGO). An experienced development practitioner and scholar, her areas of specialization are employment, gender and poverty with a focus on the working poor in the informal economy. Before joining Harvard in 1987, she had two decades of resident field experience in South Asia: in Bangladesh in the 1970s, working with BRAC, an NGO which has gained world-wide scope and reputation; and in India in the 1980s, where she served as field representative of Oxfam America.

Francis Cheneval holds the Chair of Political Philosophy at the University of Zurich. He is the author of books and papers in the field of democratic theory, property rights theory, human rights and on various topics of the history of political thought. From 2006–2008 he served as Rapporteur for Property Rights of the *Commission on Legal Empowerment of the Poor* (UNDP, New York).

Robert Cooter, a pioneer in the field of law and economics, was educated at Swarthmore College, Oxford University and Harvard University. After receiving his PhD in Economics in 1975, he joined the economics faculty at Berkeley. In 1980 he joined Berkeley's law faculty, where he is currently Herman F. Selvin Professor. He was a founding director of the American Law and Economics Association and its President in 1994–1995. He co-founded the Berkeley Electronic Press (BEPress) in 1999. In 1999 he was elected to the American Academy of Arts and Sciences. Besides numerous articles, he is co-author of *Law and Economics* (6th ed., 2011, with Tom Ulen; also translated into Spanish, Portuguese, Italian, Hungarian, Japanese, Chinese, Korean and Farsi); *The Strategic Constitution* (Princeton, 2000) and *Solomon's Knot: How Law Can End the Poverty of Nations* (Princeton University Press, 2012, with Hans Bernd Schäfer). Cooter has published a wide variety of articles applying economic analysis to private law, constitutional law and law in developing countries.

Rowan Cruft is Professor of Philosophy at the University of Stirling. His work focuses on the nature of rights, and the relations between human rights and property rights. He edited a symposium on Rights and Directed Duties in *Ethics* 2013, and co-edited *Philosophical Foundations of Human Rights* (Oxford University Press, 2015). His monograph, *Human Rights, Ownership, and the Individual*, is forthcoming with Oxford University Press, 2019.

Christopher Freiman is the Class of 1963 Distinguished Term Associate Professor of Philosophy at William & Mary. He is the author of *Unequivocal Justice* and over two dozen articles and chapters on topics including democratic theory, distributive justice and immigration. His work has appeared in venues such as the *Australasian Journal of Philosophy*, *Philosophical Studies*, *Philosophy and Phenomenological Research*, *The Journal of Ethics and Social Philosophy*, *Politics, Philosophy, and Economics* and *The Oxford Handbook of Political Philosophy*. Chris received a William & Mary Alumni Fellowship Award for Excellence in Teaching in 2016.

Amanda R. Greene is Lecturer (Assistant Professor) in the Department of Philosophy at University College London. Her research examines the nature of legitimate political authority, and especially whether democracies can make a special claim of political legitimacy. She has held research fellowships at the University of Chicago Law School, Princeton University and IHEID (Geneva). She received her PhD at Stanford University, MPhil at Oxford University and BA at the University of North Carolina. Before entering academia, she worked as a strategy consultant in the private and non-profit sectors in the United States, India and Australia.

Nien-hê Hsieh is Associate Professor of Business Administration at Harvard Business School where he teaches and writes about the responsibilities of managers, the role of business in society and ethical issues in economics more generally. His work has been published in *Business Ethics Quarterly*, *Economics and Philosophy*, *The Journal of Political Philosophy*, *Philosophy and Public Affairs*, *Social Theory and Practice*, *Utilitas* and various other journals. He serves on the Faculty Advisory Committee for the Edmund J. Safra Center for Ethics at Harvard University and is a past president of the Society for Business Ethics. Before joining Harvard University, he taught at the Wharton School of the University of Pennsylvania, where he was Associate Professor of Legal Studies and Business Ethics and served as co-director of the Wharton Ethics Program.

Dan Moller is Associate Professor of Philosophy at the University of Maryland. He is the author of *Governing Least: A New England Libertarianism* (Oxford, 2019).

Carol M. Rose is Professor of Law Emerita at Yale Law School and the University of Arizona. Her research concentrates on the history and theory of property, environmental law, natural resources and intellectual property, and has appeared in numerous journals and anthologies, including translations in Italian, Spanish and Chinese. Her books include *Perspectives on Property Law* (4th ed., 2014, with R C Ellickson and H E Smith), *Saving the Neighborhood: Racially Restrictive Covenants, Law, and Social Norms* (2013, with R W Brooks); *El Derecho de Propiedad en Clave Interdisciplinaria* [The Right to Property in an Interdisciplinary Key] (2010) and *Property and Persuasion* (1994). She is a member of the American Law Institute and the Academy of Arts and Sciences.

Fernando R. Tesón, a native of Buenos Aires, is Eminent Scholar Emeritus at Florida State University College of Law. He is known for his scholarship relating political philosophy to international law (in particular his defense of humanitarian intervention), political rhetoric and global justice. He has authored *Debating Humanitarian Intervention* (Oxford University Press, 2018, with Bas van der Vossen); *Justice at a Distance: Extending Freedom Globally* (Cambridge University Press, 2015, with Loren Lomasky); *Rational Choice and Democratic Deliberation* (Cambridge University Press, 2006, with Guido Pincione); *Humanitarian Intervention: An Inquiry into Law and Morality* (3rd ed. fully revised and updated, Transnational Publishers, 2005); *A Philosophy of International Law* (Westview Press, 1998); and dozens of articles in law, philosophy and international relations journals and collections of essays.

John Thrasher is Assistant Professor in the Philosophy Department and the Smith Institute of Political Economy and Philosophy at Chapman University. His research draws on the findings and methods of politics, economics and psychology in an attempt to understand long-standing philosophical problems. He is the author, with Dan Halliday, of *The Ethics of Capitalism* and many articles and chapters on the open society, norms, the social contract, honor and violence, Adam Smith and Epicurus, among other topics. His work has appeared in many journals spanning several disciplines, including *The American Journal of Political Science*, *Philosophical Studies*, *Nature Communications*, *Synthese* and the *Journal of Moral Philosophy*.

Index

Printed in the United States
by Baker & Taylor Publisher Services